Understanding
TROUBLED
MINDS

SIDNEY BLOCH

MELBOURNE
UNIVERSITY
PRESS

MELBOURNE UNIVERSITY PRESS
An imprint of Melbourne University Publishing Limited
187 Grattan Street, Carlton, Victoria 3053, Australia
mup-info@unimelb.edu.au
www.mup.com.au

First published 1997
Second edition, fully revised, 2011
Text © Sidney Bloch, 2011
Design and typography © Melbourne University Publishing Limited, 2011

Text design by James Curran
Typeset by J&M Typesetting
Printed by Griffin Press, South Australia

National Library of Australia Cataloguing-in-Publication entry

Bloch, Sidney, 1941–

Understanding troubled minds: a guide to mental illness and its treatment / Sidney Bloch

2nd ed.

9780522857542 (pbk)
9780522860320 (epub)

Includes index.

Mental illness.
Mental illness—Treatment.

616.891

FSC
www.fsc.org
MIX
Paper from
responsible sources
FSC® C009448

Contents

Illustrations   vii

Preface   viii

Acknowledgements   xi

1   The History of Psychiatry   1

2   Making Sense of a Life   12

3   Defining and Classifying Mental Illnesses   25

4   The Psychiatrist at Work   35

5   Stress, Crisis and Coping   53

6   The Spectrum of Anxiety   64

7   The Highs and Lows of Mood   83

8   The Mind Talking through the Body   102

9   Eating Disorders   116

10   Disturbances of Personality   124

11   The Psychoses   143

12   Alcohol and Drug Abuse   163

13   Gender Identity and Sexual Disorders   181

14   Children and Adolescents   192

15   Women   219

16   The Elderly   234

17   Suicide and Deliberate Self-harm   255

18   Drugs and Other Physical Treatments   273

19   The Psychotherapies   288

20   Promoting Mental Health   322

21   An Ethical Dimension   344

A Select Guide to Further Reading   356

Index   360

Illustrations

The black and white engravings, all glimpses from the history of psychiatry, are from the Wellcome Centre Medical Photographic Library in London. Michael Leunig's cartoons were first published in the Melbourne *Age*. Pictures of the brain are from the Mental Health Research Institute in Melbourne and the Royal Melbourne Hospital Illustration Department. The paintings are from the Cunningham Dax Collection. University of Melbourne.

Preface

In 1994, Professor Bruce Singh and I emerged from the offices of Melbourne University Press clutching a newly printed copy of *Foundations of Clinical Psychiatry*, a book we had edited for medical students. It dawned upon us then that another readership, the general public, was in need of a clear, well-informed, objective account of the nature of mental illness and its treatment. We were especially mindful of the pervasiveness of stigma, essentially due to sparse and distorted knowledge about the subject. For people suffering from a mental illness, the most unwelcome features of their experience continue to be discrimination, inaccurate portrayal in the media, and ridicule.

We first checked whether a book of this kind was available. What we found was a vast range of popular psychology texts, most of them written by non-professionals or by professionals presenting the subject idiosyncratically. These books raised readers' expectations by promising so much—and then, in our view, left them vulnerable to disappointment on discovering that mental illness does not respond to simple remedies.

So, we decided to take the plunge, with the proviso that we would keep our own biases in check and prepare an honest, objective account of the subject. Where the message was an optimistic one, we would convey that sense, but where progress was slow and treatment at an early stage, we would not disguise the reality. We were much heartened later when one reviewer described our book as 'leagues away' from 'the countless books on mental illness which emphasise a particular syndrome or ride some modish hobbyhorse' and 'often exploit as much as inform'.

Why did we use 'troubled minds' in our title? The phrase reminded us of the blurred boundary between the ordinary experiences of disappointment, sadness, anxiety and bewilderment on the one hand, and formal psychiatric disturbance on the other. The distinction between mental health and mental illness is not a matter for easy definition and, by its nature, cannot be.

We struggled to find the right word to precede 'troubled minds'. The notion of understanding appealed to us, as it refers to the sensitive concern that one person has for another. Mentally ill people have not always been regarded as deserving of such concern, and have therefore not benefited from the altruistic impulses usually available to people in need. We would try to help readers resonate with the sentiment expressed in the old saying that to understand a person, you must walk a mile in their shoes.

Both intellectual and emotional understanding is crucial, given the stark facts about how common mental illness is. The figures are astonishing. Even when using rigorous criteria, as in a large Australian survey carried out in 2007, one in five people suffered a diagnosable mental illness in the previous 12 months, the most common being anxiety, depression and substance abuse. Moreover, a quarter of them had more than one condition. In the light of these figures, it is no surprise that only the exceptional family remains unscathed.

The catalyst that finally committed us to the challenge was a series of personal experiences involving friends and acquaintances who were confronting the reality of mental illness in themselves or in their loved ones—an adolescent son with panic attacks and his bewildered parents; a mother with ghastly suicidal impulses; a family's distress at witnessing their mother's inappropriate, disinhibited behaviour; a daughter's descent into overwhelming preoccupation with her weight. All these people were generally competent and confident in their personal and professional lives, but had been reduced to a state of bafflement, fear and uncertainty. *Understanding Troubled Minds* was intended to meet the needs of these people and thousands like them who face the spectre of mental illness, often without preparation or warning.

The book was warmly received. We were particularly pleased that the Royal Australian College of General Practitioners distributed copies to its members for use with their patients. Dr Peter Joseph, its president in 1998, commented: 'The book has been quite a hit with doctors and patients. I enjoyed my copy and have loaned it to patients already with good effect.'

In 2009, our publisher nudged us into thinking about a new edition. We could see the point—psychiatry had advanced on many fronts and a rigorous update was clearly necessary. Unfortunately, Bruce Singh was caught up in a new appointment and was not able to commit himself to the task. I was apprehensive about going solo. We had worked admirably together on the original edition, benefiting from a lively exchange of ideas. My confidence was boosted by two factors. Bruce and I had edited a new edition of our book for medical students, published in 2007. We had learned much from our contributing colleagues and we were confident that they had done a splendid job of updating their area of expertise. Moreover, they granted me permission to apply the fruits of their labour in preparing a new edition of *Understanding Troubled Minds*.

I have retained the same structure as the original, since it seems to have worked well. Chapters 1 to 5 encompass general aspects of psychiatry: its historical context; how psychiatrists think about patients, using Vincent Van Gogh's life as an illustration; how psychiatrists carry out their work; the essential concepts of coping, crisis and stress; and the classification of mental illnesses. Chapters 6 to 13 lead the reader through the range of psychiatric problems encountered in clinical practice. Chapters 14 to 17 are concerned with particular groups: children and adolescents, women, the elderly and self-destructive people. Chapters 18 and 19 cover the range of available treatments, both physical and psychological. The book ends with chapters on promoting mental health, the ethical dimension of psychiatric practice and a select guide to further reading.

A word about references. To avoid cluttering the page with names of authors and dates of publication, I have simply referred in my text to the author and book from which I am quoting a passage. Online search engines are so comprehensive nowadays that details of publication and accessibility are easy to track down.

I have had a longstanding conviction that troubled minds are not the exclusive province of the psychiatrist as medical scientist. Artists of every kind, philosophers and the humanities generally all contribute richly, so complementing scientifically based knowledge. A poem by William Blake on infancy, a description of the life cycle by Shakespeare, Edvard Munch's painting *The Scream*, a view of the human condition by Jean-Paul Sartre and Franz Schubert's grief-laden song cycle *Winterreise* can tell us as much about the mind and human behaviour as the systematic findings of the scientist. I have woven the human dimension into the text through the stories of real people (thickly disguised to prevent them being identified), the testimony of sufferers and their families, and the insight of writers, poets and philosophers. I hope that I have done justice to both the science and the art of psychiatry.

Acknowledgements

Understanding Troubled Minds is based on the textbook for medical students, *Foundations of Clinical Psychiatry*, which I co-edited. I am indebted to my colleagues who contributed to it and who gave me permission to use their material as a scaffold for this book. I shall couple their names with the chapters to which they contributed, and I take great pleasure in expressing my thanks to them:

Norman James and the late Robert Barrett (The History of Psychiatry), George Szmukler (Making Sense of a Life), Assen Jablensky and George Mendelson (Defining and Classifying Mental illnesses), Nicholas Keks, Ken Kirkby and Bruce Singh (The Psychiatrist at Work), Graham Burrows, Fiona Judd and Ruth Vine (The Spectrum of Anxiety), Gordon Parker and Issy Schweitzer (The Highs and Lows of Mood), Philip Boyce, David Clarke and Graeme Smith (The Mind Talking through the Body), Phillipa Hay and Stephen Touyz (Eating Disorders), Sandra Hacker, Edwin Harari, Henry Jackson and Jayashri Kulkarni, (Disturbances of Personality), Stanley Catts and Patrick McGorry (The Psychoses), Paul Brown, Glenys Dore, Paul Holman, John Saunders and Ross Young (Alcohol and Drug Abuse), Richard Ball and Alan Cooper (Gender Identity and Sexual Disorders), Robert Adler, Pia Brous, Helen Driscoll, Philip Hazell, Joseph Rey, Bruce Tonge and Garry Walter (Children and Adolescents), Anne Buist, Lorraine Dennerstein and Sarah Romans (Women), David Ames, Henry Brodaty, Edmond Chiu and Daniel O'Connor (The Elderly), David Copolov and Philip Mitchell (Drugs and Other Physical Treatments) and Edwin Harari (The Psychotherapies).

I am indebted to the following colleagues who read selected chapters with a constructively critical eye: Ehud Bandel, Stan Catts, Peter Congerton, Janice Eloni, Andrew Gleason, Joel King, Nichola Lautenschlager, Sarah Romans, Julie Sharrock and Gary Walter.

I was well served by the staff of St Vincent's Hospital Medical Library, and wish to record my thanks to Jeremy Taylor and his colleagues for their kindness whenever I needed assistance.

I hope *Understandinging Troubled Minds* will attract the reader's eye through its pictorial dimension. I thank Michael Leunig most sincerely for permitting me to use his cartoons. Michael is a brilliant observer of human behaviour, as is so well demonstrated by the selection in this book. The late Eric Cunningham Dax, a role model for me for many years, was a distinguished psychiatrist who made an enormous contribution to psychiatry in Australia and Britain. Among his many accomplishments is his collection of psychiatric art that can be seen to great advantage in the gallery named after him in Melbourne. Julie Jones is a doyenne of child psychiatry in Australia and has always emphasised the relevance of non-verbal expression in her patients. I thank her for granting permission to use pictures from her collection of child psychiatric art. The staff at the Wellcome Centre Medical Photographic Library in London were extremely hospitable when I sought photographs to illustrate the history of psychiatry. Dennis Velakoulis of the Mental Health Research Institute, Melbourne, has a great talent in developing computer graphics of the brain, and I thank him for helping in this area.

The late John Iremonger was the director of Melbourne University Press when Bruce Singh and I first came up with the idea for this book. His eager response and wise guidance spurred us on. At MUP, Foong Ling Kong and Cinzia Cavallaro have similarly given me support and encouragement. Jean Dunn did a marvellous editing job on the first edition and an equally good one this time. She has the knack of turning convoluted prose into straightforward English, a distinct advantage when writing on the complicated subject of psychiatry. I am immensely indebted to Jean for the hard work she put into the project and for her warm colleagueship.

Finally, I would like to express my heartfelt gratitude to my family for their splendid support; they have unhesitatingly provided cogent advice whenever I have needed it.

Sidney Bloch, May 2011

CHAPTER 1

The History of Psychiatry

Psychiatry has, by and large, made steady progress towards scientific enlightenment and better treatment for the mentally ill. However, insights from the past remain useful. While psychiatry's past is littered with the corpses of ineffective, and at times hazardous, treatments, certain progressive social approaches to mental illness may have been lost sight of and need revisiting. Thus, critical appraisal of contemporary enthusiasms is again demonstrated to be a useful function of the study of history. In the words of the philosopher George Santayana, 'Those who cannot remember the past are condemned to repeat it'.

Attempts to understand and treat the mentally ill go back centuries. Name changes reflect the diverse ways in which mental illness has been regarded. For example, 'lunacy' is derived from the belief that people's mental states deteriorated at full moon; 'insanity' from the Latin *insanus*, meaning unsound mind; and 'psychiatric' from the Greek words for soul, *psyche*, and healing, *iatreia*.

Possibly the earliest account of a disturbed mind is recorded in the Ayur Veda, a 3500-year-old Hindu text. A man is described as 'gluttonous, filthy, walks naked, has lost his memory and moves about in an uneasy manner'. In the first Book of Samuel we read that King David simulated madness in order to gain safety: 'And he changed his behaviour ... and feigned himself mad in their hands, and scrabbled on the doors of the gate, and let his spittle fall down upon his beard'. In the Book of Daniel we find a vivid description of King Nebuchadnezzar's mental state: 'And he was driven from men, and did eat grass as oxen, and his body was wet with the dew of heaven, till his hairs were grown like eagles' feathers, and his nails like birds' claws'.

The ancient Greeks went beyond mere description of madness. Their explanations of the causes centred about an imbalance of bodily humours or fluids. Hippocrates, in the fourth century BC, viewed it this way, but also invoked environmental, physical and emotional causal factors. The Greek physician Galen, who practised in Rome 600 years later, persisted with the concept of fluid imbalance, postulating that depression was caused by an excess of black bile (hence the term 'melancholia', from *melan*, black, and *khole*, bile), though he also took emotional influences such as erotic desire into account. Modern psychiatry conceptualises disturbances of mood in strikingly similar ways to those of the ancients. Indeed the term 'melancholic features' resurfaced in the twentieth century to cover the biological changes seen in depression.

During the Middle Ages, the monasteries preserved the view of madness as an illness and of those afflicted as blameless. At the same time, the more sinister belief that the principal cause of the troubled mind was possession by the devil prevailed. Sufferers were taken to sanctioned healers, usually priests or shamans (a practice still carried out today in some cultures).

People who failed to respond to such routine treatment might then seek out a celebrated expert. The case of Hwaetred, a young man who became tormented by an 'evil spirit', is a clear example. So terrible was his madness that he attacked others with his teeth; when men tried to restrain him, he snatched up an axe and killed three of them. Taken to several sacred shrines, he obtained no relief. His despairing parents then heard of Guthlac, a monk who lived a hermit life north of Cambridge. After three days of prayer and fasting Hwaetred was purportedly cured.

Sin was rarely seen as causing mental illness. Rather, it was a visitation from without, affecting even righteous people. A particularly harrowing period was the seventeenth century, when religiously inspired persecution of the mentally ill was justified by the clerical hierarchy, who designated them as witches. Fortunately, this coincided with the medical profession's claim to exclusive practice of the healing arts, such as they were, and its withdrawal from former links with the priesthood. A new fairness in treatment of deranged people resulted both from the church's emphasis on charity and medicine's growing agreement that the cause of insanity was physically based.

Life before the Industrial Revolution has been portrayed as one of tranquillity, the countryside supposedly scattered with picturesque villages whose inhabitants tilled the fields, celebrated festivals and cared cooperatively for one another. The reality was otherwise. Thomas Hobbes, the social philosopher, described their lives as 'solitary, poor, nasty, brutish and short'. The insane were depicted as 'miserable individuals, wandering around in village and in forest, taken from shrine to shrine, sometimes tied up when they became too violent'.

Death by public drowning was once the not uncommon fate of mentally ill women branded as witches (from The Remarkable Confession and Last Dying Words of Thomas Colley, *London, undated).*

The late eighteenth century was a watershed in the history of psychiatry. The insanity of England's King George III revealed society's ambivalence to the mentally ill (vividly captured in the film *The Madness of King George*). In France, Philippe Pinel released the chains that had fettered the 'lunatic' for centuries, ushering in an unprecedented phase of benevolent institutional care. Moral therapy was the most significant advance of this era. It supplanted earlier physical treatments such as purging, bleeding and dunking in cold water. Moral therapy worked instead on the intellect and emotions, and was designed to achieve internal self-restraint and mental harmony. The approach was taken up with fervour by the Quakers who established the York Retreat; the humane movement was soon championed in the United States.

Literary descriptions of mental illness

An evocative description of mental illness by Honoré de Balzac appears in his novel *Louis Lambert*, published in 1832. The main character, a highly intelligent young man, becomes infatuated with a childhood sweetheart but once married plunges into a world of insanity. The narrator, a childhood friend of Louis, notes on seeing him:

> … his body seemed to bend beneath the weight of his bowed head. His hair, which was as long as a woman's, fell over his shoulders and surrounded his face, which was perfectly white. He constantly

rubbed one of his legs against the other with an automatic movement which nothing could check, and the continual rubbing of the two bones made a ghastly noise. Beside him was a mattress of moss, laid on a board. He was a remnant of vitality rescued from the grave, a sort of conquest of life over death, or of death over life. Suddenly Louis ceased to rub his legs together and said slowly, 'The Angels are white'.

Nikolai Gogol, the Russian novelist, published *Diary of a Madman* around the same time. Gogol himself was destined to succumb to what was probably severe depression, manifesting as pervasive guilt, social withdrawal, despair and finally death by self-starvation. The story paints a frenzied picture of madness and the final plea is heart-rending: 'Mummy, save your poor son! Shed a tear on his poor battered head and look how they are tormenting him! Press your orphan boy to your breast! There is no place for him on earth! He is persecuted! Mummy, have pity on your sick little child!'

Guy de Maupassant, the French writer, recorded the essence of the disordered mind in a short story, *The Horla*, offering this vivid description:

I ask myself whether I am mad … doubts as to my own sanity arose in me, not vague doubts, such I have had hitherto, but precise and absolute doubts. I have seen mad people and I have known some who were quite intelligent, lucid, even clear sighted in every concern of life, except at one point. They could speak clearly, readily, profoundly, on everything, till their thoughts were caught in the breakers of their delusions and went to pieces. There, they were dispersed and swamped in that furious sea of fogs and squalls which is called madness … Was it not possible that one of the imperceptible keys of the cerebral fingerboard had been paralysed in me? … By degrees however, an inexplicable feeling of discomfort seized me. It seemed to me as if some unknown force were numbing and stopping me, preventing me from going further and calling me back.

Eventually the narrator comes to believe that he can fend off his persecutor only by setting fire to his house. But his torment persists to the final lines: 'No—no—there is no doubt about it—he is not dead. Then—then—I suppose I must kill *myself!*'

The era of the asylum and advent of physical treatments

The sheer numbers of mentally ill people in burgeoning urban slums demanded action. An institutional solution emerged. Asylums (from the

Greek word meaning refuge) were built in rural settings with the best of intentions, planned to be havens in which patients would receive humane care. In the serenity of the countryside, and through carrying out undemanding tasks, they could be distracted from their internal torment and find dignity far from the madding crowd. Daniel Defoe, the English writer, remained unconvinced: 'This is the height of barbarity and injustice in a Christian country; it is a clandestine Inquisition, nay worse'.

Though conceived in a spirit of optimism, asylums tended to deteriorate into centres of hopelessness and demoralisation. They soon became overcrowded dumps. Institutions originally built for a few hundred people were soon holding thousands. Very few residents were discharged; many stayed for decades. Brutal oppression replaced anything that might have resembled treatment; malnutrition and infectious disease became rife. In the grim environment, people were shut away and forgotten. Family contacts were often lost, especially as the asylum was frequently at a distance from the patient's home. Out of sight and out of mind, a loss of public interest and political neglect became the norms. A fascinating exception is the York Retreat in England, established by the local Quaker community.

The brooding building on the hill came to symbolise the fear of mental illness and the stigma with which it remains associated—alas, even to the present time. By the mid-nineteenth century, critics were voicing concerns that asylums had evolved into human warehouses in which mental illness inevitably became irreversible. The combination of powerless patients, hospitals run more for the convenience of staff than for the benefit of the sick, inadequate inspection by state bodies and lack of resources led at times to quite disgraceful conditions. Unwittingly, the spread of asylums also triggered the movement of psychiatry away from the mainstream of medicine. This regrettable divorce was reflected in the term 'alienist' for doctors who practised in the asylums. Attendants and medical staff were also often cut off from the rest of society in that they lived with their families in the hospital grounds.

The conditions are evocatively described in Henry Handel Richardson's Australian novel, *The Fortunes of Richard Mahony*. We read of Richard's decline, probably from neurosyphilis, which at that time afflicted a large proportion of mental patients. Towards the end of the novel his wife comes to visit him in the asylum:

> She hung her head, holding tight … to the clasp of her sealskin bag, while the warder told the tale of Richard's misdeeds. 97B was, he declared, not only disobedient and disorderly, he was extremely abusive, dirty in his habits … would neither sleep himself at night nor let other people sleep, also he refused to wash himself, or to

eat his food ... But she had to keep a grip on her mind to hinder it from following the picture up: Richard, forced by this burly brute to grope on the floor for his spilt food, to scrape it together and either eat it or have it thrust down his throat ... she had heard from Richard about the means used to quell and break the spirits of refractory lunatics ... There was not only feeding by force, the straitjacket, the padded cell. There were drugs and injections, given to keep a patient quiet and ensure his warders their freedom: doses of castor oil so powerful that the unhappy wretch into whom they were poured was rendered bedridden, griped, thoroughly ill.

Although such a decline was often the result of years of confinement, the concept of a degenerative process in the brain became widely accepted as a likely explanation and gained added impetus from the rise of pathology as a branch of medical science. The search for causes of mental illness in the brain proved fruitful in some areas, especially in identifying neurosyphilis and the neuropathology of Alzheimer's dementia.

So compelling was the organic paradigm that all major forms of mental illness were assumed to be caused by a degenerative brain process. Thus, when the clinical syndrome of dementia praecox was mapped out through the careful scientific work of the great German psychiatrist Emil Kraepelin, it was assumed that it also had a degenerative basis and that the outcome was inevitable decline. So too with the Swiss psychiatrist Eugen Bleuler, who in 1911 renamed dementia praecox with the term we use today, schizophrenia. Though most understanding towards his patients, Bleuler propagated the idea that they could never fully recover. This was undoubtedly related to the fact that many of his patients were hospitalised for decades without effective treatment.

Great and desperate cures

In the asylum, too, psychiatry turned into a medical discipline. The accumulation of thousands of patients provided the first opportunity to study mental illness systematically. But the priority was the suffering of overwhelming numbers of disturbed patients. Psychiatrists grasped for 'great and desperate cures'. Henry Rollin, an English psychiatrist and medical historian, captures the intense zeal:

The physical treatment of the frankly psychotic during these centuries makes spine-chilling reading. Evacuation by vomiting, purgatives, sweating, blisters and bleeding were considered essential ... There was indeed no insult to the human body, no trauma, no indignity which was not at one time or other piously prescribed for the unfortunate victim.

Treatments were sometimes based on rational grounds. Malaria therapy, for instance, was launched as a treatment for syphilis affecting the brain by the Viennese psychiatrist Julius von Wagner-Jauregg in 1917, earning him a Nobel Prize ten years later. The rationale for inducing a high fever using the malarial parasite was the heat sensitivity of the spirochete that caused neurosyphilis. Von Wagner-Jauregg may have had a point; substantial improvement occurred in the nine cases he reported on a year later. But the hope that it would be equally effective for other forms of psychosis was soon dashed. The wished-for panacea was not to be. In any event, malarial therapy was hazardous and difficult to apply.

Insulin coma therapy was introduced into psychiatry by Manfred Sakel in the 1930s in Vienna and was soon being used in many countries to treat schizophrenia. An insulin injection was administered six days a week for several weeks, producing a state of light coma lasting about an hour, because of reduced glucose reaching the brain. Many years later, an investigation carried out in the Institute of Psychiatry in London, a leading research centre at the time, showed conclusively that the coma itself was of no therapeutic value. The benefits noted were probably attributable to the conscientious attention given to the patient by dedicated staff over an extended period.

The first widely available and effective physical treatments for mental illness were developed in the asylum. The discovery in 1938 of electroconvulsive therapy (ECT) by Cerletti and Bini, two Italian psychiatrists, led to a dramatically effective treatment for people with severe depression. ECT was eagerly adopted in practice but its history illustrates a typical pattern of treatment in psychiatry, where unbridled early enthusiasm is later tempered by a protracted process of scientific evaluation. Exactly the same can be said of psychosurgery—or surgical procedures—on the brain to modify psychiatric symptoms. This was pioneered in 1936 by a Portuguese neurologist, Egas Moniz (another Nobel Prize winner in the field of psychiatry) and a surgeon, Almeida Lima. It has been a source of controversy ever since. Regrettably, the negative image of both treatments still hampers their usefulness for carefully selected patients (see Chapter 18).

A momentous breakthrough was the report in 1949 by John Cade, an Australian psychiatrist, of lithium as a treatment for manic excitement. The lithium story is an illuminating one in revealing how the incorporation of a new medication into psychiatric practice is not always accomplished smoothly. Cade was not the first person to detect the potential benefits of lithium for the mentally ill. In the 1870s, two American clinicians separately prescribed it for 'nervous excitement'. A Danish psychiatrist then described its role in severe depression in 1894. All these initiatives were ignored for decades, in fact until Cade's observations. Yet another long period followed before studies were undertaken, again in Denmark, to examine the role of lithium to prevent the recurrence of severe changes of mood (its principal application in contemporary practice). The definitive research report was only published in 1967. Notwithstanding, two leading British psychiatrists expressed, unjustifiably, their disdain for lithium, emphasising the poor scientific methods that had been deployed in studying it and the dangers in its use.

Major tranquillisers were discovered fortuitously in 1953 when an anti-histamine noted to calm patients undergoing surgery also reduced the torment of psychotic patients, but without making them sleepy. Shortly after this, Nathan Kline discovered that a drug being tested for its effect in patients with tuberculosis had anti-depressant properties—the forerunner of medications for depression. All these drugs radically transformed the practice of psychiatry (see Chapter 18).

The advent of psychological therapies

A very different aspect of psychiatry arose in the 1890s, independently of the asylum. Concerned with neurotic illnesses, the new treatment grew chiefly out of neurology but was also influenced by a scientific interest in hypnosis and the unconscious. Sigmund Freud conceived of a dynamic model of the mind in which, through the mechanism of repression, painful or threatening emotions, memories and impulses are prevented from escaping into conscious awareness. Psychoanalysis grew to become an integrated set of concepts about normal and abnormal mental functioning and personality development, and spawned a novel method of psychologically based treatment. Psychoanalysis has emerged as a major theoretical underpinning of contemporary psychotherapies, and its influence has spread far beyond psychiatry, as evidenced by the number of Freud's ideas that have entered everyday thinking (see Chapter 19).

Both world wars profoundly influenced psychiatry. The high incidence of 'shell shock' in World War I drove home the lesson that psychiatric disorder could affect not only those genetically predisposed, but even the supposedly robust. It soon emerged that anyone exposed to traumatic experiences could suffer a psychiatric disorder as a consequence. A positive outcome from World War II was the development of techniques for screening large numbers of recruits, these providing a picture of the widespread prevalence of psychiatric disorders among young adults. The need to treat large numbers of psychiatric casualties led to the development by military psychiatrists of group therapy. Given that group members were not only helped by the therapist but also learned from one another, group therapy had the effect of breaking down the rigid hierarchy of psychiatric institutions. It also paved the way for the so-called therapeutic community, based on the idea that an entire ward of patients could in itself be an integral part of treatment.

The idea of deinstitutionalisation began to gather pace in the 1960s, driven by a burgeoning civil rights movement. *Asylums*, an influential book at the time by sociologist Erving Goffman, containing his minute observations of the sense of oppression experienced by patients in these 'total institutions', was also a catalyst for their closure. Hundreds of thousands of long-stay patients have been transferred to alternative accommodation since the 1960s, a process still in progress. Specialist psychiatric care in the setting of the community is becoming the norm, at least in more wealthy countries.

The contemporary scene

I grab every available opportunity to instil in my students training to become psychiatrists the sense of excitement I feel about the contemporary state of our profession. So many developments are taking place in every sphere, whether it be new technology to study how the brain works, new treatments—both physical and psychological—or innovative systems of delivering mental health care (for example, mother–baby units). Let us consider medications to illustrate. A new class of anti-depressants, the selective serotonin reuptake inhibitors (SSRIs), has enabled us to relieve depression with far fewer unpleasant side-effects and with a vastly reduced risk of death through overdose than their predecessors. The older anti-psychotics have been replaced by a new generation of medications that do not produce the former's serious purposeless bodily movements. A massive effort is being devoted to the production of effective but safe medications for all psychiatric conditions. Alzheimer's disease, for example, has long been regarded as untreatable, with progressive deterioration the inevitable course. Even here, the decline in cognitive and social functioning may be delayed in a proportion of patients with the use of certain drugs.

Psychological therapies, too, have become more refined so that their effectiveness can be measured in research studies designed in a similar way to drug trials. Psychoanalytic psychotherapy has moved towards briefer forms of treatment that focus on more circumscribed problems. Cognitive-behavioural therapy (CBT) has emerged as an effective form of treatment. Initially devised to treat depression, it is also finding a place in the treatment of such conditions as anxiety, panic attacks, phobias and hypochondriasis.

Combining SSRIs and CBT for depression has been repeatedly shown to lead to superior outcomes compared with either treatment given on its own. Family therapy has evolved substantially, especially in the area of child and adolescent psychiatry, as a way of treating problems which, though they are identified in one person, are actually an expression of maladaptive relating that pervades the entire family.

There is an accelerating pace of change in how psychiatric services are provided. Many governments have accepted the view that most resources should be placed in the community, and that admission to hospital should be brief, lasting on average a couple of weeks, in contrast to the lengthy periods of the past. Emergency assessment is carried out largely by community-based teams; other professional teams have evolved to assist more disabled patients.

There has been a steady expansion of the numbers of general hospital psychiatric units. These provide a much less stigmatising setting than a psychiatric hospital, and are usually situated much closer to patients' homes. Enduringly ill patients may be cared for in supervised homes in the community rather than in long-term wards of psychiatric hospitals, most of which have been closed or greatly reduced in size.

Impressive as this sounds, community-based psychiatry is not problem-free. To a large extent it has been driven by an ideology that, although differing in crucial ways, nonetheless resembles that associated with the rise of the asylum. The creation of the asylum in the countryside was based on a set of values driven by nostalgia for a 'natural' place of healing. The concept backfired because it isolated the mentally ill, and the costs involved were huge.

Today, the community is positively valued and institutions are derided. But parallels prevail. The same search for a natural place of healing is evident—not the countryside this time but the human community in cities and towns. Unfortunately, just as the asylum idea backfired so too has that of community-based care. The mentally ill have been isolated yet again, with many of them homeless and living in temporary, often unsuitable accommodation such as a boarding house in a poor area.

Partly as a reaction to the asylum as human warehouse and, later, to defects of community care, a consumer movement has been gathering momentum since the 1960s, to represent people who suffer from mental illness and their families. This network of support for its members has taken on a prominent advocacy role that has influenced the shape of psychiatric care, especially the development of local community-based services and the empowerment of the mentally ill themselves. At the same time, the plight of the mentally ill is raised more easily in the social and political arena.

A mixed picture

Governments are increasingly recognising the social and financial costs of mental illness. *The Global Burden of Disease*, a major study commissioned by, among others, the World Health Organization, has had a huge impact by showing that in 2020 mental illness will be a major cause of continuing disability. In terms of specific conditions, heart disease will rank first, depression second. These predictions have noteworthy implications for health economists and politicians. In many countries there is a glaring disparity in the proportion of the health budget dedicated to mental illness compared with other illnesses. The challenges to create a just system are immense. While an optimal system of mental health care remains elusive, ethical principles concerning decent care—such as those contained in the 1992 United Nations Charter on the Rights of Mentally Ill People—have prodded some governments to carry out reforms.

Mentally ill people and their families continue to face the ordeal of stigma; psychiatric illness is still seen as shameful. Fear associated with the history of the asylum is an enduring influence. People may hesitate to seek medical help or accept referral to a psychiatrist. Stigma also affects recovery, since the prejudice of others and the person's own negative expectations affect opportunities for work and social integration. The tabloid media aggravate the situation by running sensationalist stories about the danger to society of people with mental illness roaming around in the community. In fact, they are no more likely than the general public to act violently. On the contrary, they are more often victims of aggression.

These, sadly, are indisputable facts, and call out for attention. Equally indisputable, however, are the impressive strides that psychiatry is making in the twenty-first century. I have already mentioned some of these accomplishments and will highlight others throughout *Understanding Troubled Minds*, particularly in the two chapters on treatment. Astonishingly, more has been achieved in the past fifty years than during the entire twenty-four centuries since the ancient Greeks inaugurated the systematic study of the disturbed mind. We can be quietly confident that scientific research as undertaken now in many countries will lead to considerable progress and to the development of still more effective treatments in the years to come. However, we must be patient. Scientific progress tends to be incremental; the 'Eureka, I have it' discovery is rare. In the meantime we must be vigilant so that we do not repeat past mistakes. In this regard, the ethical dimension will always be as central as the scientific and the clinical.

CHAPTER 2

Making Sense of a Life

In 1879, a 26-year-old man began to evangelise with great fervour, gave away all his possessions, lived in a hovel, wore shirts made of sackcloth, and deprived himself of the basic necessities of life. A decade later, he sliced off a bit of his left ear and gave it to a prostitute saying, 'Keep this object carefully'.

How can we make sense of such unusual behaviour? In the practice of psychiatry, we attempt to do so by using what are usually referred to as perspectives. Several are available but two stand out—understanding and explanation. In this chapter, the tragic story of one of the greatest artists of all time, Vincent van Gogh, is used to show how these perspectives help us to do our job.

In day-to-day life, all of us try to make sense of our own behaviour and that of others. We give little thought to how we do this but are quite adept at the task, enough to feel we understand what makes ourselves or others tick. One vital means we use in trying to understand other people is empathy (from the Greek *em*, into and *pathos*, feeling); we place ourselves in the other person's shoes and try to imagine what they are experiencing. The information we draw on includes their statements about what they believe, feel, intend, wish, and so on, and the reasons they give for their psychological functioning and behaviour. We also consider their past experiences, customary ways of feeling and thinking, and current circumstances. We then arrive at a 'commonsense' understanding of how it is that a person acts in a particular way.

By using empathy and related understanding, we tackle the world of other people from the inside and seek meaning in their behaviour. A specific life event, say failing an exam, may well have different meanings for different people depending on their previous experiences, future aspirations, competing interests, and the like. Each of us can determine, through

empathy and related understanding, how one psychological event stems from another. For example, we can appreciate that a hardworking student who is intensely anxious not to disappoint her parents and teachers by doing poorly in her favourite subject, feels utterly devastated on failing even though this was due to her misreading of a pivotal exam question because she was in the midst of a severe bout of flu but had stubbornly insisted, against all advice, that she was fit enough to take the exam. Consider another student who is entirely sanguine about failing; in his case he has never found the subject appealing, had been planning to drop it the whole semester, and now feels a sense of relief that he has found a way to justify his decision to abandon studying the subject.

The capacity to empathise with and understand another is a marvellous asset generally and an indispensable skill for the psychiatrist, but it has its limitations. When a person's experience or behaviour lacks any sense of meaning and there are no clear connections between psychological events, we have to resort to looking in from the outside. For example, if a person is adamant that they are being hounded by the devil, psychiatrists will regard them as deluded if they hold that belief with absolute conviction and without adequate reason, and resists obvious evidence that the belief has no foundation; these are the specific features of delusions regardless of what they are about. The person could be convinced that they are being hounded by the CIA or all their teachers or the United Nations; the content is not relevant to determining what is going on in them.

This explanation-based perspective, which focuses on the form of an experience or behaviour and not its content, enables psychiatrists to diagnose a specific disorder; this in turn informs them about its cause, likely outcome and what treatments are bound to be effective. Use of the perspective has resulted in pivotal discoveries about the nature of mental illness—distinguishing between various types of illness, the role of genetics, the link between brain dysfunction and abnormal mental states, and helpful treatments.

Let us now return to Van Gogh to see how understanding and explanation are used by psychiatrists in their work. Why select him? Not only because he was a great and well-known artist but also because his life is richly documented through letters he wrote and the meticulous descriptions by others. We start with the major dates and events in Van Gogh's life shown below.

Vincent Van Gogh's life

Van Gogh grew up in an austere Dutch middle-class family led by a pastor father of limited talent who was assigned to peripheral parishes. His mother was a strong woman, unusually gifted in writing and painting. Two professions dominated in the family—the clergy and art-dealing. The family tree reveals a striking presence of mental illness. Van Gogh's uncle, also named Vincent, was subject to nervous complaints, frequently fleeing to the southern sun to recuperate. A family history of epilepsy existed on his mother's side.

Vincent Van Gogh's life history

Age	Date	Event
	1853	March 30: Born in Zundert, Holland one year to the day after his mother gave birth to a still-born son, also named Vincent
11	1864	Oct: Sent to boarding school
13	1866	Sept: Sent to new school
16	1869	Mar: Left school, returned home
		July: Moved to The Hague to serve as apprentice to an art dealer; arranged by his Uncle Vincent, a partner in the firm
20	1873	Transferred to the firm's Brussels branch in Jan and London branch in June
21	1874	June: Proposed marriage to Eugenie Loyer but was rejected; lost interest in art; solitary and absorbed in religion
23	1876	Mar: Dismissed from the firm due to poor performance
		Apr: Obtained post as assistant teacher at small school in Ramsgate, UK

Age	Date	Event
		July: Assisted a Methodist minister at Isleworth, UK
		Dec: Returned to Holland with the intention of becoming a priest
24	1877	Jan: Worked in a bookshop in Dordrecht
		May: Moved to Amsterdam to study for entry to the university's Faculty of Theology
25	1878	July: Abandoned studies and went to a mission school, but was rejected after a three-month trial
26	1879	Jan: Appointed as unqualified preacher in a poor mining district in Belgium
		July: Dismissed because of embarrassing behavior; starts a 'vagabond' existence, regarding himself as an 'outcast'
27	1880	Aug: Decided to become an artist
		Oct: Lived in Brussels, mainly drawing
28	1881	Apr: Returned to parental home
		Aug: Rejected by widowed cousin Kee Voss
		Dec: Left home again, moving to The Hague where he stayed with a cousin; the relationship between them became tense
29	1882	Apr: Met Sien, an alcoholic and pregnant prostitute, lived with her and devoted himself to her and her children
		July: Began painting in oil
30	1883	Sept: Broke up with Sien and wandered about purposely
		Dec: Returned home where he remained for the next two years; relationships generally strained; distressing affair with a woman resulted in her suicide attempt; painted productively
32	1885	Mar 26: Father died
		Nov: Moved to Antwerp
33	1886	Jan: Registered as a student at the Academy of Art in Antwerp
		Mar: Left Academy; moved to Paris where he stayed with his brother Theo (an art dealer) for two years; met painters including Gauguin and Toulouse-Lautrec; drank heavily
35	1888	Feb 20: Moved to Arles in Provence
		Sept 20: Gauguin visited him there; relationship soon became strained

Age	Date	Event
		Dec 23: Sliced off part of his ear and deposited it with Sien; admitted to hospital the next day, where he spent two weeks
36	1889	Jan 21: His friend the postman, Roulin, transferred to Marseilles
		Episodes of mental illness requiring re-admission: 4–19 Feb; 26 Feb to mid-April
		Mar 19: Placed in a hospital cell after a petition alleging that he was a dangerous madman was presented by neighbours and upheld by the Mayor
		Apr: Theo married; Johanna soon pregnant
		May 8: Entered an asylum voluntarily; stayed there for a year
37	1890	Feb I :Theo's son born and named Vincent
		May 21: Moved to Auvers-sur-Oise, just north of Paris, under the supervision of Dr Gachet who had a special interest in art
		July 27: Vincent shot himself, dying two days later
		Theo died of chronic renal disease six months later

Accounts of Van Gogh's childhood are inconsistent. Some suggest an unremarkable child whereas others portray him as solitary, 'not like other children', and estranged from his family. He was passionate about nature. He briefly attended the village school and then from eleven to sixteen was educated in boarding schools. His progress was unexceptional, but he read prolifically and had a knack for languages.

Despite excellent connections, his career was erratic. Through the mentorship of his wealthy uncle, he became an apprentice art-dealer. The prospect of inheriting his uncle's mantle was obvious. However, after rejection in love by his landlady's daughter, he lost interest and became fanatically religious. Attempts to study theology in Amsterdam and become an evangelist were unsuccessful, largely due to his provocative behaviour. Nonetheless, he was appointed as a lay preacher in a poor region of Belgium. His extreme selflessness soon led to his dismissal. After almost a year of miserable solitude, he announced his intention to become an artist. He returned to his parents' home for two years and then lived with his brother Theo (who had become a successful art-dealer like his Uncle Vincent). Van Gogh's only close relationship then was with his brother, although it was not free of tension. They corresponded frequently and by 1886 he was entirely financially dependent on Theo. Later, he moved to Arles in Provence and finally to Auvers-sur-Oise, just outside Paris.

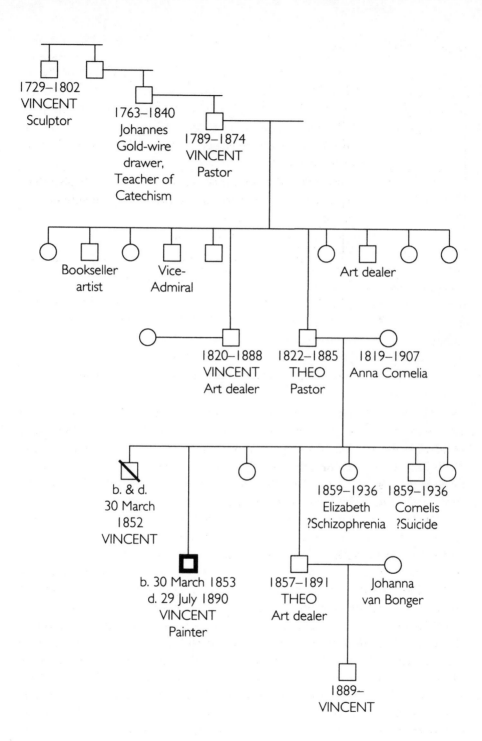

Vincent Van Gogh's family tree

Van Gogh's four key relationships with women all ended in humiliation. In London a passionate proposal of marriage was rejected by Eugenie Loyer, who was already engaged to another. He fell in love with Kee Voss, a widowed cousin, but again she did not reciprocate; his persistence resulted in much family bitterness. The following year he formed a liaison with Sien, an unmarried, pregnant prostitute. She was already the mother of a 5-year-old girl. Despite his care for her, Sien lapsed into her old ways and he felt no alternative but to leave her. Finally, he was the subject of an infatuation of a lonely spinster ten years his senior. Her family bitterly disapproved of Van Gogh. In the ensuing crisis she attempted suicide and was sent to a sanatorium.

Other relationships also collapsed. The most crucial was that with Paul Gauguin in Arles, where the atmosphere between them was 'electric' and culminated in Gauguin's departure. Van Gogh became severely disturbed, complaining that he was ugly, coarse ('as thick skinned as a wild boar') and demoralised. As he put it: 'a terrible discouragement gnawing at one's very moral energy ... fate seems to put a barrier to the instincts of affection, and a flood of disgust rises to choke one'; 'I am a prisoner in I do not know what horrible, horrible cage'.

On the other hand, Van Gogh felt remarkably energetic at times: 'The emotions are sometimes so strong that one works without knowing one works'; 'Ideas for my work come to me in swarms'; 'I go on like a steam engine at painting'; 'I only count on the exaltation that comes to me at certain moments, and then I let myself run into extravagances'. But after bursts of energy, melancholy invariably followed. Then he neglected his appearance, exposed himself to the elements in Herculean hikes, sometimes slept in the cold and often neglected to eat. He also drank heavily: 'If the storm gets too loud, I take a glass too much to stun myself.'

His medical and psychiatric history

Suffering from gonorrhoea, Van Gogh required a three-week admission to hospital in 1882. He may also have suffered from syphilis in 1886. He often complained of physical symptoms including stomach trouble, anorexia, dizziness and headaches.

At least seven episodes of severe mental disturbance occurred between 24 December 1889 and mid-April 1890. The first followed his acrimony with Gauguin in Arles, when he sliced off part of his left ear and deposited it with Sien. Most attacks began abruptly, with confusion, rambling talk, frightening hallucinations and religious-type delusions, and others of being poisoned. He acted aggressively without provocation. He made frenzied attempts to eat his paints and to drink kerosene. He later described these experiences as 'frightening beyond measure' and the thought of recurrences filled him with a 'fear and horror of madness'. There were associated 'moods of indescribable anguish', and he was sometimes observed to sit immobile for many hours. He voluntarily spent a year in a mental asylum, although he remained productive much of the time. Finally, he committed suicide at the age of thirty-seven.

What can psychiatrists make of all this?

Psychiatrists will see in Van Gogh's story unusual behaviour that might prove understandable, but also aspects better accounted for by an unravelling of its causes. His mood disturbances, the cutting of part of an ear, the psychotic episodes and his suicide are the subjects of particular interest.

Let us start with his mood. From the age of twenty Van Gogh suffered from swings of mood, predominantly depression but also excitement. In an effort to understand these, various psychological interpretations have been proposed. One biographer suggests that the key factor was domination by the stillbirth of his older brother Vincent, one year to the day before his own birth. His mother continued to grieve the loss and proved unable to devote her affections to the new child. He had to compete with an idealised lost child whose tomb he saw every day in the adjacent graveyard. This led to a profound sense of being unloved as well as unlovable, and a sensitivity to rejection. These sentiments were later played out in, and reinforced by, his unsuccessful love affairs. The failed relationships were followed by depression typified by self-punishment and estrangement from an apparently hostile world. Nonetheless, he still craved intimacy, but made intolerable demands on others; in effect he sought an unreserved love that he felt had been denied him earlier. He sought solace in a loving God, which required further suffering through self-denial and service to others. In this manner he could also give to those rejected like him the love he had never himself received. Van Gogh's estrangement from his family is further supported by an absence of affectionate remarks about his mother in his letters.

He began to identify with Christ, who also suffered, was misunderstood, and dedicated to the oppressed. This identification offered him the comforting possibility of remaining aloof from mankind yet eventually of being universally loved. The liaison with Sien can be understood as a consequence of his poor self-regard, but she was also his Mary Magdalene, who would be transformed by compassion into a good woman. He rejected the conventional church and its hypocritical 'Pharisees', like his father. Periods of exaltation and frenzied work accompanied spiritual labours. Finally, his decision to become an artist represented a fusion of his, and his family's, spiritual and artistic heritage. His intense immersion in his paintings, often accompanied by a numbing of his senses through starvation, exposure, exhaustion and alcohol, acted to ward off distressing feelings.

This interpretation, based on understanding, clarifies many aspects of Van Gogh's personality but seems inadequate to account for his profound mood swings. At times he was oblivious to everything around him, stared bleakly into space, and ceased to eat. At other times his mind was seemingly in tumult, he dressed outlandishly, and talked and laughed embarrassingly; then he worked frenetically at strange projects, such as a simultaneous translation of the Bible into four languages. Van Gogh described his moods as sudden 'unaccountable but involuntary emotions'. Others did not doubt that he had at these times passed from eccentricity to insanity.

The psychiatrist would now turn to the explanatory perspective—proposing a biological basis for his vulnerability to mood swings and, at times, clear-cut manic-depressive illness. His experiences and behaviour are consistent with typical features of what psychiatrists recognise readily as depressive and manic episodes. Genetic factors may have played a predisposing role, while unhappy events and physical ill-health were no doubt triggers.

Van Gogh's mutilation of his ear is perhaps the most tantalising episode. None of the many interpretations fully accounts for this bizarre act. A psychotic illness is the likely explanation for the form his mental state assumed. It was probably sparked off by heavy consumption of absinthe (which contained a neurotoxin known to be associated with mental disturbances). Van Gogh's poor nutrition and physical self-neglect may also have contributed.

We must consider the timing and the content of his madness as well as its form. His vulnerability was readily manifest in his deteriorating relationship with Gauguin. The weather was miserable and the two spent a number of enforced days in close proximity. Christmas was always a dangerous time. Vincent probably also knew about Theo's forthcoming marriage, and could see the risk of losing his only real source of support. Immediately before the episode he had quarrelled with Gauguin, throwing a glass of absinthe at him, and later he was reported as having threatened him with a razor. Gauguin, like so many others, had 'betrayed' him. In guilt, Vincent directed his anger inwards, mutilating himself.

Why the ear and why present it to a prostitute? Several possible and plausible explanations come to mind. Bullfights, a popular pastime in Arles, culminated in the ear being sliced from the vanquished animal by the toreador to be presented to his favourite lady. Stories about Jack the Ripper's dismemberment of his prostitute victims, sometimes involving an ear, appeared in the local paper at the time. Van Gogh was much preoccupied with the story of Christ in the Garden of Gethsemane, and destroyed two canvasses on this subject because they frightened him. In the episode of betrayal of Christ, Peter had cut off the ear of Malchus, a servant of the high priest, who had come to seize Christ.

Why the psychotic episodes?

There were several sources of intense stress in Van Gogh's life at the time of his descent into madness. The threatened loss of Theo's support, undivided until then and on which he was entirely dependent, was pre-eminent. Between January and April 1889, Theo had become engaged, married and an expectant father in rapid succession. Seeking solace in religion is not surprising given his past inclinations in that direction, but his religious ideas then were quite bizarre, totally beyond the comprehension of others (and, in retrospect, of himself). Eventually, he felt unable to look after himself and took to the suggestion of a period of asylum. Psychiatrists would examine the form of Van Gogh's breakdowns in terms of our accepted classification of mental disorders. A dysfunctional brain is possible given his confusion, loss of memory and the relatively brief duration of the psychotic episodes. Alcohol, the absinthe he consumed, also may have contributed to his mental state.

The suicide

What about Van Gogh's mental state at the time of his suicide? He continued to be buffeted by melancholia in Auvers. A month before he shot himself, he wrote: 'My life is threatened at the very root, and my steps are also wavering'. His painting, *Crows over the Wheatfields,* reflects evil foreboding. Fear of losing his sanity again plagued him. He had lost faith in his doctor and described him as being as sick as himself. There were inexplicable explosions of anger directed at him, during one of which the doctor feared that Van Gogh might use his pistol upon him.

The threatened loss of Theo's support had become more urgent. Theo then had a child with the perhaps ominous name of Vincent who, to make matters worse, had fallen ill. Theo's own health was declining, he had money worries, and he was considering quitting his job. Although Van Gogh repeatedly begged Theo to spend his vacation at Auvers rather than in Holland, Theo declined. Van Gogh had on several occasions declared that his 'life or death' depended on Theo's help. He could not easily express his resentment, and it is understandable, particularly in the light of previous self-destructive acts, that he turned his hostility inwards.

For the first time, Van Gogh was praised for his paintings. His response shows how events desirable to one person may disturb another. He wrote: 'But when I had read the article I felt almost mournful, for I thought—I ought to be like that, and I feel so inferior'. Guilt-ridden, he could not tolerate success; it was another burden to endure.

Combining understanding and explanation

It is clear from Van Gogh's story that the perspective of understanding has its limits. Despite psychiatrists' diligent efforts to find meaning in a person's narrative, we hit a snag when it becomes incomprehensible. We then have to accept that his experience is meaningless, even crazy, and that he might well have entered the world of mental illness.

The perspective of understanding has further limitations. We have no way of proving that a particular explanation, or interpretation, is correct. Equally plausible interpretations may be constructed in which certain features are given greater prominence in one than another. In the case of Van Gogh, for example, one interpretation may place more weight on his psychological dependency on Theo, another on the role of his religion convictions. On the other hand, a sound interpretation is not a fiction since it can be critically tested against the evidence on which it is based—how it fits the facts of the story. A convincing interpretation will survive close scrutiny, and one may be chosen as superior to its competitors.

Interpretation may be revised as new information comes to light. A new behaviour or experience may lead to previous ones now seen as having a meaning. The new information may also contribute to a richer understanding and to a wider range of meaningful connections. In clinical practice an understanding is constructed in the interaction between subject (patient) and interpreter (clinician) and each contributes to and may influence the other in shaping the emergent story. A risk exists that the interpreter will see in the subject a confirmation of connections that they are looking for, perhaps based on a favoured psychological theory. In turn, the patient may, if the clinician is seen as an authority to be pleased, produce material to support the interpretation.

Understanding does not lead to the formulation of general laws, nor is it a reliable way of predicting behaviour. People with similar experiences may share similar patterns of meaningful connections, but there will always be individual variation, and for some the patterns will be quite different.

Limitations of explanation

The methods of the natural sciences have made a crucial contribution to psychiatry, and will continue to do so through rapid progress in, for example, the neurosciences. However, this approach, especially in the minds of its more fervent advocates, can be overstated. Some claim that only through this method can real knowledge be acquired and that most, or all, of psychiatry will one day be reduced to causal explanation.

While this method may have useful things to say about people who find themselves in predicaments easily understood in terms of life circumstances (for example, grieving the loss of a near one), such a person is likely to be better understood in psychological terms, and more appropriately helped through such means. Even when a person suffers from a clear-cut mental illness, the nature of which is best elucidated through causal explanation, contact is made through appreciation of them as a subject rather than object. Understanding what it means for that person to have the experiences arising from the illness is essential. Even if an important treatment is prescription of a drug, compliance with it will often be determined by the quality of the relationship between patient and clinician. The impact of the illness on the person and their family, and key processes in recovery, will often be best appreciated through understanding.

Psychotherapy, the cornerstone of much treatment in psychiatry, is conducted between two experiencing subjects, and ultimately is concerned with a search for meaning. What is the meaning of the person's distress; how does it emerge from their life story; how can these meanings be recast or altered so as to allow distress to be alleviated?

Some other perspectives used in psychiatry

When thinking about a patient's narrative, psychiatrists select from many other perspectives in addition to understanding and explanation. They all help to shed light on what underlies the narrative. Some widely accepted options are the psychoanalytic, dimensional, family and cultural. Their rationale and application will be encountered in many of the chapters that follow.

Psychoanalysis clearly involves the method of understanding, given that it seeks meaningful connections between thoughts, feelings, memories and fantasies that lie concealed in the unconscious, and that the psychiatrist encourages the patient to uncover through the process of free association. The typical psychoanalytically oriented psychiatrist operates on the basis that theoretical concepts guide the pursuit of these meanings. For instance, a dream that on first sight seems to lack any meaning must be looked at beyond its manifest content, since the ego's dream censor has disguised what Freud called the 'latent' content lest it frighten or threaten the dreamer. Vehement critics of psychoanalytic theory contend that all interpretations derived in this way cannot be proven to be right or wrong, which therefore makes it a useless means of learning about the psyche, of an individual or in general. Psychoanalytic concepts are certainly problematic to define, measure and examine experimentally. But as we shall see when we consider the ego and its mechanisms of defence, or the effectiveness of psychoanalytic treatment, the scientific study of these aspects of psychoanalysis is possible if we are not overly dogmatic about how we define science.

What do we mean by the dimensional perspective? Psychiatric disorders are generally seen as either present or not, but this cross-sectional perspective tends to neglect two aspects of the human condition. The first is that people often have a varying measure of a particular psychological quality. For example, Van Gogh's mood cycles could have represented the changes that most of us experience in the face of unwelcome life events like a bereavement, a physical illness and the loss of a valued job. Feeling down does not necessarily equate to a diagnosis of melancholia. Personality traits like impulsiveness, dependency and volatility may reflect a disposition to react in certain ways, but again the degree to which they manifest lies on a spectrum. These traits are especially relevant to the understanding approach, for it is in the interaction between personality and life circumstances that meaningful connections with current problems emerge. We will look at the role of personality factors in many psychiatric conditions in later chapters, and at the concept of personality problems in their own right.

As in the case of Van Gogh, studying a person in their family setting is a key part of the psychiatrist's job. What it was like to grow up in a family falls within the scope of understanding. Ways in which a family functions are best viewed in terms of the family as a system rather than as individual members—how members typically relate to one another; what sorts of boundaries exist between sub-groups, such as parents versus siblings; whether a person's symptoms keep the family together; what patterns of behaviour pass from one generation to the next. Van Gogh's family shows striking repetitions of names used and the destinies these imply, and of relationships between brothers (strong devoted to weak: Theo supported Vincent; their father Theo was supported by Uncle Vincent).

How we experience the world is strongly shaped by our cultural identity. Van Gogh's Calvinist environment was central to many aspects of his life. The ways in which distress or symptoms of illness are expressed may be culturally conditioned or coloured. In many cultures the idiom for the expression of psychological distress involves the experience of bodily unease, and the person's symptoms may be somatic rather than psychological. The content of symptoms may reflect cultural values even when their form is determined by brain dysfunction; thus Van Gogh's delusions were of a religious nature in keeping with his social background.

Conclusion

When a psychiatrist asks why a particular person has become ill, both *understanding* and *explanation* play a role. They guide the clinician towards a comprehensive elucidation of causes, in so far as they are known, and of meaningful connections unique to that person. The other perspectives mentioned above further clarify the person's problems.

CHAPTER 3

Defining and Classifying Mental Illnesses

Psychiatry is the branch of medicine that deals with the diagnosis and treatment of mental illness (also commonly referred to as psychiatric disorder). The question of what is and is not a mental illness is complicated and often contentious. Most of us experience emotions such as anxiety and depression at some stage in our lives, but they do not amount to a clinical diagnosis and are entirely understandable in the light of the trials and tribulations of life. As not all unpleasant emotions point to a mental illness, psychiatrists (and other mental health professionals and various forms of counsellors) may also help people who do not suffer from a diagnosable condition but who nevertheless feel distressed or are not functioning effectively in their daily lives. (One of the two classifications we will look at in a moment gets over this hurdle by adding a category called 'Other conditions that may be a focus of clinical attention' and including in it rather vague entities like religious or spiritual problem, acculturation problem and phase of life problem.)

The following widely accepted definition helps us to a degree to distinguish between a disorder and what is commonly referred to as problems of living: a psychiatric disorder is a psychological syndrome (or pattern) that is associated with distress (unwelcome symptoms) or dysfunction (impaired functioning in one or more key areas of day-to-day life) or with an increased risk of death or disability.

Most mental illnesses in psychiatric practice are defined in terms of the pattern of clinical features observed, the nature of their onset and how they progress. Another view that every disorder is a distinct disease has been criticised as reflecting an overly restricted medical model that cannot be applied to psychiatry in its present stage of evolution. We could say this about only a very few psychiatric conditions, although it is likely that the picture will change as the scientific foundations of the subject become more solid.

A body of psychiatric opinion posits that a diagnosis of mental illness can be confirmed only in the presence of objective evidence of disturbed psychological functioning, whether of thinking, learning, perceiving, remembering or feeling. Behaviour that is deviant or unconventional is seen as indicating a mental illness only if it is associated with such disturbed psychological functioning. Sir Aubrey Lewis, a leading figure in British psychiatry, put it this way: 'If non-conformity can be detected only in total behaviour, while all the particular psychological functions seem unimpaired, health will be presumed not illness'.

The risk of applying a label of mental illness inappropriately is sharply illustrated in Emily Dickinson's poem:

> Much madness is divinest sense
> To a discerning eye;
> Much sense the starkest madness.
> 'Tis the majority
> In this, as all, prevails.
> Assent, and you are sane;
> Demur,—you're straightway dangerous,
> And handled with a chain.

Another illustration comes from mid-nineteenth century Black America. In a report entitled 'On the Diseases and Physical Peculiarities of the Negro Race', Samuel Cartwright, a physician from Alabama, introduced two new psychiatric conditions encountered in slaves and graced them with florid Greek names. The main diagnostic feature of Drapetomania was the wish to run away from servitude; slaves should be treated kindly and humanely to prevent the symptom. If that did not work, whipping should follow. Dysaesthesia Aethiopis, also called Rascality, manifested in slaves who were idle, unproductive, thieving and destructive! The condition was more prevalent in 'free Negroes' who lacked supervision by a white person.

The issue of nonconformity as problematic in determining what is and is not a mental illness emerged as a crucial theme in my own career. In the early 1970s I stumbled across disturbing media reports which alleged that many political and religious dissenters and human rights activists in the former Soviet Union were being labelled as mentally ill and detained in mental hospitals indefinitely or until they renounced their 'disturbed ideas'. What ideas were these? A good example of a prominent dissenter during this period, General Pyotr Grigorenko, publicly espoused the rights of a particular minority group. This constituted a source of considerable embarrassment, even threat, to the Soviet authorities—a Red Army general acting in such disloyal fashion! The State's response was to declare his thoughts as those of a gravely disturbed mind in urgent need of treatment. I had the opportunity to meet several dissenters, both prominent and ordinary, and to determine for myself that they were mentally normal and unusual only in adopting the role of human rights activist out of deep conviction and courage and despite the threat of severe punitive action by the State.

How could such a travesty of medicine have come about? Soviet psychiatry was totally hierarchical at the time and led by a coterie of psychiatrists who owed their power in part to satisfying the requirements of their political masters. Moreover, their view of mental illness, particularly the psychoses, was so broad as to allow for even the most subtle of psychological changes to be construed as evidence, and then discernible only to the expert eye. Sluggish schizophrenia was a uniquely Soviet psychiatric creation. In a Kafkaesque way, the noble aspirations of thousands of dissenters over a 40-year period were recast as delusions of reformism. It would take a chapter unto itself merely to outline the story of this misuse of psychiatry. The interested reader may turn to a book I co-authored with Peter Reddaway, an academic expert in Soviet politics, suitably entitled *Russia's Political Hospitals* (Gollancz, London, 1977), to describe and analyse the practices.

A sociological model of mental illness, known as anti-psychiatry, went so far as to question whether mental illness exists at all and argued that psychiatry is nothing more than an instrument of society (and psychiatrists its agents), which uses the label of mental illness as a means to exert social control. RD Laing, the foremost psychiatrist of the movement, asserted that it was an abnormal society that had driven people diagnosed by mainstream psychiatry into their ways of experiencing the world.

The vast majority of psychiatrists rejected this radical view, although Laing and his colleagues in the United Kingdom and Thomas Szasz in the United States did act as gadflies in stirring many psychiatrists, including myself, to ponder about the complexity of our role in society and the ethical conundrum of multiple loyalty. Instead, most of us supported an expanded concept of mental illness by applying the biopsychosocial approach. This is the basis of the perspective adopted in *Understanding Troubled Minds*; it looks not merely at symptoms but embraces many aspects of a person's psychological and social world.

Why is classification necessary?
Even in the face of the problems encountered in defining mental illness and the potential misuse of diagnostic labels and pigeonholing of people, it is vital for the practice of psychiatry to attempt to classify. As in other fields

of medicine, we group together illnesses on the basis of their similarities and differences. Classification is important for both patient and psychiatrist because:

- it makes for effective communication between mental health professionals and between them and patients and families;
- it provides a framework for the study of the outcome of mental illnesses, which gives patients and families some idea of what to expect;
- it allows for prediction of the effects of treatment and helps patients and families to understand the rationale for selecting one treatment over another;
- it facilitates scientific research into possible causes of mental illnesses and, indirectly, their treatment—with obvious potential benefits for patients.

The task is a lot easier in medicine than in psychiatry, since we can identify and classify most diseases on the basis of their known or likely physical causes. For example, the provisional diagnosis of a heart attack—based on the typical pattern of severe chest pain of sudden onset, associated with sweating and nausea—can be confirmed by specific tests such as an electrocardiogram (ECG) and elevated levels of specific blood enzymes. In psychiatry, neither are the causes of most conditions known nor objective tests available. Classification is therefore based on how clinical features cluster together to constitute 'syndromes' (from the Greek, meaning to run with).

The complaints conveyed by a person seeking treatment—called symptoms—may be physical, like pain, shortness of breath and palpitations, or psychological, such as sadness and intrusive thoughts. Clinical findings are referred to as signs. Again they may be physical, such as an irregular heart rate or an abnormal mental state like disorientation for time and place. A cluster of symptoms and signs, the syndrome, tends to have a predictable course and response to particular treatments; the syndrome is given a name and then incorporated into a systematic classification.

Traditionally, the classification is so arranged that there is no overlap between categories. This is exceedingly difficult to achieve in psychiatry as more than one diagnosis may apply in the same person, each of which may share a number of clinical features. The co-existence of depression and anxiety is a common example.

Of the available classifications of mental illnesses, two are widely used. The *International Classification of Diseases* published by the World Health Organization (WHO) is in its tenth edition (1992) and is known as ICD-10. The *Diagnostic and Statistical Manual of Mental Disorders* (DSM-IV), published by the American Psychiatric Association (APA), is in its fourth edition (1994). Both are under revision, but the process is taking considerably longer than envisaged as committees of experts in their respective fields grapple with what to include or exclude, and what to group together under one diagnostic umbrella and what to split into smaller diagnostic units. For example, debate continues regarding the diagnoses of autism and Asperger's—are they distinct from each other or variants of the same underlying condition? We cannot be sure since we do not know the cause of either. Among the eating disorders a number of clinical syndromes do not fit readily into the main two disorders of anorexia nervosa and bulimia nervosa and are grouped as 'unspecified' (in ICD) and 'not otherwise specified' (in DSM). Many other instances occur in both classifications of this lumping vs. splitting dilemma, the product of a process that depends on using syndromes rather than causes as the basis for diagnosis.

Another reason for the need to revise classifications is that many psychiatric diagnoses are, in varying measure, social constructs. A clear-cut illustration is homosexuality. This was traditionally listed as a sexual deviation in both ICD and DSM but came under marked scrutiny in the wake of the civil rights movement in the United States in the mid-1960s. In 1973 the APA, clearly influenced by the huge shift in society's attitude towards the idea of freedom of sexual expression, put the issue to a vote of its membership. The result was predictable—homosexuality would no longer be regarded as a psychiatric condition. A new diagnosis of 'persistent and marked distress about sexual orientation' was devised as a substitute. The ICD made similar change by referring to psychological problems stemming from a particular sexual orientation. The story seemed to have ended. Not so; the American Psychological Society, in the wake of pressure from religious conservatives, felt the need to voice its opposition to so-called reparative therapy whose aim is to change sexual orientation. The 150 000 member association concluded that there was no 'solid evidence' for the effectiveness of such treatment and that homosexuality is a normal variant of sexuality.

Ironically, a new sexual disorder was under consideration at about this time, namely sexual addiction; moreover, an organisation called Sex Addicts Anonymous was launched in 1997 to cater for those afflicted. Hypersexual disorder has been proposed to cover the case of people who alienate themselves from family and friends because of their compulsive sexual behaviour.

A quite different form of addiction has been identified, which coincides with the advent of the internet. Problematic Internet Use (or pathological use of electronic media) has been recommended by some psychiatrists as the name for what they regard as a bona fide form of addiction, where the affected person cannot resist the impulse to use the internet and, as a result, fails to fulfil social and other major obligations. To ascertain how common the condition is, internet addiction scales have been developed. One per cent of the general population were determined to be addicted and another 5 per cent at risk. A range of medications and psychological therapies have been proposed for PIU despite the absence of a consensus that it actually exists!

One final example of a new mental illness is utterly intriguing and extraordinarily difficult to understand. The condition lacks a name but its hallmark is a longstanding (since childhood or early adolescence), intense need to have one or more limbs amputated. Typically afflicted people are mostly men of middle age who seek desperately to recruit a surgeon to remove an entirely healthy arm or leg. They are not deluded and realise that their request is exceptionally unusual. Nonetheless, they have to have the amputation in order to restore their true identity. Once done, they are entirely satisfied, indeed feel better than they have ever felt. Needless to say, surgeons are not inclined to fulfil their wishes. The awful snag is that the person himself may then attempt to carry out the amputation. Psychotherapy and medications do not help in the slightest. I encountered my first case after four decades of clinical practice. He had managed to obtain the operation and was feeling on top of the world. Yes, it was impossible to empathise with or understand him, but it was abundantly clear that he was 'cured'!

The basis for the ICD-10 can be traced back to 1885 when the Congress of Mental Medicine, held in Antwerp, established a working group to develop a classification that psychiatric associations around the world could adopt. This was a radical step. Until that time, all systems stemmed from the theories of an assortment of influential leaders in psychiatry. At a follow-up congress in 1889, eleven categories were adopted. Following publication of the seventh edition of the ICD in 1955, the WHO invited Erwin Stengel, then Professor of Psychiatry in Sheffield University, to establish principles for a truly international system. His report formed the basis of subsequent versions of the ICD.

Marked differences in diagnostic practice were still apparent—the result of psychiatrists deploying differing theories about the nature of mental illness (some quite idiosyncratic, like the Soviet schema I have described). Dissatisfaction with this state of affairs led the APA in the mid-1970s to explore a new approach. Its three innovations were classification of illnesses according to their observable clinical features rather than to their assumed cause (with the striking exceptions of post-traumatic stress disorder and acute stress disorder); explicit criteria to improve diagnostic agreement between psychiatrists; and a 5-axis system to provide for a more comprehensive evaluation, including the presence of any physical conditions, the role of life stressors, and a quantitative estimate of the person's level of psychological and social functioning.

For an example of the use of explicit criteria, we can look at the diagnosis of schizophrenia. The psychiatrist has to establish that the patient has two or more of five listed clinical features (for example, hallucinations, disorganised thoughts) lasting for a month or more, plus major social or work dysfunction. A number of conditions that present similarly, like drug-induced psychosis, have to be excluded. Such specificity is designed to generate a greater level of agreement among practitioners, but this does not mean that the diagnosis is any more scientifically sturdy. This method also leads to a categorical decision that a person is either suffering or not suffering from a particular condition. What about someone who does not fulfil all the stipulated criteria but is clearly still suffering and needs professional help? And the person who satisfies some criteria from one diagnostic category and some from another? Does that person have two mental illnesses?

DSM has obviously not solved all the quandaries that psychiatrists face in seeking accurate diagnoses. On the other hand we are better off with it, at least when it comes to conducting research and talking the same language among ourselves.

The core groups of mental illnesses

Certain core groups of mental illnesses are part of the two main classification systems. Psychiatrists depend on these groups but recognise that they in no way do justice to the complexity of either the clinical picture or the uniqueness of the suffering person. Moreover, the ICD and DSM do not have the same groupings throughout and terminology differs in many places.

Let us look at the ICD, since this is the official classification of the World Health Organization and used universally. We will, however, refer to both ICD and DSM in later chapters devoted to specific psychiatric conditions. The tenth edition of the ICD contains ten main groups, referred to as blocks. These are subdivided further. So, for example, the first block, organic disorders, includes Alzheimer's dementia, vascular dementia, other forms of dementia, delirium, other mental illnesses due to brain damage, and personality and behavioural changes due to brain disease or brain damage.

Here is a brief account of the ten blocks, each of which will be dealt with in detail in the chapters that follow.

Organic disorders Here the person's psychological state or behaviour is affected by an identifiable physical process involving either the brain directly (for example, injury, stroke, Alzheimer's disease) or the body as a whole (for example, liver failure, under-active thyroid) with indirect effects on the brain. In some cases we know the actual cause, for example, delirium induced by withdrawal from alcohol; in others we do not (at least, as yet), for example, Alzheimer's dementia.

Misuse of drugs (prescribed or illicit)   This can produce a range of psychiatric states through direct effects on the functioning of the brain. Alcohol is certainly the most common example worldwide. Other drugs widely misused include benzodiazepines, marijuana and amphetamines. Their effect can take many forms, ranging from the easily reversible state of intoxication to permanent loss of memory and of other higher mental functions.

Schizophrenia and related delusional disorders   These are the classical psychoses. The word 'psychosis' has a long history and many meanings. In effect, it means impaired mental functioning to a degree that grossly interferes with the person's ability to maintain contact with reality and consequently to meet the demands of everyday life. In schizophrenia, the person's thinking, perception and emotional state are highly disturbed, leading to a sense of fragmentation of the self (schizophrenia literally means splintering of mind). In delusional disorders, the main features are bizarre, unrealistic thoughts, most commonly the conviction that one is being persecuted or hounded.

Mood disorders   The basic disturbance is a major change in mood, either depression or elation (mania). Associated features are a variety of symptoms like abnormal thinking (for example, inappropriate pessimism in depression and unbridled optimism in mania) and level of activity (for example, apathetic inertia in depression and inexhaustible mental and physical energy in mania).

Neurotic disorders   Like 'psychosis', the term 'neurosis' is enveloped in mists of ambiguity. In fact, the APA dropped it from its classification on these grounds. Coined in the early nineteenth century by a Scottish neurologist, William Cullen, to refer to nervous disorders of psychological origin, the word has been applied so widely (and often disparagingly) as to be meaningless. In ICD-10 it is used to more specific purpose. It covers the states of anxiety, including phobia, panic, general anxiety and obsessive-compulsive disorder; conditions linked to severe stress like that resulting from a major trauma (such as torture or rape); and physical disorders with a psychological origin (Cullen's original group).

Behavioural syndromes associated with physiological disturbances   These cover basic biological functions like eating, sleeping and sexuality. In each case a wide variety of problems may arise as a result of psychological factors. The most clear-cut example is anorexia nervosa, where profound disturbance in appetite and weight, even to the point of death through self-starvation, occur without a physical cause. Sexual dysfunctions like premature ejaculation and inorgasmia are other examples.

Disorders of adult personality and behaviour   People described as having these disorders have ingrained and enduring behaviour patterns, with inflexible responses to a range of personal and social circumstances. They perceive, think, feel and relate to others in ways that differ significantly from those of the average person in the same culture. Such patterns tend to be stable and to encompass many aspects of psychological functioning, including feelings of distress and problems in relationships. The traits of people with these disorders are clearly present to a degree in all of us. The term 'personality disorder' (one I am loathe to use and have replaced with 'problematic personality' in Chapter 10) is used if these character traits lead to detrimental outcomes and are of long standing. Personality change that entails a specific behaviour reaching a diagnostic level includes pathological gambling, pathological stealing and fire-setting.

Mental retardation (or intellectual disability)   This covers long-term conditions in which development of the mind has been arrested or remains incomplete. Mental impairment ranging from mild to severe, in such areas as thinking, reasoning and language, and social functioning are the result. A clear-cut example is Down's syndrome, the result of an inherited chromosomal abnormality. (Intellectual disability is beyond the scope of this book.)

Disorders of psychological development, and childhood behavioural and emotional disorders   These are the two principal conditions occurring in childhood and adolescence. The former is divided into specific (such as reading, writing and language) or generalised (for example, autism). The latter is a hodge-podge, made up of diverse categories linked to particular areas of disturbed childhood functioning, which include conduct disorder, emotional disorder (such as social anxiety), tics (Tourette's disorder) and mixed emotional/behavioural forms.

How the classification is used
The usefulness of the ICD is clearly illustrated in the story of Jill.

A 28-year-old woman was brought by a girlfriend to the emergency department with self-inflicted superficial lacerations of both wrists. Following an argument with her boyfriend three days earlier, Jill had been unable to sleep and was 'too upset' to go to work. She decided to cut her wrists because her boyfriend had not called her since the argument. She then telephoned her friend to tell her that she was going to die, and it was this friend who brought her to hospital.

Jill described frequent episodes of feeling depressed over many years, each usually lasting for several hours and precipitated by conflict with boyfriends or family members. However, she had not experienced significant sleep disturbance, reduced appetite or weight loss at any time. She conceded that she was an emotional person by nature. Her many relationships usually ended in conflict and a dramatic gesture on her part—including suicidal behaviour.

At first Jill was tearful, but soon became animated. She told her story with dramatic flair, and seemed to want to impress the psychiatrist with the intensity of her distress. She described herself as making friends easily—she was a 'people person'. At the same time it seemed that her friendships were superficial and short-lasting, and that others thought her inconsiderate and immature. She found it easier to 'make friends' with men than with women, and apparently considered other women as rivals for her boyfriend's attention.

In making a diagnosis, the psychiatrist would first consider the episode that brought Jill to the hospital, and then whether or not she has a disorder of personality. Although describing herself as having felt depressed from time to time over many years, those episodes were brief and not associated with features of clinical depression, such as diminished appetite, weight loss or disturbed sleep. Thus, she does not meet the criteria for a mood disorder.

The episode that led to the self-harm, precipitated by the argument with her boyfriend and associated with crying and inability to work over three days, indicates a diagnosis within the neurotic and stress-related disorder block—of an adjustment disorder, and more specifically of a brief depressive reaction.

Jill's description of longstanding patterns of behaviour and of relating to others raises the possibility of a problematic personality (perhaps of the histrionic type, which includes traits like being easily hurt, seeking attention and egocentricity), although there is not enough information to make a definite diagnosis. The psychiatrist would be cautious about this diagnosis, which would necessitate specialised and correspondingly long-term psychotherapy.

In fact, the psychiatrist began brief counselling to deal with the adjustment disorder and took the opportunity, in a planned way, to assess underlying personality features. During the sessions, it became clear to both Jill and the therapist that several aspects of her personality had led to continuing difficulties in her life, especially regarding relationships, both general and intimate. They agreed that a longer course of psychotherapy was warranted.

Jill's story leads us to look at how psychiatrists go about the interrelated tasks of assessing and treating patients.

CHAPTER 4

The Psychiatrist at Work

The key tool that psychiatrists use in everyday work is the clinical interview. Our purpose is not only to listen to the patient's story, examine the mental state and reach a diagnosis, but also to understand the patient as a person and the reasons for seeking help at a particular time. The interview is also pivotal in establishing a trusting relationship, the crucible within which treatment operates. Central to this relationship are the hope of receiving help, an opportunity to share problems and a source of reliable advice.

Respect for the dignity of patients is central in medicine, but especially for mentally ill people who are so vulnerable to being stigmatised and disempowered. We may be confronted with issues relating to respect for autonomy, in that patients may have difficulty giving informed consent or determining what is in their best interests (such as the suicidally depressed). Confidentiality is another crucial aspect of the relationship between psychiatrist and patient. The Hippocratic Oath stresses that 'Whatever in connection with my professional practice or not in connection with it, I see or hear, in the life of men, which ought not to be spoken abroad, I will not divulge, as reckoning that all should be kept secret'. This is particularly important in psychiatry, given the intensely personal nature of the material revealed. Confidentiality cannot always be absolute, but should be breached only to safeguard the patient's interests and the safety or interests of others.

When interviewed, patients may well be embarrassed, ashamed and fearful of humiliation at a time of marked vulnerability. A tactful, accepting attitude on our part fosters trust. Rushed interviews inevitably jeopardise a sensitive approach. Unfortunately, we often have to make the best of less than ideal conditions. The setting may be inappropriate (for example, a busy emergency department) or there may be a lack of resources.

We begin the interview by explaining its purpose, then do our best to listen empathically and observe behaviour and emotional responses. Our apparent passivity may provoke anxiety in patients but the process is an active one. We try to be constantly alert to their story and needs and, even if not posing questions, will use strategies to promote the flow of information. Asking the person to 'go on' or 'please say more' is a simple example, as is repeating their last phrase as a question. We also use gestures—a receptive nod, an expression showing interest. We explore many areas, firstly in a non-directive way and then by using more specific questions to clarify details. While the story is being sought, we try to understand the person's circumstances. The problems facing a young mother soon after the birth of her first child are of course different to those of an elderly man who has just lost his wife.

Some aspects of the interview call for great sensitivity. For example, when inquiring about sexual experience we use considerable tact. Due to guilt and embarrassment, people may hesitate to talk about extramarital affairs, homosexual experiences, sexual fantasies and impotence. Probing these areas can wait—there is no rush. Other areas of potential sensitivity include trauma, such as sexual abuse or the death of a sibling. If the person is tearful, we acknowledge the distress and encourage them to express feelings further, within the security of growing trust.

We virtually always raise the topic of suicide, even though it may not seem relevant. Self-destructive impulses are common in mental illness and may be concealed. Given the profound nature of questions of life and death, we seek to tread gently.

No two interviews are ever the same. As mental illness has potentially disturbing effects on communication, our approaches are tailor-made. For instance, we do not interrupt an obsessional patient who needs to provide an intricately detailed account. A patient who is suspicious due to the illness may question our motives; we try to make them as explicit as possible. We recognise a patient's desperate need to retain control by seeking permission periodically to continue the interview. A patient with impaired cognitive functioning may not tolerate a lengthy interview due to mental fatigue. We put questions to the elderly as clearly as we can since their hearing may be impaired. In the case of psychotic patients we use special skills to make sense of their agitated or bizarre behaviour, and take into account that they are preoccupied with thoughts entirely unrelated to the task at hand.

Differences in values and culture can serve as a barrier to communication just as much as not sharing the same language. We modify our mode of interviewing in an effort to join effectively with such patients.

We rely on the cooperation of relatives since their perspective yields invaluable information. However, we appreciate the potentially devastating effects on them of a severe mental illness and realise that their observations may be biased because of their emotional involvement. Given our responsibility to the patient but also our wish to help family members, we may be caught in a cleft stick. We make every effort to seek the patient's consent to approach the family and to exercise discretion about family secrets.

What is covered in the interview?

After asking for the person's name, age, marital and family status and occupation, we gather details about the following:

- The main problems—when they began, how they have progressed and what is happening currently. A beginning point in the story is identified if possible—the first symptom, a notable life event. We then clarify the nature and severity of any stressors, and how they are being dealt with.
- The effect of the problems on the patient's life (work, relationships, ability to care for themselves).
- The treatment, if any, to this point—what has been tried and with what results.
- The relationship of the psychiatric features to any relevant medical condition (our medical training comes to the fore here).

The case of Lee illustrates the ground typically covered.

Lee, a 45-year-old married mother of three who works as a computer programmer, was referred by her family doctor to a psychiatrist following a suicide attempt. She described six months of depressive symptoms that began shortly after she separated from her husband. She was unable to sleep or take pleasure from her usual activities, had lost weight and was feeling worthless. She had trouble concentrating on her work because of intrusive suicidal thoughts. Two weeks before the interview, Lee stopped work and could barely care for herself or her children. Five days later she was taken by her eldest daughter to the family doctor who, following a sensitive appreciation of her plight, diagnosed her as suffering from a depressive illness, prescribed anti-depressant medication and made arrangements for her to see a psychiatrist. The day before the appointment she had, while alone, taken an overdose of the tablets and left a note describing herself as a 'failed wife and mother'.

Since many mental illnesses recur, the link between the current episode and previous ones is strong. We therefore enquire about any past illnesses, admissions to hospital and treatments received. If, as in the following case, a patient refers to a 'nervous breakdown', we seek a thorough description of symptoms and of treatment, given that the term can cover every situation from a couple of days sick leave for anxiety to a prolonged period of hospital treatment for a psychosis.

Carla described being treated in a psychiatric ward ten years previously for a 'nervous breakdown'. The psychiatrist ascertained that this had been a manic illness in that she had been excitable, elated, heard voices and thought she was Jesus Christ. She had been treated with an anti-psychotic for several months and participated in a group program. Carla had been well since then.

A focus on any medical illnesses and their treatment, past or present, follows logically, particularly when it relates to the present psychiatric condition.

Penny, aged 55, had a debilitating form of rheumatoid arthritis compounded by a feeling of despair because of an increase in pain and disability and reduced response to her anti-rheumatic medication. But her despair had increased immediately following the introduction of a new drug and, given its potential to induce a depressed mood as a side-effect, her medications were reassessed and the likely offending drug withdrawn.

'The person who has the illness is more important than the illness the person has' sums up the value of family and personal background. A patient's life story begins with the family of origin—a description of parents and their relationship; siblings, their order of birth and the nature of their relationships; the family atmosphere especially as it affects and is affected by the patient; and any history of mental illness in other family members. The patient's life story is a hallmark of the psychiatric case history. We gather a broad body of information in order to build up a picture of the uniqueness of the person and their world—akin to a vivid biography. While no list can be complete, this is the kind of information we look for, with different emphases depending on individual circumstances:

- complications of the mother's pregnancy, feeding problems, achievement of normal milestones;
- childhood hyperactivity, bed-wetting, phobias, friendships, major childhood illnesses like asthma;
- school performance, disciplinary trouble, peer relationships;
- adolescent adjustment difficulties;
- employment record and satisfaction;

- age at first menstruation, menstrual problems, age and complications of menopause;
- sexual attitudes, activities, orientation and dysfunction;
- courtship, relationship with spouse or de facto, state of current marriage, past marriages or divorces;
- children and their relationship with the patient;
- social network—family and friends.

Here are two examples of central aspects of the pictures built up by this process:

Jean, an 18-year-old university student and the youngest of three daughters, sought help for severe bingeing and vomiting. Her mother was a 45-year-old primary school teacher, her father a 50-year-old electrician. Jean described both of them as exceedingly strict with the children, a result of their strong religious beliefs. She stressed that the marriage was 'a farce—they never talk or touch'. The atmosphere at home was usually tense. She was not close to either parent but had confided in her sisters until they had left the family home a year earlier.

A young man was referred by the university counselling service because of his difficulty in concentrating and deterioration in his academic performance. He was extremely shy, had been a loner throughout school and as an adult had no friends. He had never had a girlfriend, had not had any sexual contact and pursued solitary activities such as model-making. He had little contact with his family. 'I'd rather be alone, people don't interest me.' But his lack of social links did trouble him—'Maybe I shouldn't be like this'.

We usually draw a family tree to track graphically the details of family relationships (see Van Gogh's family tree as an example in Chapter 2).

Examination of the mental state

While drawing out the person's life story, we also examine their mental state—that is, current psychological functioning. The psychiatric history may date back years, but the mental state provides a view of how the person is at the present time. We depend on it in just the same way as the doctor in general medicine relies on the physical examination.

To begin with, we take careful note of general appearance and behaviour, from dress and grooming to demeanour, eye contact, over-familiarity, withdrawal, and the like. Even apparently trivial behaviours—'closes his eyes when talking about his wife' or 'laughs uproariously at his own joke'—provide clues.

A 45-year-old woman is dressed in brightly coloured clothes, wears heavy make-up and has purple nail polish. Her general personal care is clearly inadequate, her hair unwashed and tousled. She has trouble remaining seated and constantly fidgets. She lacks appropriate restraint as she winks and tries to touch the psychiatrist. (All these features alerts us to a likely manic state.)

We pay particular attention to the rate, volume, quality and tone of speech.

He displays minimal spontaneous speech and answers questions briefly. When he does speak, he does so softly and slowly, with long pauses. This pattern seems to reflect his extreme shyness, which suggests an avoidant personality.

As speech reflects thought, we examine them closely together. Two aspects are teased out—form and content. Form refers to the organisation of thought—how logical it is. The typical abnormality is the thought disorder in schizophrenia, where loose links between thoughts amount in severe cases to incoherence.

Thoughts are disorganised with evidence of loose associations, jumping from one idea to another and the occasional made up word: 'In the case of cats, it is always to be said. Why did you go? Following the archensivism, God will triumph.'

Content covers aberrations of thinking such as obsessions and delusions. The latter are false ideas, held with unshakeable conviction, which do not fit with the patient's cultural background. For example, a person firmly believes that secret police are ruining his business; a mother has the horrid thought that her newborn baby is the devil and must be destroyed.

Disturbed perception of one or more of the five senses is one of the most prominent features of the mental state in many severe mental illnesses. Hallucinations are false perceptions—a person sees, hears, etc. something that is not there. Auditory forms are the most commonly experienced.

A man describes hearing two male voices arguing with each other, commenting on his actions and commanding him to do things like 'punch your brother'. He hears them often during the day, every day, and at times they lead him to assault his brother. He often looks over his shoulder during the interview, appearing to respond to the voices.

Every psychiatric illness has an effect on mood, a person's enduring feeling state. Its quality, range and appropriateness are therefore of particular relevance. The terms we use to describe mood include elevated, depressed, suspicious and perplexed. And the mood may be labile (swinging), restricted or flat. The appropriateness of the mood to the person's circumstances is all-important.

She conveys a pessimistic and mournful demeanour, does not respond to any humorous cue, and displays a restricted range of feelings. She is slumped in the chair and speaks in a monotonous voice.

Our higher mental functions are extremely vulnerable to psychiatric disturbance, particularly in conditions associated with brain damage, such as dementia and head injury. Neuropsychologists usually assess these functions in detail. Problems occur in concentration, orientation for time and place, recent and remote memory, intellectual ability and judgement (capacity for rational decision-making). One popular test, used particularly in the elderly, is the mini-mental state examination (see below).

Mini-mental state test

Orientation
What is the (year) (season) (date) (day) (month)?
Where are we: (country) (town) (hospital) (ward)?

Registration
Name three objects. Allow one second to say each. Then ask the patient to repeat all three. Repeat them until the patient learns all three.

Attention and calculation
Serial 7s (that is, subtract 7 from 100 and keep subtracting 7 from the answer you get). Stop after five answers.
Alternatively, spell 'world' backwards.

Recall
Ask for the three objects introduced previously.

Language and copying
Name a pencil and watch.
Repeat the following: 'No ifs, ands or buts'.
Follow a three-stage command: 'Pick up a paper with your right hand, fold it in half and put it on the floor'.
Read and obey the following: CLOSE YOUR EYES.
Write a sentence.
Copy a design.

Finally, we assess the person's understanding of their illness—its likely cause, implications for them and the role of treatment. This is one of the most important parts of the mental state because it will determine to what extent the person can cooperate with treatment.

Max experiences florid, elaborate delusions (that the police want to detain him because of his 'exceptional powers' to tune in to their coded messages) and auditory hallucinations. He shows a complete lack of insight into his condition. He insists that he is 'perfectly well', does not require medication and is only in hospital because the government and police have conspired to imprison him; he intends to contact the media to expose this 'devilish' plot and demands to be released.

Physical examination and special investigations
Because physical and mental illness often co-exist (an obvious example is alcoholism), a physical examination is appropriate, although it is not necessarily done by the psychiatrist. Special investigations may be required to confirm clinical findings or to pursue a possible diagnosis.

Bringing it all together
Having assembled the patient's history and the results of the mental state examination (and the findings of a physical examination and any special investigations), we then summarise the material in order to crystallise our thoughts regarding diagnosis and treatment. Who is this person with the illness? What are his or her central clinical problems? How did they arise? The answers to these questions are brought together like this:

A 45-year-old, previously well, married lawyer gradually developed a series of bodily symptoms whose cause remained a mystery to her doctors. These occurred in the setting of major losses, including the death of her sister to whom she was very close. She has a family history of major mental illness, her mother having suicided when the patient was ten. She has few friends and an unsupportive husband.

The next step is making a diagnosis; this is a judgement about which category in the classification of mental illnesses (see Chapter 3) best reflects the clinical findings. When this is not feasible because the assessment is complex or incomplete (for example, neuropsychological testing is indicated), we juggle with a set of provisional diagnoses until a definitive decision can be reached.

As in the rest of medicine, diagnosis points to prognosis—the shorthand prediction of the likely outcome, with or without treatment. In psychiatry, this is by no means clear-cut. Many factors, such as personality, social support, cooperation with treatment, and the presence of stress play a role. Prognosis is often conditional on one or more of these factors, so that even though the natural course of the illness may be generally favourable, certain factors in a person's life may affect their particular outcome adversely—or indeed positively.

The formulation

Psychiatrists well recognise the inadequacy of a diagnostic category to capture the richness of a person's condition. We compensate for this by preparing a formulation. This is an account in which we consider factors—biological, psychological and social—that predispose to, precipitate and maintain the illness. All these elements, along with empathic understanding, and attempts at explanation where possible, are brought together to make sense of the clinical material.

Formulating is one of the crucial skills we psychiatrists have to master, and the three case histories below illustrate the process. A brief summary of the clinical story precedes the psychiatrist's formulation. The formulations for Janine and Walter illustrate the utility of a framework table.

Kemal, a single 25-year-old storeman and the eldest son in a Turkish family, presented with an eighteen-month history of altered eating behaviour and subsequent weight loss to the point of physical collapse. His symptoms developed in the context of family conflict, but there was no family history of mental illness.

After failed out-patient treatment, Kemal was admitted to a psychiatric unit with continuing weight loss and prominent suicidal ideas. A diagnosis of anorexia nervosa was arrived at, based on his failure to maintain body weight appropriate to age and height, a morbid fear of gaining weight and a disturbed body image (he regarded himself as obese). The plan of management was to set immediate objectives including close observation, particularly since he expressed suicidal ideas. This was judged as best done in hospital because of concern about Kemal's deteriorated physical state. A thorough physical investigation was done, as was correction of nutritional and metabolic deficiencies. After his psychiatric and medical safety had been attended to, a re-feeding program was proposed during which his relationship with the psychiatrist would be consolidated and his family assessed.

The formulation: Although anorexia nervosa is rare in men its emergence in this case is understandable. Major family issues, particularly the place of traditional values, are central in appreciating his condition. Kemal's illness evolved in the context of longstanding family disharmony. The clash between cultural tradition and assimilation led to immense tension between son and father. Kemal's divided loyalties meant that he was a partial member not only of his family but also of the Turkish community. On the other hand, his position in Australian society as an immigrant whose first language is Turkish was ambiguous.

Kemal found himself precariously straddling two cultures with no opportunity to share his concerns, resulting in ever-spiralling distress. His personality while well balanced is not assertive; expressing his frustration in a hostile family was therefore not easy. Furthermore, such expression may have been culturally inappropriate.

Kemal's view of himself as 'too fat' may have been precipitated by prevailing societal attitudes. His dieting may also have been a means of rebelling against a Turkish culture that tends to associate a large physique with strength, prosperity and attractiveness.

As he saw himself reflected as a failure in the eyes of his father, his success as a dieter may have perpetuated this behaviour. It was difficult to give up something in which he had finally succeeded. And his illness had a major impact on the family. While they were busy caring for him as the ill member, this may have served as a distraction from issues revolving around his striving for independence and their difficulties in responding. His illness could also be seen as expressing the family's troubles. His indirect ventilation of anger towards the family may also have maintained the pattern, as unexpressed anger is often a prominent emotion in anorexia nervosa.

Janine, aged 21, was brought up by her mother, Emily, after her father abandoned the family when she was three. Emily was treated for depression around that time and subsequently had to go out to work. Janine was often left on her own or with a range of Emily's friends. Emily had a number of affairs. None endured; moreover, the men often abused her verbally and physically. Although academically gifted, Janine grew up timid, with poor self-esteem and low self-confidence. Sexually exploited by several boys at school, she became pregnant at sixteen. She left home soon thereafter and has had difficulty bringing up her daughter, who is frequently ill. She came to the attention of the child welfare agencies. Despite their efforts to help, Janine perceived all but one social worker as 'putting her down' and telling her she is a 'bad parent'. She presented with a three-month history of general ill-health, tearfulness, lowered mood, insomnia, anorexia and inability to cope. She overdosed with sleeping tablets the previous evening; this was only discovered accidentally. Her boyfriend of six months had left her a few weeks earlier. She thinks she might be pregnant. Janine meets the criteria for a major depressive episode. Key features are low mood, poor sleep, anorexia, diminished self-worth and a suicidal act (presumably following suicidal ideation).

The formulation: Emily suffered from depression, perhaps increasing Janine's genetic vulnerability. Early childhood, characterised by an absent mother and several caregivers with limited commitment to providing a consistent stimulating environment, contributed to a sense of not feeling valued. Seeing her mother abused by a series of men left her feeling insecure and convinced that she too would be unable to resist such abuse. Faced with evidence of limited parenting skills, and a fear that if she acknowledged these she would lose custody of her child, Janine found the prospect of another child, without the support of her boyfriend, overwhelming. This led to the suicide attempt.

A framework to formulate Janine's presentation

	Biological	Psychological	Social
Predisposing	Mother treated for depression	Poor self-esteem, limited confidence, no consistent close relationship, mistrusting	Disrupted family, no consistent parent, poor role models, sexual exploitation
Precipitating	Pregnancy?	Sense of incompetence re future child	Left by boyfriend
Perpetuating	Current poor physical health	Lack of trust in others	'Surveillance' by child welfare
Protective	High IQ	Persistence and commitment to her child	Better relationship with one social worker

Janine's difficulty in accepting authority figures, and repeated abuse, means that gaining trust and accepting help will be pivotal. Since she will be sensitive to perceived put-downs, it will be crucial that treatment is negotiated carefully. We will boost her self-esteem by improving her childcare skills, helping her to use appropriate support services and reinforcing her academic ability. The latter may provide opportunities to train for a satisfying career. We also need to focus on her daughter's needs in order to break the pattern of transgenerational neglect.

We can treat depression with cognitive-behavioural therapy; this would be another way to help her gain an increased sense of mastery. If she is more severely depressed than appears at first, she may need anti-depressants.

First impressions might suggest a gloomy prognosis for Janine, but with effective treatment, appropriate further support and employment, the potential exists to turn the crisis into a new starting point for both her daughter and herself.

Walter, aged 64, lost his wife, Joan, ten months ago, after she had suffered with breast cancer for several years. He retired as a bank manager so he could provide nursing care over the last couple of years, and has lost touch with former colleagues. During the final weeks, Joan and the three children, particularly their daughter Amy, were keen that she be at home, but Walter insisted that she remain in a private hospital 'so she could have expert care'. The children have not seen much of him since the death. He felt lost and disorganised. He found this worrying, having always regarded himself as efficient and methodical, the one who made decisions for everyone else. His father had died of Alzheimer's disease, and he was fearful of developing it too. He lay awake ruminating about this and how he could repair relations with his children. He lost weight, withdrew socially and spent much time thinking about Joan. However, while he did little during the day, he described his mood as 'neutral' and said he retained an interest in financial affairs, reading the relevant section of the newspaper. It is not clear at this stage whether Walter's symptoms meet criteria for a major depressive episode and whether the cognitive problems are due to his mood change or some other process.

The formulation: Walter's obsessional traits and willingness to make decisions for others may have been valued in his workplace, but have limited his colleagues' willingness to maintain social ties with him in the longer term. He may have transferred this style of interaction into his caregiving, leading to family tensions. With the loss of Joan and his own premature retirement, he has lost his role and related self-esteem. His social isolation compounds this. He is encountering difficulty organising his life and, given his father's experience in later life, fears Alzheimer's disease, although his cognitive impairment may well be associated with depression.

A framework to formulate Walter's presentation

	Biological	Psychological	Social
Predisposing	Father's death from Alzheimer's disease	Obsessional and domineering personality	Isolation during Joan's illness
Precipitating	Possible cognitive decline	Grief at Joan's loss, guilt regarding children	Apparent rejection by children
Perpetuating	Increasing age	Loss of purpose	Social isolation
Protective		Sense of having done the right thing for Joan	Possible reconciliation with the children

This is clearly a *provisional* formulation to guide further assessment. A detailed account of his personality style and relationships with his family are required, together with a meticulous evaluation of the features of depression and cognitive impairment. It is possible that these may co-exist. Since his customary role of 'being in charge' may make it difficult for him to accept advice, it is crucial that he participates actively in considering treatment options.

All three formulations are multi-layered and complex. By no means are they the last word but rather a framework to guide our further work with both patient and family. They may well have to be revised as the clinical picture becomes more elaborate.

How does the psychiatrist tackle therapy?

Having completed a formulation, how does the psychiatrist set about the therapeutic task? The first step is to devise a plan, using the biopsychosocial framework, in which immediate, short- and long-term strategies are mapped out.

The rights of patients to be fully informed about their condition and its treatment, in terms they understand, is implicit in the duty of doctors to obtain informed consent. Patients must be familiarised with the nature, purpose, benefits and risks of the proposed treatment, and of any alternative ones. Limits of confidentiality should be specified, and care taken to ensure that consent is given freely, without duress.

Informed consent is especially problematic in psychiatry. The person's mental state may interfere with their capacity to comprehend the information given. We must therefore determine whether a patient is sufficiently competent to make an informed judgement about a proposed treatment and, if not, will usually obtain it from a close relative or guardian.

The particular problems affecting respect for autonomy and informed consent are sharply drawn in psychiatry when patients must have medication or other physical treatment as part of their care. Medications may cause unpleasant side-effects and some disorders may result in poor judgement and loss of insight, so that people fail to appreciate the need for treatment or do not believe it will help. Some conditions, like mania, are experienced as pleasant and people may resist treatment in order to hold on to their feeling of elation.

The process of treatment varies considerably. For instance, the emphasis is quite different for a person presenting for the first time than for one suffering recurrences of a longstanding illness. Who treats, where they treat and the ingredients of treatment depend on the nature and stage of the illness, the person's strengths and vulnerabilities, available social supports and current stressors.

Where and by whom?

Psychological distress is often dealt with initially by the family doctor, who determines whether referral to a mental health specialist is called for. Common reasons for choosing a psychiatrist are that the diagnosis is uncertain, the person has failed to respond to the family doctor's treatment, or a coexisting medical condition is complicating matters.

Treatment takes place in diverse settings ranging from a quiet office to the hectic atmosphere of a busy hospital admission unit. We may function individually or in a multidisciplinary team, usually comprising psychologists, nurses, occupational therapists and social workers.

A major decision facing us is whether admission to hospital is warranted. Several factors operate in this judgement. Perhaps the most crucial is the need for a protective, supportive setting for people who may be extremely perplexed, disorganised, depressed, psychotic or dangerous; there may be a need to remove them from a destructive social environment. Hospital-based care provides a place in which acute symptoms can be treated and attention given to the overall needs of patient and family. Other reasons for admission are less urgent—to permit a comprehensive assessment or to initiate complex treatment.

Long-term residential care has become relatively rare. When required, it is more commonly delivered in community residential settings aiming at rehabilitation. Such care is needed by people who, because of the enduring effects of their illness, loss of social skills and marked dependency, cannot cope independently or are liable to be exploited by others (such as ruthless landlords).

Compulsory treatment

People with a mental illness may be deprived of their liberty and treated against their wishes. This is a remarkable situation, unlike any other aspect of medical practice. In the not too distant past, virtually all psychiatric admissions to public hospitals were involuntary and, although psychiatry has moved rapidly towards a state where mentally ill patients are treated similarly to any other patient, the spectre of compulsion still looms.

Why are the mentally ill subject to laws that override their civil rights? The first reason is that it is in their best interests. Mental illness may affect the capacity to judge what is in one's interests. Thus, depressed people often consider themselves guilty and worthless, see no future and believe that this is an accurate judgement rather than the product of an illness. In this state of mind they may attempt suicide or neglect to care for themselves. We are aware that they will take an entirely different view once the depression lifts. We therefore accept the duty to protect them from themselves and to promote recovery by offering treatment even in the face of possible resistance. Given that the world is full of people who act against their own best interests, concern for the mentally ill relates to the fact that it is not the person but rather the disorder itself that generates self-damaging behaviour. The second reason for compulsion in certain circumstances is that psychiatric disorders may lead to behaviour that endangers others.

Mental health laws vary in terms of when compulsory treatment is justified. They usually allow compulsory treatment of people considered a danger to themselves or to others. Some laws require concrete evidence of aggressive or suicidal behaviour. But most consider potential risk, such as people stating their intent to harm themselves or making preparations by accumulating lethal substances.

Detention in the interest of the person's health is a more difficult matter. Some laws do not define health whereas others provide criteria in terms of people's inability to care for themselves to the point where their health and safety are threatened. The health criterion is controversial in that it provides wide powers of compulsion on the basis that anyone with a treatable psychiatric disorder impairs their health by refusing help.

Many mental health laws also provide for long-term committals that allow supervision and compulsory treatment of people, both within hospitals and in the community. These sometimes impose treatment on people who are relatively stable, on the assumption that they will deteriorate without supervised treatment or have done so repeatedly in the past.

Safeguards to protect patients' rights have been an important development in mental health law. Tribunals automatically review all committals, and patients can appeal to them for reassessment. The tribunals usually have legal, medical and lay representatives, though the role is sometimes assigned solely to a magistrate or judge. Committal removes the right of people to determine their place of residence and treatment. Many laws place constraints on seclusion, psychosurgery and electro-convulsive therapy (ECT) both for committed patients and, to some extent, for voluntary patients. In the case of ECT the objective is to ensure that it is properly and appropriately used.

The multi-disciplinary approach

Psychiatric patients have complex and varied needs, and a multi-disciplinary approach has been devised to meet them. A range of mental health professionals—psychiatrists, psychiatric nurses, clinical psychologists, occupational therapists and social workers—contribute their complementary skills in both assessment and therapy. The psychiatric nurse plays a pivotal role in carefully observing the person's mental state and behaviour; the psychologist tests mental abilities; the occupational therapist assesses vocational and living skills; and the social worker investigates family and other social circumstances.

In the past, the patient's family were not seen as potential aides to the professional team, but we now see them as vital participants and welcome their contribution. This is not to disregard the need of family members for support in their own right or for bolstering their capacity as continuing carers. Families of people with long-term conditions are particularly in need. The demands and difficulties of frequently recurring or worsening illness are enormous.

That people take an active part in their own care—to which many professionals contribute—is fundamental to the notion of treatment. And self-help groups, which may include family members, are a valuable source of support. They offer strength in numbers and reduce feelings of isolation, alienation and stigma. In Australia, for instance, the first such organisation, GROW, began in 1957; many have developed since, some helping patients with any mental illness and others focusing on a particular condition. Groups for relatives include the Arafmi Mental Health Carers and Friends Association.

How long should treatment continue?

The course of a mental illness may assume several forms. It may be brief with full recovery. Improvement may be followed by recurrent episodes. It may be long-term, either stable or relentlessly progressive.

For a person with an illness from which full recovery is expected, we intervene actively to identify and possibly remedy the factors contributing to the illness, to shorten the episode, and to minimise or prevent complications. By contrast, people with a progressive condition need continuing treatment to limit symptoms, to provide support especially at times of stress, and to minimise deterioration. For illnesses that recur, long-term treatment focuses on maintaining stability between episodes and preventing relapse.

Let us consider the following person and his treatment to illustrate these points:

A middle-aged man with symptoms of depression also describes problems with his marriage; he has recently begun treatment for high blood pressure, and admits to drinking excessively to 'block out problems'.

Immediate aspects of this man's treatment include:

- determining whether treatment for the blood pressure is a factor in the onset of the depression (some anti-hypertensives can cause depression);
- estimating his alcohol intake and judging its effect on his physical health;
- assessing his physical health generally (physical illness may accompany depression);
- assessing the severity of the depression, particularly the risk of self-neglect or suicide;
- searching out details of treatment of any past episodes of depression;
- interviewing his wife about the mood change and their marital difficulty, with particular attention to exploring cause and effect.

If the man is severely depressed, he will be admitted to hospital for further evaluation, to ensure his safety, to help him give up alcohol, and to begin treatment. His initial treatment in hospital will include:

- treating alcohol withdrawal, should symptoms emerge;
- prescription of anti-depressants if the diagnosis of depression is confirmed;
- individual psychotherapy to explore contributing stress factors;
- psychotherapy with the couple to clarify and lessen difficulties in their marriage.

His continuing treatment may include:

- further prescription of anti-depressants to prevent relapse, with its possible long-term use if he has had previous depressive episodes;
- individual psychotherapy to encourage and assist more fundamental change, supported by couple therapy if conflict continues.

In this chapter I have set out the psychiatrist's tasks in the most general terms. In the following chapters, which deal with the range of mental illnesses encountered in psychiatric practice in more detail, we will look at how each of them is assessed and treated.

CHAPTER 5

Stress, Crisis and Coping

Epictetus, the Roman philosopher, once remarked that 'Man is not disturbed by events but by the view he takes of them'.[1] If only this were entirely true. Events may be so traumatic or painful that even the most resilient and psychologically robust person suffers their effects. These effects may range from mild anxiety to a temporary mental breakdown. Before describing this group of conditions we must unravel the concepts of stress, crisis, coping and defence.

Stress

Derived from the Latin *stringere*, which means to draw tight or compress, this word has been in use since the seventeenth century to describe human

experiences of hardship, adversity or affliction. It conveys the idea of being subjected to extreme forces, of resisting their distorting effects in an effort to maintain physical and psychological wellbeing, and ultimately of returning to the original state. Stress usually refers to situations that place excessive physical or psychological demands upon us and threaten to unbalance us. Major life events are sources of stress to which we must adjust.

Crisis

Related to stress is the notion of life crisis, which in psychological terms is an imbalance between the demands presented by a particular problem and the resources available to deal with it. Our usual methods of handling the situation do not work, and neither do attempts to minimise the problem. There are two kinds of crisis, developmental and accidental. Transitional periods in the life cycle—such as adolescence (vividly illustrated in JD Salinger's *The Catcher in the Rye),* mid-life and retirement (beautifully captured in the film *On Golden Pond)*—are typified by emotional upheaval, which leads to a loss of personal equilibrium. These developmental crises are predictable and are experienced by everybody. Accidental crises, on the other hand, are sudden, unexpected and distressing life events involving loss, threat or conflict, and our psychological reactions to them.

Crises, while they do overlap, can usefully be divided into these categories:

- Loss, which covers a wide range of life events both physical and abstract, including loss of a loved one, of one's health, of a bodily part or function (e.g. following a stroke), or even of one's sense of pride and self-confidence. The typical reaction is grief, in which a shifting between psychological states is experienced.
- Change, in which new life circumstances such as marriage, retirement or migration throw up difficulties and so threaten our psychological wellbeing.
- Interpersonal relationships, where difficulties either in the family or beyond, intimate or superficial, are the source of substantial stress.
- Conflict, where we are immobilised by a dilemma and unable to choose between options for fear of making the wrong decision. The conflict may operate beyond our immediate awareness. Hamlet's indecisiveness is a perfect example:

> Whether 'tis nobler in the mind to suffer
> The slings and arrows of outrageous fortune,
> Or to take arms against a sea of troubles.
> And by opposing end them?

Coping

The strategies we use to grapple with a crisis help us to reduce our distress and to adapt more effectively. Coping is a problem-solving effort that enables us to return to a balanced state so as to be able to face and manage the continuing tasks and challenges of life.

In order to cope with stress, we must first be aware of the nature of the stress and of its implications. 'Coping' comes from a Greek word meaning to strike. This suggests a deliberate response and covers a range of activities from everyday, realistic problem-solving to more elaborate manoeuvres. Skilled coping is a flexible, rational attempt at mastery.

Coping has been classified in many ways, depending on whether it is cognitive (that is, adopting a specific way of thinking), or behavioural (that is, taking a certain action). However, people in crisis usually resort to several strategies, a blend of the cognitive and the behavioural. These are some common examples of coping strategies:

- realistically avoiding the source of stress, either by distraction or withdrawal;
- seeking appropriate help from family, friends or professionals;
- reducing tension and other unpleasant stress-related emotions by using various methods of relaxation;
- recognising the challenging features of a stressful situation;
- applying problem-solving manoeuvres—identifying the problem, clarifying its nature, mapping out possible options for dealing with it, choosing the most appropriate option and monitoring its effectiveness;
- drawing on past experience relevant to the stress;
- using humour to achieve a more balanced perspective ('It could be worse');
- adopting a stoical attitude ('What will be will be, getting upset won't help').

Despite this array of options, when we are faced with a major crisis where intense feelings predominate, the coping skills of even the most psychologically robust person may well become less flexible and adequate.

Defence mechanisms

Defence, which is a form of coping, has developed a specific meaning derived from its origins in psychoanalytic theory. The so-called mechanisms of defence are unconsciously determined—that is, they are beyond our immediate awareness. We consciously choose and voluntarily implement the coping strategies described above, but we are not directly aware of the defences we use. Except for a small group of 'mature' mechanisms, they tend to operate inflexibly. They protect us from unpleasant emotions such as anxiety, guilt and shame, which are themselves the result of conflict or other forms of threat. Defences also provide a breathing space, particularly in an emergency, so that other methods of coping can be explored. Judging whether a defence helps or not can in some circumstances be very difficult.

Defences have been classified in various ways, first by the child psychoanalyst Anna Freud, the daughter of Sigmund Freud. Freud himself recognised the vital role of defences in maintaining psychological balance, and he described several types. But it was Anna Freud who expanded this work and systematically grouped the defences. In her classic text, *The Ego and the Mechanism of Defence*, she took each defence in turn and vividly showed how they operate in everyday psychological life and in abnormal mental states. Freud, the proud father, acknowledged her contribution in this charming quote:

> ... the ego makes use of various methods of fulfilling its task, i.e., to put it in general terms, of avoiding anxiety, danger and unpleasure. We call these devices defence mechanisms. Our knowledge of them is as yet incomplete. Anna Freud's book (1936) has given us our first insight into their multiplicity and their manifold significance.

An ingenious system building on Anna Freud is that of George Vaillant, an American psychiatrist who has contributed much to our understanding of defences. He groups them according to their level of maturity, ranging from 'psychotic' (level 1) through 'immature' and 'neurotic' to 'mature' (level 4). The mature mechanisms closely resemble the coping strategies already described. Since Vaillant's scheme is complex I will list only some representative examples, with brief illustrations from everyday life or from a medical setting.

Denial is the process by which we minimise unacceptable thoughts, feelings or impulses, and so keep distressing and threatening aspects of reality at bay. For example, a woman told that she has a terminal illness behaves as if she is unaware of the diagnosis, or a man returns to strenuous work following a severe heart attack, against medical advice.

Repression is the mechanism by which an unacceptable impulse or idea, or a painful emotion, is pushed out of consciousness and so is actively forgotten by being excluded from awareness. The repressed material is still active, and continues to affect our behaviour. Common examples are when we forget a well-known name, particularly when the name has some unpleasant association—or are unable to recall a vivid dream we had last night.

Regression is the return to an earlier stage of psychological functioning. We behave in ways more appropriate to that stage, usually child- or infant-like, when there were no responsibilities and when dependence on a parental figure was appropriate. For example, a 5-year-old boy reverts to thumb sucking and babble talk upon the arrival of an infant sibling—a reflection of his jealousy and feelings of rejection.

Rationalisation is plausible but invalid thinking used to avoid stressful reality. For example, a man in a coronary care unit declares, on the death of a neighbouring patient, 'He was very old and I suppose too frail to deal with his heart attack'. Or someone facing retrenchment murmurs, 'I'm sure Mary was fired because she wasn't up to the job'.

Intellectualisation is the reliance on a bland account of an important personal matter with much attention to trivial detail and avoidance of expression of feelings in order to keep them at bay. For example, a woman talks about her illness as if she was reading about it in a dry textbook—as if it was not really happening to her.

Displacement is the redirection of feelings towards an object, person or situation that is less threatening than the actual source of the feelings. This eases the distress, although the underlying issues persist. For example, a woman awaiting the results of the biopsy of a lump in her breast tells her surgeon, 'I don't know whether you noted my husband in the waiting room; he's a very sick man, he has terrible asthma. I'm really worried about him.' Or a mother, whose marriage is full of tension, is constantly focused on her daughter's handling of school pressures.

Projection is the unconscious attribution of our own unacknowledged feelings, thoughts and qualities to other people. Disturbing feelings such as shame, fear and disgust are avoided by projecting them on to others. For people with schizophrenia, projection takes the form of frank delusions, that is, false beliefs held with conviction and usually concerned with persecution. In most situations, it is a tendency to see our own distress through others. For example, a renal dialysis patient who states, 'I have to conceal my shunt because people are disgusted by it', is really saying, 'I am disgusted by my shunt'. Or a woman with a lump in her breast who exclaims, 'I don't like the expression on your face, you look very concerned', is really saying, 'I suspect something awful, and I am very concerned', and so avoiding learning the truth.

Introjection is the taking on of qualities of either a feared or an admired person. Thus a young man takes on the characteristics of his deceased father to lessen his sense of loss and to relieve any tension arising out of mixed feelings towards his father.

Sublimation is satisfying an impulse by transforming it from a socially unacceptable to a valued form of activity. So, for example, an unconsciously angry man excels in vigorous contact sport.

Compensation or *counter-dependency* is an extreme form of denial that usually shows in the way in which a person acts. With an intense need to be active, energetic and joyful, the person compensates for limitations imposed by illness by going flat out. For example, after a heart attack and having been near to death, a man takes on extra responsibilities at work and plays new sports, reassuring himself that he is fully alive and will remain so. His reprieve makes him live life to the full. A bereaved woman instead of grieving the loss of her husband indulges in many more social activities than before his death, and so avoids the distress of mourning.

Adaptation, or bringing it together

'He knows not his own strength that has not met adversity' wrote the dramatist Ben Jonson nearly four hundred years ago. His observation about our everyday responses to life events lies at the heart of a model devised by the American psychiatrist Gerald Caplan. The model brings together the concepts of stress, crisis, coping and defence.

When we are dealing with normal situations, Caplan assumes that we operate consistently and with minimal strain. When faced with circumstances requiring a response, we bring into play both habitual and previously effective coping mechanisms. Before we make this response, we experience a state of increased tension that helps us to resolve the issue and thus return us to a balanced state. A crisis occurs when an imbalance develops between the difficulty and/or importance of the problem and our habitual problem-solving responses. If a new stress, either developmental or accidental, cannot be dealt with by these usual means, tension escalates further and we feel lost, helpless and ineffective. The persisting tension then stimulates us to call upon our reserves—our internal and external resources—and we attempt new methods of problem solving. We may, for example, define the problem in a new way so as to find different features that we can then approach. We may decide that certain goals are unattainable and, by trial and error, identify new goals worth pursuing.

Our own resilience and the social support available to us play a crucial role in crisis. Resilience is our capacity to act with determination in the face of adversity, to call on a range of useful coping strategies and to enlist mature defences. By contrast, vulnerability is a state of inadequate resilience—our ability to battle 'a sea of troubles' is diminished and we depend on more immature defences.

Social support is the aid provided by our immediate and extended families, by our community of close friends and colleagues, and by the broader

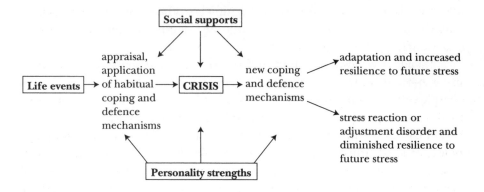

A model for the relationship of factors bearing on crisis

human network in which we function, including professional and non-professional helpers. The availability, adequacy and helpfulness or otherwise of social support are powerful factors in either enhancing or worsening the effects of stress.

We may well be able to deal with the problem by drawing upon our various resources. And our success will, as Ben Jonson implied, increase our resilience and our capacity to cope with future stress. But if we cannot manage the problem, or we avoid it by such means as giving up, tension mounts further and leads to psychological disorganisation. This in turn diminishes our resilience to future stress, and leads to the clinical conditions soon to be described.

Stress and physical illness

Just as life events and psychological factors have major effects on health, so the experience of medical illness can lead to profound changes in a person's emotional state. They are common in general hospital settings as people attempt to come to terms with illness ranging from the sudden and life threatening to the chronic and disabling. The reactions bring much distress in their own right as well as interfere with the ability of people to comply with medical treatment.

People with physical illness face stresses imposed by the condition's inherent pain and incapacity, by the threatening hospital environment, and by discomfort involved in investigation and treatment that can be painful, even mutilating (for example, the surgical removal of a breast). Perhaps the main source of stress is the uncertainty posed by illness—its severity, the possibility of death, long-term effects and the overall outcome.

Psychological reactions include both the defences we have discussed (such as denial, regression and rationalisation) and coping strategies like seeking relevant information, turning to others for support, setting realistic goals, adopting a stoical attitude or finding meaning in the experience.

Maladaptive responses that may occur include demanding or aggressive behaviour, depression, anxiety, dependency and withdrawal. A failure to comply with treatment may result from any of these reactions. Certain services in the hospital—including intensive care, coronary care, cancer wards and burns units—present specific problems, both in the nature of the conditions treated, and because they are highly stressful environments.

Adjustment disorders

Adjustment disorders are the result of major life changes leading to continuing distressing circumstances. Exceptionally traumatic life events may produce an acute stress reaction (see below).

As I pointed out earlier, life events may precipitate and contribute to the continuation of a wide range of mental illnesses. The link between stress and illness is not always clear and often depends on a person's vulnerability. Thus susceptibility is again a factor, as is social support, in determining whether or not stress is managed successfully.

The key feature of adjustment disorders is an ineffective reaction to an identifiable stress. The reaction occurs within a few weeks of the experience of that stress and persists for several months. As mentioned earlier, crises are of two sorts. They may be developmental (such as starting school, leaving home, getting married) or accidental (threatening and unexpected events such as car accident, robbery, rape). These events may be single or multiple, episodic or continuing.

The following terms are used by psychiatrists to cover the variations we see in clinical practice: adjustment disorder with anxious mood, with depressed mood, with physical complaints, with withdrawal, with work and/ or study difficulties, and various combinations of these. The entire range of psychiatric symptoms described in later chapters may occur as a result of stress. Symptoms impair people's everyday functioning and their social and intimate relationships.

Acute stress reactions

This is a temporary but severe state that develops in a previously well person in response to exceptional stress, and that usually subsides within hours or days. The stress may be an overwhelming trauma involving serious threat to a person's security or safety or that of a loved one (such as a natural disaster, war or physical assault) or an unusually sudden, threatening change in circumstances (such as multiple bereavement in a car accident).

Immediately afterwards, a sense of unreality prevails. The person is dazed and disoriented, and the mechanism of denial is obviously in play. A mix of emotions quickly takes over, including grief, fear, despair and anger. Over the next few days or weeks the person works at understanding and coming to terms with the event, after which a new level of adaptation is reached. The stages of denial, emotional arousal, 'working through' and resolution are basic responses to a variety of stressful circumstances.

The most disruptive reaction is a state of acute psychosis in which the person loses touch with reality. This is what many people refer to as a nervous breakdown. Its features are like those of any psychosis—that is, delusions, hallucinations and bizarre behaviour—but they occur suddenly in a person exposed to severe trauma. Symptoms vary considerably, fluctuate in intensity and usually subside when exposure to the trauma ceases or within a few weeks of the experience. Here is an example of the rare but dramatic acute stress reaction that presents as psychosis:

Jane was the 35-year-old wife of a diplomat on an overseas posting. The couple had been posted a year before her breakdown to a politically unstable African country, but she had managed to adjust to her new circumstances. This adjustment began to fragment when a political crisis occurred; Jane felt herself floundering in her efforts to cope. The outbreak of civil war proved to be the straw that broke the camel's back. She became acutely disturbed one evening, publicly accusing her husband of being a spy for one of the warring parties. She heard voices passing secrets to her, and made an attempt on her life in response to a voice commanding her to slash her throat as the only way to stop the war. Within a week of being sedated and evacuated to her home country, Jane's symptoms disappeared completely and she could barely recall the details of her ordeal. In discussion with a psychiatrist she was able to put this ghastly episode in perspective, recognising that her coping strategies had been challenged and then overshadowed by the frightening events. She had regressed to a 'primitive' emotional state in which everyone was a threat to her, even her husband.

Treatment and long-term problems

The expected improvement of adjustment disorders and acute stress reactions does not imply that treatment is not important. On the contrary, intervention at the time of the crisis makes for the best possible outcome and minimises the risk of future vulnerability. The tasks of treatment are to deal with acute symptoms and to help the person return to a balanced state or to a workable level of adaptation to a continuing stress, such as the restrictions imposed by a stroke. The key is that people are offered support while they mobilise their own resources to achieve these goals. The approach to crisis intervention is practical and brief (see Chapter 19). Limited changes in a person's environment may help, but the glib suggestion of 'taking a few days off' is unlikely to do much good.

Group psychotherapy, particularly for people who have experienced a common stress (such as a community disaster), can be valuable. Sharing memories of the experience in a supportive group brings effective release of intense feelings. For a person to go back over the trauma and look at their psychological responses and at possible alternatives is also useful. Simply to repeat the details of the stressful experience helps to make the unmentionable acceptable.

Medication may help but is usually used sparingly. Temporary use of drugs to reduce anxiety and to allow sleep may be needed, but anti-depressant tablets are not generally required. Drug treatment may be necessary to tide a person over the turmoil of a psychotic experience.

Both adjustment disorders and acute stress reactions are understandable responses to severely stressful situations, and they usually subside with time. But occasionally they persist and merge into more sustained psychiatric conditions. They then become less understandable as they continue long after the stress has faded. Post-traumatic stress disorder (see Chapter 6) is the name given to a delayed and/or drawn-out response that lasts for months or even years, either because the stress itself was so traumatic or damaging (for example, torture, rape, natural disaster, multiple bereavement or war experience) or because a person is particularly vulnerable.

A person who has not made the adjustment will repeatedly relive the trauma through memories that intrude in dreams or when awake. It is likely that their emotions and personality will be dulled and that they will be having difficulties with their relationships. They may be fearful and inclined to withdraw. The flashbacks are best understood as repeated, unsuccessful attempts to master the traumatic experience.

Our recognition of post-traumatic stress disorder since the Vietnam War has highlighted the critical importance of skilled, psychological intervention at the time of trauma, or shortly afterwards, so that people can work through the experience and so lessen the risk of later problems.

Conclusion

In this chapter we have looked at how best to understand common reactions to stress. I have described a group of conditions to which we are all susceptible, and which many of us have actually experienced when buffeted by the ups and downs of life. These responses are understandable, whether the stress is catastrophic or a fairly predictable part of the life cycle, and are a useful stepping stone to considering more complex psychiatric conditions in the chapters that follow.

1   Albert Ellis, the founder of rational emotive therapy, the forerunner of cognitive behaviour therapy, credited Epictetus with providing a theoretical basis for his school of psychotherapy.

CHAPTER 6

The Spectrum of Anxiety

Anxiety is regarded as an adaptive response when we encounter danger. Most animals, including humans, become alert and vigilant in the face of sudden and unexpected situations. Charles Darwin noted in *The Expression of the Emotions in Man and Animals* that as animals have evolved, they have benefited through their acquired ability to anticipate danger by means of the warning signal felt as anxiety. By contrast, what we might call clinical anxiety occurs in the absence of a realistic danger, which is why we find it so puzzling and unnerving. Both adaptive and clinical anxiety are decidedly unpleasant, given that they combine a sense of foreboding and pervasive physical discomfort, both of which may severely disrupt our lives.

In a more psychological sense, Freud distinguished between objective anxiety, a signal of danger emanating from the external world, and neurotic anxiety; he theorised that neurotic anxiety was associated with the imminent eruption into consciousness of repressed emotional conflict. Ernest Jones, one of Freud's protégés, later drew attention to the related phenomena of anxiety, fear, dread, fright, panic and apprehensiveness, and to the disproportionateness of anxiety to life circumstances.

Anxiety is regarded by contemporary psychiatrists as a target of treatment when a person experiences symptoms, both physical and psychological, in the absence of any threat or grossly disproportionate to a threat. An intense sense of fear or a more sustained pattern of worrying hamper the person's normal life, do not lessen with reassurance, and may be accompanied by thoughts and actions that are exaggerated, even ridiculous. For example, many of us fear snakes but we are unlikely to quit walking in the countryside in case we encounter them; by contrast, a person with a phobia of them may never venture beyond the city. Fear of flying is also widespread but few people would not take an overseas holiday for this reason alone; a

person with a flying phobia may have to give up a job entailing travel because they are so affected by this fear.

Certain patterns of anxiety can be readily understood by everyone. Immediately after a car accident, it is natural to feel apprehensive about driving a car, to have nightmares about the crash and to avoid the place where it happened. Psychiatrists refer to such an experience, usually short-lived, as an acute stress reaction or adjustment disorder with anxiety, and anticipate that it will improve with time and require minimal, if any, external help. Indeed, we would find it puzzling if these features lasted for more than weeks or, at the most, a few months.

All negative emotions, like those stemming from a car accident, inevitably affect the way we see the world and our future. Abnormally anxious people, however, make assumptions that lead them to interpret a broad range of life situations as posing a danger to themselves. Their constant sense of anxiety draws their attention to aspects of the world they view as hazardous, and so the pattern becomes entrenched. For example, people who suffer from panic interpret bodily sensations as indicating that they are about to die: breathlessness points to impending death, palpitations to a heart attack, dizziness to collapse. Both external stimuli (returning to the site of military combat where panic once occurred, for instance) and stimuli from within the person (thoughts, images, bodily sensations) may then precipitate an anxiety attack. Once the tendency crystallises, people become hypervigilant—monitoring their physical state and noting sensations that they would usually ignore.

Anxiety disorders are marked by psychological symptoms that reflect mental disturbance, and by bodily sensations and experiences. The core psychological feature is an oppressive unpleasant fear of dying, losing control, entrapment, embarrassment, humiliation or losing one's mind. The fear may be vaguer—a sense of foreboding, an expectation that something awful is about to happen. Closely linked is an inner tension and restlessness and a ceaseless scanning of what is seen as a threatening world. People may also experience actual distortions of the sense of oneself (called depersonalisation) and of the world (called derealisation); they feel unreal or perceive the world as strange. Not surprisingly, higher mental functioning—concentration and thinking—are disturbed. Sleep provides no escape—a pattern of insomnia, restless sleep and vivid dreams is typical.

Physical experiences cover all systems of the body—anxious people may feel their heart beating rapidly, chest pain, laboured breathing or a sense of not being able to catch their breath. Dry mouth, nausea and diarrhoea are experienced by those who respond to stress mainly through their gut. Others have muscular tension, headaches and general aches. Yet another group of symptoms relate to the nervous system—dizziness, faintness and pins and needles.

These psychological and bodily disturbances are common to many other mental illnesses, particularly depression. Indeed, many depressed people describe associated anxiety as more distressing than the feeling of sadness. Psychotic people may also experience intense anxiety as their world fragments and they sense the terror of 'falling apart'. Anxiety is often both the cause and effect of alcohol and drug abuse. People use chemicals to blot out anxious feelings, but the anxiety worsens during withdrawal or abstinence. Also, a range of medical conditions may be accompanied by anxiety. It may arise from concern about the implications of an illness (like cancer), or may be an intrinsic part of the condition itself (as in the case of an overactive thyroid), or may result from its treatment (steroids, for example, make many asthmatics inexplicably anxious).

One anxiety or many?

Some psychiatrists consider that there are several ways in which we suffer from the core emotion of anxiety, among them panic, agoraphobia and obsessive-compulsive disorder. Others see these as expressions of a common underlying condition, pointing to the fact that anxiety disorders frequently coexist, and may change from one form to another over time. The debate is far from academic since different forms of anxiety require specific treatments.

Anxiety disorders occur throughout life and may start at any time, commonly in the wake of stressful circumstances. One in six of us will develop one or other form. Specific phobias (fear of spiders, for example) are the most common, although people with them rarely seek professional help out of embarrassment or because they can readily avoid the feared situation. Obsessive-compulsive disorder used to be considered a most rare form of anxiety, but this is not so.

The usual pattern of any form of anxiety is a long-term course marked by worsening in the face of stress, particularly in the case of general anxiety. It is not uncommon for people with agoraphobia to say that they are never fully free of it. Social and specific phobias also tend to persist unless treated. Most people with an obsessive-compulsive disorder experience symptoms episodically and can function reasonably normally, but a third never fully recover.

What causes anxiety disorders?

There are many explanations, ranging from psychoanalytic theories to biological models. Historically, psychoanalytic theory offered the first contribution to an understanding of anxiety. With the development of his structural model of psychic organisation (ego, id and superego), Freud saw anxiety as a signal to alert the ego to danger, particularly that associated with wishes in the id that seek expression. In response to anxiety, repression and other ego defence mechanisms, such as intellectualisation and rationalisation, are mobilised. The task for clinician and patient is to identify and understand underlying unconscious forces, such as aggression, that contribute to the conflict (for example, the need for control to avoid inherent feelings of inferiority), and the consequences the patient fears if these drives go unchecked.

Freud had an intriguing but now largely discredited view that sexual energy or libido becomes blocked and is then channelled into anxiety. But in some forms, for example in obsessions and phobias, anxiety is transferred on to a seemingly harmless object, situation or idea that can then be acted upon (through rituals in obsessive-compulsive disorder) or avoided (as in phobias). Freud later suggested that anxiety lay at the core of most neurotic states, weaving its influence in multiple ways. He pointed out that both pressures from within the psyche at an unconscious level and demands of the outside world could lead to unmanageable conflict, resulting in the formation of symptoms.

Learning theorists suggest that faulty learning is the basis of anxiety disorders—fear appropriate to one situation becomes linked to a relatively harmless or non-threatening situation or generalises to a range of circumstances. For instance, a student who fails in an examination may become apprehensive about all subsequent tests and, even worse, fear all circumstances in which they feels their abilities (academic, sporting, social, occupational and so on) are under scrutiny.

Although initially popular, this way of thinking has been overtaken by a cognitive approach in which it is proposed that a disturbance occurs in processing information. In obsessive-compulsive disorder, for instance, dysfunctional beliefs ensue when a person takes a reasonably ordinary thought (that any of us may have periodically) regarding personal hygiene, uncertainty about whether the house is locked or not, hostility to a loved one, and the like, and invests it with profound significance. To illustrate—a loving mother's fleeting thoughts of spanking her child for a minor misdemeanor becomes transformed into a persistent and intrusive thought that she will harm, or even kill, the child. A compulsive act, such as a ritual of self-purification, may then evolve to attempt to deal with the horrendous image of committing violence.

Existential theory posits that all forms of anxiety have at their core a fundamental concern about finitude, that life comes to an end (the German word *angst* is often used to cover this concern), and that meaning and purpose in life are lacking. People who dread the prospect of a state of non-being and live inauthentically as a result 'deceive' themselves by converting their angst into a range of neurotic symptoms, and in this way avoid the existential confrontation (see Chapter 19 for an account of the corresponding form of psychotherapy used to remedy these symptoms).

Alongside these psychological factors, evidence has accumulated of possible biological causes, covering neuroanatomical, neurochemical and genetic aspects. In obsessive-compulsive disorder, for example, one in five first-degree relatives has also suffered from it. Twin studies point to a similar hereditary contribution. A possible dysfunction of brain chemistry— increased sensitivity in the serotonin neurochemcial system—is supported by the observation that only one category of anti-depressant drugs, which affects this chemical messenger, is effective for obsessional symptoms (see Chapter 19). Particularly tantalising is evidence that certain parts of the brain are over-active. Some people seem to have a specific biological vulnerability to anxiety and are much more likely to respond with acute anxiety and even panic to a range of stimuli, including drugs such as caffeine, over-breathing, and infusion of certain chemicals. It is as if their brain is set at a more highly tuned level so that its readiness to respond to danger is accentuated.

Let us now look at the forms of anxiety disorder that psychiatrists distinguish according to the prominence of particular clinical features. General anxiety disorder is, as the name suggests, the most diffuse form. Panic disorder is similar, but occurs as brief but intense attacks. Three groups of irrational fears are specific (such as of spiders), social (encounters with other people) and agoraphobia (fear of being trapped in crowded places like a supermarket or cinema). In obsessive-compulsive disorders, anxiety is associated with intrusive thoughts or images (one's hands are contaminated by germs, for instance), which the person tries to deal with by carrying out a corresponding compulsive act (repeated hand washing). Post-traumatic stress disorder is a collection of particular anxiety manifestations following a severe trauma like rape or experience of military combat.

General anxiety disorder

General anxiety disorder (GAD) affects 5 per cent of the population. They suffer many and varied symptoms of anxiety that smoulder on through life, becoming more intense when life stressors impinge. The person with GAD is the typical worrier. Concerns punctuate everyday life—worrying about keeping a job, welfare of one's children, viability of one's marriage, financial affairs, a leaking roof, bodily symptoms, and myriad other trivial and non-trivial matters. With these preoccupations comes a wide array of anxiety features as listed below. Although these symptoms fluctuate in intensity, GAD tends to be relentless. Its onset is gradual, in late adolescence or early adulthood, with the sexes equally affected. As in anxiety disorders generally, people do not seek treatment until their twenties or thirties, many regarding their negative experiences as part of who they are, and not appreciating that treatment can help. Presentations include:

- excessive worrying about everyday life events that is difficult to control;
- the effects of over-arousal (e.g. feeling on edge, unable to relax, poor concentration, irritability, the mind going blank);
- muscle tension (e.g. headache, bodily aches and pains);
- light-headedness and dizziness;
- sweating;
- cardiovascular (e.g. pounding of the heart, chest pain);
- respiratory (e.g. constricted feeling in the chest, feeling of choking or a lump in the throat, over-breathing);
- urinary (e.g. urinating frequently);
- gastrointestinal (e.g. dry mouth, butterfly feeling in the abdomen, nausea, diarrhoea);
- sleep disturbance (trouble getting off to sleep and daytime fatigue);
- alcohol and/or drug abuse.

Physical symptoms tend to lead to repeated medical consultations, the process obscuring the real diagnosis. Special tests may be carried out to investigate headache and chest pain. When these draw a blank, medications are often prescribed, some of which, the benzodiazepines in particular, may bring problems in their own right. More appropriate treatment, as we shall see, combines explanation, support, a finite series of medical investigations, and avoidance or only short-term application of medications.

Teresa, a 28-year-old secretary, was referred to the hospital psychiatrist by the nursing staff who were treating her mother for breast cancer. The nurses had noted Teresa constantly seeking information about her mother's treatment and not responding at all to gentle reassurance. She admitted that she was most apprehensive about whether her mother was receiving the best possible care. When she got slightly different answers to her questions from staff, she became all the more flustered. In her general life she worried about everything under the sun; her work colleagues referred to her as a worry-wart. She had been seeing a masseur over the preceding eighteen months for incessant headache and neck pain. These were worse when she felt 'uptight'. Teresa had wondered intermittently for years whether she should seek help for her 'nerves'.

Panic disorder

Panic disorder, a sudden upsurge of intense fear, usually accompanied by both fearful thoughts and physical symptoms of anxiety, affects 1 to 2 per cent of the population in any one year. Symptoms are similar to those of general anxiety disorder, but attacks occur without any warning and for no apparent reason. Typically, the person feels overwhelming apprehensiveness and a variety of physical symptoms; there is a dread of collapsing, going mad, losing control, even dying, or a vague sense of imminent doom or catastrophe. Episodes last for seconds to minutes, occasionally for up to an hour. Panic-stricken people are often convinced that they have a physical disease. Medical investigations that find nothing wrong fail to reassure because the bodily symptoms are so horrible to the sufferer. It comes as no surprise, therefore, that panic disorder leads to the 'panic prone person', who tends to avoid all situations in which attacks are triggered or where help may not be forthcoming. When extreme, the avoidance is labelled agoraphobia (see below).

In attempting to allay their anxiety, people may develop hypochondriacal preoccupations, which spurs them on to consult doctors and emergency departments and be extensively investigated for a purported physical disease. Other common associations are depression, alcohol or benzodiazepine misuse, social and occupational impairment, interpersonal and marital difficulties and suicide attempts.

Len, aged 45 and married, experienced his first panic attack at the age of twenty. He drank heavily to 'control' feelings of anxiety. After a driving infringement he quit drinking but experienced a worsening of the panic attacks. Len was soon unable to drive, enter a lift or shop. He not only carried a mobile phone at all times in case he needed to summon help but also insisted that his wife do the same, as well as inform him of her every movement. He became increasingly anxious about his 13-year-old daughter's wellbeing, refusing to let her go out with friends in case a 'disaster' should befall her.

Hannah, aged 33. experienced a sudden 'strange' feeling while driving, becoming intensely fearful. She just managed to reach her destination, quivering with relief that she had reached a place of safety. Her family doctor referred her to a neurologist who, despite a normal test of the brain's electrical waves, made a provisional diagnosis of epilepsy, prescribed anti-epileptic medication, and advised her to take great care while driving. Hannah promptly concluded that she was definitely epileptic and might suffer a fit at any moment. She refused to go out, stopped working and avoided her friends. Several further episodes of the same fear finally resulted in the family doctor referring her to a psychiatrist who, with the benefit of hindsight, diagnosed panic disorder and treated her accordingly.

Phobic disorders

A disproportionate fear of an object or situation that cannot be reasoned away and leads to a consistent pattern of avoiding it lies at the heart of phobic disorders; they are differentiated into specific, social and agoraphobia.

Specific phobia, affecting one in ten people, is irrational fear and resultant avoidance of particular objects or situations, and is partially understandable on evolutionary grounds. Common objects or situations feared include spiders, snakes, lightning, thunder, flying, travelling in buses and trains, heights, elevators and blood injury. The sequence is predictable. People know their fear, and studiously avoid the object or situation. The previous name of simple phobia downplays the disruption of life that an irrational fear can cause. Think of a businessman who has to travel regularly but is afraid of flying or a woman, petrified of injections, who procrastinates in visiting the dentist despite a pressing need. This degree of fear is quite different from ordinary apprehension about encountering such things as snakes and spiders, which we would not go to excessive lengths to avoid.

A young woman, Zara, sought treatment for a fear of feathers. She had always been frightened of birds, particularly of their feathers. Not only did she avoid going out if she saw or heard birds in the area, but she was constantly on the lookout for feathers that might be blowing about. She could not visit parks where there might be birds or feathers.

Pamela, a 67-year-old retiree, described a lifelong fear of thunder but was unable to specify exactly what she was frightened of. She monitored weather reports in great detail. When a storm was forecast, she avoided going out and cancelled all scheduled commitments. During a thunderstorm she would draw every blind and curtain. If a storm was particularly severe she would literally crawl under the bed, staying put until the worst was over. She lamented how miserable her life had been but had been unaware that treatment was available; she assumed that she was just the 'nervy type'.

Social phobia is similar to a specific phobia except that the fear is linked to social situations. The onset is often in adolescence, with marked social isolation continuing throughout adulthood. Socially phobic people fear what others might think of them, and are especially perturbed by appearing ridiculous. The typical story is of intense anxiety about meeting new people, attending parties, participating in work meetings or talking in front of colleagues. These people avoid eating or drinking in public, riddled as they are with anxiety that they might vomit, be unable to swallow or that their hands might shake uncontrollably. Others are concerned about blushing or sweating in company and so avoid all social encounters. Typically, a young socially phobic person describes becoming anxious when asked questions in the classroom, and finds school trips, social events or staying with friends most unnerving. In older patients, lack of friends and close relationships and job difficulties are common. Whatever the age group, people with social phobia may seek help for one of its complications, particularly depression or alcohol misuse, rather than the phobia itself.

Psychiatrists take care to differentiate social phobia from performance anxiety as experienced in public speaking or in oral examinations, and from an avoidant personality in which a lifelong pattern of inhibition, sense of inadequacy and hypersensitivity to criticism predominate (see Chapter 10); treatments differ for each of them.

Isabel, a 40-year-old teacher, sought help for a disabling fear of vomiting in social settings. Since childhood she had been worried about doing this in front of others and thus looking stupid. She avoided holidaying with friends, travelling in other people's cars, eating in the staff canteen or inviting friends for a meal. By the time Isabel finally sought treatment, her everyday activities had become extremely sparse.

Joel, a 19-year-old tennis coach, had always felt self-conscious when 'put on the spot'. At school he had been extremely anxious, blushing and stuttering when asked questions by the teacher. In his senior years he had avoided presenting work in class, often pretending to be sick on the scheduled day. Since leaving school Joel had worked as a tennis coach. He sought treatment because of mounting difficulties speaking with his students. In particular he had trouble chatting on the telephone and had enlisted his mother as a go-between; she gave answers according to his instructions. While this ploy worked, he still encountered enormous problems relating to students on court. Increasingly they were dropping out, finding him difficult to communicate with and regarding him as rude and anti-social.

Agoraphobia, which tends to start in a person's early twenties, was first described in 1871 as the 'impossibility of walking through certain streets and squares, or the possibility of doing so only with resultant dread of anxiety'. Agoraphobia is commonly misunderstood as a fear of open spaces, but the Greek word *agora* refers to a marketplace or other place of assembly. Agoraphobic people in fact avoid situations in which they feel trapped—shops, queues, theatres, public transport, bridges, tunnels and the like. In its most restrictive form, the fear is of venturing into a public area alone; indeed, the phobia may be so pervasive that the sufferer becomes completely housebound.

Strategies people use to reduce anxiety include travelling with a companion, using a train route on which stops are frequent, shopping late at night when supermarkets are relatively empty, and sitting on the aisle in theatres and cinemas. Relatives and friends may be recruited to run errands, shop or take children to school.

Anne, aged 24, was referred for psychiatric assessment six months after presenting to an emergency department with chest pain, palpitations and shortness of breath. She had been thoroughly assessed for heart disease and discharged with a diagnosis of stress. She had since attended the emergency department four times and consulted two cardiologists.

When seen by a psychiatrist Anne described her first attack of chest pain, palpitations and shortness of breath when watching television at home. Since she was so terrified that she believed she was about to die, her family rushed her to the emergency department. Initially, the assessment reassured her, but she had further attacks. Other symptoms included dizziness, light-headedness, shaking, sweating, hot and cold feelings and 'jelly legs'.

Anne had become increasingly concerned about her health, frightened of more attacks and afraid that she had a serious illness and would die. She had significantly curtailed her activities, fearing an attack when on her own or cut off from help. She had carefully mapped out doctors' surgeries in her area, knew which hospitals had an emergency department, and travelled only within a short distance of either. She had given up driving, fearful of having an attack in the car, and now avoided crowded situations, lest she could not get out if needing help.

Obsessive-compulsive disorder

There is yet another way in which anxiety may manifest—channelled into a particular way of thinking (obsession), coupled with corresponding behavioural responses (compulsion). Obsessions are distressing, persistent thoughts, impulses or images that are experienced as intrusive and senseless but cannot be banished from the mind. They revolve around morally or sexually repugnant thoughts, uncertainty about whether one has switched off an appliance or locked the house, thoughts about being dirty or contaminated, and images of harming others (the person with obsessive-compulsive disorder, or OCD, does not, in fact, cause such harm).

John Bunyan, the seventeenth-century author of *The Pilgrim's Progress*, gives a graphic account of his spiritual obsession: 'when I have been preaching I have been violently assaulted by thoughts of blasphemy and strongly tempted to speak the words with my mouth before the congregation'.

A compulsion is a repetitive, stereotyped action that must be carried out to deal with an obsession even though the person knows full well that it is futile, inappropriate and will offer only partial and temporary relief. The person seems to have no option but to pursue a ridiculous form of behaviour in an effort to reduce the anxiety produced by the obsession. The unwelcome thought or image soon recurs, and with renewed vigour. Behaviours must thus be repeated again and again. Ultimately, they lose their power to relieve anxiety, at which point increasingly complex and time-consuming rituals evolve. Checking, washing, counting and hoarding are commonly encountered compulsions. I once treated a mother who literally scrubbed the bottoms of her two young children several times a day lest any faecal material should 'infect' the rest of their bodies. She knew her thoughts about contamination were absurd but felt helpless to resist them, and found relief, and then temporarily, only when she washed the children. It was utterly distressing for her husband and extended family to witness her unceasing suffering and the effects of her behaviour on the children.

James Boswell's description of the repetitive ritual of the writer Samuel Johnson upon crossing any threshold captures the essence of the compulsion:

... for I have upon innumerable occasions observed him suddenly stop, and then seem to count his steps with a deep earnestness; and when he had neglected or gone wrong in this sort of magical movement, I have seen him go back again, put himself in a proper position to begin the ceremony; and having gone through it, break from his abstraction, walk briskly on, and join his companion ...

Some 2 to 3 per cent of the population experience OCD, usually from early adulthood. The onset is gradual, the course enduring unless treatment is effective, with relapses commonly precipitated by life stressors. Often it occurs in people with obsessional personalities—those who have always lived an orderly, highly organised life. Obsessional traits like orderliness and punctuality can indeed serve people to meet the demands of life and are not part of the clinical picture of OCD.

John, aged 40, lived on his own and had been a worrier for as long as he could remember. He had avoided people because he was afraid of saying the 'wrong thing'. After being with people he would always check—by phone or letter—to make sure that he had not offended them. While this could reduce his anxiety, an alternative option was simply to avoid people whenever possible. He had various other obsessions and related compulsions. He was concerned on leaving the house that he might not have locked the front door and had to return to check numerous times. John feared contracting AIDS, despite having no history of behaviours that would expose him. He had had ten HIV tests, all of them negative. His need for symmetry was prominent. His clothes had to be hung in a mirror image, with suits at the end of each rack, shirts inside these and trousers in the middle. Many items in the home were arranged in a similar pattern. Any disruption to the symmetry caused John enormous anxiety, with many hours then spent rearranging objects.

Post-traumatic stress disorder

Unlike the forms of anxiety we have already looked at, post-traumatic stress disorder (PTSD) has, as the name suggests, an identifiable cause—psychological trauma. Abnormal reactions to trauma were first observed in the context of battle. 'Mental exhaustion' was described in soldiers during the American Civil War, 'shell shock' in World War I and 'battle fatigue' in World War II.

This state of mind is vividly portrayed in Pat Barker's brilliant *Regeneration* trilogy, set in World War I and its aftermath. She weaves into her narrative the historical character Dr WHR Rivers who, in an address to the Royal Society of Medicine in 1917, described victims of war neurosis he treated at the Craiglockhart War Hospital in Scotland. The case of a young wounded officer who managed to dig himself out of a mound of earth under which he had been buried is typical. Although his physical wounds had healed completely, he continued to sleep poorly and suffered from 'disturbing dreams of warfare' and anxiety about whether he would ever recover. He had tried his utmost to banish traumatic memories from his mind, as was the common medical advice at the time, but they could not be kept at bay while he was asleep; he dreaded going to bed. Dr Rivers was the first doctor to agree with his patient that it was impossible to eradicate memories of such harrowing experiences by sheer will. Encouraged by the innovative therapist to confront the unpleasant thoughts 'boldly' and 'dwell upon them in the day', the officer's mental state improved considerably and he was able to return to duty.

Dr Rivers was up against it in struggling to bring relief to soldiers severely traumatised in the trenches in France and Belgium. Consider the poet Wilfred Owen's depiction of his own experience in 'Mental Case':

> Therefore still their eyeballs
> shrink tormented
> Back into their brains, because on their sense
> Sunlight seems a blood-smear;
> night comes blood-black;
> Dawn breaks open like a wound that bleeds afresh.

Psychiatrists' interest in the effects of trauma may have begun with the casualties of battle but they have expanded enormously to take account of the psychological repercussions of both natural disasters—bushfires, earth-quakes, floods among them—and man-made trauma suffered by civilians, like torture, violent crime and rape.

The debate over whether these events could lead to marked psychological disturbance only in predisposed people was waged over many years, until more objective research seemed to point to the vulnerability of even the most robust personality. The main point, it seemed, is exposure to a horrendous traumatic event. The introduction of a new diagnosis, PTSD, in the 1980 edition of the American Psychiatric Association's classification reflected this conception of a link between profound stress and a specific cluster of psychological phenomena. (The previous edition, dating from the late 1960s, contained a category entitled 'Transient situational disturbance' and only one example among many referring to war; it read curiously: 'Fear associated with military combat and manifested by trembling, running and hiding'). The view crystallised during the 1970s that the validity of a formal diagnostic entity was reinforced by the prevalence of an identifiable cluster of symptoms in so many American veterans returning from the Vietnam War.

However, a key difficulty has persisted since the acceptance of PTSD as a psychiatric diagnosis. How severe must the traumatic stress be? The definition in the APA manual reads 'outside the range of usual human experience'. The World Health Organization uses a more diffuse criterion: an event 'likely to cause pervasive distress in almost anyone'. The debate is far from academic. Given that countless numbers of people—men, women and children all over the world—will be exposed to at least one traumatic stress during their lives, the question obviously arises as to whether they should all be offered mental health counselling without delay. Given that the need could never be met, a more practical question is apt. Is there a way of predicting who will succumb to PTSD, an often debilitating and long-term psychiatric state? So far, the answer is no. This is not surprising, given the diverse factors that could theoretically play a role: level of social support, further trauma, past trauma, the severity of the trauma, a history of psychiatric illness, degree of resilience, the depth of emotional numbing, anger, guilt, shame and other pertinent emotions—the list is infinite.

Two sets of findings can help sort how psychiatrists should act; they both involve time. The first is not to jump in with offers of treatment. So-called critical stress debriefing, which is usually done in a single session two or three days after the traumatic event, has been shown to be of no value and even to cause harm. Victims seem to need an opportunity to come to terms with the trauma in a more natural way. The other temporal factor, by contrast, relates to undue delay in providing treatment. The person who comes to suffer PTSD symptoms may not realise that this is a real psychiatric condition that warrants professional help, and may suffer privately for years; they need to be encouraged to summon help long before their symptoms become entrenched or psychiatric complications, mainly depression and alcohol misuse, arise.

People suffering from PTSD typically relive the trauma, the details of the event penetrating their consciousness unceasingly. Recurrent recollection of the situation—thoughts and images in waking life, including flashbacks, and during sleep—is prominent. Given the distress this entails, it is no wonder that people are left numbed and detached and with a sense of estrangement from others. At the same time they are hypervigilant about dangers that may be lurking in the environment and avoid situations even remotely linked with the original trauma. PTSD is often complicated by other problems, particularly sleep disturbance and depressed mood, and by the misuse of alcohol and drugs in a desperate attempt to dull the intrusive memories, and outbursts of anger.

Dean, a 22-year-old chef, was caught up in a shooting incident at work and witnessed the brutal murder of a young colleague. He himself was unharmed and even returned to work the next day. However, in the weeks and months that followed, he became increasingly irritable, gloomy and tense. Dean was so aroused that he could not stand the noise of traffic and started at any loud sound. He could not tolerate the hustle and bustle of the restaurant's kitchen and began to stay at home. He would unexpectedly see the traumatic scene replayed in his mind's eye. His disturbed sleep was punctuated by terrifying nightmares. He felt guilty about his colleague's death, believing that he should have done more to save her. Customarily a lively and gregarious fellow, Dean withdrew from friends and ultimately became a virtual recluse. He also began drinking heavily, which seemed his only means to reduce his distressing thoughts.

Treating the anxiety disorders

Whatever form anxiety assumes, psychiatrists elicit an accurate narrative from the patient and, if appropriate, from family members, in order to establish the nature of the condition. Steps are also taken to ensure that any possible physical cause has been excluded (for example, low blood sugar, an over-active thyroid, excessive caffeine, withdrawal from substances that act on the brain). If other psychiatric symptoms coexist, especially depression and misuse of alcohol or drugs, we clarify whether the anxiety is the primary or subsidiary clinical syndrome, since treatment will differ. We also look for factors that aggravate and maintain the anxiety symptoms because they will be targets for therapeutic intervention; these include interpersonal conflict, pressure at work, adverse life events, and excessive use of caffeine, nicotine or alcohol.

We explore the effects of the person's anxiety on family members, since they may influence the situation for good or for ill. For instance, children whose mother is virtually housebound because of agoraphobia, or spends many hours a day decontaminating the house, will not be unscathed. Likewise, a spouse may be making considerable adjustments to accommodate their partner's phobias. Paradoxically, the illness may suit the family—an emotionally insecure husband may inadvertently foster his anxious wife's dependency and thus block any chance for her improvement.

When Lisa, a 24-year-old student, began to experience classic features of panic disorder, her father took to accompanying her to classes in case she might suffer an attack. Having recently been retrenched and feeling an abject failure, he found that his daughter's vulnerability gave him a sense of being needed. In parallel with Lisa's treatment, the father was advised about the nature and treatment of panic disorder and alternative daily activities were devised for him.

Since many people with anxiety states harbour unrealistic beliefs about their physical state, a central facet of treatment is reassurance that they will not die or go mad. The therapist provides information about the nature of anxiety symptoms, dispels common misconceptions and myths, and points out what can be done in terms of treatment. For example, it is helpful for people to learn which symptoms are produced by over-breathing and to experience how these can be produced voluntarily by hyperventilating. This is the first step in achieving controlled breathing—slowing the rate and avoiding excessively shallow or deep inhalation. These are typical aspects of therapeutic breathing:

- Hold your breath and count to ten.
- Then breathe out and say 'relax'.
- Breathe in and out through the nose over a 6-second cycle—breathe in slowly over 3 seconds, breathe out slowly over 3 seconds.
- At the end of each minute (i.e. after 10 breaths) hold your breath again for 10 seconds, and then resume breathing over a 6-second cycle.

Printed information on these topics helps immensely as the person becomes a partner in the treatment, and is available from self-help organisations. Many anxious people use the internet to good purpose—provided they are guided to reliable sites and cautioned about quick and/or costly fixes.

Learning to achieve a state of calm offers people a sense of mastery over physical symptoms and a welcome alternative to a perpetually worried psyche. This can be accomplished in many ways. The benefits of music, meditation, Tai Chi and yoga have been known for centuries. A commonly applied method known as progressive muscular relaxation consists of monitoring muscle tension and then alternatively tightening and letting tension go in specific muscles. This is often combined with visual imagery and the person is encouraged to imagine a scene from their own experience that brings inner tranquillity. Popular images are beach scenes, gentle waves, shady glades and billowing clouds; these may be complemented by recordings of soothing music or sounds of nature.

Stress management uses many approaches. The strategy of structured problem solving assists the person to identify sources of anxiety related to life pressures and their possible remedies, assess the potential value of each in turn, choosing the most pertinent one, plan how to carry it out, and review progress. Associated measures are exercising regularly, participating in recreational activities, and counselling for a targeted problem, like financial difficulties or a strained marriage.

Psychoanalytically based psychotherapy had its heyday in the 1950s and 1960s and is still relevant for certain people. Freud's classical case histories of Little Hans and the Rat Man centre around phobic and obsessional symptoms that he thought had symbolic significance and were therefore open to psychoanalytic interpretation. But while such symbolism is clear (for example, the obsessional person with thoughts of harming others is often grappling with powerful underlying aggressive drives), extended psychoanalyses have been shown to be ineffective.

Cognitive and behavioural approaches target symptoms directly. Here, therapy aims to improve people's psychological and social functioning and to promote more effective ways of coping with stress.

A combination of these various approaches is the mainstay of psychological treatment. First, peoples' irrational beliefs and false assumptions are identified. They are then guided to challenge and replace them with a more realistic view of themselves and their world.

Sam, a 21-year-old student, developed a fear that he would faint while travelling on a bus. Although he had never actually done so and accepted the therapist's explanation for the symptoms, his level of anxiety still rose dramatically when he boarded a bus. As part of therapy, Sam was provided with a cue card that read, 'You have never fainted. What you are feeling is anxiety and it will not make you faint. Anxiety goes away. Sit on the bus and wait.' He read this card repeatedly while waiting for the bus and was able to get on and prove to himself that he would not faint.

Specific behavioural techniques can be combined with the cognitive approach for particular anxiety disorders. Once panic attacks are controlled, graded exposure to feared situations helps people with related agoraphobia to overcome avoidance of them. PTSD and simple phobias can also be effectively treated in this way. As the words 'graded exposure' suggest, the person is gradually brought into contact with the object or situation or memory that brings on the anxiety. People are first trained to relax and then led through a series of steps until each anxiety-provoking stimulus has been mastered. The purpose is to bring the patient into contact with the feared object or situation in order to break the pattern of avoidance, the main factor that perpetuates the condition.

In the past, the very opposite was done. People were immersed in the worst of their fears, their pleas for relief ignored. This seemingly callous procedure was intended to prove that they could both survive the ordeal and recognise the irrational basis of their fears. So-called implosion therapy or flooding has been superseded by graded exposure, since the procedure was obviously unpleasant and the outcome equivocal.

For people with social phobia, a helpful set of strategies known as social skills training has been devised. People can improve their social interaction by learning, for example, how to initiate and sustain conversation, read non-verbal cues emitted by others, and be appropriately assertive.

Obsessions may respond to the simple technique of thought stopping. People learn to recognise when a thought is assuming an obsessional quality and to counteract the related self-absorption through sheer will. Response prevention is the name given to a simple strategy of learning not to perform the compulsive action or ritual even though feeling very anxious; in so doing the person comes to realise that the obsession-grounded anxiety does not last indefinitely.

Hypnosis would seem to be a reasonable treatment for some anxiety disorders given that in a suggestible state, fears can be induced and just as readily eradicated. However, it has proved of limited value.

Drugs may be required for more severe cases of any anxiety disorder, to complement the treatments we have mentioned (see Chapter 18). The benzodiazepines were widely used in the past but, because they are potentially addictive, they are used for short periods only and then tapered off. Their main advantage is rapidity of action. Anti-depressants such as the selective serotonin reuptake inhibitors (SSRIs) and tricyclics are effective in treating anxiety-related conditions, including panic attacks, PTSD, obsessive-compulsive disorder, generalised anxiety and social phobia. Beta-blockers, used to treat elevated blood pressure, prevent physical symptoms of anxiety like tremor, sweating and palpitations, and are sometimes helpful for specific and social phobia. The SSRIs are used especially when depressive symptoms co-exist with anxiety.

On extremely rare occasions, OCD may be so disabling, and unresponsive to years of both psychological and drug therapies, that psychiatrists have to consider the most radical procedure in their repertoire of treatments—psychosurgery (see Chapter 18). Cutting specific circuits in the brain that may be the site of the hypothesised abnormality brings a degree of relief.

Because family members can powerfully reinforce the maladaptive behaviour inherent in an anxiety state, drawing them into treatment programs has distinct advantages. For example, they may be taught how to help the phobic person to tackle the avoidance, which is the core of the disability, by encouraging the person to confront the fearful situation rather than giving bland reassurance—in other words, being cruel to be kind.

Conclusion

Research since the 1980s has focused on defining anxiety disorders, investigating their causes and identifying effective treatments. Psychological therapies, particularly cognitive-behaviour therapy, together with new advances in medication, have greatly improved the long-term outlook of people who are buffeted by anxiety, whatever its form.

CHAPTER 7

The Highs and Lows of Mood

I have of late—but wherefore I know not—lost all my mirth, foregone all custom of exercises; and indeed it goes so heavily with my disposition that this goodly frame, the earth, seems to me a sterile promontory; this excellent canopy, the air, look you, this brave o'erhanging firmament, this majestical roof fretted with golden fire—why, it appeareth no other thing to me than a foul and pestilent congregation of vapours.

Shakespeare's *Hamlet*, Act 2, Scene 2

We all have good and bad days—that's normal. Indeed, it is not unusual for our mood to vary considerably over a single day. In response to the ups and downs of life, we experience joys and disappointments, successes and failures. And our mood may also be affected by many physical factors, like premenstrual hormonal changes, a viral infection (the flu virus is a regular culprit), alcohol and drugs.

There is no precise dividing line between ordinary sadness and what psychiatrists call clinical depression. We use this term when lowered mood persists, brings intense distress, and interferes with the person's ability to cope with the ordinary demands of living, whether of work, study or personal relationships. This lack of a clear division is typical of many areas of our mental health. It is equally the case, as we saw in the last chapter, with anxiety in its various manifestations. Similarly, many physical disorders—such as high blood pressure—are also on a continuum from close to normal to what we call illness.

Extremes of mood have been considered as a malady since antiquity. In the Old Testament, the Book of Samuel tells of Saul's tendency to depression, which was responsive to music: 'And it came to pass, when the evil

spirit from God was upon Saul, that David took a harp, and played with his hand: so Saul was refreshed, and was well, and the evil spirit departed from him'.

Hippocrates was the first, in the fourth century BC, to describe mania and melancholia. The idea that disordered mood does not take a single form is therefore centuries old. The Greek physician Arataeus (120–180 AD) first referred to endogenous and reactive types, suggesting that some forms were biologically based whereas others were due to psychological and social factors. As early as the mid-nineteenth century, French psychiatrists described the alternation of melancholia and mania. A few decades later, the noted German psychiatrist Emil Kraepelin distinguished what he called manic depressive insanity from dementia praecox (later re-labelled schizophrenia) according to the course and outcome of the illness. The former was episodic with recovery between attacks, the latter a progressive decline. Today, psychiatrists have built on this distinction, and further noted that some people may suffer from either depressive or manic swings (unipolar mood disorder) or experience both over time (bipolar mood disorder).

Clinical depression manifests as a cluster of symptoms and observable mental and physical signs that commonly occur together. At least two weeks of lowered mood is regarded as the minimum period to warrant the diagnosis. Most people have experienced symptoms for much longer before they consult their doctor. People with milder forms may not feel bad all day but still describe a dismal outlook and a sense of gloom. They may be cheered up by a pleasing event but are then dragged down by even a minor disappointment. The degree of severity extends from mild, blurring into ordinary sadness (minor depression, although it is debatable whether depression can ever be labelled as minor, certainly not in the eyes of the sufferer), to extreme (major depression), where the risk of suicide is high and health may be seriously affected by poor nutrition and self-neglect. A severely depressed person may also lose touch with reality and be buffeted by hallucinations and delusions (psychotic depression).

Psychiatrists have not yet resolved the debate about whether depression is a single condition that varies only in severity, or is best seen as of a number of separate types. The proponents of the second view focus on two principal types—one is largely biological (also called endogenous) and points to a genetic origin; the other is reactive to adverse effects of a stressful event in the life of a person who is vulnerable because of certain personality features (is sensitive, dependent, pessimistic, irritable, for example). In my view, we are unlikely to sort this out until we discover what is going wrong in the brain and how genetics plays a role.

In the meantime, behind every case of depression, whatever the claimed type, lies a state of mind that has always ravaged humankind and continues to cause an immense amount of suffering in the affected person, with distressing repercussions for family and friends; this is especially so when the risk of suicide prevails or the prospect of many relapses over several years is likely. In my work with hundreds of depressed patients over the years, the toll on everyone involved has been painfully palpable. Indeed, little has changed in the way depression is experienced since Richard Burton provided the first detailed account in *The Anatomy of Melancholia*, published in 1621:

> Being then it is a disease so grievous, so common, I know not wherein to do a more general service, and spend my time better, than to prescribe means how to prevent and cure so universal a malady … that so often, so much, crucifies the body and mind.

Crucifying body and mind may seem hyperbole but, as any of us who have suffered a clinical depression can testify, it is often harrowing in the extreme.

A persistent elevated mood occurs far less commonly than clinical depression. Here, a similar continuum prevails, with milder states difficult to disentangle from normal joy or exuberance. Moderately severe (hypomania) or very severe forms (mania) are more clear-cut— the person's behaviour then has serious consequences if treatment is not promptly initiated. Most people with mania also suffer depressive swings as part of the condition of bipolar mood disorder.

Depression requiring professional help is common. The rate of major depression over a person's lifetime is as high as one in eight women and one in twelve men. But many people remain both undiagnosed and untreated. Bipolar disorder is much rarer, with a lifetime rate of about 1 per cent. The two forms may occur at any point in the life cycle but the usual age of onset is in a person's twenties; they are far less common during childhood, but certainly present then and need to be identified so that the necessary treatment can be promptly initiated. Over half the people who have had an episode of disordered mood suffer from one or more recurrences; that proportion goes up to 80 per cent in those who have suffered from severe depression or bipolar illness.

What is clinical depression?

Tom, a 32-year-old bus driver, went to his family doctor complaining of tiredness and disturbed sleep over the previous six weeks. His appetite was poor and he had lost 3 kilograms. Although well liked and highly regarded at work, he felt incapable of performing his duties and suspected that his workmates were ignoring him. He denied any previous emotional problems. He and his wife were expecting a baby but this was planned and they were both delighted about the prospect of parenthood. There had been no tension between them but he had lost interest in their sexual relationship. His father had had an alcohol problem and deserted the family when Tom was four. A maternal aunt had once been treated in a psychiatric hospital and had suicided later.

A physical examination was normal, as were tests to exclude any physical illness (especially an under-functioning thyroid, any infection or anaemia). The doctor prescribed anti-depressant medication, provided encouragement and reassurance, and arranged to review Tom the following week.

Tom disappeared a few days later. With the aid of the police he was found comatosed in his car, which was parked in a deserted paddock. An empty bottle of whisky and an empty packet of anti-depressant tablets lay by his side, as well as a note to his wife expressing regret at leaving her and the baby. A hose had been connected to the exhaust but, luckily, loss of consciousness had prevented him from starting the ignition. He was most fortunate to survive this determined suicide attempt.

Admitted urgently to hospital, the psychiatrist diagnosed major depression of so serious a degree as to warrant electro-convulsive therapy (ECT). Together with general psychological support and the use of anti-depressants, he responded extremely well. He was able to return to work six weeks later.

Tom suffered two further depressive episodes during the next two years but his wife alerted the psychiatrist, as planned, at the first appearance of symptoms. He was again treated effectively with ECT. Due to Tom's vulnerability to these serious episodes, a mood stabiliser was prescribed, a treatment designed to reduce the rate of recurrence. He was still well and free of any serious mood swings after twelve years.

As is obvious from Tom's case, where his life was almost lost, depressed people feel so miserable that they view the future with despair. They judge their circumstances to be hopeless, believing their prospects are bleak or that they burden their family and others. A *New York Times* journalist draws this picture of her own depression: 'the thick black paste of it, the muck of bleakness'. Later in her heart-rending essay (*NYT*, 10 May 2009) she writes about her state as the 'quiet terror' that 'hovers', waiting to 'slither back in'. Friends or relatives may reveal a more favourable picture, but depressed people persist in seeing their situation in the blackest of terms. They often describe their mood as one of endless misery, quite different from ordinary sadness; those who have also experienced bereavement say that grief is consolable whereas when they are clinically depressed they feel utterly forlorn and beyond comforting. Given this state of despair, it is not surprising that depressed people are unable to take any pleasure in their usual activities—a cardinal feature that is illustrated poignantly by Hamlet's account at the beginning of this chapter, or vividly in Theophile Gautier's poem, 'Tristesse' (Melancholy):

> April is back,
> the first rose,
> with its lips half-parted,
> smiles at the first fine day,
> the blessed earth
> opens and burgeons,
> everything loves, everything enjoys,
> alas! there is a fearful melancholy in my heart!

> The drinkers in merry mood
> in their rosy songs
> celebrate beneath the vine-trellises
> wine and beauty,
> the joyful music
> with their clear laughter
> scatters itself through the air,
> alas! there is a fearful melancholy in my heart!

In scanty white dresses
the young maidens
go away under the arbours
on the arms of their swains,
the languorous moon
silvers their long-held kisses,
alas, there is a fearful melancholy in my heart!

For my part, I no longer love anything,
neither man nor woman,
neither my body nor my soul,
not even my old dog:
go and say that they are digging
beneath the pale turf
a nameless grave,
alas! there is a fearful melancholy in my heart!

Loss of interest touches everything, ranging in degree from an unwillingness to join in everyday activities such as sport or hobbies, through neglecting oneself and one's family, to not caring whether one lives or dies. Severely depressed people cannot concentrate, stop working and neglect personal hygiene. Irritability is common and may cause alienation from family and friends. If the condition remains untreated, physical health may suffer. Extremely depressed people can even die from starvation or dehydration.

People with milder depression share their misfortune; those more severely affected tend to experience a sense of guilt and of failure. They blame themselves for their situation, regarding themselves as bad and undeserving of care. Guilt may reach delusionary proportions, with people convinced they have committed crimes or grievous sins. Rarely, such people take their own lives as well as those of their family in order to 'save them from a world of evil'.

Suicide is obviously the most serious outcome. Of all people suffering from clinical depression, two-thirds have thoughts of dying, and 15 per cent of those who have been treated in hospital for depression take their own lives. Those lost to depression include many a famous figure: Vincent Van Gogh, Ernest Hemingway, Sylvia Plath, Primo Levi, Virginia Woolf, Robert Schumann, and many more. Abraham Lincoln may well have killed himself too if he had not been assassinated. Vulnerable to melancholia, he wrote a poem in his late twenties entitled 'The Suicide's Soliloquy' which reveals his deep anguish:

Here, where the lonely hooting owl
Sends forth his midnight moans,
Fierce wolves shall o'er my carcase growl,
Or buzzards pick my bones.

No fellow-man shall learn my fate,
Or where my ashes lie;
Unless by beasts drawn round their bait,
Or by the ravens' cry.

Yes! I've resolved the deed to do,
And this the place to do it:
This heart I'll rush a dagger through
Though I in hell should rue it!

Three years later, Lincoln sought medical help but to little effect. He wrote:

> I am now the most miserable man living. If what I feel were equally distributed to the whole human family, there would not be one cheerful face on the earth. Whether I shall ever be better I cannot tell; I awfully forbode I shall not. To remain as I am is impossible; I must die or be better …

The fact of Lincoln's survival may be ascribed to his determination to achieve self-awareness and ways of comforting himself.

John Stuart Mill, the nineteenth-century philosopher, captures the despair that overwhelms even the most rational mind, with suicide the only means of relief. In his autobiography he poignantly shares his descent into hopelessness:

> It was in the autumn of 1826. I was in a dull state of nerves, such as everybody is occasionally liable to; unsusceptible to enjoyment or pleasurable excitement … the whole foundation on which my life was constructed fell down … At first I hoped that the cloud would pass away of itself; but it did not. A night's sleep, the sovereign remedy for the smaller vexations of life, had no effect on it … Hardly anything had power to cause me even a few minutes oblivion of it. For some months the cloud seemed to grow thicker and thicker. The lines in Coleridge's 'Dejection'—I was not then acquainted with them—exactly describe my case:

A grief without a pang, void, dark and drear,
A drowsy, stifled, unimpassioned grief,
Which, finds no natural outlet or relief
In word, or sigh, or tear.

… there was no one on whom I could build the faintest hope of assistance. My father, to whom it would have been natural to me to have recourse in any practical difficulties, was the last person to whom, in such a case as this, I looked for help. Everything convinced me that he had no knowledge of any such mental state as I was suffering from, and that even if he could be made to understand it, he was not the physician who could heal it.

Mill's feeling of isolation is echoed by the novelist William Styron in *Darkness Visible* (1990), a powerful account of his own depressive experience:

Depression is a disorder of mood, so mysteriously painful and elusive in the way it becomes known to the self—to the mediating intellect—as to verge close to being beyond description. It thus remains nearly incomprehensible to those who have not experienced it in its extreme mode, although the gloom, 'the blues' which people go through occasionally and associate with the general hassle of everyday existence are of such prevalence that they do give many individuals a hint of the illness in its catastrophic form.

Although depression is foremost a disturbance of emotion, bodily changes may predominate. A group of so-called vegetative symptoms occur in severe cases. Less interest in food is common, leading to substantial weight loss in the severe forms. More atypically, a depressed person eats for consolation and may gain weight. Marked sleep disturbance, particularly early morning waking (typically about three o'clock), also points to a severe state. Difficulty in falling asleep is more typical of milder cases. Excessive sleep is yet another pattern. Variation in intensity of mood is a classic finding, the morning being the worst time with improvement towards evening (diurnal variation). The slowing down of thinking and movement, sometimes to the point when speech may be impossible to follow or the person is mute and the body totally immobile (retardation), contrasts with another abnormal presentation—restlessness that leads to incessant pacing, wringing or rubbing of hands, tearing skin and pulling at hair (agitation). Paradoxically, retardation and agitation can coexist, with the latter coming on episodically.

Rarely, psychotic features like delusions and hallucinations occur. The delusions typically cover themes of worthlessness, guilt for sins committed, persecution or nihilism (a belief that the person does not actually exist). Hallucinations are usually auditory. These psychotic features parallel the severity of the depression, and cease when the person recovers.

All sorts of features may conceal an underlying depressed state. For example, depressed adolescents may exhibit disturbed behaviour, truancy, sexual promiscuity or poor academic performance. Elderly people may focus on physical symptoms like constipation and weakness, or show excessive concern over their general health. Pain may dominate the picture. These situations have been referred to as masked depression, but the term is misleading as careful enquiry invariably uncovers the depressive symptoms. Sometimes the person may not refer to sadness, although appearance and behaviour—withdrawal, poor sleep, weight loss, no interest in life—indicate otherwise.

How does the depressed person look?

It is easy to spot a severely depressed person. He or she looks downcast and has a drawn appearance, furrowed brow and stooped posture. There may be evidence of poor self-care and loss of weight. Activity is often slow, with limited spontaneous movement and speech. Or the person may be extremely agitated, with hand-wringing, restlessness and pacing.

People with milder forms appear less miserable, and the change in mood is apparent only to family or friends. Depressed people often shed tears and tell of frequent spontaneous periods of crying. But tearfulness in itself is neither an indicator of depression nor more likely to occur in severe compared to milder forms. Indeed, more severely depressed people may be quite unable to cry and show little in the way of emotional response.

Less affected people often find relief at being able to 'get things off their chest', particularly if given the chance to vent their feelings. On the other hand, people with deep depression find little or no benefit in sharing their experience. They may have minimal insight into their circumstances, failing to understand that they are suffering from an illness and are in need of treatment. Instead, they may believe their condition to be justifiable punishment for their 'misdeeds'.

Mania—the other side of the coin

Alex, a 28-year-old teacher, was referred to a psychiatrist by a police doctor after he had assaulted the school principal. The principal had confronted Alex following reports that he had made sexual advances to several female students. He had recently bought an expensive car he could ill afford and announced his plan to lecture at prestigious universities. On admission to hospital (compulsorily, because of his total lack of insight into his condition) he was irritable, excessively active and brimming with grand ideas. He proudly spoke of his influential political contacts and of his intention to issue Supreme Court writs against the principal and the doctors. His speech was so rapid at times that it was barely intelligible. He had not been mentally ill in the past but his mother had been hospitalised for a mood disorder after the birth of his younger brother. Alex was immediately treated with an anti-psychotic drug while in a supportive ward environment, and made a full recovery within three weeks. Sadly, he was not able to return to his previous job: the ugly force of stigma had triumphed. However, with the help of his psychiatrist he managed to re-establish his career elsewhere and put the unpleasant experience into perspective.

Such an episode of abnormally high mood usually begins rapidly, over a matter of days. It may follow a depressive period and can, paradoxically, be triggered by treatment with anti-depressant drugs. People report feeling unusually happy and optimistic. Their sense of self is highly inflated, many regard themselves as unusually gifted, and there is an obvious grandiosity to their manner. This euphoria has an infectious quality. However, if their wishes are thwarted, they may become prickly and irritable, even aggressive. They are excessively energetic, hyperactive and barely sleep. Speech is rapid, loud and pressured, punctuated by jokes, puns and plays on words. In more severe cases, speech is so fast that an almost continuous flow of ideas occurs (flight of ideas), with jumps from one thought to the next; speech may become incomprehensible. Judgement is so distorted that the social consequences can be devastating. People spend vast sums of money, drive recklessly, make foolish business decisions or perform sexual indiscretions. Delusions such as a belief of having extraordinary power, or hallucinations like hearing God assign them a special mission, occur in especially severe states. All these abnormalities improve rapidly as the mood disturbance resolves.

Spike Milligan, the great humorist, vividly portrays the essence of mania in conversation with the psychiatrist Anthony Clare, who records it in his book, *Depression and How to Survive It*:

The best scripts I wrote were when I was ill. I've just recalled this— the ones that I wrote best were when I was ill—a mad desire to be better than anybody else at comedy, and if I couldn't do it in the given time of eight hours a day I used to work 12, 13 and 14 … I was four feet above the ground at times, talking twice as fast as normal people. Working on this with great fervour to write this stuff … I once did write 10 000 words in one day, like Balzac! I was pressured inside. I couldn't sleep. I just wrote and wrote. I couldn't sleep. I just couldn't stop, couldn't control it.

Probably one of the most illuminating accounts of mania (and bipolar) is that by Kay Redfield Jamison, a person who has suffered terribly from its effects for most of her life and is at the same time one of the most renowned researchers of the malady. Her medical memoir, *An Unquiet Mind*, takes us into both the magnificent highs and the desperate lows as she shares with us her own harrowing experiences. Here is her revealing description of what it is like to be manic:

> When you're high it's tremendous. The ideas and feelings are fast and frequent like shooting stars, and you follow them until you find better and brighter ones. Shyness goes, the right words and gestures are suddenly there, the power to captivate others a felt certainty … Sensuality is pervasive and the desire to seduce and be seduced irresistible. Feelings of ease, intensity, power, well-being, financial omnipotence, and euphoria pervade one's marrow. But, somewhere, this changes. The fast ideas are too fast, and there are far too many; overwhelming confusion replaces clarity. Memory goes. Humor and absorption on friends' faces are replaced by fear and concern … you are irritable, angry, frightened, uncontrollable, and enmeshed in the blackest caves of the mind. You never know these caves were there. It will never end, for madness carves its own reality.

Occasionally, in what is known as a mixed affective state, people experience features of both depression and mania in a single episode. They have a dejected mood but are grandiose and hyperactive and may have flight of ideas.

Mood disorders in clinical practice

Mood disorders are regarded by most psychiatrists as a group of conditions with certain similar, overlapping features. The classifications to which I alluded earlier emphasise different aspects, including clinical features, severity, the course of the illness, its response to treatment and psychological factors that precipitated it. For example, the chief criteria for a major depressive episode in DSM-IV (the American system described in Chapter 3), are listed in the table below.

Criteria for a major depressive episode (DSM-IV)

At least five of the following have been present during the same two-week period and represent a change from previous functioning; at least one symptom is depressed mood or loss of interest or pleasure:

- depressed mood (or irritable mood in children or adolescents) most of the day, nearly every day;
- marked loss of interest or pleasure in activities most of the day, nearly every day;
- significant weight loss or weight gain when not dieting (e.g. more than 5 per cent of body weight in a month), or decrease or increase in appetite nearly every day;
- insomnia or alternatively excessive sleep nearly every day;
- agitation or retardation nearly every day;
- fatigue or loss of energy nearly every day;
- feelings of worthlessness or excessive or inappropriate guilt (which may be delusional) nearly every day;
- diminished ability to think or concentrate, or indecisiveness, nearly every day;
- recurrent thoughts about death and suicide.

A major depressive episode usually begins gradually, over weeks. Some people recover completely and suffer only a single attack during their lifetime. Over half will have one or more recurrences but are usually symptom-free between episodes. Sometimes many years will pass before a relapse, but other people have only a brief respite. Typically the period between episodes diminishes with age. Untreated mania lasts about three months, and untreated major depression between six and twelve. Some people experience depression regularly during autumn or winter with recovery in spring and summer (called seasonal affective disorder). Others have intense episodes of depression lasting only a few days and occurring about every three weeks—their symptoms tend to be severe and often involve suicidal thinking.

To refer to 'minor' depression, as I commented earlier, is not an accurate designation since it can thoroughly disrupt a person's life, including work performance and interpersonal relationships. In the past, this form was called reactive depression, to emphasise that mood responded to environmental influences. Also, milder types of depression are often accompanied by anxiety.

Dysthymic disorder is an enduring low-grade depressive state, more common in women than men, marked by a pessimistic view of life and of the future, low self-esteem, indecisiveness and lack of energy. It usually begins in late adolescence or early adulthood, adversely affecting study or adjustment to work. Clear-cut bouts of depression, breaking the continuing dysthymic pattern, may propel the person to seek professional help.

Cyclothymia is a pattern in which people experience distinct but relatively mild mood swings—from exuberance to despondency. But the changes, in both directions, may disrupt their lives, with harmful effects on career and relationships. The swings are largely uninfluenced by life events.

Finally, lowered mood clearly resulting from well-defined stress, such as a marital break-up or loss of a job, is referred to as an adjustment disorder with depressed mood. As the stress lessens, so do the symptoms.

What causes mood disorders?

There has been much research, and it points to many potential causes within three broad groups—biological, psychological and social. One group will be more important than the others in any particular form of disordered mood.

Biological factors

The fact that disordered mood runs in families suggests that genes play a role. Their contribution is particularly well established in bipolar. For example, twin studies show a higher concordance rate in identical twins compared to non-identical twins. Searching for a single gene has proven futile making it likely that many genes are involved, including some that predispose to risk factors like poor coping with stress and certain personality traits.

A promising theory to explain mood disorders was based on the observation that reserpine, a drug once used widely to reduce high blood pressure and that caused marked depression in some people, lowers the levels of certain chemical messengers in the brain. By contrast, anti-depressant drugs increase the levels. As chemical messengers influence the secretion of hormones, endocrine abnormalities might be expected in people with mood disorders. Those with certain endocrine disorders, particularly an under-functioning thyroid or an over-functioning adrenal gland, often experience mood disturbance.

Neuro-imaging scans show shrinkage of the brain of some depressed patients, especially elderly folk and those with bipolar, but the pattern is not universal. Such inconsistency also applies to lower activity in the frontal brain. The advent of several powerful investigatory tools brings with it the strong likelihood of finding out a lot more about the biological foundations of depressive states.

Psychological and social factors

People with certain personality traits, especially if dependent and obsessional, are more vulnerable to developing depression, but it occurs in even the most well-adjusted and sturdy person.

Loss of a parent during childhood is associated with an increased risk of depression in adult life, but the link may be non-specific since such loss is also linked with other disorders, including alcoholism and anti-social personality.

One life experience intimately linked to depression is the death of a loved one. Grief and depression share a number of features, but grief differs in being a normal response to loss with the psychological purpose of enabling the person to adapt.

Uncomplicated grief typically follows a broad pattern. The first effect, disbelief, really a state of shock, is followed by recognition of the reality of the loss and the first painful feelings. People who are grieving will, like people with clinical depression, experience intense sadness, disturbed sleep, loss of interest and social withdrawal. But grief does have distinctive features. They are preoccupied with the dead person and may even imagine seeing or hearing them. They may lose interest in food, but marked weight loss is rare. Any guilt concerning the deceased (for example, not having done enough for them in a terminal illness) does not extend to feelings of failure and worthlessness.

Working through the loss and surrendering ties with the deceased happens gradually. This grief work entails a step-by-step accommodation of the intense emotions experienced and concludes with a phase of acceptance. The bereaved person finds ways to live with the loss and restructures their world accordingly. So normal grief is limited by time. Given support from family, friends (and sometimes professionals), the bereaved person will accept their sense of loss. Recovery does not mean forgetting the deceased; rather, memories are no longer accompanied by emotional turmoil. The past is recalled with sentimental pleasure while, at the same time, new interests and friends are cultivated.

CS Lewis's well-known account of his personal agony after losing his wife, *A Grief Observed* (filmed as *Shadowlands*) illuminates the essence of grief, especially when he rails against fate and tells how grief pervades everything:

> They tell me H. is happy now, they tell me she is at peace. What makes them so sure of this ... why are they so sure that all anguish ends with death ... why should the separation which so agonizes the lover who is left behind be painless to the lover who departs ...?

We are under the harrow and can't escape. Reality, looked at steadily, is unbearable … How often—will it be for always?—how often will the vast emptiness astonish me like a complete novelty and make me say, 'I never realized my loss till this moment'? The same leg is cut off time after time. The first plunge of the knife into the flesh is felt again and again … Grief is like a long valley, a winding valley where any bend may reveal a totally new landscape.

This brief account helps us to understand the psychoanalytic view of depression, which suggests that it may be a form of abnormal grief. Grief responses are not confined to death. They may, for example, follow a break-up of a relationship, the loss of a job, diminution of status or deterioration in health. These are all experiences of loss and may be accompanied by the psychological reactions of grief. Even the shattering of an ideal can cause grief in the broader application of the concept.

Stress deserves special mention in considering the causes of depression. Depressed people often experience major stressful life events immediately before their illness. It had been thought that this pattern was more typical of milder reactive forms, but stressful events accompany severe depression just as often. Stress may also precede the beginning of other psychiatric states like schizophrenia and anxiety. An underlying vulnerability to a particular disorder is probably the crucial factor. Stress is a personal experience—what one person finds unnerving may not be perceived as such by another. And stress is so common that it may simply coincide with the beginning of depression.

Behavioural theories to explain depression arose from animal experiments. If an electric shock is applied to an animal, it will attempt to escape. After repeated shocks, with no means of escape, the animal will eventually give up, in a state of helplessness resembling depression (learned helplessness). Similar helpless states may arise as part of the human condition. Aaron Beck, a former psychoanalyst who was one of the first to propose the role of faulty information processing, further suggested that repeated setbacks occurring in childhood pave the way for pessimistic patterns of thinking—a so-called 'negative cognitive set'. People in this situation view the world, themselves and the future in a bleak light and so misinterpret life events and deprecate themselves harshly.

There is scope for thinking about causal factors in an integrative way. Consider a few of the points we examined above. People who suffer mood disorders may be genetically predisposed in the face of stress because a number of chemical messengers do not function normally; the dysfunction then affects certain hormones, which in turn has a deleterious influence on the immune system. All this may pave the way for damage to nerve cells. On the optimistic side, we do know that effective treatment reverses the hormonal and immune abnormalities.

Physical illness and depression

Physically ill people commonly develop depressive symptoms—at the rate of about a third of all medical in-patients and out-patients. The link here between mind and body may be confusing, as some general symptoms of a physical illness may be very like depressive features. Tiredness, insomnia, anorexia, weight loss, apathy and loss of libido are common both to many physical disorders and to depression. For instance, the first phase of an illness such as glandular fever may be misdiagnosed as low-grade depression.

The fact that serious physical illness is a critical life event and therefore a potent source of stress is another complicating factor. The physically ill may suffer many losses, including physical function, a bodily part or organ, self-esteem, earning capacity and friends. In fact, grief reactions are a normal response to illness, and their severity is usually consistent with the degree of stress. If the reaction is so marked and/or persistent as to interfere with recovery, psychiatrists regard it as a disorder in its own right—an adjustment disorder with depressed mood (see Chapter 5). A person who is predisposed to depression may also suffer a major depressive episode precipitated by a physical illness.

The biological effects of a physical disease may directly cause a depressive syndrome known as an organic mood disorder. A classical example is depression following an endocrine abnormality like an under-functioning thyroid. Conditions affecting the central nervous system, such as stroke, Parkinson's disease, multiple sclerosis and epilepsy, may also have this effect.

Drugs that act on the brain's chemical messengers (I referred earlier to reserpine as a classic instance) can cause depression. Steroid medication may lead to disordered mood (usually depression, occasionally mania). Many women on oral contraceptives experience mildly lowered mood and may choose not to continue taking them for this reason.

Treating the depressed person

Depressed people usually seek help initially from their family doctor, who is well placed to make the diagnosis if they have been patients of the practice for a long time. The doctor will know what the person is usually like and that the psychological and bodily changes reflect a mood disturbance. Psychiatrists, who are often consulted in more severe cases, make a thorough evaluation, asking about past history of psychiatric illness, its treatment and the response, past suicidal thoughts and acts, family history of mental illness and current physical health. At the heart of this pursuit is consideration of biological, psychological and social factors that could be contributory. Information about current life circumstances is central in assessing psychological and social domains. Physical examination may suggest the need for investigations such as thyroid function tests, blood examination and a CT scan of the brain.

In assessing the depth of depression and the risk of suicide, an interview with a family member or friend is vital, since someone who has known the person can gauge the level and quality of change. This assessment is a crucial part of treatment, particularly to prevent suicide. The following questions are always considered: Is there a suicide risk? Does the person's mood vary with external influences? Is the mood disturbance an understandable response to life circumstances? Is there evidence of 'vegetative' symptoms such as weight loss? Does the person express inappropriate guilt? Are there any psychotic symptoms?

Whether or not a person is admitted to hospital depends on their level of social support, physical health and degree of suicide risk. A serious suicide risk calls for urgent referral to a psychiatrist. If the person cannot recognise that they are ill and refuses treatment, compulsory care and close nursing observation are essential, indeed can save life. Because it takes at least two to three weeks before people respond to anti-depressants, ECT may be recommended.

Psychological treatments

People with milder forms of depression are often helped by a brief course of psychotherapy (10 to 20 sessions). There are several forms of effective psychological therapy. In the most commonly applied model, cognitive behaviour therapy (CBT), the therapist carefully teases out patients' negative thoughts, attitudes and beliefs about themselves, their relationships, and the future. By completing a daily record, the patient monitors their mood and life events, and responses to them. The therapist challenges the validity of any negative thinking by asking the patient to judge its appropriateness, and also encourages a more realistic appraisal of life situations. The patient may also be given specific tasks from which to gain a sense of mastery. We look more closely at CBT in Chapter 19. In mindfulness-based CBT, a variant of the original approach, the patient receives the same therapy but is also taught how to become more aware of him or herself in the 'here and now', in terms of psychological and bodily changes, as well as how to tolerate any distressing emotions and thoughts.

Interpersonal therapy, another well-researched form of brief psychotherapy designed to treat depression, focuses on current family and social relating, on the premise that the negative mood arises from complications in these relationships. Examples are ambivalent feelings towards a relative who has died, a retiree's painful transition to a non-working role, the empty-nest scenario, poor interpersonal skills, and marital tension due to the loss of a job, illness or other life event.

Crisis intervention is appropriate when the depression began suddenly and is linked to an obvious stressful life event. People with a longstanding complex pattern of depression, poor self-esteem, conflicted relationships and pervasive self-defeating attitudes may benefit from intensive psychoanalytically oriented therapy. Depressed people with marked marital or family problems may be helped by one of several types of family therapy.

Physical treatments

People with more severe forms of depression usually do not respond to psychotherapy alone, although it is helpful in combination with medication or electro-convulsive therapy (ECT), and after recovery. Please turn to Chapter 18 for an account of the anti-depressants, mood stabilisers and ECT and their application in the treatment of mood disorders.

Managing bipolar disorder including mania

Acute mania and hypomania

Treating people with mania poses a challenge for the psychiatrist in that they usually need urgent admission to hospital, often against their will. Feeling on top of the world, the last thing on their mind is the need for treatment. Fortunately, a number of medications are now available to induce a state of calm and a return to reality. Curiously, anti-epileptic drugs (referred to as mood stabilisers in the context of bipolar) in combination with anti-psychotics do the job in most cases. Lithium, the first anti-manic drug discovered, remains an effective option, but only at high concentrations that carry a risk of toxicity. ECT may be required in severe cases where the high proves intractable.

People with a less severe form of mania may not require admission and can be treated with a mood stabiliser alone, although their mental state can deteriorate suddenly. Cooperation may be limited, requiring a relative to assist. Milder forms of mania may even resolve without medication, provided relatives are there to keep a close eye on the person.

Preventing recurrence over the long term

Most people with bipolar illness need mood stabilisers to prevent the recurrence of either depression or mania. Whether to start such a program depends on the severity and recurrent nature of the disorder, as well as the risks and side-effects of continuing medication. Usually, two episodes in two years warrants maintenance treatment. Since bipolar can disrupt a person's life markedly, some psychiatrists launch therapy after a single attack of mania. Mood stabilisers prevent both highs and lows in the majority of patients. Again, recruiting a relative is desirable since the patient lacks full insight into the seriousness of their condition. Educating everyone about the long-term nature of bipolar, its treatment and especially the early signs of recurrence is pivotal.

If one stabiliser is inadequate, a combination of two, even three, may help. Since the illness is generally lifelong, patients need considerable support and counselling. Poor compliance remains the principal reason for the failure of treatment. Psychotherapy improves cooperativeness and helps to prevent recurrence.

Bipolar depression

Symptoms in bipolar depression are similar to depression unassociated with mania, as is the response to anti-depressants, ECT and lithium. Lithium has a profound role in reducing the risk of suicide. Anti-depressants may precipitate a switch from depression to a high. Mood can shift from depression to mania and back again over a brief period (called rapid cycling).

Conclusion

The story of the treatment of mood disorders mirrors that of modern psychiatry in one notable way. The consignment of people to the gruesome fate of months of sheer agony has been replaced by early detection and effective treatment. The distress of hundreds of thousands of people has been eased by continuing research advances in both medications and psychological treatments. Although the causes of mood disorders remain elusive, there are grounds for optimism as we gain more and more knowledge about the subject.

CHAPTER 8

The Mind Talking through the Body

Many people who suffer physical symptoms actually have emotional problems that they are expressing through their body. They may or may not have a medical condition, but even if they do it is not enough, in the doctor's judgement, to explain their health problems. Such situations of psychological distress are common in medical practice and affect about a third of people attending family doctors.

Two words are often used to describe these situations. In hysteria (an ambiguous word with a rich history), there are physical symptoms but no physical basis for them. In hypochondriasis, people are preoccupied with a fear of having, or are convinced that they do have, a serious illness. Bodily symptoms with an emotional basis may also be part of the so-called psychosomatic illnesses, where physical conditions are certainly present but are heavily influenced by psychological factors.

In all these circumstances, physical symptoms arise from psychological forces of which the person is mostly unaware. Defence mechanisms that are deployed at an unconscious level transform the emotional state into bodily dysfunction, and this shows itself as physical symptoms. People interpret these physical symptoms in vastly different ways. One person may put a headache down to stress whereas another is convinced that it is due to a brain tumour.

If symptoms are under voluntary control, then the person is regarded as faking illness or malingering to attain an obvious purpose. A student may be trying to avoid the pressure of an examination or a person may be determined to gain financial compensation after a minor accident

Why the mysterious leap from mind to body?

This is how many observers have described the puzzling transformation of one form of experience into another—the emotional into the bodily.

Personality factors, and defence mechanisms as outlined in Chapter 5, have been particularly valuable in helping us to understand the process, but the most illuminating concepts have come from medical sociologists. Their ideas of the 'sick role' and 'illness behaviour' provide a useful social and cultural perspective from which to approach the subject. In all societies, people who become ill are granted certain privileges—they are exempted from work and other responsibilities and cared for by family and friends. They are also expected to meet certain obligations—to seek medical help and to accept the recommended treatment in order to recover as soon as possible.

'Illness behaviour' describes people's responses in the sick role, particularly how they perceive, evaluate and act on bodily symptoms. These responses vary greatly, from the stoic to the dramatic, from communicating distress in words to displaying it through gesture and action. People who are preoccupied with physical symptoms have been described as showing a form of abnormal illness behaviour, at least in the eyes of the doctor. Issy Pilowsky, the Australian psychiatrist who developed the concept, summarises it as an inappropriate or maladaptive mode of experiencing, evaluating or acting in relation to one's own state of health.

When such behaviour is combined with denial in the face of psychological distress that is obvious to the astute professional observer, then the psychiatric states described below come into play.

Some of the variation in people's responses is linked to social factors and may be particular to an ethnic group, social class or family. Social context is relevant generally—for example, a severe injury in a football match may go unnoticed whereas a relatively trivial injury at work may bring intense distress. Similarly, a work injury may be a badge of honour in one family, a symbol of weakness in another.

Who is likely to express emotion through their body?

People who express emotions through the body often share certain personality traits, although it is difficult to know whether these have always been there or have resulted from prolonged distress. The tendency to be needy and demanding of others is a good example. Masochism—obtaining satisfaction through painful experience—is another trait that may work strongly against a return to health. People may relieve feelings of guilt by linking a sense of punishment to suffering.

Anger is common in the medical arena. It is more obvious when directed externally, say to medical staff for their 'uselessness'. When kept within, it may take the form of refusing to take medication, co-operate with treatment, undergo necessary surgery or ultimately get better. Analgesics have no effect on pain, prescribed medications produce intolerable side-effects and surgery fails to bring relief.

These people challenge the doctor by continuing to return for treatment until there is little or nothing else to offer. This sometimes leads to desperate measures like surgery, which in turn bring their own complications. Generally, such people are long suffering. They may, if delicately questioned, tell of having had their own needs unmet as children when they had to care for a younger or ill sibling or an ill parent. They have come to deny their own needs and grown up into compulsive carers, feeling overly responsible and tending to others. Then, often triggered by a minor illness or injury, their role is radically reversed. Quite unexpectedly, as they are oblivious of their own underlying psychological needs, they become long-term users of health care.

One way to bring all these elements together is by applying psychoanalytic ideas. Freud believed that responding through the body is an unconsciously determined manoeuvre to deal with a deeply embedded psychological conflict. The symptom that arises symbolically reflects that conflict—is, in essence, a disguised form of it. The reduction in anxiety that results from this compromise solution (the somatising response) is called primary gain. Secondary gain refers to the more obvious advantages of having a physical illness—sympathy, care and relief from responsibility.

Anna O, one of the best-known cases in all of psychoanalysis, is highly relevant in this context. She was treated by Freud's mentor Josef Breuer, a celebrated physician in Vienna, in the early 1880s. Freud later became involved in trying to unravel her seemingly inexplicable physical symptoms; *Studies in Hysteria* (1895) was the outcome of this pioneering research. Anna O helps us to understand the conversion of emotional conflict into bodily symptoms. A young attractive woman, she had nursed her dying father and in the process developed a number of physical symptoms, including paralysis of her limbs and her neck, a squint, and difficulty in talking and swallowing.

In treatment with hypnosis, Anna O re-experienced the intense feelings she had had while at her father's bedside. In recalling, in the hypnotised state, these experiences in which her symptoms had originally occurred, it became clear how each one of them related to events surrounding her relationship with her ill father. Through this sort of detective work, Freud and Breuer were the first to propose that psychological forces, operating unconsciously, could affect bodily function, so mimicking physical disorders. Freud advanced his thinking by emphasising the sexual nature of the underlying conflicts, and so shaped the long-term direction of psychoanalysis. Although the sexual dimension did not find favour with many of Freud's contemporaries (a position that still pertains), his contribution to an understanding of conversion phenomena remains as compelling today as it was a century ago.

Werner's experience throws further light on the influence of the psyche on bodily function:

A 35-year-old teacher of the intellectually disabled awoke one morning with a paralysed right arm after observing his wife flirting with a close friend at a staff party the evening before. When tests in hospital ruled out a stroke or other physical disorder, a psychiatrist was consulted. It soon emerged that the symptom represented both Werner's wish to hit his wife and its unacceptability given his high moral standards. His parents had been members of a fundamentalist sect, and the children were expected to conform to its tenets—notably, expressing any emotion was frowned upon. Always resentful of these constraints, Werner had unwittingly channelled his anger into dedicated involvement with a disadvantaged group.

The family as a crucible

A somatising response tends to run in families, probably due to their original illness behaviour and their beliefs about illness. For example, people who as infants or children suffered the loss of a key figure tend to remain sensitive to how family and friends relate to them. Following a later experience of loss, they may show their distress in the form of either psychiatric or physical symptoms. Then, the care given by family and health professionals may become an alternative source of gratification that compensates for the earlier loss but paradoxically perpetuates the symptoms.

To understand the meaning of an illness for a particular person, the doctor has to appreciate that early experience of illness and the way it was handled in the family may powerfully determine later illness behaviour.

How the psychiatrist approaches the somatising response

Talking through the body is a feature in many psychiatric states, but sometimes the physical symptoms are so prominent that the underlying psychological disorder is masked. Thus, depressed people often experience fatigue, constipation, aches and pains, and preoccupation with physical symptoms. In people with clinical anxiety, bodily changes such as palpitations and tremor may predominate. Loss of weight is central to anorexia nervosa. Less commonly, unexplained physical symptoms like an unshakeable belief that one's intestines are rotting occur in the psychoses as the content of bizarre delusions.

A regular dilemma for the psychiatrist (and for any doctor) is to determine whether a set of physical symptoms are mainly organic or psychological in origin. This is a meaningless distinction, as in most illnesses both elements, together with social factors, make a combined contribution. In practice, the task is to sort out to what extent each one of the three elements bears upon a particular disorder. The following case is a typical clinical conundrum.

Mrs Johnson, aged 74 and with previously documented heart disease, had been living alone since the death of her husband eighteen months previously. Her daughter phoned to say she was going overseas. Mrs Johnson immediately developed chest pain and feelings of panic. On admission to hospital it was unclear whether the symptoms were an episode of angina, conversion of her concern about being left on her own into chest pain, chest discomfort typically associated with anxiety, or malingering—that is, simulation of angina in order to gain her daughter's attention. All were possible in the circumstances.

Hypochondriasis

The hallmark of hypochondriasis is the fear of having, or the belief that one has, a serious disease, when a thorough clinical check-up does not support the diagnosis of a physical disorder that would account for the symptoms. Over three hundred years ago, the French playwright Molière gave a vivid account of hypochondiasis in his satire, *Le Malade Imaginaire*. The central character, Argan, is so incessantly preoccupied with matters of ill health and disease that his life is consumed by them, with unpleasant results for his family. At one point, he rebukes his daughter: 'Ah! She has entirely put me … out, and I shall want more than eight doses of medicine and 12 enemas to put all this right'.

The hypochondriac is imprisoned by morbid preoccupations. There is no room for a commonsense view or even a touch of humour. Indeed, these health concerns and imperviousness to reassurance make the person the butt of humour. A 'Wizard of Id' cartoon illustrates this nicely. The nurse informs the doctor that the hypochondriac has arrived for a consultation. 'Why are you so concerned about your health?' the doctor asks (rather naively, one would think). 'Death runs in our family', the patient responds in all seriousness!

People with hypochondriasis are on a never-ending vigil in obsessing about every detail of their bodily function, being exquisitely sensitive to physical sensations that they interpret as evidence of a serious disease. But this behaviour occurs in many situations, especially in the elderly and as a response to actual physical disease. A specific diagnosis of hypochondriasis is made when these concerns linger on for months despite repeated medical reassurance. The person may worry about multiple diseases or fixate on a single condition. For instance, in 'cardiac neurosis' the person's fear is of having heart disease; in 'cancer phobia' the concern is of a hidden tumour. The classical hypochondriacal pattern is illustrated well in the case of Ellen.

Ellen, 57 years old and married, consulted her family doctor in an agitated state, complaining of headache and dizziness and convinced she had a brain tumour. Her fears were calmed temporarily after a thorough physical examination. The doctor's sensitive inquiry drew out the following story. Ellen was the youngest of a family of ten children. Since her father's death when she was fifteen and her sisters' departure from home, she had had to care for her mother. Her mother had died of cancer six months previously. A brother and a niece had also died of cancer, while one of her own daughters had survived it in childhood. In the preceding month both of her unmarried daughters had revealed plans to leave home. The doctor concluded that all these stresses had led to marked anxiety and hypochondriacal concerns. A sense of potential abandonment had highlighted Ellen's own emotional needs, which had been inadequately met as a child. Her fears were closely associated with her experience of family members suffering from cancer and her mother's fatal illness.

Hypochondriacal features can also occur as part of depression or long-standing anxiety. The conviction of having a disease can reach delusional intensity and, on occasion, constitute a sign of a psychotic disorder.

It is tempting to try to understand what leads a person with what we may call a pure form of hypochondriasis to spend virtually all their emotional energy on their bodily concerns and fears of disease. The approach of the American psychiatrist, Harry Stack Sullivan, has always made sense to me. He posits that the 'physical ailment, bizarrely enough, is a means for augmenting security in interpersonal relations. Without it, the patient would feel abased, inferior, and without any merit for the consideration of others.' And it certainly is true that hypochondriacal people engage with the world through discussion of their ailments; there is always a doctor listening even if the person needs to traipse from one to another to ascertain the nature of the symptoms. Moreover, so long as the body is the subject of the concern, more painful emotions like impoverished self-esteem are kept at bay.

Body dysmorphic disorder is a particular form of hypochondriasis in which a disturbance of body image is the central feature and takes the form of an obsessive concern about a defect in appearance. Common complaints are facial flaws (for example, a prominent nose), but hands, feet or breasts may be involved. On occasion the intensity of the concern verges on the delusional. Repeated consulting of cosmetic surgeons may not be recognised as being based on a delusion and may lead to ill-advised surgery. The result is often unsatisfactory, leading the person to pressure the surgeon to re-operate.

I had occasion once to supervise a trainee who offered a young woman long-term weekly psychotherapy after we hypothesised that her 3-year preoccupation with the thickness of her eyebrows was symptomatic of a underlying unease about herself as a person. We were ambivalent about inviting her to commit herself to what we envisaged would be a distressing therapeutic process. On the other hand, the eyebrow problem was devastating to her and disruptive of social life. It emerged that as a child she had never been praised for any achievements by her parents; they were a misanthropic pair when it came to anything celebratory in family life. After eighteen months of looking at herself in a secure, non-judgemental environment, she developed a measure of self-understanding which led her to appreciate that she was a person of worth and had something to offer the world. The eyebrows were then seen as perfectly normal.

Conversion disorder

Formerly called hysteria, conversion disorder was first described by Hippocrates over two thousand years ago and assumed to occur only in women and be due to a floating womb. Psychiatrists apply this diagnosis when a disturbed bodily function suggests a medical diagnosis but thorough examination reveals nothing abnormal and the symptoms appear to be a response to stress. Conversion is likely when the doctor's findings do not match any known patterns of bodily dysfunction—for example, paralysis of a leg with nothing to indicate damage to the nerves supplying the leg.

Conversion disorders were much more common in the nineteenth century, reflecting their close links with social and cultural influences. That they are more common in women, and in developing countries, also points to socio-cultural links. A conversion symptom may affect an entire community. The classical example is dizziness or vomiting in a school. The usual explanation for such an 'epidemic' is the effect on the whole group of a stressor like the death of a student. Almost 300 staff members of the Royal Free Hospital in London were stricken with a flu-like illness in 1955 and suffered from persisting fatigue. Was this an infectious disease that spread rapidly through the hospital or a classical example of 'epidemic hysteria'. The arguments for conversion were that symptoms occurred in many more women than men, special tests were all negative, malaise was prominent rather than an objective finding like elevated temperature, and symptoms resembled a previous epidemic of psychogenic over-breathing. On the other hand, Melvin Ramsay, then a consultant in infectious disease at the 'Free', concluded from his studies that a variant of myalgic encephalitis was at work. We shall never be sure.

The diagnosis of conversion is always difficult to make since it involves a judgement that symptoms are not physically based. A complicating issue is the occurrence of conversion symptoms in association with genuine physical problems. Thus, people with epilepsy may present with fits that mimic their true fits but do not show up on special tests. The likelihood of a conversion disorder is strengthened by a story of psychological stress preceding the onset of symptoms.

Claudia's 8-year-old son had died tragically in a boating accident. At first, she was grief-stricken, cried uncontrollably and experienced vivid images of the accident. On the morning after the funeral she complained of weakness in her legs to the extent that she found it difficult to walk. Neurological examination found nothing abnormal. Claudia's symptoms were no doubt due to the conversion of grief into weakness in her legs. The significance of the death was intensified by the struggle she had had in conceiving her son and by reawakened memories of her husband, lost five years previously in a car accident. As is often the case, Claudia did not share this pivotal information with her doctors as she was so preoccupied with her paralysis and worried that multiple sclerosis might be the culprit.

Hilda, a woman in what she regarded as the prime of her professional career, was referred for a psychiatric opinion after an ear, nose and throat specialist could not detect any physical basis for the hoarseness and feeling of a lump in her throat she had experienced for several weeks. She had had a dispute with her senior manager a year earlier in which she felt harassed and bullied. Feeling totally humiliated she had sought, but failed to obtain, an apology. At her wit's end, she felt she had no choice but to initiate legal proceedings. After a drawn-out procedure she did obtain financial compensation for income lost and personal suffering. Hilda was supported through this ordeal by a therapist, who also helped her to achieve insight into the link between her symptoms and the severe stress she was under. Much to Hilda's relief, her symptoms gradually waned and then disappeared.

The commonest form of conversion involves pain. This is severe, prolonged, causes much distress and functional impairment, and has no obvious physical basis. Pain is the best example of the adage that the relevant question is not either/or but how much of each. This may be a difficult decision, with clinicians reluctant to make the diagnosis of pain conversion for fear that the patient may react negatively. Patients and clinicians alike prefer physical rather than psychosocial explanations. Repeated investigations are often done in the quest of a treatable state. Minimal or no improvement is the result. The two parties then become entangled in an emotion-ridden tussle. Chronic pain is a major cause of disability, contributing to much personal and family misery.

Linda, aged 36, fell at work and had had relentless back pain since, unrelieved by analgesics. At first no physical changes were found. However, following several series of X-rays in eighteen months, the third orthopaedic surgeon she consulted diagnosed a protruding disc and recommended surgery. When reviewed two years after the operation by a psychiatrist, Linda was still physically disabled, entirely dependent on her husband, and thoroughly demoralised. The psychiatrist drew out a story that gave a good understanding of her plight.

As a child Linda was responsible for her younger sister when both parents worked. Following primary school she was sent to boarding school, a move she resented bitterly. After completing a university degree she joined the public service and was quickly promoted to a managerial position. She soon married a man much younger than herself. Thus, with her emotional needs in childhood unmet, she responded as an adult by striving for positions of superiority (and therefore invulnerability) in both work and marriage.

A minor event, the fall, forced Linda to resume a dependent role. Her doctors experienced many negative feelings about her, seeing her as punishing and belittling. The psychiatrist put this understanding to effect in psychotherapy, where she was encouraged to address the issue of her anger towards her parents and resultant guilt. This, combined with a physical rehabilitation program, led to gradual improvement.

Psychogenic amnesia and fugue

Confusing as it may be, psychiatrists include under the umbrella of conversion disorders a number of psychiatric states in which a conflict of one kind or another is transformed not into physical symptoms but rather into disturbed mental functioning, such as loss of identity or of memory. Dissociation, a term coined by French psychiatrist Pierre Janet, is used to cover the unconscious process involved.

A typical dissociative state is psychogenic amnesia—that is, psychologically induced memory loss. A sudden inability to recall personal information is its hallmark. Related is depersonalisation, in which people feel unreal, detached from themselves, as if in a dream-like state. Less common but most dramatic is psychogenic fugue, where the person typically wanders away from home without any sense of who they are and is found days or weeks later—in rare cases having assumed a totally new identity.

Although depersonalisation is experienced by many people during anxiety-provoking events, amnesia and fugue usually occur only in extremely stressful situations such as war or disaster. These psychological states may also occur in the face of overwhelming and unresolvable internal conflict. The case of Sophia, one my own most intriguing patients, is a perfect illustration of the latter.

Sophia, a 21-year-old student from a traditional Greek family, was found by police wandering in the centre of the city, confused about who she was. When brought to the emergency department, it emerged that she could not remember her name, where she lived or any details about her family.

Over the next three days, Sophia gradually recovered her memory, by which time the police had located her parents. When she was more accessible, her story enabled us to make sense of the amnesia. Her boyfriend had been pressing for them to begin a sexual relationship; Sophia was inclined to go ahead but the prohibition of pre-marital intercourse by her parents and their culture led to an intense internal conflict. Her desire to satisfy her boyfriend's wishes seemed irreconcilable with loyalty to her family. Hopelessly stuck, her mind resorted to an unconscious manoeuvre that enabled her to forget not only the dilemma, but her entire identity. Involvement of the family allowed an open exchange of feelings about Sophia's dilemma, which paved the way for reconciliation.

The treatment of people presenting with psychogenic amnesia and fugue is insight-oriented psychotherapy, a task for skilled therapists. Most recover quickly; a minority have persistent dissociative symptoms and require longer-term therapy.

Multiple personality disorder (also referred to as dissociative identity disorder), in which two or more personalities appear to function alongside one another in the same person, but quite separately and without one being familiar with the others, is a rare and fascinating form of severe dissociation. A source of intense controversy, mental health professionals are unable to agree about whether such a condition exists at all. Some say that it results from early life trauma, particularly sexual abuse, that is forgotten for a long time but may be recovered through sensitive psychotherapy—the so-called repressed memory syndrome. Others contend that such memories are the products of the therapist's imagination and influence rather than of real events.

Psychosomatic or psychophysiological disorders

In contrast to the conditions I have described so far, psychosomatic (or psychophysiological) disorders are those in which there *is* demonstrable physical disease or alteration in physiological function, and psychological factors play a role in either causing, triggering or maintaining the disease or altered function. Certain medical conditions have classically been labelled as psychosomatic, including high blood pressure, asthma, dermatitis and ulcerative colitis, but meticulous studies have failed to demonstrate links between specific psychological factors and these conditions. For example, an association between a frustrated wish to be nurtured and peptic ulcer was claimed by some researchers for years, and peptic ulcer was regarded as a typical psychosomatic disorder. We now know that Helicobacter pylori infection is responsible, and the psychological hypothesis is dead.

On the other hand, non-specific stress does appear to trigger or aggravate many medical states. The fact that emotions can trigger common bodily changes like rapid heart rate and elevated blood pressure is one clue as to how stressful states may often bring on or worsen medical conditions. Further evidence for the link between psyche and soma is the role of various psychotherapies in enhancing the biological treatment of medical symptoms—for example, bronchodilators in asthma. Indeed, asthma is a clearcut disease in which the mind and body intersect.

Sylvie, 45 years old and with a history of intermittent asthma since her teenage years, developed more severe and more frequent attacks despite maximal drug therapy. Inquiry revealed a pending divorce and increasing repressed hostility towards her estranged husband. Treatment involved helping Sylvie to become aware of her anger and to express it, but in the context of a secure therapeutic relationship. She also became aware of long-concealed resentment towards her parents over the deprivation she felt following their divorce when she was a child. The psychological dimension of treatment led to better control of her asthma by standard anti-asthma medication.

The extreme somatising response

People who present with myriad complaints covering many systems of the body, and for all of which there is no physical basis, are severely disabled. They pose a huge challenge to the medical system, given the repeated and unnecessary investigations and treatments that are often carried out on them. They may exhibit aspects of hypochondriasis, conversion and feigned illness, and thus present complex diagnostic and therapeutic challenges. Their lives consist of their illness and the pervasive attention they pay to it;

in effect, illness becomes a way of life, seemingly the only way. The pattern, more common in women, begins in young adulthood and tends to continue throughout life. Since such 'heart-sink' patients are eternally demanding, doctors become increasingly frustrated, ultimately feeling quite helpless.

Carmel, aged 45 and formerly a nurse, presents weekly on average to her family doctor, the locum service or the emergency department. The complaint is usually of pain, in any part of her body. She sees no less than ten specialists. She presents to each of them a conviction that she has a disorder in their particular field. Carmel has had a series of operations, reflected in her battle-scarred abdomen. She is frequently admitted to a ward, where she frustrates staff. Communication breakdowns between the specialists and between them and the family doctor are common. One result is the absence of any coordinator of care.

Malingering and factitious disorder

Whereas all the above examples of the mind talking through the body are unconsciously derived, both malingering and factitious disorder are deliberately feigned. Malingering is the intentional production of exaggerated symptoms for specific gain, such as accident compensation. In factitious disorder the reason for feigning is not obvious. People with this disorder may present to hospitals repeatedly in order to receive treatment, including surgery. Their motivation is assumed to be a deep unmet need for care and affection. A bizarre variant involves a parent causing injury or apparent illness to a child (giving an emetic to induce vomiting, for example) in order to gain medical attention. It arises out of the parent's anxiety about their competence to care for a child and, again, their own unsatisfied need for affection (see the abuse section in Chapter 14).

Treating both soma and psyche

With people who speak through their bodies, we seek to shift their preoccupation from the physical to the psychological, and to assist them to deal with the latter more adaptively. The sensitive doctor does this without challenging the legitimacy of the physical symptoms. In general, the more sudden the onset of the physical changes and the clearer their link with psychological stress, the better the outcome. By contrast, longstanding forms of somatising are most resistant to change.

Confronting the person virtually never succeeds. Rather, the doctor determines if there is an adequate physical basis to explain the symptoms, and wins the person's confidence that the complaints are being taken seriously. The snags can be formidable. Repeated complex investigations are likely to reinforce the person's conviction that they have a physical disease even when the doctor suspects a psychological cause. Errors are made in both directions. People who do not have a bodily disease may end up in surgery, whereas others diagnosed as somatising may turn out to have a real physical disorder. Over-investigation is encouraged by an increasing reliance on technology among doctors, combined with a demanding or anxious patient and the possibility of being sued for negligence. A valuable rule of thumb for both patient and doctor is that once a 'work-up' is complete, no further tests are done and treatment proceeds on the basis of psychological counselling, review at regular intervals, and drug treatment as appropriate.

The place of drugs is complicated. Somatising people are often sensitive to the side-effects of medications, and drugs like anti-depressants are poorly tolerated. And, because of a concern about addiction, drugs for anxiety and insomnia are prescribed with caution. Drug treatment of enduring psychologically based pain is problematic as it tends not to respond to conventional methods. Indeed, the key to treatment is attending to psychological and social issues.

Frank, aged 60 and married, had developed irritable bowel syndrome ten years previously following an extramarital affair. He consulted his family doctor because of a recent onset of severe and disabling headache; he had been thinking of telling his wife, who had suffered a mild stroke, about the affair. Neurological examination and investigations were all normal. The headaches persisted, along with lowered mood, loss of pleasure in everyday activities, feelings of remorse and early morning waking. A comprehensive approach was adopted, to excellent effect. This combined continued drug treatment for the irritable bowel, judicious use of analgesics for the headache, a course of anti-depressant medication (biological) and both individual and marital psychotherapy (psychological).

The contribution of biological, psychological and social factors is well illustrated in Frank's case. The possible presence of depression or anxiety is relevant because they are both readily treatable. Depression, which commonly occurs alongside physical symptoms, varies from grief over the loss of bodily functions to sustained lowering of mood. Many people who are not fully aware of their inner emotional state may still benefit from specific anti-depressant or anti-anxiety treatment.

Psychological and social treatment may be hampered if doctor and patient have conflicting approaches to the problem. Indeed, they may clash over the basic question of whether the condition is physical or psychological—much to the patient's dismay. When the doctor focuses on psychological matters, the patient may vehemently resist. In any event, the doctor strives to understand the patient's point of view through empathy and discussion of practical difficulties imposed by the illness. Trust is a key to the sharing of personal concerns whether at work, in marriage or in other relationships. Frank's case shows how psychotherapy may relieve symptoms in people who accept that approach. Gains are made by shifting the focus from symptoms to adaptive coping. This overcomes the impasse and offers the person an opportunity to set achievable goals and to improve functioning and self-esteem. In more severe cases, compromise rather than cure is the only realistic option.

A striking feature of treatment is the large number of professionals who may become involved, including the family doctor, physician, surgeon, psychologist, social worker, physiotherapist, occupational therapist and psychiatrist. Such a cumbersome team may not work in unison. Opinions will differ and individuals may even offer contradictory advice. Ideally, one professional coordinates an agreed-on plan of treatment, most conveniently the family doctor. A role for the psychiatrist usually emerges when either a mental illness is suspected or the frustrations of other professionals reach a crescendo!

Conclusion

The sheer complexity of the link between mind and body is reflected in my difficulty in presenting the ideas in this chapter any more clearly than I have! Despite over a century of scholarly interest and research, somatisation remains a source of bafflement and frustration. However, one thing is clear—psyche and soma are inextricably bound, both in health and in illness. Psychiatrists' understanding of this association, at the least, enables them to adopt a coherent therapeutic approach in trying to meet the challenge of the person exhibiting a somatising response.

CHAPTER 9

Eating Disorders

Concern about the size and shape of our bodies is widespread in Western societies. Equally common is a concern about what we eat. It would be the rare teenage girl who has not experimented with dieting. However, it can go drastically wrong, to the extent of becoming a life-threatening illness.

Anorexia nervosa (AN) is one of the most dramatic of all psychiatric disorders. The typical picture is of a girl (90 per cent of cases) inexplicably starving herself, at times to the point of death. Although widely regarded as a contemporary condition, a similar picture has been noted for centuries. In the Middle Ages, cases of weight loss, celibacy and asceticism in young women were taken as evidence of sainthood. The first clear description of anorexia nervosa dates back to 1689, but the syndrome was established through the accounts of Pierre Lasègue in Paris and William Gull in Oxford (who gave the condition its name) two centuries later.

By contrast, the history of the other common eating disorder, bulimia nervosa (BN)—binge eating and vomiting—is brief. The syndrome was first outlined in 1979, reflecting then its 'epidemic' proportions and the accompanying professional interest in its treatment. It is possible, however, that features of bulimia nervosa go back hundreds of years: St Catherine of Siena made herself vomit as a form of repentance in the fourteenth century, while St Mary Magdalen de Pazzi exhibited a pattern of over-eating followed by vomiting in the early seventeenth century.

These two principal disorders of eating occur mainly in young women, usually starting in the late teens. Psychiatrists have identified other variants of anorexia nervosa, bulimia nervosa or a combination of the two. Binge-eating disorder, characterised by recurrent binge eating in the absence of extreme and regular attempts to lose weight, is the main one. We need to remember that disturbed patterns of eating are extraordinarily common in young women but that most are transitory and do not progress to clear-cut diagnosable illnesses.

Anorexia nervosa

Anorexia nervosa is the most common serious chronic disease of adolescent girls in developed countries, occurring in all socio-economic groups. The usual age of onset is 14–19, but younger children can be affected. The course is long-term with an average duration of seven years; even then many people do not return to complete health. Tragically, one in ten dies within twenty years. The risk of suicide is thirty-two times greater than expected.

We cannot talk about a specific cause, biological or psychological, although many theories have been proposed. Psychoanalytically oriented therapists have suggested that AN develops as an unconscious manoeuvre to avoid facing the challenges of moving to emotional and sexual maturity. Obviously, an emaciated girl stands little chance, if any, of being seen as sexually attractive. On the other hand, family therapists highlight recurring patterns of relating in families with an anorexic member—parental over-protection of the children, over-involvement in the affairs of one another, rigid thinking and failure to resolve conflicts. Family dysfunction of this kind is certainly observed, but it is unclear to what extent it precedes AN or results from the family's struggle to cope with an anorexic member.

Of greater practical relevance for psychiatrists are factors that predispose a young woman to develop AN. We know that exposure to an environment in which concern about weight and dieting prevails, and a family history of members who are thin or underweight, are pertinent. Genetics may be at work, given that the risk for first-degree female relatives is ten times that of the general population, and concordance much greater in identical twins than non-identical twins (55 per cent vs. 5 per cent).

Evidence of a social role comes from groups such as ballet dancers and models who are under constant pressure to maintain a trim body—for example, AN is estimated to affect about one in ten ballet dancers. When they are removed from this influence, improvement tends to follow. Adolescent dieting may be the key ingredient in these circumstances. Indeed, girls who diet have an eight-times greater risk of developing an eating disorder than those who do not. The potential contribution of cultural factors is of interest. Originally rare in Asian countries, the rate has increased in Japan, a finding probably due to the rapid and widespread permeation of traditional Japanese culture by Western influences.

The three core elements of AN are self-induced weight loss as part of the relentless pursuit of thinness, intense fear of becoming fat, and loss of periods. Weight loss is achieved through starvation as well as through over-exercising and vomiting. People fear gaining weight, even if substantially underweight, based on their grossly distorted perception of their bodies. They feel fat even at an extremely low weight; on objective testing they overestimate their current size. Associated with the starvation is an unusual fascination with food—its preparation, consumption and disposal. This includes avoidance of eating in company, odd practices such as cutting food into minute pieces, eating slowly, drinking large amounts of water, spicing food heavily and hoarding or hiding food. Many will induce vomiting and abuse laxatives and diuretics to facilitate further weight loss.

Over-activity, as common as dietary restriction and as difficult to treat, is of two kinds: over-exercise and persistent restlessness. Many exercise excessively to expend kilojoules and thus to lose weight. This may be covert (going up and down stairs on the pretext of fetching things) or overt (strenuous exercise such as aerobics, jogging and swimming). Exercise is solitary and obsessive, with a sense of guilt felt if it is not carried out. Restlessness ensues in emaciated people. Involuntary in form, it is linked to sleep disturbance; the pattern is analogous to ceaseless over-activity in laboratory animals deprived of food.

Other symptoms may include depression, loss of sexual drive, social withdrawal, poor concentration and insomnia.

Physical signs result from the effects of starvation: slow heart rate, cold extremities, low blood pressure, swollen legs and a fine downy hair on the face and trunk. Of the hormonal and metabolic changes, most are the result of weight loss. Fortunately, most changes are reversible, except for long-standing osteoporosis. Lack of potassium can lead to dangerous, even life-threatening, cardiac dysrhythmia.

All the above features are relevant in establishing the diagnosis, since weight loss can also point to other serious psychiatric (and physical) disorders. For example, the severely depressed person with pronounced weight loss has a genuine loss of appetite and is not anxious about body image. A person with schizophrenia may have marked weight loss out of a deluded belief that food is poisoned and unsafe to eat, but without the attitudes to eating and weight typical of AN.

Treating anorexia nervosa

Although AN is a deadly serious matter, people treated early in the course of the illness do well. Psychiatrists together with other mental health professionals, a dietician and a specialist physician may all be involved depending on severity and complications.

Since patients tend to be ambivalent about the need for treatment, winning their trust and establishing a solid therapeutic alliance are crucial.

The rationale of treatment is carefully explained and reassurance offered that confinement to bed, separation from family and friends and administration of high doses of drugs will not occur (anti-depressants may be prescribed for any concomitant obsessive-compulsive or depressive symptoms but otherwise have no role). The patient in turn has to agree to regain their normal weight; remaining 'a little anorexic' defeats the whole purpose of treatment.

The family is seen on the premise that they want to do their best for their relative. The clinician evaluates their strengths and vulnerabilities and seeks to relieve them of their inevitable feeling of guilt. Family therapy has been found to be effective in teenage girls who have not been ill for long. Working on new patterns of relating in the family and promoting a mature relationship between parents and daughter, based on increased autonomy, are interrelated goals.

More severely ill patients are optimally treated in specialised units. A more humane approach exploring psychological, interpersonal and family aspects has replaced a behavioural approach used in the past, in which weight gain was reinforced by incentives such as increased social contact with family and friends and freedom of movement. Beyond this, treatment involved strict bed-rest and isolation. I can recall treating young women in this way, offering them a series of rewards in exchange for agreed increments in weight. We were never comfortable doing this, but it was then broadly accepted as the definitive treatment and we were frighteningly aware of a potential lethal outcome. The ethical dilemma still prevails as to whether we should enforce treatment in a seriously ill patient who refuses to cooperate. The mortality rate in those treated compulsorily is higher than those treated voluntarily, no doubt attributable to the greater severity of the former, but both groups gain similar amounts of weight.

Day programs lasting two to three months are advantageous in that they incorporate individual, group and family therapies, as well as re-feeding strategies. Patients may then continue in one or more of these psychotherapies as well as receive further nutritional counselling.

Patients can be made worse (heart failure, fits and coma), even die, with rapid re-nutrition. Metabolism is stimulated and with it a demand for potassium and phosphates by the body's cells. Given depleted reserves, this can be met only by drastically reducing blood levels.

In general, a good outcome is linked to early intervention when weight loss is not so great, the person is motivated to change and the family is supportive. Poor outcome correlates with the reverse of these factors and significant coexisting personality problems. The following two cases illustrate how the outcome can vary in AN, notwithstanding the provision of treatment.

Trudy, the only daughter of devout, unhappily married parents, was raised in a provincial town. As a young girl she was shy, withdrawn, obedient and conscientious. Although without intimate friends, she regarded her childhood as happy. Her physical health was good, her weight normal. She went to university a year earlier than her peers and continued to live at home. Trudy met her first and only boyfriend in her second year. They grew increasingly intimate until he sought a sexual relationship which she refused, whereupon he left her. She was deeply distressed, worried that she might have been wrong to refuse him, but also felt guilty about the heavy petting that she had permitted to occur. Trudy started to diet at this time and paradoxically felt a newly awakened sense of self-confidence. Moreover, she felt in control for the first time. She soon became preoccupied with food, refusing to eat with her parents and restricted herself to food low in kilojoules. She worked out a strict pattern of eating. Her menstrual periods ceased, her weight plummeted.

Over the next twenty years Trudy enjoyed a successful academic career, but remained socially isolated. Her only real interests beyond her work were food and dieting. She developed a series of eating rituals. She accepted that she was too thin and admitted feeling hungry, but would not allow herself to eat normally. Although she knew it was ridiculous, she thought of herself as overweight, and was terrified of becoming obese. Controlling her eating and weight became the most crucial pursuits in Trudy's and her parents' lives. She literally lived in order to diet. She had five extended admissions to hospital for nutritional restoration, during which she always cooperated, but only after the fifth admission was she better able to maintain her weight.

Sally grew up in a working-class suburb and at the age of 13 won a scholarship to a girls private school to which she had to travel two hours a day. She had been conscious of being mildly chubby relative to her peers but for the first time in her life became aware of her weight and began dieting, eating just one meal a day and giving her lunch to school friends. Her parents became alarmed when she had lost 10 kilograms and was fitting into her 11-year-old sister's clothes.

The family (parents and sisters) entered a family therapy program in which the parents were encouraged to help Sally eat at regular meals. Her father's frequent absences due to work commitments and her mother's concerns were explored and addressed. Sally also had individual therapy in which she confided her loneliness and sense of not being good enough at the new school. She felt guilty since her parents had been inordinately proud of her achievement in winning the scholarship. Sally was encouraged to share this with her parents. A decision was reached that she would move to a co-ed school closer to home if she continued to be unhappy. However, six months after beginning therapy

Sally regained her lost weight, resumed a normal eating pattern, formed a close friendship with a girl in her class and decided to stay put.

Bulimia nervosa

As in AN, 90 per cent of patients with BN are women. The usual age of onset, however, is a little older, between 20 and 25. The number presenting with BN grew remarkably during the two decades that followed its first description in 1979. This was probably the result of better detection of cases, but cultural factors could also have played a role. The key clinical difference between AN and BN is that weight is not lost in the latter. The core features are repeated bouts of uncontrolled over-eating, an intense fear of gaining weight and attempts to limit its increase through extreme weight-control strategies. BN typically begins with dieting in an attempt to lose weight. A compulsion to 'give in' to urges to eat is followed by vomiting, spontaneous or induced, to get rid of the food. Over-eating high-calorie foods—chocolate and cakes are common—may end only through abdominal discomfort and vomiting. Binges are triggered by stress, and tend to occur in cycles. The manoeuvres people use to lose weight are self-induced vomiting, purging with laxatives and intensive exercising. Periods cease in a third of women.

Like AN, we are not clear about the cause and so rely on factors that put a young woman at risk of developing it—a history of obesity, past sexual or physical abuse, low self-esteem, critical comments by the family about the person's weight and shape, a family history of substance abuse or eating disorders, and parental obesity.

Cheryl, a 30-year-old mother and part-time shop assistant, had since her late teens suffered episodes of binge eating and purging associated with wide weight fluctuations. She worried that she might pass on these habits to Janine, her 3-year-old daughter. Her problem had developed in the context of a strained relationship. She had left home at 18 to live with her first boyfriend but the romance had rapidly soured when he began to drink heavily. She had always felt 'chubby'. When feeling despondent at night she began to over-eat. This soon got out of control, with binges of two loaves of bread and a few packets of chocolate biscuits. In an attempt to control her weight she would starve and ingest fifty laxatives the next day. Despite leaving this abusive boyfriend in her mid-twenties she was quite unable to quit the bingeing. She then formed a much happier relationship with the father of Janine and found a satisfying part-time job. Although the bingeing diminished, it did not cease entirely; food and weight issues still occupied her thoughts.

Cheryl was treated with cognitive-behaviour therapy by a psychologist and responded well. The therapist discouraged her from dieting, advised her to keep a diary recording the precipitants of her bingeing episodes and encouraged her to explore her overly critical view of herself. A pattern emerged of bingeing when she felt frustrated or bored, especially in the early afternoons. Strategies to deal with this were explored, such as going for a walk. After twelve sessions she was no longer bingeing or using laxatives. Thoughts of weight, body shape and food had not disappeared but no longer distressed her and did not prevent her from getting on with 'more important things in life'.

The most effective treatment for BN, cognitive-behaviour therapy (CBT), is applied on the premise that erroneous ideas about weight and body shape maintain the symptoms. Patients are counselled to quit dieting and to adhere to a healthy pattern of eating. Identifying precipitants of binges or bulimic episodes, and keeping a diary of behaviours such as bingeing and vomiting, are key features. CBT has been extended to address features like problems in relationships, mood instability and low self-esteem. Anti-depressants may relieve symptoms but relapse is common once treatment is discontinued. Combining CBT with anti-depressants (used for their direct effect on bulimic symptoms) is favoured by some psychiatrists. Half of women treated respond completely, a third partially and the rest continue to suffer.

Binge-eating disorder

Binge-eating disorder has been added to the group of eating disorders on the grounds that it can be distinguished from AN and BN and has a more benign course. Recurrent episodes of compulsive binge eating, often done secretly, without associated vomiting, purging, starving or excessive exercise is the principal feature. CBT is an effective treatment with most patients responding well, although obesity may remain as a unwanted problem.

Obesity

We all know people who turn to food as a source of comfort at times of emotional distress. Whether this behaviour, if continued long-term, leads to obesity is controversial. The medical consensus suggests that obesity is the end result of an interplay of many biological, psychological and social factors. Characterising obesity as a mental health problem requiring psychological treatment has a long history, and psychiatrists were asked to assess obese patients in the past. This is no longer the case. Instead, they are seen by family doctors, specialist physicians, dieticians and, in severe cases, surgeons (who carry out bariatric surgery such as stapling the stomach where the oesophagus joins it in order to create a small pouch; this has a narrow opening to the remaining stomach, thus drastically reducing the amount of food that can be eaten). Self-help groups and organisations like Weight Watchers also play prominent roles.

While studies have failed to detect specific psychiatric symptoms in obese people, disordered eating (particularly binge eating) and specific weight and shape concerns have been identified. Distortion of body image, a belief that others feel contempt for them, and low self-esteem are encountered in some obese children.

Losing weight is achievable by dieting programs of many types. A structured behaviourally based approach is one of them. It focuses on setting of goals and regular monitoring of eating and exercise patterns in order to identify effective strategies. Even modest weight loss, in the region of 10 per cent of initial weight, is enough to boost psychological wellbeing. There is one huge snag: preventing lost weight from being regained is most problematic. This reinforces the feeling of failure in already psychologically vulnerable people. Treatment therefore emphasises the need for enduring lifestyle changes.

Psychiatrists do have a specific role in dealing with overweight patients. Many drugs they prescribe lead to weight gain. Such patients are advised about nutrition and exercise in an effort to reduce the chance of putting on weight. On occasion, the responsible medication has to be replaced with another that is relatively free of the side-effect.

Conclusion

Much is known about the two main eating disorders, AN and BN, and this has led to useful treatments. The downside is the poor response of people who are more severely affected or who have had symptoms for an extended period. Here preventive medicine can play a decisive role. Since we know that 90 per cent of cases are in women of a young age, and that dieting is an early warning sign, their early identification becomes all-important. The longer the problem is left to establish itself, the more difficult it is to achieve a good therapeutic outcome. As a society, we need to promote public appreciation of the dangers of restrictive dieting; an obvious measure is to introduce dedicated health programs for all high school girls. More broadly, programs of early intervention in adolescent health clinics are critical.

CHAPTER 10

Disturbances of Personality

One of the most controversial areas in psychiatry is the concept and treatment of disturbed personality. Part of the controversy arises from the many definitions of personality. This in turn creates difficulties in drawing boundaries around normal personality, beyond which a person's behaviour leads to problems for them and for others. The term is derived from the Latin *persona* (mask, as worn by an actor in a play) and describes how we are perceived by others. A useful definition refers to a person's uniquely enduring and deeply ingrained qualities and corresponding patterns of behaviour, including the way that person relates to the world and to him or herself. Personality characteristics (traits) are relatively stable over time. A cluster of traits that are prominent and consistent in an individual constitutes a *personality type*. *Character* is related to personality and refers to what is deeply etched in a person; it has been used customarily to describe the moral core of a person.

The quest to determine the nature of these traits has been vexed. Indeed, one observer has suggested no less than 18 000 of them! Consider for a moment what such a list would include: extroverted, gregarious, sociable, curious, frugal, harsh, callous, irresponsible, immoral, envious, obstinate, cautious, optimistic, fearful, shallow, buoyant, flamboyant, happy-go-lucky, enterprising, creative, boring, excitable, immature, impulsive, extravagant, adventurous, persistent, reflective, rational, orderly ... the list is endless. The psychologist Gordon Allport was the first to point out, in the 1930s, the many definitions of personality—he located over fifty in the scientific literature of the time.

Social forces also have to be brought into the picture, since they exert a central influence on the evolution of personality. Culturally based differences in child rearing may explain marked variations in behavioural patterns. Some cultures reward qualities that others condemn, so leading to personality styles that are determined by those cultures. The stiff upper lip of the English is a sharp contrast with the emotional volatility of the Italians!

A particular scientific approach has evolved over the last half-century to bring order to this overwhelming subject. In brief, the aim is to group personality traits systematically, so reducing them to a manageable number of distinct dimensions. A linked task is devising measures so that people can be rated on these dimensions and their personality profile mapped out. An American psychologist, Raymond Cattell, pioneered this method in the 1940s by studying thousands of students and then applying elaborate statistical techniques to the data he obtained. A set of sixteen primary and eight subsidiary factors emerged. These were set out as bipolar scales with the extremes of the dimension at either end. For example, Cattell's questionnaire includes introversion–extroversion, dominance–submissiveness, stability–emotionality, adaptability–rigidity and venturesomeness–timidity.

Other psychologists found this unwieldy. Hans Eysenck of the University of London, for instance, reduced the dimensions to a mere pair—stability–neuroticism and introversion–extroversion. Like many other personality researchers, he used a range of explicit and implicit questions requiring yes or no answers. Questions covering the stability–neuroticism dimension include 'Do you often worry about things you should not have said or done?' and 'Are you an irritable person?' Examples of introversion–extroversion questions are 'Do you enjoy meeting new people?' and 'Do you have many different hobbies?'

The challenge of producing a coherent array of traits that capture the richness of personality continues, with distinguished contributors wrestling with the subject. The common figure seems to be five, and the so-called five-factor model is in the ascendancy; as shown in the table below.

A more refined approach to what distinguishes one person from another in terms of personality links dimensional traits with biological attributes. An American psychiatrist, Robert Cloninger, has shown persuasively that this can be done. In his model, he differentiates between two groups of characteristics: temperament and character. Temperament refers to dimensions that we mostly inherit, appear early in life, remain stable through life, and involve unconsciously determined ways of learning and developing habits. Character, by contrast, is strongly influenced by early learning, matures in adulthood, influences social and personal effectiveness and relies on our capacity to learn from experience.

The four dimensions of temperament are seeking novel experiences, risk-taking, depending on rewards from the environment, and persistence. People scoring highly on novelty seeking take every opportunity to explore their environment, make decisions impulsively and avoid frustration. Risk-taking covers worry and fear of uncertainty. Reward dependence is about reliance on the approval of others and the need for social attachment. And persistence, as the term suggests, entails perseverance and resoluteness.

The five-factor solution to grouping personality traits

To a high degree		To a low degree
anxious, tense, irritable, perfectionist	**Neuroticism**	bland, lacking concern
talkative, inappropriately self-disclosing, attention-seeking, dramatising	**Extroversion**	socially isolated, lacking zest, inhibited, shy
eccentric, rebellious, fantasising, impractical	**Openness**	intolerant, bland, conformist, aesthetically insensitive, has narrow interests
gullible, indiscriminant, trusting, open to being manipulated	**Agreeableness**	cynical, suspicious, quarrelsome, arrogant, exploitative
over-achieving, workaholic, compulsive, over-scrupulous	**Conscientiousness**	under-achieving, disregarding of rules, aimless, lacking self-discipline

The three dimensions of character are self-directedness, that is, striving to achieve goals and overcome challenges through self-determination; cooperativeness, or identifying with others and feeling concern and compassion for them; and self-transcendence, having a sense of spirituality.

So far, we have looked at the attempt to bring a sense of order to the range of normal personality types. People at the extreme ends of the personality dimensions are of particular interest to psychiatrists, since they tend towards patterns of behaviour marked enough to affect their lives detrimentally. Psychiatry at the coalface rather than in its research function has always had to deal with people who have been labelled as dysfunctional in their personality (in addition to a disturbed mind, as in psychosis, or a deficient intellect, as in intellectual disability).

This ostensibly reasonable system of grouping personality types by dimensions immediately throws up the controversial question of when a personality pattern crosses the boundary from normal to problematic (if indeed such a boundary exists). Psychiatrists tend to adopt a pragmatic position—even if only because people whose personality traits lead them to have troubled lives seek their professional assistance. In general, they show longstanding inflexible, maladaptive patterns of functioning that affect their lives deleteriously and often distressingly, in the spheres of relationships, work and recreation.

The psychiatrist tries, as with any patient, to understand why these people behave the way they do, rather than trivialise or dismiss their problems. Unfortunately, the term 'personality disorder', the one used in formal psychiatric classifications, tends to be used more widely in a derogatory way—which is paradoxical as the people so diagnosed genuinely need professional help. Moreover, they are vulnerable to the full range of psychiatric maladies, and these are often difficult to detect since they may be masked by the personality type. The psychiatrist needs a depth of understanding and skilled observation to unravel the specific contribution of personality factors, since they will greatly affect the person's outcome and treatment.

Types of problematic personalities

You will not find this label elsewhere. I have devised it to avoid value-laden alternatives. I have a marked aversion to the term personality disorder; to me it is derogatory and enveloped in pessimism concerning change.

Interest in problematic personality types has a long history, with clear descriptions found in great literary works. We have only to think of a Dickensian character like Fagin, Shakespearean ones like Iago and Richard the Third and a Biblical figure like Esau. It was only in the nineteenth century, however, that methodical efforts were initiated to study them. The first group of people to be looked at were those who showed patterns of behaviour that suggested the absence of a conscience—that is, lying, stealing, assaulting, even killing, without remorse. Dr John Prichard in England suggested in 1835 that this pattern might reflect an illness, with an aberrant moral centre in the brain. 'Moral insanity' was the term he gave to this new condition and he included among its features 'angry and malicious feelings, which arise without provocation' and elicit 'the greatest disgust and abhorrence'.

This questionable act of creating a psychiatric condition based on behaviour alone—which makes it essentially a social construct—has continued to bedevil not only psychiatry but society as a whole. The profession (along with other social institutions, particularly the legal system) has wrestled with the thorny problem of whether people labelled as psychopathic are responsible for their actions. To put this dilemma most starkly, does the psychopath who kills without remorse deserve punishment or medical treatment?

The psychopath was soon joined by other categories of problematic personality, culminating in the 1920s when a renowned German psychiatrist, Kurt Schneider, grasped the nettle and attempted to bring order to the chaos. His classification still forms the core of the section on personality disorders in the International Classification of Diseases of the World Health Organization. The 1992 version (ICD-10) subdivides problematic personalities into eight types: paranoid, schizoid, anti-social, emotionally unstable, histrionic, obsessional, anxious and dependent. The manual of the American Psychiatric Association (DSM-IV) more usefully groups them into three clusters, each with an underlying theme (an approach popular with psychiatrists). In addition, each has certain criteria:

- Cluster A, marked by odd, eccentric behaviour, includes schizoid, paranoid and schizotypal patterns.
- Cluster B is typified by dramatic, explosive, emotional and erratic behaviour; it includes histrionic, anti-social, narcissistic and borderline patterns.
- Cluster C consists of avoidant, dependent, obsessive-compulsive and passive-aggressive types; they show anxious, fearful, dependent and introverted behaviour.

DSM-IV places personality disorders on a separate axis from formal psychiatric disorders in order to encourage psychiatrists to consider the role of personality in any mental illness. By contrast, ICD-10 considers personality disorders as one group of diagnoses among many. Both specify *categories* of personality disorders, but there is no universally agreed definition of each category, no objective biological findings, no causal theory that distinguishes one category from any other, no clear conceptual boundary between categories, and uncertainty as to the number of categories. In effect, the classifications we use merely reflect professional consensus at a point in time. Certain categories have disappeared and new ones have emerged in successive editions of DSM and ICD.

Clinical experience and research suggest that while people may fulfil criteria of a problematic personality, many cannot be assigned to a specific category, and a large proportion have features of more than one category.

The argument could be made that the subject of problematic personalities is in disarray. On the other hand, there is at least a practical advantage in attempting to classify various types in that it enables people who have grappled for years with their patently maladaptive and ineffective forms of coping to seek appropriate help, and psychiatrists (in concert with other mental health professionals) to do their bit to improve their lives.

We shall consider the eleven DSM types, but first devote attention to how common they are and what factors in general lead to people having them.

How common are they?
One in ten adults, both men and women, shows features of one of the problematic personalities. When we move to psychiatric groups presenting with

conditions like depression, anxiety and substance abuse, the rate of personality problems jumps to about a third. In the general population, the prevalence of specific problematic personalities is about 2 per cent (except obsessive-compulsives, where the rate is double that). While a proportion of personality disturbed people improve in middle age, and the rate may therefore decline, they have often alienated their families, friends and colleagues to such a degree that they still lead troubled lives. Given the lifelong pattern of maladaptive behaviour that the diagnosis of a problematic personality portends, psychiatrists are reluctant to apply the construct in children and adolescents. Moreover, adolescence is a time of fluctuating changes in personality, which could be a problem of mood or an early psychosis.

What leads to problematic personality types?

Just as we are fascinated about what makes someone the person they are, so are we curious as to the basis of problematic personalities; many theories compete—genetic, temperamental, psychological and social. Animal breeders can select for desired behaviour patterns through controlled breeding (for example, making a dog tamer), which suggests that personality traits may well be inherited too. Evidence for a genetic contribution comes from comparing twins—identical twins have the same personality traits to a much greater extent than non-identical twins. Certain personality patterns seem to occur more often in families. More clues for a genetic basis come from studies on what happens to children of a parent with an anti-social personality who are adopted by psychologically healthy families; they still tend to exhibit a higher rate of delinquent behaviour than their step-siblings.

Physical damage to the brain, like tumours and infection early in life, may be associated with problematic personality. People with anti-social personalities have been most closely studied in this regard, and investigations have shown irregular brain waves and minor neurological abnormalities, but they do not amount to anything consistent. I once worked for Sir Denis Hill, an eminent British psychiatrist, who thought he had stumbled on a brain-wave abnormality in people serving a prison sentence. The finding was intriguing but came to nothing. Like so many medical researchers, he had entered a cul-de-sac. Clearly, brain changes may affect a child's behaviour, which in turn may lead to learning or relationship difficulties, all these features combining to produce anti-social traits and delinquent behaviour. Similarly, brain damage resulting from severe head injury may be followed by marked personality change—but not necessarily anti-social.

In the middle-aged or elderly, a change in personality, including exaggeration or loss of longstanding traits or the emergence of new uncharacteristic ones, calls for a careful search for an underlying physical illness, mood disorder or early dementia. Typical features of these may be masked by use of alcohol or the effects of prescribed and over-the-counter drugs. A corroborating history from those who have known the person for a long time is needed to unravel all these possibilities.

Several theorists assert that problematic personalities are mainly psychological in origin. Freud regarded personality development as resulting from the interplay between basic sexual and aggressive drives and ways of dealing with them. Since these drives are primitive in form, their expression may not mesh with family and wider social expectations. The person may then deal repeatedly with the resulting conflict in one of many ways—for example, by blaming others (paranoid response) or by developing attention-seeking behaviour (histrionic response). The dominant response moulds the emerging personality (paranoid and histrionic personalities respectively in these examples). Another example is that people who have been emotionally deprived during their early years often have difficulty in forming trusting relationships in adult life.

Erik Erikson, one of Freud's most brilliant students, extended what had been a rather narrow view of personality development when he devised a model encompassing psychological and social aspects, as well as mapping out a series of eight tasks, each of them emerging from achievement of the previous one. These tasks are shaped by reciprocal links between psychological development and social forces such as mothering, family, religious faith and work. The first task for instance involves trust—the experience of being cared for by an empathic parental figure in infancy leads to gaining a sense of basic trust in the world. A later task ushered in by puberty is the attainment of a stable sense of identity. Any task not dealt with paves the way for personality problems.

A derivative school of psychoanalysis, self-psychology, posits that healthy development requires a consistent empathic response from the principal caregiver, usually the mother, to her baby and, later, young child. The child in turn internalises the experience of the empathic parent as a form of self-soothing and becomes endowed with an integrated sense of self. If this response is lacking or distorted (for example, because the mother has post-partum depression and therefore is not emotionally attuned to the needs of the baby), the sense of self fails to evolve; this in turn may lead to one or other form of marked problematic personality (borderline and narcissistic in particular—see below).

In another theory stemming from psychoanalysis, namely attachment theory, John Bowlby applied the study of animal behaviour to describe emotional and behavioural patterns by which an infant and later young child forms a secure *attachment* to its mother. The securely attached young child develops the capacity to be alone; this depends on the internalised presence of the mother regardless of any physical presence. Insecure attachment in early childhood renders the child vulnerable to personality disturbance in adulthood. Other investigators have studied the consequences for personality development of continuing emotional deprivation in childhood (for example, through depression or physical illness in the mother), or childhood physical or sexual abuse. According to this view, the child shapes his or her evolving personality to deal with the effects of unempathic traumatising parents (who often were themselves traumatised and hence unable to empathise with their child). DW Winnicott, an English child analyst, termed this unconscious personality distortion the 'false self'.

Neuroscience research suggests that connections between the brain's nerve cells may be strengthened or weakened, and new connections formed, throughout life (so-called plasticity) in response to emotionally charged experiences. Thus, child abuse and other adverse life events may lead to neuronal loss whereas positive experiences stimulate interconnectivity.

Problematic personalities and the psychiatrist

Psychiatric help is sought either by the troubled person or by distraught relatives or friends at a time of crisis—family conflict, breakdown of a key relationship, tussles at work, financial pressure and the like. Various offences, such as assault, drink-driving and shoplifting, may lead to the police or courts initiating the process. The person may be intoxicated with alcohol or drugs and threatening further harm to themselves or others. Particularly with borderline people, an impulsively taken overdose or self-inflicted lacerations of the arms or legs are the route to medical attention. They often have a history of many presentations of this kind, to several clinics or hospitals. Alternatively, help may be sought for associated psychiatric difficulties, to which the person with a problematic personality is particularly vulnerable. In a patient diagnosed with a mental illness, failure to respond to adequate treatment may indicate a hitherto undetected problematic personality, which aggravates the severity of the mental illness.

Less dramatically, people with a problematic personality may seek help for persistent low morale, anxiety or self-doubt from a family doctor or mental health clinic, which may have noted a series of failed relationships or other repeated emotional difficulties about which the person feels impotent. Medical presentations include preoccupation with inadequately explained physical health and bodily symptoms, especially enduring pain. A previously unrecognised personality disturbance associated with a known physical illness or a formal mental illness may reveal itself in the wake of a failure to cooperate with treatment, conflict between medical staff and patient, and litigious threat.

The psychiatrist takes a detailed history from the person in order to capture as complete a picture as possible. An account of childhood and early relationships within the family and with significant other people is at the heart of the inquiry, as are the methods of dealing with conflict and current problems. This emphasis on gathering information about many aspects of the person's life contrasts with a symptom-focused approach more typical of a discreet mental illness. Relationships, self-esteem, coping with life's vicissitudes, motivations and aspirations, for example, are carefully explored.

Pinpointing the specific problematic personality type requires identifying particular lifelong maladaptive patterns of behaviour. A cross-sectional snapshot is not enough. For example, a severely depressed executive in charge of a large company may be utterly reliant on family and professional staff for even the most trivial decision. These dependent features could be part of the depression rather than reflect a longstanding dependent personality. Talking with the person alone may not yield enough information to reach the correct diagnosis. People are not always the most objective observers of themselves; the psychiatrist therefore needs to seek additional observations from parents, siblings and friends.

A further source of knowledge is more intangible—the psychiatrist's own reactions to the person. Take the histrionic type. Because people in this group are typically vain, demanding, dependent and sexually provocative, the psychiatrist may well feel manipulated and come to resent this. The borderline personality tends to idealise or denigrate rather than see people as a complex admixture of both positive and negative qualities. A common result within a hospital is splitting, in which certain staff are treated with great reverence whereas others are sharply criticised and devalued. The two staff groups may (if they have no insight into what is happening to them) come to verbal blows about how best to approach the person.

In addition to questionnaires devised to distinguish between the personality types I have already described, systematic methods have been tried to measure problematic personalities. They are generally not that useful and less informative than the thorough psychiatric evaluation I have presented above. There is certainly no shortcut to reaching an accurate diagnosis of personality problems. Clinical skill and time are essential, and nothing less will suffice.

Specific problematic personalities

We are now in a position to look at each form of problematic personality covered in the three DSM-IV clusters, together with case illustrations.

Cluster A

We undoubtedly consider this group as strange, unusual or eccentric. Although expressed in various ways, the gist is oddity. People in this group may also develop delusional disorder or a paranoid form of schizophrenia.

People with *paranoid personalities* have an unwarranted belief that others are deliberately untrustworthy and potentially devious, react with hostility to a perceived threat, hold longstanding grudges and easily feel slighted. Unjustifiable jealousy is common. They show few affectionate qualities and rarely have intimate relationships. Playfulness and tenderness are scorned as showing weakness. Their lack of basic trust of the world makes them hypervigilant—especially in new situations, where they assume that other people will conspire against them; they may even experience psychotic symptoms in these circumstances. Not surprisingly, they tend to be regarded by others as secretive and brittle. They are prone to litigious action against employers, neighbours or State bureaucracies. Their childhood is often one of punitive parenting. Repeated experiences of humiliation compounds the person's resentment and confusion about the reasons for their suffering.

Fiona complained that people at work disliked her and contemplated seeking legal advice as she thought that they wanted her to resign. She had recurrent disagreements with the pay office about her salary. She felt that other people were inferior and that she had married a man who was socially and academically far less accomplished than herself. When she saw a psychiatrist, having been referred by her family doctor for problems at work, she was angry, rejected the help offered and complained bitterly about the rigidity of health professionals.

People with *schizoid personalities* are timid, aloof and anxious when close to others—indifferent to them and their opinions. They have few if any friends, preferring to live alone. Since they are incapable of deep emotions, they come across as detached and remote. Because of poor social skills and their disinclination for intimacy, they rarely develop close relationships. They are solitary in their interests, finding pleasure in intellectual abstraction and communing with nature. An apparent self-sufficiency masks a wish for closeness. Socially, they experience themselves as awkward, which leads to a pre-emptive withdrawal from intimate ties. They may succeed in a job that requires relative isolation and tend to avoid occupations involving interaction with others. Relationships of the schizoid world are a central theme of the playwright Samuel Beckett, particularly in his plays *Endgame* and *Waiting for Godot*.

Marjorie, a nurse, worked the night shift in a small hospital. She lived with her six cats and saw her family only on Christmas Day, a gathering she anticipated with dread. Born of elderly parents, she had always been a quiet, timid and compliant child who seemed to need no company. In adult life she found it difficult to understand other people's need for friends and believed that an emotional life was 'unnecessary'.

People with *schizotypal personalities* have patterns of peculiar thinking, appearance and behaviour, but not to the extent encountered in psychosis. They have odd beliefs, are frequently suspicious, and may become excessively fascinated by magic and the occult. Although their speech is often vague and idiosyncratic, one can still follow their train of thought. They often dress eccentrically and are stilted in their mannerisms. They classically have no friends, as their lack of social skills unnerves them in unfamiliar social situations. They may break down with the emergence of a psychotic illness, including schizophrenia. Conversely, a proportion of people with schizophrenia have first-degree relatives with schizotypal features. These associations point to a shared genetic vulnerability.

Mr Johnson lived alone following his retirement from a position as a clerk in the Public Service. In the belief that people looked at him as if he were strange, he always wore dark glasses. As he grew older Mr Johnson became more reclusive. Although he wrote letters to all his previous doctors seeking treatment for his facial tics, he refused to consult them directly because the prospect of going out was too disconcerting.

Cluster B

People within this cluster are excessively emotional and act it out in ways invariably distressing to themselves and disturbing to others. The pattern occurs much more commonly in men, and not infrequently among offenders.

People with *anti-social personalities* exhibit pervasive, irresponsible and socially deviant behaviour. Their childhood is characterised by lying, truancy and vandalism. As adults, they cannot hold a steady job or maintain intimate relationships. They are reckless, impulsive and unable to plan effectively. They act aggressively and show scant regard for the rights and property of others. They are in constant trouble with authority figures and the law. They rarely experience remorse for such anti-social activity. Abuse of both legal and illicit drugs to relieve feelings of tension, boredom or anger is common.

They may come across as charming, even helpful, but these are a means to disarm and exploit others.

Biological factors may account for the much higher prevalence of anti-social patterns of behaviour in men, and in their association with substance abuse, criminality and attention deficit hyperactivity disorder. Family life tends to be marked by inconsistent parenting and ineffectual or excessively harsh discipline. A dog-eats-dog world where only the most ruthless survive and others are a means to survival may underlie the behaviour. The concept of the criminal psychopath as a category distinct from the anti-social personality has been a source of controversy for decades. Chillingly portrayed by Anthony Hopkins as Hannibal Lecter in the film *Silence of the Lambs*, such a person may assault, kill or torture without remorse.

Joe lived in a de facto relationship with a woman with three children from a previous relationship. She had retreated to women's refuges many times in the wake of his violent outbursts. He had been institutionalised as a child after his father was gaoled for assaulting the family. Joe had never held a steady job and was inevitably fired following an angry episode, sometimes going on the rampage. Apparently unconcerned at the havoc he caused, he pointed instead to his shabby treatment by others. Once he had burnt down his employer's warehouse after being sacked, and was subsequently convicted.

People with *borderline personalities* are perhaps the most challenging of all, both for the family and professionals. The term reflects the position it was regarded originally as occupying in terms of severity—between neurotic and psychotic. Such people lack a sense of self, and feel empty and confused about their identity, goals and values. Their relationships are typified by intense contrasts, either idealising or denigrating others. They are over-whelmed by terrifying feelings of abandonment if left alone, even briefly. They also experience intense, short-lived mood changes with depression, anxiety and anger prominent among them. Impulsiveness leads to such behaviours as substance abuse, violence and recurrent deliberate self-harm (wrist-cutting is the most common). Their tendency to inflict physical damage on themselves may paradoxically serve the purpose of proving that they are actually alive and capable of feeling. The response may counteract the characteristic continuing sense of an inner void. When they become depressed, this may be so severe as to lead to suicide. Health professionals often feel frustrated at what they feel are excessive demands, presentation of many unexplained physical symptoms, 'doctor-shopping' and poor adherence to treatment recommendations. A vicious cycle is set up in which the professional's reactions are perceived by the person as insensitive and rejecting, and any hint of a therapeutic alliance is lost; this may well lead to worsening of their mental state.

In terms of causal factors, many borderline people have suffered childhood sexual abuse or marked emotional neglect; others have experienced their parents as alternating unpredictably between emotional intrusiveness and neglect. Whatever the case, the result is a fragile sense of self.

I have had the pleasure of attending workshops with a colleague who I regard as the most original contributor to an understanding of the causes of borderline personality and its treatment. Otto Kernberg, an American psychoanalyst, has devoted his entire professional life to the subject. Most noteworthy is his shift from the notion of grouping certain personality traits together to offering an account of the borderline personality that reflects the likely organisation of psychological experience. He refers to three problem areas in this regard: sense of identity, unconscious defences against psychological threat, and the capacity to stay in touch with reality. His observations make a lot of sense.

Consider identity first. Typically, the borderline person is a total stranger to themselves and unable to retain a consistent integrated concept of the self over time or in various aspects of their life. Their use of primitive defence mechanisms in the face of anxiety and threatening situations is in keeping with the lack of a sense of identity. Splitting and projective identification are the two prominent defences used. In the first, the person fails to integrate positive and negative aspects of themselves and others. In a pleasing relationship, they develop such strong fantasies that they revere or idealise the other person. If frustrated, negative fantasies abound with obliteration of any memory of positive features. The result is total denigration of the other. With sudden shifts between these two states, the other is not seen as a person with realistic assets and liabilities. In projective identification, the borderline unwittingly ascribes to another person what they cannot tolerate in themselves and then proceeds to maintain a link with the feature that has been projected. For instance, the person may project their own aggressive impulses into a therapist and then complain bitterly that the therapist hates them. Reality testing is defective in that the borderline person cannot differentiate between psychological stimuli that hail from within and externally, and is unable to empathise with others applying customary social criteria. But unlike a psychotic person, these states are fleeting and episodic.

Kernberg is of the view that the sort of personality organisation he has mapped out for the borderline also applies to some of the other problematic personalities in DSM-4, including narcissistic, schizoid, schizotypal, antisocial and histrionic. The debate among psychiatrists continues more generally as to whether these types are separate entities, especially since so many of their features overlap and, in many cases, people cannot readily be assigned to a particular type.

Alice had been raised in a chaotic household where she had been physically abused by her mother and sexually abused by her stepfather. She escaped at fifteen and supported herself to an extent, but also depended on her sister both financially and emotionally. Following the sister's marriage, Alice took multiple 'minor' overdoses while intoxicated. She also began to mutilate herself by burning her skin with cigarettes and cutting her abdomen with a razor blade. She entered into intense but short-lived relationships with men, feeling devastated when these ended. She would readily plunge into self-condemnatory despair. Her teaching career was disrupted by many admissions to hospital, where she poured out feelings of alienation and abandonment, and the fear that her needs would never be met.

People with *histrionic personalities* (confusingly and disparagingly labelled 'hysterical' in the past) show exaggerated but superficial emotional reactions and attention-seeking behaviour. Acting vainly and egocentrically, they have a constant need to be conspicuous. They are prone to exaggeration, even lying, in an effort to be noticed. Moreover, they have to be satisfied immediately. They also have a pervasive wish for novelty and excitement, this leading to a stormy interpersonal life. Any relationships begin seductively and remain shallow and unpredictable. A variety of physical complaints, dramatically presented, are often a central feature. The childhood of the histrionic type, in the case of women, is typified by a perception of mother as cold and not caring, and father as demanding of his daughter's affection.

Paula was always in crisis. She had left her marriage after years of turbulence in which she could never wring from her husband the affection she believed due to her. On the other hand, she told others about her exemplary behaviour as wife and mother. She never felt appreciated in the workplace and changed jobs frequently. She always imagined that the next intimate experience would be the answer to her needs. When problems surfaced, Paula would feel distraught but show no flexibility or perseverance; bitter complaints about the unreasonable and cruel treatment she received at the hands of others would follow. Her children, weary of her excesses, left home as soon as they could, which led to further outbursts about 'my wretched lot'. She dressed flamboyantly even when at her lowest ebb. She ingratiated herself with all who tried to help her, however ineffectual she felt them to be.

People with *narcissistic personalities* are entirely self-absorbed and vain. They have major difficulties appreciating the feelings of other people despite professing humility and thoughtfulness towards others; this failure of empathy leads to dislocated encounters that invariably dissolve in ill will. They will enter into a friendship only with someone who admires their own unique qualities. They have an exaggerated belief in their own importance, accompanied by an acute sensitivity to criticism. Feeling special brings with it a drive for excellence, but gross disappointment when an expected sense of entitlement is inevitably not affirmed by others. Envy of others' accomplishment is intense, pushing the narcissist to seek increasingly ambitious goals. High principles are invoked whenever they criticise rivals whose success threatens their own need for admiration. While constantly desiring reassurance, they respond to any slight with profound disappointment, rage or chilly withdrawal. Threats to self-worth, including fair criticism, the breakdown of a relationship or a temporary setback in ambition, are interpreted as catastrophic and may result in profound shame, depression, vengeful rage or despair.

In childhood, parental empathic failure is common, similar to what occurs in the borderline. A child may be treated as an extension of, or consolation for, the parent's own needs. Denial protects the narcissist against the vulnerability caused by such empathic failure, but denial is not foolproof. In Ovid's poem, Narcissus suicides on realising that his image is illusionary and that he is not a genuine person. Tragically, such is the core state of all narcissistic people.

Stephen, a merchant banker, always believed that his next scheme would make him his fortune. He had little patience with the dreariness of ordinary people and would only befriend those whom he thought would advance his prospects. His endless preoccupation with his own successes, combined with pervasive thoughtlessness, rapidly alienated other people; he then reacted furiously at their lack of appreciation of his special qualities. He never found a woman worthy of him, flitting from one relationship to the next. Always dissatisfied and never feeling that he had to offer anything more than his wonderful self, Stephen was unable to understand why others could not recognise his charms.

Cluster C

The people in this group would in the past have been labelled neurotic—the chronic worriers for whom life is a relentless trudge. They are the tense, fearful and unhappy members of society who find coping with life's demands and challenges a constant ordeal.

People with *avoidant personalities* suffer from constant feelings of inadequacy, self-denigration, fear of the negative judgment of others, and inhibitions in their chosen activities. Despite an intense desire for approval, they have limited social relationships and work in settings that are not likely to bring unpredictable social encounters lest they might say or do something inappropriate. They commonly feel demoralised and aware of their limitations but too fearful to advance beyond them. As a result of these attributes, they are reluctant to assume responsibilities, take risks or engage in activities where there is even a remote possibility of failure. Unlike the schizoid they consciously desire closeness, but also fear it. Some psychiatrists regard the avoidant type as a social phobia.

Magda had always lived with her parents and had worked at the same secretarial job in a small office for years. She had always been painfully shy and envied those she knew who had married and had raised families. She rarely visited her small circle of associates, too concerned that she might offend them with her intrusiveness. She had never holidayed away from her parents, yet was an avid reader of travel books and dreamed of visiting exotic places. After her parents died she continued to live in the family home and, despite financial security, remained unable to venture out into the world.

People with *dependent personalities* submit to others and seem incapable of making decisions without advice and approval. They transfer responsibility to others, quite unable to work and live independently. They often feel anxious when alone. Consequently, they cling to established relationships and are most concerned that they might come to an end. They are sensitive to criticism and often deny their own views rather than disagree with others. They have a general lack of self-esteem.

Christina always sought advice. She found it impossible to do anything without seeking approval—she could not even shop for clothes for her children without taking her sister along. Her husband was extremely demanding but she seemed oblivious to this and welcomed any opportunity to serve him and his extended family. She had always wanted to learn the piano but, since her husband thought this a frivolous pursuit, had abandoned the idea for fear he would disapprove of her spending time and money doing something for herself.

People with *obsessive personalities* are typically orderly, punctual, dutiful and conformist to a degree that limits their capacity to respond to situations that call for flexibility or compromise. They display a rigid perfectionism that interferes with their ability to complete anything. Rarely do their achievements or those of others measure up to their required ideal standards. While obsessional qualities may be advantageous and socially desirable in particular circumstances, their moralising and inflexibility inevitably lead to difficulties. Their preoccupation with rules, procedures and social order overrides the pleasure of accomplishment or the company of others. They are often emotionally cold and judgemental. Their need for control leads to dealing with others in a formal and unspontaneous way. Resentment and fear of their potential destructiveness are controlled by keeping all emotions under firm control. Problems are ruminated over with little likelihood of resolution, leading to further disorganisation; this in turn causes more biting self-criticism.

David, a successful lawyer, ran an independent practice because he was unable to delegate work. The only son of organised and distant parents, he had been meticulous as a child. He had been a model student with few friends, since he was always preoccupied with homework or avidly collecting stamps. He did brilliantly at university but recalled the time as empty, with pressure of study leaving no room for participation in student life. David eventually married a librarian who shared many of his qualities. He found the arrival of children stressful as they disrupted his previously ordered life and gave him little pleasure. Whenever difficulties occurred he pondered over how he could control things or people better in future.

People with *passive-aggressive personalities* are stubborn and appear intentionally forgetful and inefficient, usually causing inconvenience to others. They become sullen and resentful if criticised, and often feel that they are treated unreasonably and are the innocent victims of authority. They have difficulty in accepting responsibility for the problems they cause and are more likely to see fault in others, and thus alienate them. Relationships are often stormy. Their childhood experience is invariably one of fearful submission to punitive parental authority. They apply an unconscious strategy in which they express considerable anger as a result of their unmet needs to be cared for, and fear of punishment for criticising parental figures.

Ed was always in strife with his wife, and crossed swords with his boss who he felt made unreasonable demands. The electricity, phone and gas were cut off many times because, despite endless reminders from his wife, he forgot to pay the bills. His employer found him constantly obstructive, but when confronted about his inefficiency he became argumentative and shifted the blame to others.

Most of his friends had withdrawn from his company over the years, irritated at his inability to keep arrangements for social activities.

Principles of treatment

Given that disturbed personality functioning is invariably complex, long-standing and well entrenched, short-term measures do not suffice; psychotherapy proceeds over several months or years. The choice of therapy (see Chapter 19 for details of these therapies) is influenced by the psychiatrist's view of the factors that have contributed to the problematic personality as well as by its degree of severity, the person's motivation and capacity to engage in a psychologically based process, and any concurrent psychiatric disorder.

People diagnosed as borderline or narcissistic are particularly challenging, requiring long-term individual therapy to accomplish enduring improvement. Setting clear limits, agreeing on a realistic contract, exploring childhood events and their associations with current difficulty, and interpreting the evolving relationship between therapist and patient are derived from psychonanalytic insights and are vital facets of treatment. The work involves a high level of skill to deal with the many dilemmas that inevitably arise. A trusting relationship between patient and therapist is pivotal, offering a secure base to help people overcome the emotional storms they typically experience in their lives. This occurs through their feeling understood as well as learning to examine their own contribution to their difficulties. Therapist empathy and thoughtful feedback boost the person's capacity to reach an understanding of their inner motivations and feelings, their ways of relating to others, both current and in the past, and the links between the two spheres.

Supportive psychotherapy, required for the more severe forms of personality disorder of whatever type, focuses on the person's strengths to make realistically attainable changes and to limit any self-destructive behaviour. Establishing a co-operative alliance and providing a consistent structure are central ingredients.

Behavioural techniques such as social skills and relaxation training are helpful to those who are socially anxious. Cognitive therapy may be indicated when depression is a prominent feature, and has been tried as a complementary school to the psychoanalytic one.

Group therapy may complement an individual approach when the person is likely to benefit from feedback by peers; for schizoid, dependent and avoidant people in particular, sharing of distress and mutual support play a helpful role. Family therapy involves a combination of supportive and interpretative strategies to gain the support of the family in order to help the person change and cope better with life's problems.

Brief admission to hospital may be required to defuse a crisis, but a long-term stay there tends to increase dependence on professionals and so undermine whatever coping skills already exist. On the other hand, since the 1980s specialised units have offered a comprehensive treatment program for marked disturbances of personality, but are not the norm given their costs and the expertise needed; combined individual and group therapies play a prominent role, over a period of several months.

In the United Kingdom, a day-hospital treatment program, using individual and group psychoanalytically oriented principles, has been effective over a sustained period in reducing the rate of deliberate self-harm and improving interpersonal functioning. In another British study, a brief in-patient admission followed by a year of weekly individual psychotherapy resulted in reduced rates of deliberate self-harm and readmission. Similar results have been achieved with twice-weekly out-patient psychoanalytic therapy over twelve months. Dialectical behaviour therapy, developed in Seattle in the 1970s and consisting of behavioural and meditation strategies applied twice-weekly, either individually or in a group, also yields these benefits.

Skilful use of medication may be called for, particularly in treating the borderline person. Drugs are directed to the relief of symptoms and not in the expectation of producing personality change. For example, people with borderline functioning may develop psychotic symptoms in the face of marked stress; anti-psychotic drugs are a crucial addition to psychotherapy in these cases. Similarly, people with obsessive-compulsive, avoidant or dependent personalities may become anxious or depressed following stress and therefore benefit from short-term anti-anxiety or anti-depressant drugs. In prescribing any drug, the psychiatrist emphasises that such treatment is secondary to psychotherapy or is a temporary means to tackle an associated psychiatric disorder, especially depression of mood

Conclusion

I may have conveyed the impression that all problematic personalities are severe and resistant to treatment. This tends to be the view of psychiatrists, since they usually see people at the extreme end of the spectrum. But the whole group is varied in at least two senses. Firstly, some are much less disruptive than others (for example, dependent, avoidant and obsessional people). Secondly, in each of the eleven types many more people will be mildly rather than severely affected. Those who do get to receive treatment for their difficulties, whatever the degree of severity, may well be helped to lead less troubled, even fulfilling, lives.

CHAPTER 11

The Psychoses

Although it may seem a trivial matter, the shift from the indiscriminate use of the term 'madness' to the more specific 'psychosis' had profound implications for psychiatric practice. The word was introduced in 1845 by an Austrian psychiatrist, Ernst von Feuchtersleben, to indicate a serious mental disorder affecting both body and mind. So, from the morass of human mental suffering was extracted a series of conditions that could be dissected and systematically studied.

But after more than a century and a half of painstaking and often frustrating inquiry, psychosis continues to be one of the most perplexing challenges confronting medicine, psychiatry, and indeed society itself. The key dilemma is our difficulty in comprehending the internal world of people when they have literally lost their mind and contact with reality. Our bewilderment and fear of losing our own sanity combine to reduce our capacity to empathise with, and to understand, the psychotic person. This often causes us all, including psychiatrists, to seek explanations for the inexplicable behaviour. The history of psychiatry is riddled with such attempts, from the scientific to the bizarre, from witchcraft to viruses. Unlike most other psychiatric presentations, a commonsense approach comes up against a chasm in our ordinary day-to-day experience.

What is psychosis?

The term originally referred to a range of mental disturbances but has come to have a much more specific use, namely reference to a group of conditions in which misinterpretation of the nature of reality is the hallmark; this is reflected in impaired perception (hallucinations), false beliefs tenaciously held (delusions), and disorganised patterns of speech (thought disorder). A direct outcome of these defining features is that the person's competence as a person is called into question, at least temporarily.

The psychoses are a major public health problem. About 3 per cent of people are affected by a psychotic disorder at some time in their lives. Schizophrenia, the most common form, occurs in just under 1 per cent of the population, in the sexes equally, and in every ethnic and cultural group.

Rivalling other prominent diseases of modern times like diabetes and heart disease in rate and risk, they represent even higher economic costs to society because they mostly begin in late adolescence or early adult life, and the disability they bring is often prolonged and marked.

Psychotic disorders, particularly schizophrenia, have been seen as occupying a special place in psychiatry. In general, we do not consider psychotic people to be like ourselves. It has been argued that a psychiatrist's inability to understand a person's psyche suggests that they may be dealing with psychosis—in other words, that a subjective judgement points to the diagnosis. Karl Jaspers, an eminent philosopher and psychiatrist, developed this principle as part of existential philosophy, using the term 'abyss' to reflect our complete failure to understand the mental world of the psychotic person. This brings to mind Churchill's frustration in trying to grasp the Russian mentality: 'It is a riddle wrapped in a mystery inside an enigma'.

I vividly recall my first encounter with a psychotic patient after just a matter of days as a junior trainee in psychiatry. I had seen a few patients with psychosis during my brief attachment to a psychiatric clinic as a medical student, but these were fleeting contacts. Anne was an attractive student who looked like any other young woman of her age on the campus across the road from the hospital where I was working. She had been brought to the emergency department by two of her friends who noted that she had been acting bizarrely and quite out of character. She made no sense at all as she referred to a voice that instructed her to take on a special role to save the world. Only she had the power to do this. I ascertained that she had been acting unusually for a couple of weeks—not sleeping most of the night, laughing inappropriately, revealing to all her friends that she had been summoned by a higher power for a special mission, and neglecting her studies.

Over the next few days, it became abundantly clear that she was in the throes of a first-episode psychosis, although it took another week to determine that this was more likely than not to be florid schizophrenia. We were able to rule out a drug-induced or physically based condition, but bore in mind the possibility of mania. I was overwhelmed by my encounter with Anne. Here was a bright, intelligent person, about my own age, potentially a sister or a friend, who was inaccessible even on an ordinary level of social intercourse and totally impossible to comprehend. I certainly could not make any sense of her grandiose delusions, no matter how much I tried to empathise with her. This failure to connect with a fellow human being came as a shock; for me it was tantamount to us coming from different planets.

I have seen hundreds of people like Anne since then, and still become disconcerted that they can lose their minds so profoundly. But I have also been reassured on countless occasions that they can return to the world of reason with treatment, allowing a human bridge to be re-established. When you read the account of Sandy Jeffs' experience later in this chapter, you will, I am confident, appreciate this point.

The Jasperian view has been challenged periodically, notably by the radical Scottish psychiatrist RD Laing, who launched the so-called anti-psychiatry movement in the 1960s. He clearly recognised the danger of giving up trying to reach the person with a label of schizophrenia. As he put it:

> I think it is clear that by 'understanding' I do not mean a purely intellectual process. For understanding one might say love. But no word has been more prostituted. What is necessary, though not enough, is a capacity to know how the patient is experiencing himself and the world, including oneself. If one cannot understand him, one is hardly in a position to begin to 'love' him in any effective way … No one has schizophrenia, like having a cold. The patient has not 'got' schizophrenia.

He went on to propose the controversial alternative view that the experience of psychotic people could be best understood as their retreat into a private world in the face of intolerable reality. Modern psychiatry does accept the Laingian position in one specific way. It uses the label 'brief reactive psychosis' for those psychotic states in which an obvious precipitant, such as overwhelming stress, is thought to be a contributing cause. In observing Hamlet as he struggles to deal with his father's murder, Polonius obviously can attach a measure of meaning to his seemingly bizarre behaviour when he observes: 'Though this be madness yet there is method in it'. As for the vast majority of psychotic states, no 'method' is discernible and Churchill's word 'enigma' is not far off the mark.

Our main focus will be on schizophrenia; the psychotic forms of mood disorder are covered in Chapter 7.

What causes psychosis?

Most psychiatrists adopt a model that links a biological predisposition on the one hand, and precipitating and perpetuating environmental influences on the other, to explain the onset and course of a psychotic state. Since psychosis is experienced only by a minority of people, even among those exposed to extreme stress, a specific vulnerability presumably operates. The greater this vulnerability, the less stress is required to trigger the illness.

Each of the psychoses may have several interrelated causes. Most research has been carried out on schizophrenia. Here, studies of families, twins and adoptees show compellingly a role for genetic factors. An exponentially increased risk occurs as biological links become closer, shifting from 2 per cent in uncles and aunts to 10 per cent in first-degree relatives and 50 per cent in identical twins. Only a model that assumes a role for many different genes and environmental factors can predict this enormous spectrum of risk.

A theory concerning an excess of the chemical messenger dopamine is widely accepted by psychiatrists. Receptors for this messenger are blocked by anti-psychotic medication, and therapeutic doses correlate with the blockade. Prolonged exposure to amphetamines (especially methamphetamine or 'ice', which are indirect dopamine agents) may produce psychotic features, further supporting the dopamine theory. Indeed, the picture induced by drugs of this kind can be identical to acute paranoid schizophrenia. Methamphetamine users are at a ten times higher risk of developing psychotic symptoms than the general population. On the other hand, not all users develop psychosis, suggesting that additional vulnerability factors are at work, among them younger age and people with odd, eccentric or anti-social personalities.

Problems with dopamine are unlikely to be the only dysfunction, given that certain symptoms of schizophrenia are relatively unimproved by anti-psychotics. Serotonin has been implicated, in that hallucinogens like LSD have serotonin-like actions. Moreover, abnormal pathways in the nerve cell, and lack of regulation of key physiological processes related to brain maturation, probably have a role to play.

Although specific pathology has not been found in the brains of schizophrenic patients at post-mortem, reduced weight and volume in several areas, especially the temporal lobe, are notable; sophisticated X-ray findings are consistent with what is found at dissection. All in all, the story is utterly frustrating. For decades, psychiatrists have looked for distinct brain pathology in the hope that this might lead to determining the cause. Many cul-de-sacs mark the research terrain.

Gender influences vulnerability, and also has a marked effect on timing and severity. The peak age for the onset of schizophrenia is several years later in women (25–35 compared to 15–25 in men), and women usually respond better to medication. Pregnancy tends to protect against psychosis; on the other hand, the risk is higher than normal following birth (see Chapter 15). For women with established schizophrenia, symptoms tend to worsen before menstruation. The pattern of symptoms also differs between the genders, with women likely to be more socially functional and less apathetic. In this case, but not other psychiatric states, female sex hormones offer some advantage.

As already alluded to, several illicit drugs, especially amphetamines (speed) and hallucinogens (like LSD), cause psychoses in their own right. This is unlikely to be the case with marijuana (cannabis) but, in people who are vulnerable to psychosis for other reasons, cannabis may influence the timing of a relapse and the ultimate course of the illness. The stable rate of schizophrenia since the 1950s in Western countries—despite the massive increase in cannabis use—suggests that it is not a cause of the illness but only a trigger.

A disturbance in the development of the nervous system could well be a key factor. Disordered function of nerve cells and their interconnections possibly distorts normal thinking and feeling. Brain-imaging studies demonstrate intriguingly that in some cases these changes predate the onset of illness. Major changes in brain structure during adolescence, a process known as pruning, are thought to play a role in the timing of onset of initial symptoms.

Controversial evidence suggests that some psychoses result from the effect of viral infection on an immature brain. People born in late spring and early winter, or after a major viral epidemic, are somewhat more likely to develop schizophrenia later, but no one would claim that it is a viral illness.

Myriad life circumstances contribute to increasing a person's vulnerability to a psychotic illness, though the evidence is by no means clear-cut. Early life trauma, like child abuse or incest, particularly if severe and protracted, is an example of a general risk factor for psychiatric disorders in adult life. During the heyday of psychoanalysis, this source of vulnerability was thought to be the principal explanation for schizophrenia. Psychoanalytic theory then saw psychosis on a continuum with neurosis—it being a more severe form of neurosis. Poor self-esteem, and an incomplete sense of who one is, may be other general sources of vulnerability.

Reassuringly for many families already stigmatised by the fact of mental illness in a member, past theories that parents and families are capable of causing psychosis in relatives (for example, the so-called 'schizophrenogenic mother' as coined by Frieda Fromm-Reichmann, a psychoanalyst who bravely attempted to analyse patients over periods of years) are dead and buried. Certain personality types are probably more vulnerable to psychosis, particularly the socially withdrawn, the distrustful and the grossly unstable.

That there is a relationship between stress and the timing and outcome of psychotic disorders is likely. Demanding life events—bereavement, a car accident, a bitter disappointment—may trigger relapse. Living in a continually stressful environment certainly predisposes a person to relapse, particularly in the case of schizophrenia. A compelling illustration is the impact of family atmosphere on the course of this disease. Family stress may become evident in terms of expressed emotion, which has three components: critical comments about aspects of the person's behaviour, expressions of hostility towards the person, and emotional over-involvement by the carer that inappropriately restricts autonomy. Patients belonging to families with high levels of expressed emotion have higher rates of relapse despite adequate drug treatment. Where families undergo stress-modifying interventions (see sections on treatment below) relapse rates decline markedly.

The broader social environment also appears to influence the course of psychosis. Interestingly, people with schizophrenia may do better in developing countries. A number of explanations have been suggested. Is it the lower expectation to perform? Is it a stronger sense of family cohesion? Is it a more accepting community attitude? These questions have thoroughly challenged both sociologists and psychiatrists.

What can we say in summary then about causality? In the case of schizophrenia, it is possible that an interaction between the inheritance of an assortment of genes and environmental stressors impact on brain development. Those stressors occurring close in time to the onset of the illness presumably act as triggers. This model is common to many complex diseases, but when affecting an organ like the brain during several stages of development, numerous chemical and anatomical systems are involved. During adolescence, hormonal changes may also play a role.

How do psychiatrists classify the psychoses?

Up to the late nineteenth century, psychiatrists lumped the psychoses together under unhelpful labels like madness and lunacy. This 'unitary theory' was first challenged by Emil Kraepelin, a noted German psychiatrist, who meticulously described the many features that were found in psychotic patients and attempted to find an underlying causal disorder in the brain. Failing in his quest he turned to another method of classifying the psychoses, based on their trajectory. He detected two chief patterns: progressive mental deterioration or a series of relapses with recovery between them. The first he labelled dementia praecox (renamed schizophrenia by his Swiss colleague Eugen Bleuler in 1911), the second manic-depressive psychosis. This model has out-lasted its competitors and remains the main way of classifying the psychoses. Contradictory findings—good outcome in up to a third of people with schizophrenia, and progressive decline in some people with bipolar disorder—have not shaken Kraepelin's categories.

Little has changed in our ability to distinguish between various forms of psychosis. Laboratory tests are frustratingly still unavailable and treatment is given according to constellations of symptoms rather than for a specific diagnosis. Imaging of the brain also supports this approach, since findings correlate more strongly with clinical features than with diagnosis. For example, reduced blood flow to certain parts of the frontal lobe is associated with negative symptoms (see section on schizophrenia below), whereas abnormal findings in the temporal lobe and hallucinations correlate.

We cannot even assume that schizophrenia is a discrete entity. There is no clear point of separation, for instance, between it and the psychosis encountered in mood disorders. The term 'schizoaffective disorder' covers the grey area between them. Schizophrenia also is related clinically and genetically to several adolescent-onset non-psychotic diagnoses, especially personality patterns typified by oddities of speech and eccentric behaviour. A continuum has been found between schizophrenic symptoms and psychotic-like experiences in about 6 per cent of the general population. Fortunately, these do not progress and do not point to a future mental illness; what they do represent remains a mystery.

We now turn to the features that people with different psychoses manifest, starting with schizophrenia, the most common.

Schizophrenia

Schizophrenia is defined by the presence of what have been called positive symptoms—delusions, hallucinations and disorganised thought—and negative symptoms—blunting of feelings, constricted mental activity, poor motivation and social withdrawal. Negative symptoms can also be a response to the psychotic experience itself and to putative therapeutic forces (for example, involuntary admission to hospital, enforced drug treatment). The full range of other psychiatric symptoms may occur as a reaction to the upheaval of the psychotic experience.

People with schizophrenia typically experience bizarre delusions (false beliefs held with total conviction, which cannot be shaken by logic and are foreign to the person's background). Their content is usually influenced by cultural and personal factors, and is persecutory, grandiose or pseudoscientific (for example, computer chips implanted in the head). They tend to explain disturbing, subjective experiences in which people believe their thoughts are being read by others (thought broadcast), are being put into their head from outside (thought insertion), or are being taken away (thought withdrawal).

Hallucinations are common in schizophrenia, the person hearing, seeing, tasting, feeling or smelling things that are not there; most people hear voices.

Disorganised thinking and speech, loosening of associations, manifest as the person jumps from topic to topic with no obvious connections between them; complete incoherence may result.

Cognitive impairment manifests as a slowness to react mentally, impaired memory, poor planning and an inability to maintain focus. Even in stable patients, planning a task may prove too demanding. Cognitive deficits respond poorly to anti-psychotic medication and are key targets for psychosocial rehabilitation.

A change in the way the person experiences and expresses feelings is another common feature. Inappropriate emotion, where a person's facial expression does not correspond to what they are saying, is often associated with disorganised thinking or due to an emotional response to hallucinations.

Despite experiencing many of these features, a large proportion of patients do not accept that they are ill and ascribe the symptoms to the treatment given to them or the way they are dealt with by mental health professionals.

The core features—as agreed in one widely used classification system—are reproduced in the table below. Not all of these are necessarily present and indeed the picture varies substantially. The diversity may be magnified by severe depression, even leading to suicide (about 10 per cent of schizophrenic patients take their own lives). Some people slide imperceptibly into psychosis over a period of months or even a couple of years, whereas others descend abruptly into a world shorn of a contact with reality. Psychoeducation—providing information about symptoms, causes, treatment and prognosis in an understandable and user-friendly form to patients, families and other carers—improves knowledge of mental illness and self-management. It is best conducted over multiple sessions. Relapse prevention strategies are included.

Core features of schizophrenia

Acute phase

- delusions of a bizarre type, involving a belief that the person's cultural group would regard as totally implausible;
- prominent hallucinations, throughout the day for several days or several times a week for several weeks; for example, a voice keeping up a running commentary on the person's behaviour or thoughts, or two or more voices conversing with each other;
- disorganised thinking, so that it is difficult to follow the person's train of thought;
- flat or grossly inappropriate emotional response.

Preceding or residual phases
- social isolation;
- impaired functioning as, for instance, wage-earner, student or home-maker;
- peculiar behaviour, such as talking to oneself in public or hoarding food;
- impaired personal hygiene;
- blunted or inappropriate emotional response;
- vague or impoverished speech;
- odd beliefs influencing behaviour, e.g. superstitiousness, belief in clairvoyance, telepathy, 'sixth-sense' and 'others can feel my feelings';
- unusual perceptual experiences, e.g. sensing the presence of a force or person not actually present;
- lack of initiative and interests;

Psychiatrists have been much influenced in recent years by a series of honest accounts by people and their families of their experience, including the stigmatising attitudes of society. Even health professionals, despite their training, have not always been free of prejudice. These personal testimonies are therefore all the more vital, especially in that they break longstanding taboos.

Sandy Jeffs, an Australian arts graduate and a poet, has written vividly about her long struggle with schizophrenia. Her book, *Poems from the Madhouse,* has won several awards and her poems have appeared in many anthologies. She has the striking ability to convey the bewilderment and suffering of the schizophrenic experience. As she herself puts it, 'I am one of the lucky ones … so many are silenced by their illness'. Her poem 'Psychotic Episode' illuminates the experience amazingly well:

> When the chilled, icy wind blew,
> in went I,
> into a world I knew nothing about,
> into a space for which I could
> never have prepared myself even if
> I had been warned of its existence.
> Down, down, down went I,
> tumbling into an abyss filled
> with a myriad spooks and phantoms
> which preyed upon my unsuspecting self.
> There was no room for rationality,
> only chaos upon chaos upon chaos,
> and flowing rivers of turbulent waters flanked
> on each side by Gothic mountains of angst.

And I was immersed in something
deeper than a huge black hole,
from which I did not emerge
until the haze was blown away
by all manner of processes that acted
upon my distraught, disturbed self.
But as the wind wuthered about my cardboard face,
a chill had set in and frozen my life force forever.

Elsewhere, she gives rich descriptions of some of the features listed in the table above. Among her delusions have been: 'Beethoven had stolen the nine symphonies from me'; 'The devil had raped me and was waiting for me every time I went to bed'; 'My friend was trying to poison me with her pumpkin soup'. Her hallucinations have included voices, visual images and smells:

I hear voices which say different things. I hear voices which tell me among other things that I am evil, the most horrid person in the world—that I am capable of contaminating whole societies with my evil and I won't let people touch me for fear of causing their death. Imagine trying to have a conversation with someone while at the same time there is a person in each ear talking to you and saying different things. I have smelt God; I could never describe the smell but it was most sublime and at the time undeniably God.

She also recalls the initial phase of her illness, leading into her first actual breakdown:

Early university days were … characterised by growing unusual behaviour … I used to have 'turns' when I would thrash around violently and lapse into unconsciousness. These happened for quite a few years. When I was under quite a bit of stress I started doing crazy things. I thought I was a grand person who could do and say anything without any consequences. Eggs became important in the way they were arranged in the fridge because there was a great cosmic plan associated with their order. Finally I stopped talking, eating and drinking and retired to the bed of a person I did not even know. After some time I was taken to hospital and voices started to insinuate themselves in my mind. One of the voices was my father who would call me and I would answer. I began to hear voices that would tell me I was evil. This was the beginning of a terrible journey which has touched me with a profundity like nothing else I have known ... In one respect it was a relief to be given the label because it explained to me and my friends what my behaviour had been about ... why I had been so bizarre ... and that there was a possible way of ameliorating the condition with treatment. The first months of schizophrenia were frightening and bewildering because no one knew what was happening. People thought I was pretending or trying to manipulate the system. It turned out I was one of the lucky ones who responded to medication and had a reasonable outcome, but I cannot over-emphasise the fear of madness and its bizarre machinations and the reverberating consequences it has to all who come into contact with its spectre.

Despite Sandy's relief at being given a diagnosis, psychiatrists are reluctant to apply the label of schizophrenia until at least half a year has elapsed lest the psychosis is a more limited illness, such as that induced by drugs, and to avoid the stigma that, sadly, is still attached to the term. But even for people diagnosed with schizophrenia, the fact is that the outcome still varies and is more positive, particularly over the long term, than is widely believed. A study in Vermont in the United States demonstrating this is the follow-up of a large group of patients who had been hospitalised for many years. When the hospital closed, many of them made a successful transition to community living, much to the astonishment of their professional carers.

Considerable variability applies to the pattern of recovery from an acute episode, ranging from the emergence of lifelong negative symptoms through to early remission. About one in five patients achieves a good outcome with full remission after a single episode; most experience recurrences. Looked at more positively, about half of all first-episode patients maintain interpersonal relationships and many hold competitive employment five years later. Crucially, 99 per cent of patients require continuing anti-psychotic medication to sustain improvement. Vulnerability to relapse is most evident in the early years of the illness. This critical period combines a peak in biological vulnerability with the need to adjust to facing a potentially lifelong illness. Better outcome correlates with female sex, onset at a later age, married status, adaptive functioning prior to the breakdown, onset preceded by an identified stress, and a good response to medication. Suicide risk is highest in the first years following diagnosis when the person becomes increasingly aware of the implications of having such a severe illness.

The other psychoses

Schizophreniform disorder

This cumbersome term, meaning schizophrenia-like, is applied to people whose illness is abrupt in onset, responds well to treatment and does not have enduring symptoms. This diagnosis is much preferred to schizophrenia, with all its sinister connotations. Whether it is an extremely mild variant of schizophrenia or a condition in its own right remains unanswered.

Psychotic mood disorders

The psychoses related to mood disorders are covered in Chapter 7, but are briefly mentioned here since in some cases of mania and depression the disturbance is so severe that psychotic symptoms predominate. Particularly in depression, a gradual worsening of the mood state may lead to delusions of guilt and self-deprecation. On the other hand, psychotic features develop abruptly in mania. The psychosis usually reflects the person's mood disturbance with the delusional belief, for example, that one has the power to influence world leaders (in mania). Less often, delusions are not clearly linked to mood, such as a conviction of being persecuted or of one's mind being interfered with by satellites.

Psychotic mood disorders are difficult to distinguish from schizophrenia and schizophreniform disorder, particularly in adolescence, which is a reason for frequent changes in diagnosis. When a person has both a mood disorder and psychotic features but there is no clear-cut relationship between them, the concept of schizoaffective disorder is considered (see below).

The psychiatrist's difficulty in establishing a clear diagnosis in the wake of an evolving psychiatric disturbance experienced by a person for the first time is well illustrated in the story of Michael.

Michael, aged 19 and unemployed, was brought to a community mental health clinic by his parents who, with the help of their family doctor, had had to persuade him to come.

He had been well until nine months previously when, following success in his examinations, he gained a place in an applied science course at university. During the first semester, Michael tended to spend more and more time on his own. Appearing preoccupied and moody, he became erratic in his attendance at classes, stayed awake at night and slept late into the day. Michael failed dismally in every one of his university subjects, his tutors struck by his inability to carry out assignments. Much to his parents' dismay he was uncharacteristically abusive. He began to use marijuana regularly.

Michael soon became progressively more withdrawn and suspicious. He began to hear voices that threatened to kill him. Reckless driving brought him to police attention on two occasions. He proclaimed to them that God had appointed him as the chosen one but that there were many people who were out to thwart him. The parents' concern naturally escalated in the face of the increasingly bizarre behaviour. At first they sensed Michael was 'not quite right', but as his condition worsened they reluctantly resigned themselves to the fact that something was horribly wrong. Discarding a series of plausible explanations—adolescent turmoil, transition from school to university and recreational drug use—the spectre of severe mental illness loomed large. The family doctor had also expressed uncertainty at first, but after some months confirmed the parents' worst fears. Michael was admitted to a psychiatric ward.

Physical conditions and recreational drugs were ruled out as a cause of his abnormal mental state. Following three weeks of treatment comprising anti-psychotic medication, psychoeducation and psychological support of the family, the psychotic features gradually waned. During this period Michael appeared stunned by what had befallen him and demoralised about his future. His emotional expression was blunted. He displayed no interest in activities like playing his guitar, a previously enjoyable pastime. He resented being a patient, even denying that he had a psychiatric problem of any kind. He then became overtly depressed, continuously lamenting that 'my life is ruined'. Adding anti-depressants and initiating weekly psychotherapy helped to alleviate this morbid state although he remained emotionally detached and socially withdrawn for the next few months. He described being 'cut-off', as if 'living underwater'. Michael gradually resumed some of his old interests and felt sufficiently confident to return to his course; he also began to reconnect with family and friends. He continued to be seen intermittently by both his psychiatrist and the family doctor.

Schizoaffective psychosis

Disturbed mood and psychotic symptoms may evolve in such complex ways as to challenge even the most seasoned clinician. The nature, sequence, prominence and relative duration of mania or depression then have to be carefully assessed. When a person has disordered mood and psychotic features but no clear relationship exists between them, schizoaffective disorder is a possibility; the symptoms of schizophrenia and mood disorder either occur together or sequentially.

Robyn, a 50-year-old divorced ex-nurse, lived with her two teenage sons. She had suffered bouts of depression and mania over ten years. Recently, she heard her sons talking to her and a faint voice she believed was that of her priest, who lectured her about virtue and sin. These voices persisted when her mood was stable. Robyn responded only partially to mood stabilising drugs. She still had breakthrough episodes of mania or depression about twice a year, requiring involuntary treatment. When well, Robyn was most cooperative and exceedingly apologetic for her psychotic behaviour.

Psychosis as a reaction

Brief reactive psychosis is the only form of psychosis that is linked with a specific identifiable cause. Clear psychotic symptoms follow shortly after major stress, in presumably vulnerable personalities, the trigger being well beyond their customary life experience. Emotional turmoil, with fluctuating mood and perplexity, is a hallmark. Typically it lasts a matter of weeks, with full recovery.

Jane was the 35-year-old wife of a diplomat on an overseas posting (I have also used her story in Chapter 5). The couple had been sent a year before her breakdown to a politically unstable country, but she had managed to adjust. However, she felt herself floundering when a political crisis took place, and the outbreak of civil war proved to be the final straw. She became acutely disturbed, accusing her husband of spying for one of the warring parties. She heard voices passing secrets to her, and made an attempt on her life in response to a voice commanding her to slash her throat as the only way to stop the war. Within two weeks of evacuation home and anti-psychotics, Jane's symptoms waned almost entirely and she could barely recall her ordeal. In discussion with a psychiatrist she was able to place the harrowing episode in perspective, understanding that her coping resources had been challenged and then overwhelmed by the frightening events. She had developed a severely compromised psychological state in which everyone posed a threat to her, even her husband.

Delusional disorder

This condition, in which one or more false beliefs predominate but there are no other psychotic symptoms, tends to occur in the second half of life. It either develops abruptly or, more commonly, gradually over months, even years. The beliefs may be of several kinds—for instance, erotomanic (that one is loved by a prominent person), grandiose (that one has special powers), morbidly jealous (that one's partner has been unfaithful, but without reason), paranoid (that one is being persecuted) or hypochondriacal (that one has a serious illness). The delusion often evolves in a sensitive personality buffeted by everyday stresses. It makes some sense and can be intuitively understood. Delusional disorders are thus a clear exception to the notion of the abyss in psychotic illness, which helps the psychiatrist to distinguish them from schizophrenia. As their roots lie within the personality, they often resist treatment, particularly if the condition has evolved gradually.

Maude, a 68-year-old widow, had been living on her own for seven years since the death of her husband. She had managed well and was in good physical health apart from increasing deafness. However, her family noticed that she wrapped aluminium foil around the roses, and kept the curtains drawn day and night. Maude had complained to the local council that neighbours were poisoning her roses, and revealed a belief that unspecified people were spying on her.

She had no history of mental illness. The persecutory delusions were the only psychotic feature. There was no evidence of a mood disorder and she was cognitively intact. Physical examination and investigations for dementia were normal, apart from longstanding deafness, for which she wore a hearing aid.

The family went with Maude to her family doctor, who she had known for twenty years. She was willing to share her suspicions for the first time. In collaboration with a psychogeriatric service, she was assessed in her home and diagnosed with delusional disorder. Treatment included an anti-psychotic in low dosage. Her hearing aid was checked regularly. Although the delusions persisted, Maude became less preoccupied by them and was able to enjoy gardening without fear of the neighbours interfering.

Drug-induced psychosis

Amphetamine is the classic culprit. In large amounts over a brief period it can produce psychosis even in normal volunteers. The psychosis may be preceded by irritability and restlessness. Delusions are usually persecutory in type. Associated visual and auditory hallucinations are common. Although the psychosis usually resolves when amphetamine intake ceases and the drug is excreted from the body, relief for acute symptoms may be needed.

Treating acute psychoses

Since the experience of psychosis, especially a first episode, is so shattering, psychiatrists have to be exquisitely sensitive to both the sufferer and their family. Not surprisingly, given people's loss of contact with reality, they have trouble accepting that they are ill and in need of care. Some general principles of treatment apply to all forms of psychosis, but the details vary according to the specific diagnosis. I shall focus on schizophrenia, since it illustrates well the aspects of treatment that are intrinsic to sound clinical care.

Our first task is to carry out a thorough psychiatric and medical assessment. This is necessarily done in a staged way in the highly disturbed person, and only the briefest history and physical examination may be possible initially. Interviewing the family and friends is most helpful to fill in any gaps. Occasionally these inquiries have to be done without the person's consent in order to promote their best interests.

Establishing rapport is crucial to effective treatment. A friendly, non-judgemental tone is used. When probing for symptoms, we start gently: 'Has anything happened lately that has upset you?' or 'What is the most important thing you would like help with?' These sorts of questions reveal disorganised thinking as well as offering people the opportunity to share their concerns. More specific questions are posed later: 'Have you noticed anything suspicious going on around you?'; 'Have you felt like people are talking about you, or watching you in an unusual way?'; 'Has anything on the TV or radio seemed to refer to you personally?' and 'Have you heard people talking to you or about you when there was nobody there?'

Noteworthy matters in the assessment are: current and past risk of self-harm or harm to others; need for involuntary treatment; substance abuse; history of not taking prescribed medicines, their side-effects and negative attitudes towards treatment generally; and degree of insight into the implications of suffering from schizophrenia.

Since certain types of epilepsy and pathology in the brain occasionally mimic schizophrenia, an electroencephalogram (an examination of the electrical patterns of the brain) and a CT or MRI scan are done in those presenting for the first time. Other tests to exclude physical causes include thyroid function, HIV status and vitamin B_{12}. Since all anti-psychotics have adverse effects, baseline measures of thyroid, liver and various other bodily functions are done in patients starting medication, and repeated every six months if indicated.

With the assessment more or less completed, the next most vital task is to relieve the person of their distressing, often terrifying, symptoms. If effective treatment is delayed, potential support and cooperation from family and friends may be lost. This is particularly so at the time of a first episode, when everyone is feeling confused, fearful and helpless. Similar failure to recognise the early signs of any later episodes may prolong the agony for both patient and family.

Acute psychosis, particularly when it occurs for the first time, is a psychiatric emergency. The first step is to ensure the safety of the person and those around them by admission, if necessary, to a secure, non-threatening environment, usually a hospital ward. Sometimes compulsory hospitalisation is essential when people are a risk to themselves or to others through their inability to recognise that they are ill. The person's feelings, particularly of fear and hostility, are sensitively explored in order to gain their trust.

The first phase of treatment extends for days into weeks. Anti-psychotic medication, the mainstay of treatment, is introduced in a step-wise way and kept to the minimum effective dose. We may turn to another type of anti-psychotic or increase the dose if the person does not respond or there are intolerable side-effects. The latter—particularly restlessness, involuntary bodily movements and a spaced-out feeling—can be most unpleasant and jeopardise a fluctuating willingness to follow professional advice. To relieve associated anxiety, insomnia or depression, anti-depressants and benzodiazepines may be needed (see Chapter 18).

Long-acting anti-psychotics given by injection, usually every two weeks, are a boon in people with impaired insight or gross disorganisation. This so-called depot medication is applied only after oral treatment fails. In about 15 per cent of schizophrenic people, conventional anti-psychotics prove ineffective and a variant called clozapine is considered. The huge snag is that this unique anti-psychotic can have serious side-effects, including suppression of the bone marrow and an inflammatory condition of the heart's muscle—both potentially lethal. A strict protocol is put into place when clozapine has to be used; this involves a baseline blood and cardiac assessment, and regular monitoring of white cells for at least eighteen months.

When the psychotic symptoms recede, as they do in up to 90 per cent of people with a first episode in response to medication and supportive care, other needs come into focus.

Supporting the person and their family

Once the acute illness has subsided, we take special note of the impact of the psychosis on the person's sense of identity and perception of their world. This experience is influenced by many factors. In young people, for instance, their sense of who they are is fragile and, understandably, they are reluctant to accept the fact that they are now severely mentally ill. Indeed, many resist the label, at least at first. Some lose any sense of who they were prior to the psychosis, engulfed as they are by the intensity of their recent experience.

Informing the person in clear language about symptoms, triggers of relapse and how to avoid them enhances self-sufficiency. A continuing relationship with a mental health professional (psychiatric nurse, clinical psychologist, psychiatric social worker or occupational therapist) who is acting as a care coordinator (more commonly called case manager—a ghastly term that should be consigned to the dustbin) can accomplish this psychoeducation. People with persisting cognitive difficulties also need help with budgeting and the activities of daily living. A structured form of training, incorporating repeated practice of graded cognitive tasks, tackles this aspect more directly.

Training in social skills is commonly used to help people who have lost the ability to function in the domains of work, leisure and family and other relationships. Complex social processes are broken down into their basic elements, such as eye contact, volume of speech, conversational etiquette. Through practice, as well as modelling by the therapist, suitable skills are developed into a repertoire of key social functions.

Only about one in ten people with enduring psychosis returns to a full-time job. Traditional approaches assumed that acquiring pertinent work skills had to be step-wise, and guided by a comprehensive vocational assessment. The return-to-work rate was negligible, and mainly to protected employment. A more promising approach, supported employment, entails a briefer assessment, prompt placement in a paid job and, importantly, intensive support in the workplace itself. The program works optimally when mental health and vocational aspects are integrated, allowing a better match between level of function and type of work.

Non-government support groups and organisations offer a range of social services, such as club houses (patient-run day centres) and transitional employment schemes. They are also instrumental in gaining political influence, leading to greater awareness of the plight of the severely mentally ill and better funding for mental health care.

Substance misuse occurs in about half the patients with psychosis; treatment is targeted specifically at this problem. Although many understand that using illicit drugs, most commonly cannabis, poses a risk to their mental health, they will contend at the same time that they feel better on them. Psychiatrists apply a range of strategies to help their patients reduce or eliminate drug use, but have no alternative other than to accept that their efforts will commonly be to no avail. Anxiety and depression, also common in the psychotic person, are easier targets of treatment. Physical conditions such as obesity, heart disease and diabetes need to be tackled vigorously. Special efforts are required to ensure good antenatal care for patients who become pregnant. Continuation of anti-psychotics during the pregnancy is usually advisable, since the dangers of relapse in the mother far outweigh the very small potential risk to the foetus of adverse drug effects.

For people who persistently fail to cooperate with community-based care, compulsory treatment can be legally instituted in many parts of the world. This can play a crucial role in reducing the chance of a relapse, enabling the person to spend less time in the more restrictive setting of a hospital ward and experience less intense symptoms and disability. However, as many patients regard compulsory community treatment as a violation of their civil rights and much prefer not to be on an 'order', every effort is made to resume voluntary care as soon as possible.

Family interventions, ranging from relatively informal (for example, giving relevant information) to structured family therapy have a pivotal place. Measures include helping families to deal with upsetting events related to their relative's illness (their acting bizarrely in a public setting, for instance), teaching them strategies to manage stress and family tensions, replacing destructive emotions with constructive action, encouraging sharing of difficulties with trusted friends, and maintaining social support.

Anne Deveson's book, *Tell Me I'm Here*, an account of her family's experience in coping with her son's battle with schizophrenia—culminating in his suicide seven years after the diagnosis at the age of twenty-five—reveals how crucial is the need for family measures of this kind. She gives her reasons for writing the book in the preface:

Jonathan is dead. But our stories need to be told. How else can we know that others tread the same pathways? How else can we find our healing? So I write this book for Jonathan, who was graceful and funny and lovely, but who for his last seven years lived a life of torment. I write it for those millions of others with schizophrenia, who daily walk a tightrope, courageously trying to balance between their world and ours. I write it for their families who struggle to hold on to hope when often they are scourged by despair, and who suffer from our ignorance and neglect.

Deveson's book is mandatory reading for any family grappling with the challenge of trying to help a family member afflicted with a psychotic illness, particularly schizophrenia. Although the outcome in Jonathan's case was tragic, Deveson's searing honesty serves as a source of inspiration for family carers.

At its best, the treatment program I have outlined is a combination of a stable, caring living environment, a supportive partnership with dedicated mental health professionals and family doctors, and assistance to participate in appropriate social and work pursuits. Although it may not be possible to achieve all the inherent goals, the measures we have discussed can make an enormous difference to quality of life.

Treating the first episode

The link between how long psychosis remains untreated and the long-term outcome is strong. The greater the delay in people receiving active and extended treatment, the more adverse the illness's effects on study, work, family and other relationships. Any disruption in the sensitive period of adolescence and early adulthood affects adjustment. Both medication and psychosocial treatments are less effective as the complications of the illness become more entrenched.

However, there is one caveat. We cannot be sure that this is the case for the adolescent presenting with what appear to be early features of a psychotic illness; social withdrawal, poor study habits, decline in academic performance and the like may reflect a difficult adjustment to the challenges of separation and individuation. Premature labelling of the struggling young person as 'first-episode psychosis' and commencement of treatment, especially medication, may be unnecessary and may generate unwanted ill-effects of stigma and anxiety about what the future may bring. A mammoth research effort to identify accurately the predictors of psychosis has been under way since the 1990s; we can be confident that we will gain information in due course, although the ideal of an objective physiological test seems a long way off.

In first-episode patients, a medication-free trial is considered after about eighteen months in those whose symptoms have disappeared entirely. On the other hand, psychological and social measures are continued, combined with a careful check for any hint of a relapse. If two or more episodes have occurred or a firm diagnosis of schizophrenia has been reached, medication is prescribed for at least five years, but often much longer.

Conclusion

We have achieved a growing understanding of the psychoses in recent years, paving the way for advances in drug and psychological treatments. This understanding encompasses an exciting research opportunity to determine causality. Until we gain this knowledge, psychiatrists must make best use of available therapy options, despite their limitations. Not only will these efforts improve the lives of patients and their families, but they will also contribute to breaking down the stigma these diseases have historically attracted. Models of health care in the twenty-first century are definitely better attuned to the needs of the person and their family. Integrating specialist mental health and primary health care has the potential to meet many of the needs of people with psychosis living in the community—the vast majority of those with enduring illness.

CHAPTER 12

Alcohol and Drug Abuse

Substances have been used for their pleasurable effects since time immemorial and feature prominently in many cultural traditions. However, the use of some of them, and misuse of all, are linked to a range of unwelcome experiences for the consumer and pose pervasive problems for contemporary society. Psychiatrists apply the term 'substance abuse' to cover addiction and its associated physical, psychological and social complications. Alcohol, opiates (for example, heroin), stimulants, cannabis (marijuana), benzodiazepines, hallucinogens and solvents are the main substances that lead to problems; their misuse contributes to hospital admission, suicide, crime, marital and family disharmony and industrial accidents.

The move from medicinal to recreational use of drugs is best illustrated by the story of the opiates. These were prescribed for clinical purposes well into the nineteenth century. By the 1890s, however, opiates were increasingly recognised as dangerous because of their addictive properties. In recent decades their recreational abuse has reached epidemic proportion, spawning a drug culture, drug-related crime and the spread of AIDS and infective hepatitis. These developments have required growing cooperation between governments, law-enforcement agencies and health services and led to a call for changes in drug legislation.

Recreational use of alcohol was spurred by its ready availability—for example, cheap gin in eighteenth-century England. The term 'alcoholism' was coined in 1849. Throughout the nineteenth century the temperance movement gained momentum in a number of countries. Prohibition in the United States, launched in the early twentieth century, failed dismally and was repealed in 1933. This was the year of the founding of Alcoholics Anonymous (AA), also in the US, which is still the principal support group.

What is substance abuse?

A distinction is made between substance dependence or full-blown addiction and substance abuse that falls short of dependence. Substance abuse is typified by recurrent social, work, psychiatric and medical problems. Examples would be a university student bingeing on amphetamine every weekend followed by a day of missed classes because of 'crashing', or a middle-aged man driving when intoxicated with alcohol. Substance dependence, on the other hand, is typified by the following:

- the substance is taken in large amounts, and over a long period;
- there is a persistent desire to use the substance and efforts to cut down are unsuccessful;
- much time is spent in obtaining, taking or recovering from substances abused;
- intoxication and withdrawal effects may occur when there are social or work roles to be fulfilled, or when it is hazardous (e.g. driving);
- important responsibilities are given up or neglected;
- use continues despite awareness of a substance-related problem;
- tolerance occurs—increased need and/or diminished effect with the same amount of the substance;
- symptoms are experienced on withdrawing from the substance;
- the substance is taken to relieve or avoid these withdrawal symptoms.

Medical and psychiatric assessment of substance abuse extends beyond distinguishing between dependence and abuse. It includes an estimate of the quantity used, diagnosis of related psychiatric and medical disorders, and attention to family, work and legal problems. Clinical states that commonly require medical attention are:

- intoxication that may result in serious medical problems or even death;
- withdrawal, which is a typical set of physical and psychological symptoms (especially in the case of alcohol and other sedatives);
- delirium, characterised by disorientation for time and place, agitation and hallucinations;
- dementia, a diffuse loss of memory and intellectual function (occurring mainly in alcoholism);
- drug psychosis, usually transient (occurring mainly with amphetamines, cannabis and the hallucinogens);
- panic, frequently associated with cannabis and stimulants like amphetamine and cocaine;

- flashbacks, the unwanted recurrence of a drug effect (occurring with hallucinogens and cannabis).

What causes substance abuse?

Several interacting factors—biological, psychological and social—contribute to the onset, course and outcome of substance abuse. In general, people use a substance because it offers rapid pleasure without obvious short-term harm, or relieves physical symptoms or emotional distress. The potential for its abuse relates to the drug's intrinsic properties and to the mode of administration. Drugs that are smoked or injected intravenously produce effects within seconds and are therefore highly reinforcing.

Studies of identical and fraternal twins, and of children adopted away from substance abusing families, point to a genetic factor in alcohol abuse. Moreover, people with a family history of alcoholism share certain biological traits, particularly the body's capacity to break down alcohol readily so that they need ever-higher 'doses' to feel its euphoric effect. Animal research confirms this biological pattern—it is very easy to breed rats susceptible to alcohol dependence, and to condition them to seek out alcohol.

The search for a so-called addictive personality has proved futile, since teasing out cause and effect is virtually impossible. On the other hand, certain personality traits and behaviours that confer a risk of misuse have been identified in children as young as three; they are impulsive, moody, aggressive, relate poorly to peers and struggle academically. Parents may also serve as poor role models for their children when resorting to alcohol and drugs in the face of adversity. Factors that predispose people to substance abuse include past deviant behaviour, delinquency, emotional trauma, long-term painful physical illness and crises (such as death of a spouse, marital strife, work-related stress, combat exposure, and incest and rape).

The association between mental illness and substance abuse is of marked relevance to psychiatrists, since their coexistence (referred to as 'dual diagnosis') complicates the treatment of both. In one survey, a third of those with a mental illness—particularly schizophrenia and mood disorders such as depression and bipolar illness—were also diagnosed with substance abuse. Conversely, a quarter of patients attending drug and alcohol clinics have an associated psychiatric diagnosis.

A crucial reason for substance use in the psychiatrically ill is self-medication to achieve specific effects. For example, they may take stimulants to motivate themselves and lessen a depressed mood, alcohol or cannabis to take the edge off psychotic symptoms, albeit temporarily, and benzodiazepines to reduce anxiety.

People with dual diagnosis have higher rates of relapse, admission to hospital, disruptive behaviour, unemployment, financial difficulties, isolation and homelessness. Difficult to treat, they are frequently referred back and forth between mental health and drug and alcohol clinics, both of which feel ill equipped.

The negative psychological effects of alcohol and other drug abuse—poor self-esteem, guilt, shame and anger—reinforce addictive behaviour.

The pattern of substance use is largely determined by substance availability and social attitudes. There is no doubt that the greater the access to alcohol and drugs, the greater the level of abuse. This is clear, for example, in statistics of deaths from alcoholic liver disease, which increase when alcohol is cheaper and more widely available. The effects of a range of social forces are equally clear. Young people, for instance, are susceptible to peer pressure, reinforced by glamorous media advertising. Others at risk are socially isolated people, particularly in deprived urban environments where families are fragmented and drugs and alcohol readily available. By contrast, but also at risk, is the so-called Type A personality—typically a driven, achievement-oriented man in whom personal expectations of success are paramount and social conventions to drink common. Patterns also vary from culture to culture; the Irish typically binge whereas the French tend to imbibe more continuingly.

The cycle of abuse

The 'career' of a person with substance abuse is determined by a web of personal and social factors. To make sense of it, we need to look at the addiction and family life cycles.

The addiction cycle has six stages—pre-initiation, initiation, continuation, escalation, cessation and relapse. Influential in the pre-initiation phase are antisocial behaviour, a family history of disharmony and substance abuse, and a deprived social environment. Initiation is linked to availability, experimentation, peer group pressure and self-medication of physical and emotional pain. Continuation is promoted by continuing stress leading to the development of a drug habit. Escalation is linked to inadequate coping and to crises related to substance use, and leads to dependence. Cessation, if it occurs, is temporary and related to periods of relief from stress. Relapse, triggered by a combination of demanding life events and poor coping, is usually typical of 'stable' addiction. Repeated cycles of abuse and quitting result in progressive ill-health, and possible premature death.

The family cycle runs alongside the addiction cycle and they intersect in recognisable ways. Addiction in early marriage, for instance, often leads to divorce but, should the marriage survive, the substance abusing person progresses to stable addiction in mid-life. Mid-life crises may result in escalation of the abuse, often leading to marital conflict and divorce. The pattern in later life is typified by either continuing addiction, stable abstinence or controlled drug use.

Likely outcomes

Long-term follow-up studies suggest that about 50 per cent of substance abusers achieve stable abstinence. A major study of alcoholism in London, for example, showed that after ten years 40 per cent of people had a good outcome while half were still drinking uncontrollably.

Most of those who become abstinent make the decision independently. How they do it remains uncertain, but these seem to be important influences towards recovery:

- acquiring a substitute dependence such as compulsive working, exercise or eating;
- a consistent threat such as probation;
- a medical condition that deters continuing use;
- forming a new, supportive relationship or 'inspirational' group membership, the most effective of which is Alcoholics Anonymous (AA).

Some substance abusers simply become weary of their habit, realising that the many negative effects heavily outweigh any benefits. This change in attitude is often triggered by support from a respected figure, often a friend, doctor or AA member.

Seeking help

A key moment for anyone abusing alcohol or other drugs is when they seek help or are pressured to do so, often by a spouse or employer. A comprehensive assessment is then critical; it encompasses a thorough medical and psychiatric history, and meticulous physical and psychological examination, which focus on these points:

- The reasons for referral can be vital in planning treatment and rehabilitation (e.g. many large firms have active programs for early identification, and may insist that an employee seeks help).
- The details of alcohol and drug use will include over-the-counter, non-prescription substances, given that polysubstance use is common.
- Although people are often unable to explain why they use drugs, it is important to clarify where they are in the addiction cycle, and to pinpoint situations and emotions that reinforce the abuse.

- Some people have legal problems and may seek a favourable court report, with the psychiatrist determining whether marked antisocial behaviour preceded or followed the onset of drug-taking.
- The question of whether psychiatric disorder was present before or only after drug abuse is of crucial interest.
- Examination of the mental state is possible only after any drug effects or intoxication have waned. In fact, the 'real' person may not emerge for weeks or even a few months.
- A thorough physical assessment is vital, including laboratory tests of liver and blood function.

What can be done to help those who abuse substances?

Substance misuse is treated in various settings dependent on the particular needs of the person (and of the family); they include family doctor surgeries, hospital emergency departments and wards (for people who develop a severe withdrawal syndrome), out-patient clinics, psychiatrist offices and specialist alcohol and drug clinics. Psychiatrists have a distinct role where mental illness accompanies the substance abuse, especially when psychiatric symptoms persist after the abuse has been remedied.

Treatment is a challenge due to two characteristics of substance abusers: they tend to deny the problem and so waver in their commitment to deal with it, and they drop out from therapy in the face of even minor setbacks. Because of the difficulty in engaging the person's cooperation, a relationship of trust with the therapist is pivotal in any program of counselling. Skill in tactful confrontation is required to deal with the pervasive denial. Positive feedback bolsters morale.

Treatment is typically repeated over several years because of recurrent relapses. The idea of a cure is not helpful, since vulnerability to relapse is life-long. The aim therefore is to help people minimise the harm they can do themselves as a result of their habit while maximising the quality of their lives between relapses.

Motivational interviewing is a highly regarded counselling approach; its mnemonic FLAGS (feedback, listen, advice, goals, strategies) encapsulates its key ingredients. The therapist provides objective **feedback,** especially information about harms related to abuse, with empathy and understanding. Labels such as 'alcoholic' or 'addict' are avoided. While giving this feedback the therapist **listens** to the person's concerns. Considering the level and pattern of abuse and its severity, and any physical or psychological symptoms, the therapist offers **advice** on the consequences of continued use. Mapping out **goals** revolves around abstinence, substitution therapy or reduced consumption to safe levels. **Strategies** to achieve goals set include administration of anti-craving drugs, substitution therapies (such as methadone), ways to avoid high-risk situations, involvement with a self-help group, and one of the psychotherapies.

Commitment to treatment is considered in terms of *stages of change*. Those who do not wish change (*pre-contemplation*) may see it as too demanding or not appreciate the seriousness of the abuse. People expressing ambivalence (*contemplation*) admit to difficulties associated with abuse. Motivational interviewing identifies discrepancies between current substance use and future goals in order to move the person to a stage of *action*. At this point he or she has not only made a decision to change but has also tried to implement relevant strategies. The next stage, *maintenance*, emphasises changes such as reduced consumption or continuing substitution therapy.

The sequence may well be disrupted by *relapse*. Indeed, few people succeed without faltering. They may go around the stages of change cycle several times before achieving enduring improvement.

Recruiting the family may be pivotal because of their potential to aggravate or improve their relative's condition. Self-help groups are available for them—AA or NA (Narcotics Anonymous) for patients and Al-Anon or Alateen for spouse and children respectively. Families can be a vital crucible within which effective treatment is built.

Different forms of substance abuse

Alcohol

Alcohol has always been viewed ambivalently by society, given that it enhances the pleasures of life but also causes immeasurable harms. Shakespeare knew this well:

> Come, come; good wine is a good familiar creature if it be well used …

> Oh God! that men should put an enemy in their mouths to steal away their brains: that we should … transform ourselves into beasts …

> *Othello*

Alcohol use ranges from occasional social drinking to severe alcoholism with medical complications. International recommendations on safe drinking are based on standard drinks or units and their alcohol content as shown in the table below. Alcohol intoxication initially causes disinhibition; then, as the blood level increases, sedating effects predominate, ranging from impairment of mood, cognition and coordination to coma and death.

Safe drinking is up to four units a day for men, two units for women. Women achieve higher blood alcohol concentrations for a given dose than men for two reasons: less alcohol is broken down in the stomach and less is distributed throughout the body. Harmful drinking is more than six and four units respectively. About one in five men and one in fifty women drink at an unsafe level, making alcohol by far the most abused substance in Western societies.

A practical guide to standard drinks

Drink	Quantity	Standard drinks
Beer	285 ml glass	1
Beer (light)	375 ml can/stubbie	1
Wine	120 ml	1
Spirit	30 ml nip	1
Wine	Bottle (750 mls)	8
Spirit	Bottle (700 mls)	22

Note: The average restaurant serving of wine is 150 mls.

People abusing alcohol seek treatment only when they are forced to do so. The usual reasons are medical, psychological, social or legal complications. Alcohol is unique in having the capacity to cause widespread tissue damage; most bodily systems can be affected. Physical complications may also be due to withdrawal from alcohol, nutritional lack and reduced immune function, and correlate with level of consumption and frequency of binge drinking. Falls and road accidents during periods of intoxication are common.

Social complications like lateness or absenteeism at work can push people to consulting a doctor. Coming up against the law is the fate for drink-driving and disinhibited behaviour while intoxicated. The social damage of alcohol abuse is disastrous for the family—domestic violence, behavioural problems in children, financial embarrassment and distress in the spouse. The Australian author MJ Hyland makes the family problems excruciatingly palpable:

> I came home from school … and found my father lying on the kitchen floor next to the fridge. He was wearing his pyjama bottom and a white singlet.

There was an empty packet of Serepax on the floor next to his arm, like a business card: While you were out, Serepax called by.

I stood over him and wondered whether he was dead yet. I made Vegemite on toast. When my mother came home from work she said, 'I'm going to call an ambulance.'...

'Maybe we should just leave him,' I said, and I think by saying this I blew it. I turned what was a mutual unexpressed desire into something criminal and premeditated.

'Oh no,' she cried. 'God forgive you. We can't just leave him.'

'Why not?'

'Because he's your father.'

'Oh,' said I. 'I thought he was a fucking hopeless alcoholic.'

From 'Asylum Elegy', Meanjin, vol. 63, no. 4, 2004.

The precise relationship between psychological complications and alcohol abuse remains unclear but several clinical pictures are recognised by psychiatrists. Given that alcohol has a temporary euphoric effect, it should come as no surprise that long-term drinking often leads to unstable mood. Most people treated for alcohol abuse are depressed. Although some improve within two or three weeks of withdrawal, many continue to experience lowered mood. Importantly, even when alcohol abusers are not clinically depressed, persistent gloominess and irritability tend to cast a pall over their lives and those of their families.

About 15 per cent of suicides are committed by people who abuse alcohol. Only a small proportion of them are medically depressed, but the disinhibiting effect of alcohol, together with the frequent crises that accompany its abuse, are key factors. Anxiety and panic are other common consequences. Continuing social discomfort tends to pave the way for excessive drinking, a strategy used to lessen that discomfort. Alcohol abuse is also a major complication of the specific form of anxiety known as post-traumatic stress disorder (see Chapter 6). The drug dampens down its distressing features, particularly the re-experiencing of the trauma. In Vietnam War veterans, for example, half of those with post-traumatic stress disorder were also abusing alcohol and other addictive drugs.

Alcoholic hallucinosis is a peculiar psychotic state that typically arises during the withdrawal period. Hearing voices that have a critical or intimidating quality exerts a dramatic but fortunately temporary dislocation of the person's life.

The most damaging psychological long-term effect of alcohol abuse is undoubtedly cognitive impairment, or brain damage, which if left unchecked leads to progressive dementia. The Wernicke-Korsakoff syndrome, named after two prominent Russian psychiatrists, is a particularly serious form of brain damage. Consisting of confusion, unsteady walking and disturbed vision, it results from a deficiency of thiamine (vitamin B6), which must be replaced immediately if serious memory impairment is to be avoided.

Martin had had things go wrong for a while. He felt tense when he got up each morning. He had had a rotten time with his chest, having to take three courses of antibiotics. His feet had been feeling peculiar and he had nearly fallen while walking down a slope. He got no help from his family, his wife having run off with another man and his two children living in another city. But fortunately a good mate gave him casual work. Things were not too bad until he had an attack of pain in his right abdomen, which landed him in hospital. The doctor told Martin his liver was swollen. For some reason he kept asking him about his drinking. He seemed surprised when Martin said a 24-can slab of beer would last him most of the day.

Treating alcohol abuse

The sheer number of complications due to alcohol demands a range of treatments matched to the phases in which people come for help. These include detoxification, strategies for controlled drinking, chemical aversion, relapse prevention and self-help groups.

Detoxification, an unfortunately derogatory term, refers to the process of minimising the physical and psychological symptoms resulting from withdrawal. A specialised treatment setting is the best way to achieve this. Diazepam, a tranquilliser, is the best treatment for withdrawal when medication is required, using progressively reduced doses over seven to ten days.

Treatment with anti-craving drugs is considered before completing the detoxification program. Naltrexone blocks the euphoric effects of alcohol and is well tolerated, but cannot be given if the person has chronic liver disease. Acamprosate also suppresses craving and is well tolerated except if there is renal impairment (it is excreted through the kidneys). A combination of the two drugs may be more effective than either drug alone.

In chemical aversion, a drug, for example disulphiram (Antabuse), is prescribed that produces unpleasant effects like flushing and nausea when alcohol is consumed. The threat of experiencing these symptoms is the basis of its effect. Interest in aversive techniques has declined over the years, with many doctors reluctant to prescribe a potentially unpleasant (and potentially fatal) procedure.

Relapse is associated with emotional states like boredom, anger and depression, with relationship conflicts and with social pressure to drink. To prevent it, people are taught to monitor any pessimistic thoughts and feelings, identify personal and social situations (avoiding usual haunts such as pubs) in which the risk of drinking is high, think afresh about life goals, and overcome the spiral of guilt, self-blame and return to uncontrolled drinking by finding constructive ways to deal with a temporary lapse.

Finally, Alcoholics Anonymous (AA), a worldwide social form of therapy, is regarded by many people as the foundation on which they have built a life of abstinence. Its Twelve Steps (see table below) give a philosophical direction as well as practical pointers to recovery and better daily living.

AA's Twelve Steps

1. We admitted we were powerless over alcohol—that our lives had become unmanageable.
2. Came to believe that a Power greater than ourselves could restore us to sanity.
3. Made a decision to turn our will and our lives over to the care of God as we understood him.
4. Made a searching and fearless moral inventory of ourselves.
5. Admitted to God, to ourselves, and to another human being the exact nature of our wrongs.
6. Were entirely ready to have God remove all those defects of character.
7. Humbly ask Him to remove our shortcomings.
8. Made a list of all persons we had harmed, and became willing to make amends to them all.
9. Made direct amends to such people wherever possible, except when to do so would injure them or others.
10. Continued to take personal inventory and when we were wrong promptly admitted it.
11. Sought through prayer and meditation to improve our conscious contact with God as we understood Him, praying only for knowledge of His will for us and the power to carry that out.
12. Having had a spiritual awakening as a result of these steps, we tried to carry this message to alcoholics, and to practice these principles in all our affairs.

The main value of AA is the strong bonds forged between its members, who maintain a strikingly cohesive network based on loyalty, responsibility and obligation. But there is a caveat—AA does not suit everyone in that it calls for a commitment to a strong philosophical position centring on spirituality.

Continuing controversy surrounds the question of 'controlled' drinking. Its supporters contend that for people unwilling to abstain completely, a level of safe drinking is achievable. This approach applies best to drinkers early in their 'careers', that is, before problems have become entrenched. The most appropriate intervention is along the lines of the FLAGS model outlined earlier. Feedback of the score on a screening test like AUDIT enhances motivation.

Setting limits is in accordance with World Health Organization guidelines, namely less than four standard drinks a day for men and less than two for women, and two alcohol-free days a week. Treatment also focuses on the person understanding situations that trigger hazardous drinking, developing strategies to avoid them, and planning in advance the amount to be consumed.

Benzodiazepines

In the 1960s, the benzodiazepines, a new class of tranquilliser drugs, looked set to revolutionise medical practice. They were remarkably effective in the treatment of anxiety, stress-related symptoms and insomnia and, unlike their predecessors (the 'nasty' barbiturates), seemed to be non-habit-forming. Millions of people were treated with the prototype—Valium (diazepam). I remember well the excitement shared by patients and medical profession alike. At last, a safe and effective tranquilliser. Alas, this proved yet another mirage in the chronicle of the search for the perfect drug for troubled minds. The medical profession and public only become aware of the addictive potential of the benzodiazepines when they began to hear horrific stories of 'Valium junkies' who suffered horrible symptoms on trying to get off them.

These symptoms were often mistaken for a recurrence of the original complaint, and so the vicious cycle of prescribing and dependence continued. Fortunately, scientific studies and adverse publicity then led to the realisation that the use of benzodiazepines should be restricted to brief periods where rapid relief of anxiety and insomnia was needed—for example, in the midst of a severe emotional crisis. Benzodiazepines are either short- (4–6 hours) or long-acting (8–12 hours). Continuous users experience a withdrawal syndrome that peaks from two days (short-acting) to seven days (long-acting). The main symptoms are anxiety, a sense of unreality, depression, irritability, insomnia, bodily aches, nausea and diarrhoea. Since epileptic fits occasionally occur during withdrawal, severely affected people may need to be hospitalised.

Life had never been the same for Margaret after she lost her husband from cancer ten years earlier, when she was 68. She had recovered from an episode of depression with antidepressants and supportive care, but had come to rely on the benzodiazepines her family doctor had prescribed for 'just a month' for her feelings of tension. They had been so helpful that she had persuaded him to repeat the prescription. A month ago, she visited her sister for a holiday but left the pills at home. Her sister had to call the doctor because Margaret had begun to feel 'unreal' and was racked with muscular aches and nausea.

To overcome dependence, people need to learn other ways to cope with anxiety and stress. Gradual weaning over 6 to 12 weeks is recommended. At the outset, a short-acting benzodiazepine is replaced by a long-acting one and its dose tapered over several weeks. In-patient detoxification is considered when high doses have been used, there is a past history of severe withdrawal or marked psychiatric disorder, or coexisting substance misuse is present. Anti-depressants are used in some cases, especially those with an anti-anxiety action. Relaxation training is recommended if a pre-existing anxiety disorder recurs. Self-help organisations like TRANX (Tranquilliser Recovery and New Existence) are similar to AA in their approach and provide a counselling service and support for benzodiazepine withdrawal.

Opiates

Opiates are among the most powerful drugs affecting the nervous system and have been of inestimable value for the relief of severe pain. But they have also been a source of horrendous misery for millions of people who have become hopelessly addicted. Heroin, morphine, pethidine and codeine are misused because of their euphoric and sedative effects and their ability to blunt emotional pain. Use of heroin, particularly intravenously ('shooting-up'), produces a 'rush' lasting minutes; it consists of euphoria, a sensation of warmth and a feeling in the lower abdomen resembling orgasm. A floating euphoria accompanied by a sense of tranquillity follows, lasting several hours depending on dose and blood level. Signs of dependence are visible injection sites and hardened veins, intoxication (for example, pin-point pupils) and characteristic withdrawal features (overwhelming craving, nausea, cramps, gooseflesh, sweating, restlessness, watery eyes and nasal congestion).

Abusers are mainly single men in their early twenties with a record of poor academic achievement and unstable employment. The socio-economically deprived are most vulnerable, with peer pressure, family history of drug abuse and childhood trauma being additional influences. Opiate addiction may result from treatment for severe pain. Appropriate prescribing of the painkiller imperceptibly merges into dependence, with the doctor sometimes unaware this is happening. A special problem is self-medication by doctors and their families.

Suzy was introduced to heroin by her boyfriend when she was 18. Along with friends, she had experimented with a number of drugs during adolescence. She found the high from heroin more pleasurable than anything she had experienced before. Within six months, she was injecting up to a gram a day. If she went without heroin for more than a few hours she would 'hang out severely', getting runny eyes and nose, aching muscles, abdominal cramps, sweating, irritability and poor sleep. All this went away when she used more heroin. Suzy's job as a waitress could not support her costly habit, so she began to earn extra money as a sex worker. One day she bought heroin that was much stronger than her previous supplies. She stopped breathing after injecting it, but survived the overdose only to return to heroin the following day.

Treating opiate dependence is not easy. People often receive help under legal pressure (or because of drug-related complications). They are best treated by a multi-disciplinary team used to the ups and downs of opiate abuse. Withdrawal takes two to three weeks. Follow-up emphasises relapse prevention, establishing membership of a healthy social group and securing a job. Self-help organisations such as Narcotics Anonymous (NA) may help in this process. Therapeutic communities that offer rehabilitation over several months stress the difficulty of developing a sense of responsibility and self-esteem. Since success depends on a major commitment, early dropout is unfortunately common.

There are two broad approaches: substitution and abstinence. Substitution therapy means taking indefinitely a drug that removes the craving for opiates and frees the person from the many troubles and dangers of securing their habit. Methadone is the favoured substitute opiate; it is made in the laboratory and has the advantage of simple administration as a daily, single oral dose. Treatment provides a breathing space for people to improve their physical, psychological and social wellbeing. The result is fewer deaths from overdose, and lower rates of HIV and hepatitis C infection. Opiate use becomes confined to a small part of the day, thus freeing up time for more meaningful pursuits. Should a lapse occur, high doses of methadone blunt heroin's euphoric effects, so that injecting heroin while on methadone is less likely to be reinforcing. Many people do well as long as they take the methadone but there is, tragically, a marked relapse rate once it is discontinued.

Substitution treatment is provided by methadone clinics, and family doctors, psychiatrists and other specialists with a special interest and training. Methadone is more effective in higher doses when the goal is maintenance for years rather than early abstinence, and as part of a program that encompasses treatment of existing psychiatric disorders and counselling to promote effective coping and adjustment.

Buprenorphine is an effective alternative to methadone, and safer in overdose because it is less likely to cause serious respiratory depression. Another advantage is the need to take it only every other day because of its long duration of action.

Treatment aimed at total abstinence entails detoxification followed by rehabilitation. Buprenorphine is most commonly used; diazepam is another option. Very rapid detoxification under anaesthetic or sedation is also available and is induced by administering a drug (naltrexone) that counteracts the effects of the opiate. Naltrexone may also be used to prevent relapse after detoxification is complete, but there are serious risks attached to its use if the person resumes injecting heroin. The drop-out rate with naltrexone is greater than with substitution therapies.

For the addicted person who has failed conventional therapies, continued injection of heroin under supervised medical conditions is being trialled in a few trail-blazing centres. Evidence is growing that reduced illicit drug use and crime, as well as improved psychosocial adjustment, can follow. Heated debate has accompanied this radical innovation, but in my view the matter is principally a pragmatic one. Can lives be saved and better outcomes accomplished when administration of heroin is supervised, compared to leaving the treatment-resistant addict to flounder?

Given that heroin use is associated with enormous costs in terms of drug-related problems, and that a quarter of heroin-dependent people die within ten to twenty years of active use, society is duty-bound to do whatever is within its reach and to remove ideologies from policy formation.

Stimulants

Three groups are abused: amphetamine and its derivatives, cocaine and prescribed stimulants. Amphetamines were once marketed as anti-depressants and appetite suppressants. Illicit use is now widespread among young people. The predominant form is methamphetamine, which is smoked, inhaled or injected. Ecstasy (MDMA) is an amphetamine derivative popular in the 'rave' scene due to the pleasant hallucinatory experience as well as its stimulant effects; these include euphoria, increased energy, enhanced sensual and perceptual experiences and a sense of closeness to others.

Cocaine was widely used in the early twentieth century in proprietary tonics and medicines. The modern epidemic of illicit cocaine use dates from the 1970s. It can be taken orally or injected but is frequently inhaled in the form of 'crack'. Desirable effects are euphoria, and increased libido, energy and alertness.

A person may emerge from a period of stimulant use feeling relatively normal but thereafter become irascible and moody. These symptoms often pave the way for another 'run' of stimulant, and so the vicious cycle repeats itself. As with alcohol, its disinhibiting effects may lead to accidents, violence and crime.

Stimulant abuse is often associated with psychiatric states including anxiety, panic attacks and mood disorders. Psychosis, however, is the most common complication. Paranoid ideas ranging from fleeting suspiciousness to delusions of persecution are prominent, together with auditory and visual hallucinations. Treatment follows the usual principles of substance abuse.

Jeff worked long hours rehearsing and playing in a band. He had suffered from low self-esteem since childhood, when he was constantly criticised by his alcoholic mother. He found that if he snorted speed, he had more energy and confidence to perform. One weekend he and his fellow musicians used a lot more speed than usual and Jeff became very suspicious that they wanted to kill him. The police were called after he tried to attack one of them. He was sedated and admitted to a psychiatric ward until his mental state returned to normal a few days later. He was told he had had a speed psychosis. He considered the advice to quit, but thought it impossible to keep away from amphetamines while active in the music scene.

Cannabis

Cannabis is the most popular recreational drug in developed countries; an estimated 3 per cent of young adults use it regularly, half of whom are likely to be dependent. The two most common forms are marijuana (leaves and flowers) and hashish (resin). Usually smoked, it produces a feeling of well-being, disinhibition and enhancement of the senses, lasting several hours. The withdrawal syndrome of insomnia, irritability, anxiety and sweating is relatively mild, not usually requiring treatment.

Long-term use may produce changes in memory, attention and integration of complex information. Although subtle, these changes may affect everyday functioning, particularly in adolescents already struggling with their studies and in adults whose jobs require a high level of mental aptitude.

Cannabis use may be associated with psychiatric symptoms including anxiety, a sense of unreality and paranoid delusions. An acute psychosis may occur but is usually short-lived—a matter of weeks. However, it may be indistinguishable in vulnerable people from schizophrenia. Cannabis is also a notable cause of relapse in established schizophrenia. Long-term use may produce diminished drive, apathy and deterioration in lifestyle. This improves greatly if the person remains drug-free for several months.

Hallucinogens

Thousands of naturally occurring hallucinogens have been identified, particularly in various species of mushroom (for example, mescaline, psylocibin) and nuts. Synthetic variants such as LSD (lysergic acid diethylamide) became popular in the 1960s. Their compulsive use is not common nowadays. A brief account cannot do justice to the variety of psychedelic experiences. Enhancement and distortion of all the senses may occur, as well as changes in the experience of space, time and body. Some users report spiritual experiences—an illumination of the meaning of life. It should come as no surprise, however, that hallucinogens produce hazardous effects—anxiety, a sense of unreality and marked mood changes. Some users may develop an acute psychosis with visual hallucinations. Occasionally, a psychotic illness resembling schizophrenia develops. Death has resulted from risk-taking behaviour based on delusional thinking—for example, that one can fly. The term 'flashback' refers to the return of psychedelic drug effects, which are experienced as unwanted and frightening. Because of the low potential for dependence, treatment is rarely sought for a psychedelic drug habit other than for bad 'trips', when the patient is placed in a quiet environment and 'talked down'.

Solvents

Commercial solvents derived from petrol or natural gas (glues, lacquers, paints, cleaning fluids and butane) are seen in sporadic outbreaks in schools and among poorly adjusted adolescents, particularly in isolated rural settings. They have similar effects to sedative drugs—drowsiness, dizziness, lack of coordination and perceptual distortions. Death may result from breathing difficulties or cardiac arrest, or as a result of bizarre, disinhibited behaviour. Treatment deals with the problems of the adolescent under-achieving at school and socially, and recommends healthier forms of recreation.

Polysubstance abuse

Certain patterns of abusing two or more drugs are common: alternating amphetamines (to boost energy at work) and alcohol or benzodiazepines (to calm down and recover from the stimulant effects), and combining substances to accentuate the effects of each (for example, alcohol and cannabis). A high prevalence of severe problematic personality and psychiatric problems is typical, including being the victim of all manner of abuse in childhood. Polysubstance abuse is a therapeutic challenge, as the case of Lenny below highlights. Establishing a therapeutic relationship and identifying goals are extraordinarily difficult to achieve. No pharmacotherapies or psychotherapies have proven of value. If there is a predominant substance abuse, treatment can be targeted to it. If abuse is indiscriminate, setting limits on behaviour (for example, in the parental home) reduces ill-effects on others. Harm reduction strategies are valuable, including the provision of sterile injections.

As a child, Lenny had continuing difficulties with his peers and suffered bouts of depression. He felt his five siblings were better treated by his parents, although his father was generally aloof and punitive. He began to use drugs as an adolescent following the suicide of his best friend, and had a protracted binge with alcohol and cannabis. Thereafter, he often drank to intoxication. In late adolescence, Lenny found that drinking alcohol and taking benzodiazepines created a powerfully reinforcing numbness. He began to inject heroin in his early twenties, through acquaintances in the music industry. He also took amphetamines to boost his energy levels but preferred benzodiazepines for their sedating effect. Although he had used drugs intravenously for ten years he denied needle sharing and was HIV negative.

He had made several attempts at rehabilitation, managing two years on a methadone program. At age 32, Lenny sought help following a car accident in which a good friend was killed. He began treatment in a residential therapeutic community, but following graduation after eighteen months he went on two alcoholic binges. Needless to say, his treating psychiatrist was not very hopeful that Lenny would benefit from any further initiatives.

Conclusion

It is a tragic reflection on our times that the international trade in illicit drugs is second only to that in armaments—hundreds of billions of dollars annually. At international, national and local levels, societies have struggled to curb the epidemic of substance abuse. No matter whether substance abusers are considered victims or criminals, their ultimate fate is dismal. While the cacophonous debate is endless, psychiatrists can but attempt to shed light on the nature of the addictions through careful research, as well as offer their best available treatments—if not to cure, at least to ameliorate.

If the picture for illegal drug use is bleak, then the alcohol scenario brings to mind the poet TS Eliot's remark, 'Man cannot tolerate too much reality'. Here too, the psychiatric profession is playing its part, particularly in striving to deal with the physical, psychological and social consequences.

William Hogarth's engraving of a scene in Bedlam, London's notorious asylum (from *The Rake's Progress*, 1735).

A lecture on hysteria by the French physician, Jean Martin Charcot (after a painting by Andre Brouillet, 1887, in the Musée de Nice).

The Bethlehem Royal Hospital, typical of the asylums in which psychiatry was born (an engraving by Robert White, c. 1700).

The 'gallery for women' in the Bethlehem Royal Hospital (from the *Illustrated London News*, 1860).

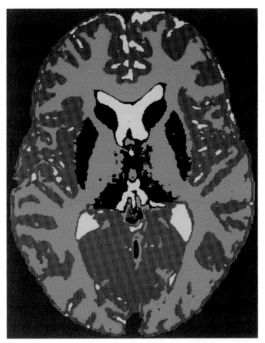

A magnetic resonance imaging (MRI) scan showing different areas of the brain (Mental Health Research Institute).

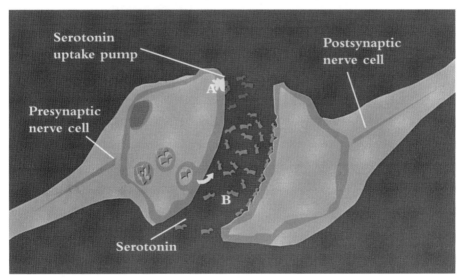

One group of anti-depressants, the SSRIs, acts by preventing the uptake pump (**A**) from removing serotonin from the synapse (the space between the nerve endings). The resulting higher concentration of serotonin in the synapse (**B**) leads to more of the chemical messenger reaching the postsynaptic nerve cell (Mental Health Research Institute).

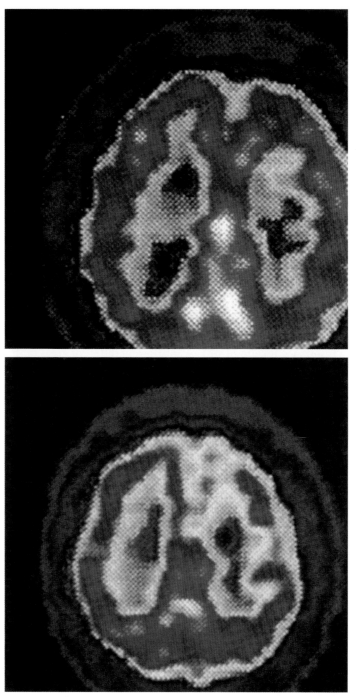

Good blood flow to the outer rim of brain tissue (red), shown in the top brain scan, contrasts clearly with the reduced blood flow (yellow) of a person with dementia in the scan below (Royal Melbourne Hospital Illustration Department).

Donna Lawrence (1973 –), *Untitled,* 2006 Cunningham Dax Collection

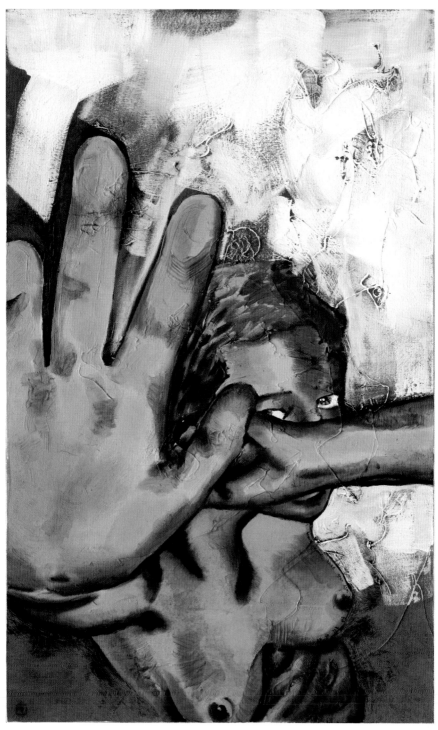

Donna Lawrence (1973 –), *Diagnose this*, 2005, Cunningham Dax Collection

Graeme Doyle (1947 –), *The Horse: 'A Poor Man's Guernica'* or *Landscape on Another Planet*, 1971/2000, Cunningham Dax Collection

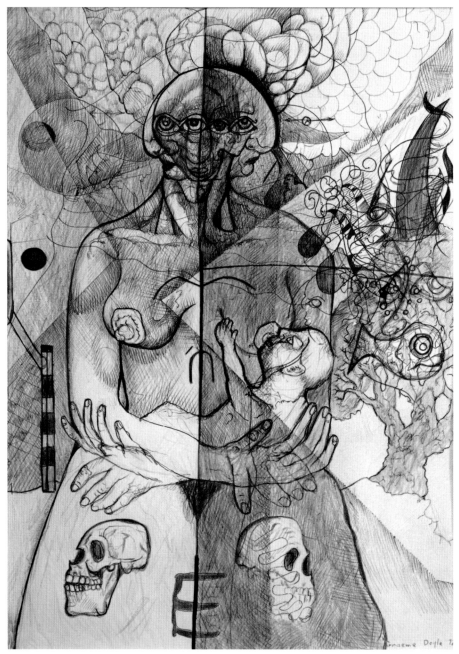

Graeme Doyle (1947 –), *Untitled*, 1978, Cunningham Dax Collection

Romy Dwosh (1978 –), *GEN, Eric,* 2007, Cunningham Dax Collection

Romy Dwosh (1978 –), *Serenity Breaking Down*, 2007, Courtesy of the artist

Julie Goodwin (1964 –), *Untitled*, 2001, Cunningham Dax Collection

Konrad Winkler (1948 –), *Julie,* 2000, Cunningham Dax Collection

Joan Rodriquez (1935 –), *Birth into Chaos,* 1987, Cunningham Dax Collection

Joan Rodriquez (1935 –), *The Vinegar Woman*, 1991, Cunningham Dax Collection

A painting by an 8-year-old-boy with severe anxiety. From the professional collection of Dr Julie Jones.

A drawing by a depressed 7-year-old-girl. From the professional collection of Dr Julie Jones.

Leah (1985 –), *My friend*, 2008, Cunningham Dax Collection

Gender Identity and Sexual Disorders

Sexual identity and sexual function are integral to the human experience. During the twentieth century the contribution of Freud, who brought sexuality into the human psychological arena, and the pioneering work of William Masters and Virginia Johnson in describing normal and abnormal sexual function, and the treatment of the latter, have helped to draw the subject into the medical sphere. Psychiatrists have contributed here in providing psychological understanding of problems that arise and in treating many of them—ranging from uncertainty about gender identity and disturbed sexual function to the so-called paraphilias (deviant sexual behaviour).

Gender identity

Gender identity is about the sense of being male or female. For most people, biological sex and gender identity are in harmony. Sexual development is shaped by both biological processes and environmental experiences, including family and social influences and cultural norms and expectations.

Problems may stem from clear biological abnormalities (for example, a child born with deformed genitalia), and early treatment can minimise long-term harm. Some children with gender dysphoria grow out of it or the features remain mild. At the other end of the spectrum, a person may be so convinced that he or she has been born the wrong sex that they seek a change to what feels natural (transsexualism). Transsexuals ultimately become so desperate that they see the only remedy as changing their gender through surgery. Before this drastic point, they may have tried to live a heterosexual life, but this is always unrewarding and ultimately abandoned. They may also have had homosexual relationships. Not surprisingly, most will be emotionally unstable and have personality difficulties. Most people are not operated on, either because their plight is not sufficiently convincing to doctors or because treatment facilities are unavailable. However, there is no doubt that many people have adapted well to their converted gender and live stable lives.

Pre-surgical evaluation is most rigorous, with candidates required to demonstrate they can live naturally and comfortably as the other sex for at least one to two years. They also have to undergo comprehensive psychiatric evaluation to confirm their suitability for this radical procedure. They need to be psychologically stable and willing to participate in a program of pre-surgical counselling. Hormone therapy may be introduced prior to surgery to promote physical changes.

Allen, aged 22, presented with a request for conversion surgery. Although raised as a boy, he had always felt uncomfortable, avoided rough and tumble play in preschool, and got out of playing contact sports during his school years. He had sought the company of girls and been rejected by boys for 'being a sissy'. In late adolescence he left his country town for the city, where he came into contact with the homosexual community and through them met other people like himself. He began taking illicitly obtained female hormone tablets and proceeded with electrolysis to remove facial hair. At interview he divulged that he had been dressing as a woman for a year and now wanted to start a new life as a woman.

A person who underwent sex realignment surgery most successfully is the celebrated British author Jan Morris, who writes in her book, *Conundrum*:

> But it all seemed plain enough to me. I was born in the wrong body, being feminine by gender but male by sex, and I could achieve completeness only when the one was adjusted to the other ... I believe the trans-sexual urge, at least as I have experienced it, to be far more than a social compulsion but biological, imaginative and essentially spiritual too. On a physical plane I have myself achieved, as far as is humanly possible, the identity I craved ... So I do not mind my continuing ambiguity. I have lived the life of a man, I now live the life of a woman, and one day perhaps I shall transcend both, if not in person, then perhaps in art. If not here, then somewhere else ...

Sexual dysfunction

Sexual dysfunctions may be lifelong or may arise after a period of normal functioning. They are generalised or situational (for example, involving only a specific sexual partner) and due to psychological, physiological or mixed causes. The most common problems in men are lowered sexual drive, difficulty in achieving or maintaining an erection and ejaculating prematurely. For women, they are lowered sexual drive, painful intercourse and inability to experience orgasm. Both men and women tend to present with overlapping difficulties. For example, a man with premature ejaculation may also have difficulty maintaining an erection. A woman may complain of lack of sexual drive as well as the inability to experience orgasm. These sorts of clinical pictures reflect their complex causes and call for individually tailored treatments.

Conditions affecting both men and women

Men and women with continuing or recurrent reduction or absence of sexual fantasies and desire for sexual activity may suffer marked distress. Cumbersomely named hypoactive sexual desire disorder is either biological in origin or occurs in the wake of stress, medical and psychiatric conditions (for example, depression and anxiety) or marital strife. Defining a precise cause can prove elusive.

George, a 42-year-old successful businessman, complained of loss of libido and of being unable to match his wife Liz's sexual interests. He felt that this was in part age-related but acknowledged that increasing pressure at work had taken his mind off sex. Sometimes, when he felt compelled to respond to Liz's sexual overtures, he had been unable to develop a firm enough erection. A key aspect in counselling this couple was to acquaint Liz with the biological reality that George's sex drive had waned relative to her own. The more he was stressed by domestic and business worries, the worse things would become. Relevant sexual education and a sensate-focus approach (see treatment section below) improved his performance substantially and boosted the frequency of sexual encounters.

Persistent or recurrent avoidance of sexual contact resulting in intense distress or interpersonal difficulties—sexual aversion—extends along a continuum from mild to severe. People may be squeamish about coming into contact with sexual fluids, experiencing them as messy; following sexual activity, they feel the need to cleanse themselves by showering. Disgust is associated with sexual interaction and appears to be ingrained. Treatment concentrates on strengthening non-sexual aspects of the relationship. Thereafter, if the couple genuinely desire it, the therapist arbitrates a sexual agreement on the frequency and type of sexual contact, nature and extent of foreplay and the use of condoms. A compromise of this kind allows the couple to engage in circumscribed sexual activities, which represents an improved quality of life.

An under-appreciated cause of aversion is homosexual, bisexual or auto-erotic orientation. A homosexual man, for instance, may marry in the belief that his sexual preference will change with heterosexual experience. His spouse may not have been aware of his homosexuality. Treatment rarely succeeds and most couples separate.

Dyspareunia, or genital discomfort on having sexual intercourse, leads to marked distress. Inadequate lubrication or insufficient stimulation by the partner may contribute in the case of women. Anxiety, anger, disgust or other negative emotions may inhibit arousal and result in painful intercourse even if stimulation is adequate. Men may fear impregnating their partner, contracting venereal disease or performing inadequately. Treatment requires an understanding of the potential dynamics so that they can be dealt with directly.

Conditions affecting women

Continuing inability to achieve or maintain an adequate response of sexual excitement, and delayed or absent orgasm following normal sexual excitement, are the principal sexual problems in women. Women vary greatly in the stimulation needed to trigger orgasm, and determining whether a diagnosis is appropriate or not is based on a judgement on what is reasonable in the light of a woman's age, sexual experience and adequacy of sexual stimulation.

Mary, aged 23 and married, had never experienced an orgasm with her husband Peter, although she was able to reach it through self-masturbation. Peter had told her she was abnormal and should get treated. Mary was exceedingly busy rearing two children aged eighteen months and five months, received negligible help from Peter and felt constantly exhausted. He had always had a much greater interest in sex than she had, indeed insisted on it every night. Intercourse was performed without foreplay, with Mary never fully aroused when Peter penetrated. The act rarely lasted more than minutes, insufficient for Mary to respond. She was invariably left 'high and dry' and felt immensely frustrated. The formulation as a guide to treatment of arousal and orgasmic dysfunction was based on inadequate foreplay, Peter's quick ejaculation, Mary's fatigue and the marital strain.

Vaginismus

When women with vaginismus are examined, the mere touch of the labia may produce spasm and pain. The entrance to the vagina may become so

constricted that it entirely prevents the entry even of the tip of a finger. The involuntary spasm may be induced by an admixture of fear (notably of pain), guilt and revulsion. Vaginismus is commonly traced to inadequate education and misconceptions about sex—that it is unhygienic, disgusting, for men only and painful. Women with severe vaginismus may also believe they have an underlying physical abnormality. They may present with non-consummation, the passive partner colluding unconsciously to maintain the sexual *status quo* (for example, virginity). Women may also use symptoms to control the relationship. It is equally true that it suits some men to be the underdog in psychological terms. Following a gentle vaginal examination to confirm the diagnosis, treatment consists of self-exploration by the woman to demonstrate the obvious patency of her vagina, followed by progressive dilatation using plastic bougies— by the patient or partner, preferably both. A good outcome is usual, although a level of discomfort may persist.

Conditions affecting men

The two main medical presentations in men are erectile dysfunction (impotence)—the failure to achieve an erection or maintain it until intercourse has ended—and problems with ejaculation, particularly premature ejaculation. We shall cover erectile dysfunction when discussing the case of Kevin below.

Problems with ejaculation

Premature ejaculation occurs with minimal sexual stimulation before, during or soon after penetration. It often occurs with a man's first attempt at intercourse or after a long period of abstinence. It may also develop after surgery or diseases affecting the genitalia, or be due to such psychological factors as anxiety and hidden hostility towards the partner.

Ed, aged 23, typically ejaculated within a minute of penetration, much to the dismay of himself and his partner. He had been prone to this with previous sexual partners. He was similarly brisk during self-masturbation. The most critical aspect in treating such premature ejaculation is the squeeze technique. The woman lightly grasps the tip of the penis and vigorously masturbates the partner until he feels he has almost reached the point of ejaculation. At this point he signals, and the partner interrupts the stimulation by squeezing the head of the penis for a few seconds. Providing the timing is right, which is achieved with practice, ejaculation is suppressed. Some loss of erection indicates that the method has been applied correctly. The process is repeated after about 25 seconds, and then several more times —over a 20-minute period. After using the technique for three weeks, Ed was able to defer ejaculation satisfactorily and the couple agreed that the time was right to attempt intercourse with his partner in the superior position. Following several minutes of alternate stimulation and squeezing, insertion was accomplished. Once Ed had become accustomed to the sensation of vaginal containment, he was able to start gentle thrusting at a depth and speed that delayed ejaculation for several minutes. If he felt he was losing control during this process, he withdrew rapidly but smoothly and his partner resumed squeezing until stability was restored.

For the person who fails to ejaculate at all, a rare phenomenon, the first step is to force emissions manually. Following intense activity to initiate arousal, direct penile manipulation by his partner is commenced. A moisturising cream helps to promote comfort during what is necessarily vigorous stimulation. In refractory cases, a vibrator may be applied. Once masturbatory ejaculations have become established, vaginal ejaculation may be considered. Again, the woman stimulates her partner using physical manipulation. When he approaches ejaculation, rapid insertion is accomplished by the woman guiding his penis. Pelvic thrusting is then started. She also provides other extra-genital caressing that her partner finds arousing. If emission does not occur, the man withdraws and vigorous masturbation resumes.

Treating sexual dysfunction

Optimal treatment requires the cooperation of both partners. If the person presenting with the dysfunction does not have a current partner, the therapist's opinion will necessarily be qualified and the treatment sub-optimal. The therapist sees each partner separately, then together. There is no place for evasion of delicate topics. Even if keep-off signs are posted, the therapist tactfully seeks sufficient detail to accurately understand the problem. Any relevant physical tests will be conducted.

Since most people with sexual dysfunction suffer a degree of apprehension, and anxiety is antithetical to pleasurable sexual activity, relaxation training—including deep breathing and visual imagery—is universal. These strategies are used before sexual engagement if anxiety is a major problem.

Optimal sexual stimulation combines psychological and physical stimuli that allow a person to respond erotically. No two people are alike sexually—what excites one may do little for another. Thus, the therapist seeks detailed information about the couple's sexual preferences.

Intercourse is initially prohibited. Instead, the couple are instructed to engage in mutual bodily pleasuring and to explore their erotic potential. No attempt is made to force arousal, since it is much more likely to occur if the man is relaxed and being stimulated by a caring partner. The couple start with non-sexual stroking of neck, arms and shoulders. As they accustom themselves to this they proceed to more sensuous caressing, which elevates sexual tension and leads to direct stimulation of erogenous zones. The watchword, however, is 'gradual'. The couple is advised to convey their preferred needs to each other. With evidence of strong sexual arousal (good erection in the man and lubrication and swelling in the woman), they allow this to wax and wane by modulating stimulation. The concern that, once aroused, intercourse must follow automatically is thus countered. Sexual arousal is enhanced by judicious use of fantasy and by stimuli such as photographs, music, perfumes and vibrators. These are broached only with a delicate understanding of the sensibilities of the partners. Progress is appraised during the course of therapy and, if favourable, new targets are set.

Relevant sexual information is provided to rectify any erroneous beliefs, and to fill in any gaps resulting from inadequate education during adolescence. Counselling comprises reassurance, explanation and encouragement. Failures are analysed and counter-measures prescribed.

Treating erectile dysfunction

Kevin, aged 44, has been unable to develop and maintain an erection. He has noted a progressive decline in his libido over five years, has fewer sexual fantasies and a reduced wish for intercourse. He requires more intense stimulation to achieve a full erection and sex is not at all pleasurable. Under considerable pressure since his promotion to manager, he has been overworking, having many late nights and drinking excessively. The sexual problem emerged when at his wife's insistence he made a half-hearted attempt at intercourse, which failed. He then experienced severe performance anxiety. Anticipating failure, he tried too hard; his erections were ill-formed and penetration difficult. Latterly, he has been avoiding sex at all costs. Feeling humiliated, he has been unable to discuss this with his wife. She has wondered if there is another woman. Communication has all but ceased and their relationship is at a low ebb.

A tailor-made treatment plan for Kevin would incorporate relevant aspects of the relaxation strategies, counselling and sexual stimulation just described.

For ageing men especially, where psychological factors are minimal, drugs like sildenafil and tadalafil that promote genital response may be of considerable benefit. A successful response confirms the functional capacity of penile blood vessels. Failure suggests a vascular or neurological cause; special investigations may be carried out to check this possibility.

The paraphilias (sexual deviations)

Controversy surrounds the question of what constitutes normal sexual behaviour. Is sexual behaviour that differs from socially acceptable norms abnormal? Where should the limits of such norms be drawn and by whom? Should variations from what is regarded as normal necessarily be labelled as deviant?

Debate about these issues is highly charged—as is clear in the changed medical and social attitude towards homosexuality since the 1960s. Homosexuality was categorised as a paraphilia until the early 1970s when, through professional consensus, it was deleted from psychiatric classifications. The only person I ever treated was five years prior to the change when a student in his mid-twenties was 'strongly advised' by the police, who had found him 'loitering' around a popular homosexual rendezvous, to undergo treatment. He arrived most reluctantly at our clinic in the belief that he would be charged unless he complied with the police. On the other hand, he was perplexed about his sexual orientation although felt that he was in all likelihood a 'natural homosexual'. A psychologist on our team unhesitatingly recommended behavioural treatment.

And so it was that we launched a program in which he was administered mild electric shocks on viewing slides of homosexual scenes but was spared the same when viewing heterosexual ones. At the end of treatment neither of us were persuaded that anything had changed although I assumed that I had fulfilled my professional responsibility as best I could. Today, I shrink back with horror on recalling the role I played. But then I was applying a new treatment that at the very same time was reported on by John Bancroft, a leading expert at Oxford University, in the prestigious *British Journal of Psychiatry*. Seven of his series of ten homosexual men had changed their attitudes 'significantly', justifying the use of an 'inherently unpleasant method'.

The concept of a person feeling uncomfortable or disturbed with his or her sexual orientation is still included in psychiatric classifications, although arguments prevail about whether or not it should be.

The main feature of the paraphilias, which occur almost exclusively in men and have their origin in childhood or adolescence, is an intense, lifelong sexual urge and fantasy involving either non-human objects or the suffering and humiliation of the person—their partner, children or other non-consenting people. Paraphilias reflect an intensity of certain aspects of normal sexuality or a grossly inappropriate choice of sexual object. If a person has acted on one of these urges or is distressed by thinking about them, then the diagnosis of a psychiatric disorder is appropriate. The sexual acting-out declines with age but the related fantasies may continue.

We need to remember that human beings may harbour a rich fantasy life without corresponding action. For most people, such fantasies accompany normal sexual arousal.

Behaviour of this kind may not be harmful to the person or to others, except, crucially, in relation to psychological and sexual risks, especially for children. Some cases of paedophilia physically harm children through penetration or in the course of restraining them. The level of emotional harm in the victim is extremely high. Murder for sexual gratification, particularly serial killing, has a morbid fascination for the public, as reflected in the popularity of films and books like *The Silence of the Lambs.*

The paraphilias take many forms, including exhibitionism, voyeurism, fetishism, cross-dressing, frotteurism, paedophilia and sadism. Other types of unusual sexual behaviour occur—especially centring on self-stimulation—but we do not know how often since most of it takes place privately and, if not distressing, may never come to professional attention. More than one paraphilia may occur in the same person, indicating a more complex psychological disturbance. By definition, a sexual impulse is involved in the paraphilias, but other motives may drive the behaviour. An exhibitionist, for instance, may expose his genitalia in his contempt for women or to gain a sense of exhilaration. Understanding these putative motives is part of optimal treatment.

Exhibitionism is a relatively common paraphilia, occurring mostly in men in their twenties. It takes the form of penile exposure to strangers, perhaps accompanied by masturbation or spontaneous orgasm during or after the event. Typically, no further sexual activity is attempted, as the person's wish is not to make physical contact but to be seen. Victims are usually female, both children and adults. Although many incidents involve passive, sexually inhibited males, this is by no means the rule.

Voyeurism, which often accompanies exhibitionism, is the observation of unsuspecting women either naked or engaging in sexual activity, or in the context of excretory functions. The person experiences intense sexual gratification, perhaps explaining why he may go to great lengths to achieve his ends.

Fetishism involves the use of non-living objects for sexual arousal, commonly women's clothing. Underclothing, shoes, and occasionally rubber or plastic items, are favoured. The objects are used for masturbatory purposes or, less commonly, to enhance conventional sexual behaviour. Cross-dressing is part of a complex pattern of deviant sexual behaviour. It can also be a feature of a gender identity problem like transsexualism.

Frotteurism concerns men deriving gratification from touching and rubbing their genitals against anonymous, unsuspecting women in crowded places or from touching their breasts and buttocks.

Paedophilia refers to sexual activity with pre-pubescent children by an adult. Particularly in the case of girls, a male friend of the family or a relative, rather than a stranger, is commonly involved. But strangers are more frequent in the homosexual situation. Such behaviour may be a product of relationship, marital or sexual problems within a family, often associated with substance abuse. Behaviour involves fondling, having the child touch the genitalia, and masturbation; attempts at penetration vary with the age of the child.

Sadism covers acts in which inflicting psychological or physical suffering is sexually exciting. In *masochism*, the person is humiliated, beaten, bound or otherwise suffers to achieve sexual gratification.

A core reflection of the person with a paraphilia is: 'I don't understand why I do these things. After each lapse, I feel guilty and remorseful and vow never do it again; but I begin to fantasise, I succumb, and the cycle repeats itself'.

The cause of all paraphilias is unknown but likely to include genetic and environmental factors. The latter may be encountered incidentally. For example, a virginal boy is seduced by an older sibling or adult; an adolescent with a burgeoning sex drive experiments with a younger boy or allows himself to be engaged by an older, experienced man or woman; an older adolescent with sexual experience imitates pornographic acts seen on the internet or at a strip club. Only a fraction of those subjected to these experiences become paraphilic, possibly because they are genetically predisposed and because robust reinforcers, including intense sexual pleasure, override inhibitory forces such as guilt, remorse and fear of detection.

Paraphilias, especially those with acting-out manifestations, may present with concurrent psychiatric disorders such as substance abuse and personality disorder. These may exacerbate the paraphilia and require treatment in their own right.

In the developed world, several paraphilias (for example, paedophilia and exhibitionism) are unlawful, and those who practise them come to clinical attention only following criminal conviction or as part of a probation order. Very few men with paraphilia seek treatment before offending; indeed, the behaviour may have continued for years before any criminal prosecution is initiated. Most men probably wish to continue to pursue their sexual preferences regardless of whether they are breaking the law. Only a few are motivated by guilt and the need for expiation and seek help accordingly. An even smaller number is compelled to obtain help by partners who can no longer cope.

Since the paraphilias are not ultimately curable, treatment depends on the needs of the specific person—for example, to reduce the chances of reoffending, improve symptoms, promote self-control and treat any coexisting psychiatric condition.

Risk management consists in identifying high-risk situations; for instance, convicted men with paedophilia are prohibited from accessing children and pornography, or a recalcitrant exhibitionist may be barred from beaches and public parks. The ultimate societal control is imprisonment, which is usually imposed for paedophilic offences on the grounds of public safety and deterrence.

Anti-testosterone hormonal drugs to diminish libido have been used for many years as a substitute to surgical castration in treating those with a high sex drive and limited self-control who have sexually offended. Their effectiveness has been shown in a number of studies but they may have to be prescribed indefinitely to reduce the rate of relapse.

Convicted sex offenders in some jurisdictions are compelled to participate in group therapy, the most common form of psychotherapy used in the prison setting. Core group therapeutic factors are the offender taking responsibility for his actions, learning how to empathise with the victim, and developing genuine motivation to change or, at least, to learn strategies to control anti-social behaviour. Group therapy is effective in reducing recidivism, albeit modestly. Many other forms of psychotherapy have been tried, with equivocal results

Family support is pivotal, and the outlook is better when the offender's family remains intact. So intervention is designed to improve family cohesion and to reduce problems in relationships that may trigger the paraphiliac behaviour.

Generally speaking, the results of treatment are uncertain. Evaluating the benefits is tricky, particularly as self-reports are unreliable (their accuracy does improve substantially when confidentiality is assured).

CHAPTER 14

Children and Adolescents

Alas, it is a myth that childhood is the happiest time of one's life. In fact, many children will, at some time, have troubled minds. Child and adolescent psychiatry, a sub-specialty of psychiatry that deals with these children, is distinctive in the following ways.

- The huge changes during childhood and adolescence mean that what passes as normal behaviour at one point may be seen as disturbed behaviour at another. For example, distress on being separated from familiar caregivers is normal in toddlers and common in children starting school, but absence from school in an older child may point to a form of anxiety warranting professional intervention.
- Children's dependence on their family evolves throughout childhood, with infants entirely reliant for survival, whereas adolescents are in transition between the family-based child and the young autonomous adult.
- Children rarely seek professional help for themselves. Usually they are brought by concerned parents or teachers. While all parents worry at some time about their child's behaviour or development, most do not seek assistance. Either the problem passes or they are reassured by the advice of family and friends. If the problem is severe or persists, parents may consult the family doctor or other relevant health service, but only occasionally a mental health specialist.

About one in seven children and adolescents (for convenience I shall refer to them all as children) experiences psychological problems that are beyond what we may call the ordinary trials and tribulations of growing up. The rate is higher in low income families. Before mid-adolescence, boys are more affected than girls, and city more than country children; those with a chronic physical illness are more vulnerable, particularly if the brain is involved or if they are intellectually disabled. There is usually no identifiable physical cause for psychiatric disorders in children. Even though we are finding relevant genetic and biological factors in certain conditions, treatment is mainly psychological rather than pharmacological. Parent counselling, family therapy and individual psychotherapy are the mainstays. Medication has a prominent role in certain conditions. Worryingly, only one in four children with mental health problems receives professional help. There is therefore a huge unmet need, one that society needs to be most concerned about.

Clinical problems fall into three broad groups:

- developmental—psychological growth is derailed; for example, intellectual retardation, autism and specific distortions or delays of speech or language;
- emotional—more common in girls and manifesting as anxiety or depression or indirectly as a bodily dysfunction, usually in the domains of eating, toileting or sleep;
- behavioural—much more common in boys, and taking the form of disruptive, defiant and anti-social conduct.

Many children have mixed emotional and behavioural presentations; the combination is particularly common among the intellectually disabled.

The critical role of development

The most dramatic changes in our lives take place between birth and early adulthood. The first three years sees the most rapid development in motor, language and intellectual skills. Play, creativity and use of symbols begin, accompanied by a growing sense of physical, personal and sexual identity. From birth, an infant can attend, perceive and respond to the environment through behaviour and expression of emotion. The responsiveness powerfully triggers adult reactions—both love and caring, and negative emotions like distress and anger. Attachments to individual caregivers develop at around 4–6 months. Young children up to about five are the most vulnerable to family disruption and experiences of separation.

Temperament is a crucial factor determining how a child relates to the environment. We define temperament in infants as being consistent patterns of response to themselves and to their world, whether of activity, persistence, emotional responsiveness, fearfulness or sociability. Infants with troublesome temperaments are more likely not to fit well with their parents' expectations of the ideal child. It should come as no surprise that it is these children who may be brought to psychiatrists with emotional problems or disturbed behaviour. As boys develop more slowly than girls and tend to be temperamentally more unsettled, they are more likely to have these difficulties.

Adolescence is at the other end of this time of great change. Opinions vary as to when it starts—at about ten years, or coinciding with either puberty or with the start of secondary school. The transition from adolescence to young adulthood is also ill-defined. In developed countries the long period of post-secondary education means that young people are often dependent on their parents well into their twenties. However, they become adults in the eyes of the law on their eighteenth birthday.

Contrary to popular opinion, most children negotiate their adolescence without major emotional turmoil. However, they do experience a range of intense feelings and their mood is often changeable. It is a time of marked transition that affects all areas of life. In his classic book *Childhood and Society*, Erik Erikson, an eminent psychoanalyst, described the core task as being to establish a sense of identity—awareness of one's separate and unique existence, and a sense of belonging to, and identifying with, a family, peer group, society and culture.

Physical and psychological changes are profound. In general, adolescents are not daunted by their emerging sexuality and enjoy the associated bodily changes and intimate relationships. The key intellectual developments are the ability to think in abstract terms, to generalise from experience and to appreciate the past and future. This often leads young people to challenge the beliefs and practices of their parents' generation.

About one-third of children move through adolescence smoothly, supported by good peer and family relationships. About half have periods of purposeful activity alternating with withdrawal, a tendency to become angry easily and to blame others. These adolescents are less confident and more prone to depression and anxiety. Concern over emerging sexuality hinders the development of their sexual relationships or, less commonly, leads to promiscuity. Their families are more likely to be affected by illness, parental conflict and divorce.

Serious turmoil with anti-social behaviour affects about a fifth of adolescents and is more common in poorer families and in those with parental mental illness and marital tension. Conflict with parents, low self-esteem, anxiety and depression are common. These adolescents often do less well academically, begin sexual relationships early, have difficulty forming stable friendships and struggle to develop a secure identity. A history of tumultuous development is often found among adolescents who later develop psychiatric, personality and social problems (such as homelessness).

Development and clinical problems—the example of divorce

The case of divorce illustrates clearly how, in children facing the same stress, psychological problems may reveal themselves in many ways according to the child's stage of development.

Divorce is experienced by many children, given that it is the fate of up to a third of Western marriages. Significant stress factors for children are the preceding marital disharmony, the actual separation and its effects. After divorce, the child's stage of development greatly influences the experience of loss. Preschool children (3–5 years) may be confused about what has happened and preoccupied with fears of abandonment by the other parent. They may regress, behaving like much younger children; there may also be angry outbursts or demands for attention.

After her father left the marriage Lucy, aged 3, began wetting and soiling despite being fully toilet-trained. At times her speech was unclear. Her mother described tantrums and clinging to her 'like a shadow'. She became difficult at bedtime, screaming when her mother left the room and needing her to return repeatedly before falling asleep.

Young school-age children (6–8 years) may be extremely sad, feel torn by divided loyalties and yearn for their parents to be together again. They may also fear abandonment and neglect and blame one parent for the other's departure.

Con, aged 6, seemed unaware of his parents' unhappy marriage and his father's many affairs. His father had left for another woman after a failed attempt at marital therapy. Con stopped playing at home and school, sitting gloomily alone. His schoolwork deteriorated sharply. When his mother found him hiding biscuits, he said he would need food when she also left. When reassuring Con that she was staying with him, he lashed out, crying: 'No, you should go away, because you made my daddy leave; then he can come back'.

Older school-age children (9–12 years), being more mature cognitively and socially, can be more detached but may deal with their insecurity by aligning with one parent against the other, particularly when the latter finds a new partner.

Danny, aged 11, was a sullen youngster whose school progress was declining and who refused to see his father. The separation was instigated by his mother.

At first they had a cooperative arrangement for his care, but this broke down when his father found a new partner. Danny angrily commented on this new relationship, which he felt meant that he and his mother were no longer wanted.

Adolescents (13–18 years) may find that divorce raises concerns about their own future relationships. Older adolescents may make a mature appraisal of their parents' situation but their anger may take the form of moral outrage. The experience may lead to disrupted emotional development or maladaptive patterns of behaviour, even delinquency.

Mario, aged 18, asserted that he could handle his parents' separation and divorce and the skirmishes that ensued because he was older than his sister and had developed a life of his own. He had shared with his girlfriend a fear that he himself might divorce one day, and his bitter disappointment in his parents. He was highly critical of his parents, who he thought were acting irresponsibly, especially when they quarrelled. He went on to express his anger indirectly by petty thieving and rebellious behaviour in the classroom.

How do child psychiatrists carry out their job?

The vast majority of child psychiatrists apply the biopsychosocial framework we discussed in Chapters 2 and 4.

The biological dimension focuses on the child's birth and developmental history, any previous illnesses or current physical symptoms, and relevant evidence of psychiatric disorder in other family members. Physical examination and investigations may be necessary, depending on the particular problem. For example, a child whose problem is bed-wetting may always have wet the bed or only after a recent stress. While the child is most unlikely to have a urinary infection or kidney dysfunction, these possibilities can be readily excluded by simple tests in order to set the minds of parents (and psychiatrist!) at rest. By contrast, a child with behavioural and learning problems who is 'going blank' several times a day would need more complex neurological tests to exclude a serious condition like epilepsy.

The psychological dimension is concerned with the child's emotional state and cognitive abilities. The psychiatrist usually assesses these through direct observation and by asking parents and teachers for their views. The child's ability to relate to the interviewer, response to separation from the parents and current mood are all revealing. Younger children in particular may encounter difficulty telling others, even their parents, that they are anxious or unhappy. The psychiatrist therefore uses a number of indirect approaches—particularly drawing (say, of a good and a bad dream) and play—to encourage children to share feelings and experiences. Many children find it easier to tell a story at one remove—that is, to tell how an imagined child may behave or feel in a situation that resembles their own. Inviting a child to describe their three worst fears or make three wishes is usually most informative, as seen in the case of Mary.

Aged 8, Mary had frequent tummy aches and was missing school as a result. Given three wishes, the first was that her mother would stop worrying so much about her younger sister, who was intellectually disabled. This turned out to reflect a continuing concern about her mother's wellbeing and the translation of this anxiety into the physical pain. Her second wish was that her parents would stop bickering, and the third that the whole family would go on a wonderful cruise.

Older children and adolescents are offered the chance to be seen on their own as well as with their parents. This is often the only way to explore sensitive subjects such as sexual abuse, suicidal thoughts and pregnancy, and also conveys a message that the psychiatrist is vitally interested to hear what the adolescent has to say. He or she is asked if there is anything they would not wish to have discussed with their parents, but the limits of confidentiality are stipulated, since risk of harm to oneself or to others and certain illegal activities cannot be kept secret.

The psychiatrist may learn about the child's cognitive development from school reports and consultation with teachers. In addition, by the simple task of the child drawing a person, their mental age, from 3 to 13, can be adequately calculated. If the child has considerable problems with learning and academic achievement, a child psychologist can be asked to assess specific cognitive abilities needing special attention. The accurate diagnosis of a specific learning difficulty such as dyslexia ideally leads to remedial teaching and relief of associated emotional difficulties. Deterioration in schoolwork may also signify serious underlying psychiatric problems.

The social dimension mainly involves looking at how the family might be triggering or maintaining the child's difficulties. For example, marital conflict, domestic violence and anti-social behaviour in other family members often have a bearing on a child who has been truanting from school. The psychiatrist asks the parents about their own experiences in their families of origin, since these may continue to affect their own parenting abilities. Of central relevance is the state of the marriage, especially disharmony, conflict or separations. In meeting the family as a group, the psychiatrist can observe interactions between the participants at many levels.

Broader social circumstances are also examined. Cultural factors may, for example, affect adolescents from a particular ethnic background; they may be torn between their parents' values and those of their peers. These issues may be less obvious but just as pertinent for adolescents at odds with the values of their friends on matters like smoking, drugs and sexual behaviour.

The case of Paul illustrates how the psychiatrist has need to consider an array of developmental and family factors.

A lanky 12-year-old, Paul has suffered recurrent headaches over several months. The family doctor cannot detect any physical basis for the symptom although abdominal migraine is a remote possibility, given a family history of it. Paul did not prompt the request for medical help but was brought by his mother because she had felt thoroughly exhausted and demoralised. He had started high school several months earlier.

Might the symptoms be a reaction to the stress of entering this new, unfamiliar environment? Have the parents' fundamentalist religious beliefs contributed to his anxiety on moving from a church to a secular school? Has his mother's depression or the growing parental conflict or his father's outbursts of anger had adverse effects on his psyche? Could his father's abuse of alcohol be compounding the already stressful family atmosphere and reinforcing a sense of duty in Paul to come to his mother's aid? The needs of two younger brothers might be making it difficult for Paul to seek his mother's care other than when they are playing with their friends.

Symptoms of distress when apart from his mother might not be new. Paul may have felt separation anxiety when he entered kindergarten, recurring at stressful times such as when his father was severely injured in a car accident. We can see readily the wide range of possible causes of Paul's pain, and how the inquiry is necessarily far-reaching to establish the nature of the presenting problems and to obtain a picture of the child's development in the context of overall family functioning. Two other areas are pertinent: the type of temperament in the child, with emphasis on responsiveness, irritability and impulsivity, and details of any psychiatric problems in the nuclear and extended family.

Classifying psychiatric problems

Diagnosing children with a mental illness, when individual development and family and social circumstances vary so much, is problematic. Moreover, difficulties are often situational or improve as the child matures. Little is known about the causes of most disorders, in contrast to risk factors and associated circumstances such as socio-economic status. Finally, some diagnoses have limited implications for treatment since their effectiveness is not yet established (for example, conduct disorder). Nevertheless, classification is essential for communication between professionals, to research causality and natural history, and to clarify response to treatment.

Psychiatric conditions in children have been mapped out in the classifications of the World Health Organization and American Psychiatric Association and are periodically revised. Several caveats prevail in their use by clinicians. Firstly, problems are seen in the context of normal development, i.e. what is common for 1-year-olds can be maladaptive for 7-year-olds (for example, nocturnal bed-wetting, separation anxiety). Secondly, disorders are often about a failure to achieve developmental milestones. The difference therefore between normality and disorder is less clear-cut than in adult psychiatry. Finally, symptoms may be diagnosable because of their intensity or persistence; temper tantrums are common in preschoolers, but deemed problematic only if they occur frequently, are of long duration and lead to functional impairment. With the exception of certain developmental disorders, discrete conditions are difficult to identify in infants. During preschool and primary school years, symptoms and disorders become clearer with age.

Conditions are divided into the following broad groups: emotional (for example, depression); disruptive (for example, conduct disorder); elimination (for example, functional enuresis); developmental (for example, autism); and so-called adult disorders that can start in childhood or adolescence (for example, anorexia nervosa, substance abuse, schizophrenia, bipolar).

PROBLEMS OF INFANCY AND EARLY CHILDHOOD (0–5 YEARS)

Social functioning evolves rapidly during the first three years, paralleling language development. At eight weeks babies respond to any face with smiling and eye contact. By six months this response is specific to the main caregivers, usually mothers and other family members, who then assume particular significance for older babies and mobile toddlers. At times of distress, hunger, illness or separation, it is to these persons that children look for comfort. These attachment figures also facilitate children's exploration of the environment. Disruption of these ties can have a profound emotional effect resulting in detachment or anxious over-attachment. Together with these interpersonal developments, the child's self-concept begins to evolve.

Infants differ considerably in terms of temperament—some are regular in their feeding and sleeping habits, placid and easy to soothe ('easy' temperament); others are just the opposite ('difficult' temperament). These qualities have long-term implications. For instance, 'difficult' infants make much greater demands on caregivers, which they may not be able to satisfy.

Problems in the first five years tend to reflect a disturbed infant–caregiver relationship or are developmental or organic in nature. For instance, a poor fit between the infant's and caregiver's personalities can generate a spiralling dysfunctional interaction, increasing both infant and maternal distress. The most common problems seen are disturbances of bodily functions such as sleeping, eating and elimination, and those that are more pervasive like autism. In all these instances, the psychiatrist pays close attention to parental functioning. Maternal depression is one noteworthy example, which during the first year after birth affects women directly as well as the rest of the family and is often an unrecognised factor in feeding, sleeping and temperamental problems in young babies.

Sleep disturbances

About one in ten children under school age has disturbed sleeping, and half of these have associated behavioural difficulties. Typically the child cannot get off to sleep, has a disrupted sleep pattern including nightmares, night terrors, sleepwalking, insomnia or, occasionally, too much sleep. Nightmares are common in the years before school and are in fact anxiety dreams. Night terrors, experienced by 3 per cent of young children, involve intense fear, screaming and an appearance of being awake but with no memory of it. Sleep-walking takes place in about 15 per cent of children and is more likely at times of stress—the child who is in a trance-like state for up to half an hour clumsily moves about and may say things that make no sense.

Poor sleepers are either children with family problems such as maternal depression and marital conflict or those who are biologically vulnerable, with a history of birth difficulties, developmental complications, awkward temperament and over-activity. Treatment ranges from attending to under-lying problems, like family tension, to introducing predictable bedtime routines and modifying behaviour by not responding to infant cries and gradually spending less time at the child's bedside.

Feeding and eating battles

Struggles between parent and child around feeding are common enough, beginning in the second or third year. When the child is temperamentally unstable and/or the parent is intolerant of normal displays of self-will (part of the toddler's new sense of independence), the scene is set for a continuing war between distraught parent and defiant child.

Newborn premature babies have particular eating difficulties, and up to a third of them require several weeks of nasogastric or intravenous feeding. As they lack practice in swallowing and sucking, they will resist taking food by mouth. A more unusual condition is pica, which is the persistent eating of non-food substances such as soil—often associated with mental retardation or parental neglect. Prolonged ingestion of substances like paint, hair or grass may cause poisoning or intestinal obstruction.

Bladder and bowel disturbance

All children lose control of bladder or bowel function intermittently, but occasionally it persists and is a matter of concern to both parent and child. Psychiatrists can help by pinpointing what is happening.

Children who have no physical disorders like urinary infection or diabetes, and who wet their bed or clothes, day or night, at least twice a month when aged 5–6 years, and once a month when older, are said to have functional enuresis. Primary enuresis is a developmental problem in which the child has never been dry for a long period. It is not usually associated with emotional or behavioural problems but distresses both child and family. Like most developmental problems, it occurs more often in boys. There may be a genetic predisposition, given that a family history of wetting is common. Secondary enuresis is wetting that follows a period of urinary control of a year or longer. It is often linked to disruptive family and life events, and accompanied by emotional and behavioural difficulties.

The psychiatrist makes a full inquiry, including a physical examination and urine testing. Behavioural treatment using a pad-and-bell alarm is most effective, particularly when a star-chart gives positive reinforcement. Parents help the child to use the toilet when the alarm goes off and reset it after changing the bed. Treatment continues until there has been a month of dry nights. Desmopressin, a synthetic variant of anti-diuretic hormone, is effective in the short term but is associated with a high relapse rate.

A similar disorder of bowel function is called functional encopresis. The repeated passing of faeces into inappropriate places like clothing may be voluntary or involuntary. Encopresis occurs in 1 per cent of 5-year-olds, and is much more common in boys. It is often due to overflow incontinence resulting from chronic constipation, which may be associated with a diet low in fibre and high in sugar. When parent and child are locked in a battle of the bowel, encopresis may follow. A punitive parental response undermines the child's desire to cooperate and increases fear of defecation. Frequently, there are disturbed family dynamics. Some encopretic children have low self-esteem and poor social skills, but these are usually due to the soiling, which causes acute embarrassment. Once organic problems are excluded, treatment focuses on achieving regular defecation. This involves rewards for sitting on the toilet at specified times, a high-fibre diet (associated with judicious use of laxatives if needed) and parental guidance to guard against negative reactions towards soiling.

Attachment problems

The normal bonding between parent and child, particularly between mother and child, may run off course, resulting in a clinging dependency or its more puzzling opposite—what child psychiatrists call reactive attachment disorder. In the 'inhibited' group, the infant consistently fails to respond to social cues such as following faces or playing games like pat-a-cake or peek-a-boo. These children are withdrawn and apathetic, showing little spontaneity or curiosity, and may show self-absorbed behaviour such as rocking and head-banging. Play skills and language development may be delayed. In the 'disinhibited' group, the child may be too friendly and show affection indiscriminately, including towards strangers. These behaviours is typically a response to inadequate care, where the child's physical and emotional needs have been neglected by parents or there have been repeated changes in caregivers (for example, many foster-home placements). The child may fail to grow and gain weight in response to marked distortions in the child–parent relationship. Reactive attachment disorder may be so severe as to be confused with mental retardation or autism.

Jack was an affectionate toddler who enthusiastically greeted every new adult entering the paediatric ward. He showed no preference for his mother, who did not visit often. He was in hospital for investigation of his failure to thrive, and at the time of admission had cigarette burns on both hands. A diagnosis of reactive attachment disorder secondary to parental abuse was made.

In treating these children, the aim is to provide care appropriate to their development and protective measures to ensure their safety. Assistance with parenting, including joint treatment in a mother–infant unit, may be necessary. Sometimes, however, the child must be removed from parental care before work with the family can begin. This intervention is crucial because of the possibility of long-term consequences, the most serious of which is the tendency for these children to reproduce their experience when rearing their own children, despite all their good intentions.

Autism

More common in boys than girls, so-called pervasive developmental disorder is a serious condition characterised by disturbed verbal and non-verbal communication, social interaction and play behaviour. It is usually associated with some intellectual disability. Autism, first identified by Leo Kanner in 1943, is the most common form. Asperger's syndrome is the label reserved for cases in which language and intellectual skills are within the normal range (named after Hans Asperger, who described it in the 1940s). The question of whether autism and Asperger's are two distinct conditions or part of the same spectrum remains unclear. In autism the core features usually manifest before the child's third birthday:

- delayed and abnormal language and speech (e.g. constantly repeating the same phrases);
- impaired social responsiveness—children are seemingly aloof and avoid eye contact;
- ritualistic behaviour (e.g. rocking, head-banging, pacing up and down);
- intolerance of change;
- limited ability to play creatively.

Parents of autistic children were once described as cold and unresponsive, leading to the child's failure to form social relationships. Indeed, Kanner unjustifiably and cruelly labelled them refrigerator parents. If a parent does lack warmth, it is understandable in the light of an unresponsive child. It is now widely accepted that the disorder is due to brain pathology, but its nature continues to mystify. Research has shown a genetic factor in some families, and an association with intellectual retardation, epilepsy (one in five retarded autistic children suffers from epilepsy) and nonspecific abnormalities of brain function. It is no surprise that a journal entitled *Molecular Autism* was established in 2010, whose principal focus is research into genetics and neurobiology.

Given that the brain is developing rapidly at the age of onset, it is crucial that autism is diagnosed as early as possible, and that graded educational and behavioural programs are begun promptly. In essence, treatment encompasses systematic training for a range of skills that normal children acquire readily. Medications can be used for specific behaviours such as sleep disturbance, hyperactivity and aggressiveness. A variety of so-called cures have been offered to vulnerable parents. Certain diets, vitamins and not immunising the child are examples of treatments that are of no value at all and can in fact prove harmful.

Although autism is life-long, two-thirds of children can live independently or in a supported community and participate in special occupational programs. A few are even able to work in ordinary employment. The outlook is best for those with higher IQs who develop functional speech. A typical autistic adult is brilliantly portrayed by Dustin Hoffman in the film *Rainman*. The character is discharged to the care of his brother, who is more and more amazed at the selective mental capacities (for example, a photographic memory) of someone who nevertheless has severe intellectual retardation. Oliver Sacks has also brought the autistic condition to life in his engaging book *An Anthropologist on Mars.*

PROBLEMS OF PRIMARY SCHOOL CHILDREN (6–12 YEARS)

Children gradually risk moving away from their parents and enter into increasingly complex relationships with other people. Social skills acquired in the years before school equip them to meet the demands of school and peers. Most children tolerate separation from attachment figures by their fifth birthday, allowing them to attend school without distress. During the primary school period, children grow in size, physical strength, agility, social skills and cognitive aptitudes. A smooth transition to school and other social settings is facilitated by a supportive family. Taking turns, sharing with others, cooperating on a task and helping distressed peers leads to a growing sense of empathy and the capacity to resolve conflict verbally.

Freud called this stage the latency period, which he saw as an interim time between the massive changes in infancy and early childhood and the manifold challenges of adolescence. Later observers have rejected this view. For example, Erik Erikson highlighted the busy-ness of the time during which children are actively learning to master the basic tools of their society. In developed countries, great emphasis is placed during this period on formal learning in school, especially of the three Rs. Failure at this task is, in Erikson's terms, associated with a sense of inferiority.

So, it is at this time that children present with learning problems. These are often associated with behavioural difficulties, which show themselves in four main ways: attention-deficit hyperactive, oppositional, conduct, and specific developmental disorders. Children with these conditions, particularly boys, make up a large proportion of those referred to child psychiatrists, reflecting the concerns of parents and teachers. In addition, a number of other specific syndromes manifest at this stage—for example, Tourette's and gender identity disorder (see below).

Attention-deficit hyperactive disorder (ADHD)

Children with ADHD typically show lack of persistence and attentiveness, and are impulsive and restless. Parents always stress the last, together with problematic feeding and sleeping from an early age. Children are typically distractible, disorganised, cannot follow instructions and have difficulty establishing routines. Toddlers are accident-prone, and kindergarten-age children often disruptive of other children's activities. Language delay and learning difficulties are common. These features usually manifest in early school years.

Up to one in twenty children shows ADHD, with boys affected three times more often than girls. The cause is largely unknown but it may well represent a final common neurodevelopmental pathway arising from multiple causes, including genetic. Diverse factors have been blamed. The most popular in the 1970s was food additives but this link has been discredited. Inconsistent parenting may play a role, although it is more likely that it compounds the brain disorder inherent in the child. Sophisticated neuroimaging investigations show disruptions in the dopamine chemical messenger system, which is consistent with the use of stimulants as the primary drug treatment.

Mrs Sherbrooke broke into tears in the family doctor's office. She had been called to the school and told that her 7-year-old son Robert had hit another boy. While not a serious incident in itself, the teacher's patience had run out after months of Robert distracting other children with his noisiness and running about the classroom. The teacher had not mentioned anything before this episode since she had hoped his behaviour would settle, but he was becoming worse instead. Mrs Sherbrooke was advised to seek professional help for Robert. Although the troubles at school were a shock to her, the news was not totally unexpected. She knew that her son was a very active boy who could not stick to a task and needed constant supervision. Otherwise he climbed trees, ran into the street without looking and left a messy trail behind him.

David, aged 5, was seen by a psychiatrist because he had lit a fire that could have caused serious damage had it not been detected. There had been many family disruptions and his mother had shortly before begun a new de facto relationship. When observed, David scarcely sat still for more than a moment and was unable to stick to any task requested of him. He had impaired short-term memory and, although his general IQ was average, testing showed defective concentration and attention.

Treatment of ADHD has many components, among them family counselling designed to reduce activities that bring the child into conflict with others. Parents are taught how to reward their child for appropriate behaviour, to offer clear instructions and to act consistently. The school is involved in assessment and informed of diagnostic decisions and treatment. Teachers ideally assist the child with learning difficulties by not overtaxing their capacity to attend, interspersing learning with periods of exercise, using cues to alert the child who has strayed from a set task and placing them close to students who concentrate well. Paradoxically, and as yet mysteriously, stimulant drugs (dextro amphetamine or amphetamine-like, such as methyl-phenidate) have a pivotal and effective role in reducing inattention, impulsivity and hyperactivity when these disrupt learning, relating with other students and family life. Symptoms may improve sufficiently by late adolescence to consider stopping the medication.

Some commentators have argued vociferously that medication is used far too liberally in children, and in the absence of genuine ADHD. Furthermore, they claim that a full assessment of the child, including developmental and family aspects, often reveals psychosocial factors that point to the need for psychological and social measures in treatment. The snag, as with so many psychiatric problems in children, is the lack of objective means to establish a precise diagnosis and its degree of severity.

Oppositional defiant and conduct disorders

As all parents know, kids can defy them and other authority figures with only the slightest provocation. When these behaviours are excessive for the child's age or markedly aberrant (such as stealing, compulsive lying, running away from home, truancy and aggression), we are heading towards what are termed oppositional and conduct disorders. These are divided into socialised and unsocialised forms depending on whether the child acts alone or in company. Some of the affected children will become serious offenders in late adolescence, particularly if they show no remorse and negligible concern for the feelings of others. A few even evolve into anti-social problematic personalities in adulthood (see Chapter 10).

Oppositional defiant disorder (ODD) is the label given to children who lose their temper at the drop of a hat, argue with adults and annoy and blame others. These behaviours disrupt relationships with family members and peers; the children are difficult to manage at school, where they are perceived as wilful and non-compliant. Oppositionality is interactional by its very nature and is sometimes explicable in terms of a particular situation, such as over-controlling parents. Conduct disorder (CD), not ODD, is the preferred diagnosis if the child exhibits anti-social or markedly aggressive behaviour, since ODD does not present with these features. On the other hand, ODD commonly evolves into CD.

Children with CD characteristically do many of the following: bully, initiate fights, act cruelly to people and animals, steal and run away from home. An isolated anti-social act does not justify the diagnosis. About 5 per cent of adolescent boys and 2 per cent of girls exhibit CD features, the prevalence increasing with social disadvantage. A clear link between CD and adult anti-social personality exists. Conversely, many anti-social children do not graduate thus, with 'good enough' mothering, higher intelligence and adequate parental supervision likely to be protective.

The question of whether children with ODD and CD are psychiatrically disturbed or simply bad has been repeatedly raised. Is society in effect medicalising badness or shifting the blame from a disturbed family or community to the child? Or is anti-social behaviour a product of alienation and social disadvantage? A medically oriented view holds that both CD and ODD constructs are valid on the grounds that their presenting features cohere and are not merely an aggregate of various forms of deviance. Nevertheless, environmental factors such as parental neglect, childhood sexual abuse, overly harsh discipline, inadequate supervision and delinquent peers are common correlates.

Treatment tends to be ineffective in the long term and anti-social patterns remain entrenched. Problem solving, parent-management training and family therapy have a place, particularly when administered as elements of an integrated program. Medication has a minimal role but may be prescribed in emergencies and for coexisting psychiatric conditions. By far the best option is to identify children at risk as early as possible and to teach their parents how to relate consistently and effectively to them.

Carlos, a 12-year-old adoptee, was assessed by a child psychiatrist after he set fire to a neighbour's house. He had shown anti-social behaviours, including fire-setting and running away from home, since his toddler years, and had continued to resist his mother's attempts to set limits. Carlos had been placed in institutional care on a number of occasions because of his parents' inability to manage his behaviour. Treatment included a special educational program, consistent limit-setting with appropriate consequences if he broke them, and participation in group therapy to build his self-esteem and promote relationships with his peers. Despite all this help, it took several years for Carlos to grow out of his problems.

Adam, a 13-year-old, lived with his mother, stepfather (a teacher) and his 8-year-old half-sister. He had occasional contact with his natural father, who had left the family when Adam was an infant. He had always been a temperamental boy who could not accept 'no' for an answer; his tantrums were legendary. Although he got through primary school without too many difficulties, he was a handful at home. He often managed to get his own way, so much so that the parents often ended up arguing between themselves rather than dealing with the source problem. The stepfather was convinced that his wife was far too indulgent, whereas she blamed him for not being more involved and for arriving home when arguments about homework and television viewing were over. The situation deteriorated when Adam entered high school. Although he did not get into trouble, his academic performance deteriorated and he truanted when an assignment he had not completed was due. He stayed at home on these days playing computer games. The atmosphere at home was electric given that he 'never' did what he was told.

Specific developmental problems

Sometimes children, more commonly boys than girls, face difficulties in a single developmental sphere; these are often associated with learning problems. Reading problems are the most common, occurring in one in ten children. Tests of intelligence requiring skill in the use of words are the best predictor of later reading ability. The term 'dyslexia' was widely used to describe these disturbances but is confusing and unhelpful.

Problems with speech (impaired articulation or production of sounds) and language (poor understanding or expression to convey meaning) are also common. Since normal hearing is essential for language development, any child with a marked language disorder will have their hearing carefully checked, and undergo an examination by a speech therapist. Mild or occasional stuttering is common in early stages of language development, and speech therapy effective in reducing it.

Specialist attention is needed when the pattern of problematic learning is severe or sustained. This may encompass speech therapy, motor-skills training, a teacher's aide to support the child, and alternative methods of learning and communication such as a computer keyboard instead of handwriting. Improvement in specific delays does occur with maturation, but without relevant professional help emotional and behavioural problems may result from social and communication handicaps.

Specific learning disorders need to be distinguished from academic underachievement. In the latter, despite an average IQ, performance in most subjects is below that expected in terms of age and intelligence. Factors other than learning disabilities, such as lack of motivation or depression, may then apply.

Tourette's disorder

In this puzzling and bizarre disorder, also known as multiple tic disorder, the child involuntarily makes brief, purposeless body movements and utters sounds that may in fact be swear words. Not unexpectedly, affected children are often shunned by their peers and even teachers because of their behaviour. The movements often respond to an anti-psychotic drug, suggesting that Tourette's is due to brain dysfunction.

Ben was 12 when first seen by a psychiatrist. He had suffered from Tourette's for a few years, with typical vocal utterances—involuntary chicken-like noises—and a tendency to fling his arms about. He had few friends and had never been invited to stay at a friend's house. Within weeks of commencing an anti-psychotic the symptoms subsided markedly and he was able to spend a holiday with a friend for the first time. His parents commented excitedly that Ben had not been so happy for years.

Gender identity disorder

By the age of four, children have a sense of their own gender and that of other children but may experiment with behaviours of the other sex, such as cross-dressing. Parents are rarely worried by tomboyishness in their daughters, but are much more likely to be concerned at their sons' girlishness. In most children, sex-role assignment by the parents, which almost always fits with the external genitalia, seems to be the key to gender identity. A few children have a strong wish to be of the other sex or, in extreme cases, a conviction that they really are of the opposite sex despite bodily evidence to the contrary. Some will seek sex reassignment surgery later in life. While the cause of these gender identity disorders is unknown, both biological and environmental factors probably play a part. (see Chapter 13)

PROBLEMS OF ADOLESCENCE (13–18 YEARS)

Puberty marks the onset of adolescence, a phase of life that brings profound changes in roles and relationships in the family, school, peer group and beyond, and reflects a shift to more independent status and greater internal control. Although the concept of adolescent turmoil is commonly mentioned, adolescence is managed effectively by the great majority and the transition to adulthood negotiated with only the occasional hiccup. On the other hand, the developmental life changes are unprecedented and challenge the young people as well as their families. The decade between 15 and 25 is also, crucially, one during which a number of serious mental illnesses have their onset, notably schizophrenia, bipolar and other mood disorders, and anorexia and bulimia nervosa. So-called identity crises are not uncommon and usually relate to perplexity about self-image, relationships, sexual orientation, religious affiliation and values. A proportion of young people who are unsure of who they are and what they value are vulnerable to potentially deleterious influences. Particularly harmful are religious cults and extremist political movements.

Early adolescence—puberty until 14—sees rapid physical development, most notably of secondary sex features. This is accompanied by a preoccupation with bodily appearance. Not surprisingly, eating disorders emerge at this time. It coincides with starting high school, a major transition and the foundation for education and one's future career as well as for close friendships. Puberty marks a point of discontinuity in psychosexual development: sexual interests, motivations and the capacity for sexual activity increase. Hormonal changes underlie much of this shift. Sexual orientation becomes clearer, with the evolution of predominantly hetero- or homosexual erotic fantasies. Although sexual interest expands rapidly at puberty, sexual activity varies markedly across cultures and times.

During *middle adolescence*—14 to 16—peer influences are pervasive, determining preferences in music, clothing and personal grooming. The notions of self-concept and self-esteem become pre-eminent, with diverse factors contributing: physical appearance, acceptance by peers, academic attainment and sporting prowess. Conflicts with parents concerning autonomy are par for the course and are not necessarily destructive.

Late adolescence—16 to the mid-20s—(the end-point is most fluid in the twenty-first century, depending very much on the culture in which the adolescent grows up)—is typified by an emphasis on education and vocational training. In many Western societies, around two-thirds of boys and a half of girls are sexually active by 18. For most, these relationships are monogamous and stable in the short term. Very early sexual activity, however, may be problematic and associated with other risky adolescent behaviours. Girls at greatest risk of early pregnancy have a background of emotional deprivation or institutional care.

Increasing self-reliance and capacity for independent decision-making, as well as the experiencing of novel life events (for example, a relational break-up, loss of job), are prominent from the mid-teens onwards.

Disorders of mood

All adolescents experience mood swings but only a small proportion will be diagnosed with clinical depression and require treatment. Atypical presentations (for example, sleeping or eating more than usual) are common, contrary to the more typical picture observed in adults. Frequently, other psychiatric problems coexist, particularly disruptive disorders, drug and alcohol abuse and anxiety. On the other hand, treatment may not be considered due to the ubiquitous misconception that unhappiness in this age group is existential or a stage of growing up. Without treatment, a depressive episode lasts an average six months. More than one in two depressed young people suffers recurrences in adulthood and about a fifth develop a full-blown bipolar illness. Recurrence is more likely in those who have had previous episodes, been depressed for an extended period, not fully recovered with treatment, face stress or suffer from other psychiatric or physical ailments.

Recognition and treatment are vital, since the link between depression and suicide is well established in this age group. Although suicidal behaviour is far more common in girls, death by suicide is four times more common in boys. It may be triggered by educational pressure, unemployment, family conflict or break-up, portrayal of youth suicide in the media, alcohol and drug abuse and the loss of a close relationship.

A particularly dramatic finding is that most adolescents who suicide have told an adult (such as their teacher or family doctor) of their distress in preceding weeks. Since about one in ten adolescents who attempt suicide will later succeed, all attempts are treated with utmost seriousness.

The mainstay of treatment is one of the psychotherapies, but antidepressants (a selective serotonin reuptake inhibitor) (see Chapter 18) are prescribed if the picture is severe. Rarely, electro-convulsive therapy is considered when all other treatments have failed.

Anxiety disorders

That anxiety is commonly experienced in adolescence is perfectly understandable, given the myriad uncertainties that come with trying to forge one's own unique identity and stepping out into a world replete with opportunities and challenges. About half of normal adolescents report feelings of apprehension, restlessness, social anxiety or bodily symptoms.

Separation of adolescents from key caring figures, who tend to be over-protective, or from familiar surroundings may lead to feelings of anxiety. Emotional distress is often accompanied by bodily symptoms like headache and abdominal pain for which no physical cause can be found. These adolescents may be overly dependent on parents, particularly mother. Although many are relatively immature with a poor self-image, they are usually of average or above-average intelligence and have not been buffeted by learning difficulties. Anxiety may relate to the adolescent's wish to protect a parent from marital strife or to support an ill or depressed parent. Up to half these adolescents will continue to have emotional difficulties in adult life, and face an increased risk of developing agoraphobia or other anxiety syndromes.

Treatment involves addressing underlying family problems, psychological therapies, and anti-depressants for any coexisting marked depression, and sometimes for the anxiety disorder in its own right.

Tina, aged 15, persistently refused to go to school and feared leaving home. She was struggling at an academically oriented school and her anxiety about her studies was reinforced by an over-protective mother. Father had left the family when Tina was ten, following which mother treated her as a substitute companion. Tina felt a strong need to be there for her mother for 'she hits the bottle hard when she is alone'. Treatment focused on both Tina and her mother. It included graded practice at leaving the house with the support of an older brother. Family therapy boosted Tina's growing independence and the family's understanding of how their difficulties had arisen in the wake of father's departure.

Younger children also suffer from anxiety syndromes especially at times of transition (for example, moving from pre- to primary school). The varied ways in which they present are similar to those in adulthood and are therefore not repeated here.

Substance abuse

Most adolescents experiment with drugs, ranging from tobacco and alcohol to cannabis and narcotics. Cannabis use is ubiquitous and perceived by most teenagers as entirely harmless. Realisation of its potential role in precipitating a psychotic illness and as a gateway to more serious drug abuse seems remote from the average adolescent's mind. Recreational alcohol is particularly common but not necessarily problematic unless it has adverse social consequences (for example, conflict with family) or leads to risk-taking (for example, accidental injury). Use of other illicit drugs, such as solvents (glue sniffing), opiates (heroin, codeine), hallucinogens (MDMA/ecstasy, LSD) and stimulants (cocaine, amphetamines) is often construed by health professionals as pathological.

Dependence is less often seen in adolescence than in later years. Adolescents most at risk of substance abuse may well be fighting with their parents, faring poorly at school, unable to hold down a job, attracted to deviant peers, suffering from another psychiatric disorder, particularly behavioural in type, and have a family history of substance abuse. The hazards of the abuse include increased risk of death through suicide, accidents or infections like hepatitis B and C and AIDS, and of criminal behaviour in order to obtain drugs.

The proportion of adolescent substance abusers who approach health services is not known but is probably very low. Abuse often emerges via other problems—psychiatric (for example, psychosis), forensic (offending), educational (for example, academic failure) or social (for example, homelessness). Treatment requires a comprehensive assessment of social and developmental factors. Most approaches emphasise harm minimisation—preventing physical disease (hepatitis C, HIV), progression to physical dependence and forensic consequences—on the premise that conventional psychotherapies have not been shown to be effective. Enhancing self-esteem through educational help with learning problems, sporting activities, and vocational and social skill training is a key goal, while family therapy sets out to reduce conflict and establish consistent limit setting that is appropriate to the adolescent's age. Drugs to reduce craving that are helpful in adults have not been systematically evaluated in adolescents.

Psychoses

Psychotic illnesses are exceedingly rare before puberty; both schizophrenia and bipolar disorder present more commonly from mid-adolescence onwards. The close association with substance abuse, as mentioned above, may be a contributing factor. While symptoms resemble those found in adults the diagnosis may be elusive, since specific features such as disordered thought and delusions may be absent at this stage. Early non-specific symptoms include declining social and cognitive functioning, and general anxiety without cause. Treatment is that for adults, although working with the family is particularly stressed (see Chapter 11 for a detailed account).

Abuse in childhood and adolescence

William, aged 14, had always been socially isolated, aggressive and threatening towards his peers, defiant and uncooperative with his carers. He had been expelled from several schools. He had solitary pursuits—swimming, reading about guns and natural disasters. He entertained grand ideas about a career in a special military unit. Shortly following his birth, William's mother had abandoned him to the 'care' of his stepfather. Tragically, this consisted of regular physical (and probably sexual) abuse until he escaped at age 11. His behaviour thereafter led to the breakdown of a series of foster placements. He also suffered symptoms of post-traumatic stress disorder related to the abuse: intrusive thoughts and panic in the company of young people, which made him want to escape or strike out. William felt safer when on his own, swimming or in his fantasy world of weaponry. He had had recurring frightening dreams in which he was as small as a 'dot' and threatened by a giant 'god-man'. When encouraged to draw a face, he saw only his stepfather. William then depicted a recurrent thought of his stepfather beating him against a wall.

Child abuse—physical, sexual and emotional—differs from all the other conditions we have covered so far since the child is the victim of an interaction with an adult, often a caregiver, that results in physical and emotional harm. Since 1961 when Henry Kempe, an American paediatrician, drew attention to the battered child syndrome, child abuse has become widely recognised as a tragic aspect of contemporary family life. Surveys since the 1980s have shown staggeringly high rates of abused children. The repercussions are dire: long-lasting impaired relationships, failure to achieve intimacy, a diverse range of psychiatric problems in adulthood and the incapacity to parent.

The family has always been regarded as the foundation of society, a sacrosanct institution to be protected and maintained—and the home as a haven, a refuge from social ills. On the other hand, women and children have until relatively recent years, at least in Western societies, been seen as possessions of the husband and father—as reflected in law, religion and economic arrangements. For many of the world's women and children, this is still the case.

It is revealing that societies for the protection of animals long preceded their counterparts for women and children. In 1871 the plight of a severely maltreated child, reported by neighbours to the Society of Prevention of Cruelty to Animals in New York, was dismissed by the courts as the child was deemed not to be an animal! This bizarre situation soon led to the formation of a society for the prevention of cruelty to children. Despite masses of evidence that the home is a dangerous place for many women and children, we are still struggling to accept that a quarter of adults have experienced abuse as children.

At first, awareness of child abuse was limited to severe physical harm, but the net then widened to include sexual abuse, emotional abuse and general neglect. Children used to be thought of as tough, resilient and able to cope with adversity. This idea has been shattered to the extent that psychiatrists invoke the concept of post-traumatic stress disorder (see Chapter 6) to cover the negative responses of children. Abused children tend to show rather than tell—that is, the effect of their experience is often seen first in changes in behaviour, emotional state, bodily functioning and learning difficulties.

Traumatic effects may follow a single catastrophic event or many forms of abuse over an extended period. Acute reactions include regression to an earlier stage of psychological development, insomnia and nightmares, a tendency to be easily startled, extreme wariness of the external world, wide-ranging fears, panic and irritability. Behaviour may change dramatically, with symptoms like bed-wetting, anxiety and aggressive behaviour. If the abuse is prolonged or there are repeated episodes, the child's self-image, relationships and view of the world are profoundly affected. Children become preoccupied with protecting themselves from environmental pressures. Abused children, like abused adults, may develop behaviour designed to appease the abuser, in the erroneous belief that they will then be better off. This invariably fails to stop the abuse, increases helplessness and, paradoxically, induces guilt.

Children need predictable and consistent nurturing by a caregiver to whom they are attached. Disruption to this 'good enough' care (a term introduced by Donald Winnicott, a British paediatrician and psychoanalyst, to suggest that parenting is not necessarily ideal) has, understandably, long-term adverse results. The nature of the difficulties depends on the quality of care the child had before the abuse, the type of abuse itself (severity and duration in particular) and the relationship of the child to the abusing adult. The closer the child to that adult, the greater the sense of betrayal, confusion and enduring ill-effects. These cover the full range of psychiatric problems: low self-esteem, relationship difficulties, anxiety, depression, and eating and post-traumatic stress disorders. A close link has emerged between childhood abuse and the later development of problematic personality in adult life, particularly of the borderline type (see Chapter 10). While most people who were abused as children will not repeat this abuse as parents, up to a third will—they seem, paradoxically, to be incapable of preventing the cycle.

Munchausen syndrome by proxy, fortunately rare because it can be so hazardous, is a most bizarre form of abuse. The caregiver, most often a mother, fabricates her child's symptoms (for example, describing fits or reporting fever in an otherwise well child) or actually makes the child ill through inappropriate administration of medications like laxatives, diuretics, even poisons. Children may be tested repeatedly until the bizarreness of the clinical picture points to this possibility. Even in the face of abundant evidence, the mother persistently denies her role. She herself usually has longstanding personality difficulties or an undetected psychiatric disorder. Moreover, she may have experienced a history similar to the one she has inflicted on her child.

Treatment of any type of child abuse calls for a high level of suspicion as the first step in the diagnosis, followed by evaluating the degree of urgency for protection. Liaison with a welfare agency occurs if there are concerns for the child's safety. The child and family are referred to a child protection unit, a paediatrician or a child psychiatrist for confirmation of the diagnosis.

In many countries, social welfare authorities must be informed of suspected child abuse, including sexual abuse. Proper protection of the abused child is a crucial step in treatment. Sometimes the child will be admitted to hospital for tests or even temporarily removed from the family. Police may have to assist with this removal and investigate criminal aspects. A formal application for protection may be vital to ensure safety. Most children do return to parental care once assessment has been completed and treatment launched.

Preventing psychiatric problems in children

One of my favourite psychiatric cartoons shows a middle-aged therapist alongside a baby lying on the patient's couch; the caption reads 'I wish I could have started my therapy when I was your age'. Mental health professionals working with children can play a pivotal role in educating the public on the advantages of prevention. In no other developmental period of the life cycle are the opportunities to prevent psychological problems so promising. Anna Freud once remarked, in a lecture on the kindergarten and psychoanalysis, that 'what the child has to acquire between his first and sixth year of life is more than he ever will in his subsequent life; never again will similarly great demands be made'. While many programs have been devised, particularly in the domains of teaching parenting skills and in working with teachers and students in schools, their effectiveness is debatable. When I edited the *Australian and New Zealand Journal of Psychiatry*, I invited a number of experts in the field to address the subject. More questions than answers were the result.

Indeed, a series of vital issues challenge policy-makers in the realm of child mental health and social wellbeing. Consider the following as illustrative. Should mental health programs be introduced for all children in the light of Anna Freud's observation, or only for those who are identified as vulnerable? Can we assume that most children have the necessary resources to develop resilience, and relevant skills to cope with the stress of growing up? Is there a danger of medicalising child development such that what should be a natural process is transformed into a clinical one? Should resources, which are necessarily limited, be dedicated only to areas of childhood experience that are known to cause psychological harm? Obvious examples are to curb bullying through educating children about the risks to the mental wellbeing of its victims, or providing emotional and practical support to disadvantaged families? Programs can be even more specifically targeted by intervening early and energetically in the case of, say, a behaviourally disturbed child; it could be argued that benefits would accrue for such children, who are on the cusp of developing serious psychiatric problems, by teaching their parents how to convey affection, apply consistent discipline and provide a stimulating home environment.

The questions I have posed also relate to another critical phase of psychological development. A growing realisation since the turn of the century that a huge proportion of mental illness has its onset in the decade from the mid-teens to the mid-twenties, and that the use of psychiatric services is paradoxically low in this period, has led to a heated debate about the best way to close the gap. In the customary model the needs of youth and young adults have tended to fall between two stools, with lack of continuity of care after age 18. The suggestion that mental health care be available to 15–25-year-olds, together with general health, drug and alcohol and sexual health services in a one-stop shop characterised by easy access and youth-friendly staff, is intuitively appealing.

An Australian Government innovation called Headspace was launched along these lines in 2006. As stated on its website, Headspace 'provides a national, coordinated focus on youth mental health and related drug and alcohol problems ... and aims to improve access for young people aged 12–25 years to appropriate services and ensure better coordination between services'. (www.headspace.org.au) Since its value is being assessed, time will tell whether the model will succeed or not. Many non-governmental organisations have started up websites on the internet in many countries to promote mental health in young people. A good example in Australia is Reach Out, one of whose aims is to 'help alleviate depression by encouraging help-seeking behaviour and coping skills among young people' and another to promote existing community agencies that support young people at risk. (http//au.reachout.com)

Conclusion

The field of child and adolescent psychiatry is at an exciting point in its relatively short history. For the very first time, the scope of the mental health needs of young people has been recognised, and commensurate attention given to clarifying the nature of the problems that afflict them and to treatments that are likely to be useful. Although there is a long way to go before we achieve a solid evidence base on both these counts, the journey taken so far has been impressive.

CHAPTER 15

Women

If I had written this book in the 1960s, it would have been inconceivable to devote a specific chapter to mental illness and women. The 1968 psychiatric classification of the American Psychiatric Association, for example, did not mention women at all. Today, it is equally inconceivable not to consider the mental health issues that are of special relevance and concern to women, particularly the severe psychiatric disorders that occur in the context of having a baby.

Why is this so? Research studies point to substantially higher rates of certain forms of mental illness in women compared to men. Moreover, many more women seek professional help or are identified as needing it. The feminist movement has highlighted the particular needs of women and how these have been neglected for centuries—the psychological effects of domestic violence, rape and sexual abuse in childhood and adolescence spring to mind. At least in part, this inattention derives from social values that were challenged vociferously from the 1960s by leading figures in the feminist movement like Simone de Beauvoir, Betty Friedan, Gloria Steinem and Germaine Greer. Many psychiatrists are sensitive to these influences and have modified their thinking on the nature of mental illness and its treatment. Much to the benefit of psychiatry (and medicine overall), many women have become members of the mental health professions; among them have been noteworthy advocates of the special problems that beset women and leading researchers into such areas as depression in the wake of giving birth, the psychological effects of infertility and the menopause, and the enduring effects of childhood sexual abuse.

I am particularly impressed with the thoughtful arguments of Deborah Leupnitz, an American family therapist and committed feminist, who has argued in her book *The Family Interpreted*, that therapists in past years tended to impose societal values inimical to women under their treatment. I would go along with her thesis. I can recall in my own professional lifetime that the social and political context, especially a prevailing sexism, was ignored in psychiatry, at a great cost to the female patient and women generally. For instance, she was made to feel culpable for the problems of her family, responsible for causing psychotic illness (the shameful labelling of the mothers of schizophrenic patients as 'schizophrenogenic' remains a stain in the history of that illness) and a failure if she were single.

The history of society's attitude to mental illness in women is intriguing and not always edifying. For example, during the Middle Ages and beyond it was believed that women who now would be diagnosed as suffering from hysterical conversion or a psychosis were witches, who could be cured only by torture or death. This is powerfully brought to life in Arthur Miller's play *The Crucible*, which relates the unsavoury historical episode known as the 'witches of Salem'. The ideas of Charles Darwin in the nineteenth century led to a view that biological factors, including genetic ones, were pre-eminent in shaping our behaviour. Theories of differences between the sexes evolved and were used to justify stereotyped gender roles. Women's functions were thus seen as primarily domestic and maternal. The male-dominated medical establishment endorsed this view, and fostered the notion that women were vulnerable to both physical and mental illness because of their genetic make-up.

Nineteenth-century 'hygiene manuals' preached that sexual transgression in women caused ill health, so re-enforcing the tie between women's social behaviour and health status. Prominent feminist writers have highlighted the link society makes between madness and femininity, and described fashions in the presentation of women's symptoms and in the (usually) male medical response. Women were consistently diagnosed with so-called mental disorders that critics claim were socially determined behaviours to deal with anxieties resulting from severe restrictions on what women could do in society. I can recall as a new psychiatric trainee hearing about two very old women who had been admitted to an old-style mental hospital literally decades earlier because of their loose moral behaviour. They had each given birth to a baby and, as a result, been shunned by their family and friends. Consignment to an institution was deemed to be the most appropriate response to their plight. Out of sight, out of mind. Years later, no one had any idea where they hailed from and what they were doing in a psychiatric ward. Unbelievable yet true.

This sort of story was not so rare in the nineteenth and twentieth centuries and has been brought vividly to life by the Irish novelist Sebastian Barry in his heart-rending novel *The Secret Scripture*. The principal character, Roseanne McNulty, is about 100 years old (no one knows for sure including herself) and a long-time resident of a provincial mental asylum when we are introduced to her. We soon learn that she was placed there as a young woman, again for 'loose moral behaviour', through the initiative of the local parish priest in his quest to help the 'disgraced' family. A novel yes, but based on events that did indeed occur and that suited all the players involved, except for the unfortunate detainee who lost her freedom for life.

The world of literature also brings forth the example of women who may not have contravened social convention, as in the case of moral insanity, but were regarded as totally dependent and passive and therefore in need of institutional care. Janet Frame, a young New Zealander and long-term resident of this kind, was on the verge of being subjected to leucotomy, a then radical psychosurgery, when it emerged totally out of the blue that she had been awarded a prize in a short story writing competition. The staff were entirely oblivious of her talent. She went on to become a celebrated author.

Freud's view of women as inherently passive and inferior (his concept of penis envy embodies his bias) influenced later psychological theories— including those that are a backlash to it. Karen Horney, a leading figure in the American psychoanalytic movement, repudiated Freud's notion, arguing that social forces were much more relevant than biological ones in determining gender behaviour.

Rigidity of positions towards gender roles (and their adverse effects) endured into the 1970s. For example, one American study found in 1970 that in considering men and women, clinicians maintained a double standard of mental health. A mentally healthy woman was seen as having quite different (stereotyped 'feminine') qualities from a healthy man. This placed women in a bind: they had to maintain these feminine features in order to be regarded as healthy!

In her controversial book with the evocative title *Women and Madness*, Phyllis Chesler, a social scientist, argued strongly that the labelling of women as mad constitutes a means of social control. Using the cases of Zelda Fitzgerald (wife of the famous author F Scott Fitzgerald) and Sylvia Plath, among others, Chesler vigorously attacked a male-dominated psychiatry. She put it most radically:

> Women are impaled on the cross of self-sacrifice ... [Their] madness is essentially an intense experience of female biological, sexual, and cultural castration, and a doomed search for potency. The search often involves 'delusions' or displays of physical aggression, grandeur, sexuality, and emotionality—all traits which would probably be more acceptable in female-dominated cultures. Such traits in women are feared and punished in patriarchal mental asylums ...

Treatments in psychiatry have been characterised by feminist critics as the attempt to return women to the very situation in which they became mentally ill in the first place—that is, their passive, dependent and submissive role—and for failing to look at the need for social change, particularly for empowerment. Others highlight psychiatry's tendency to treat disturbance in the individual person rather than examine its social causes. Of special concern is sexual exploitation of patients by psychotherapists, the ultimate abuse of the power relationship inherent in the therapeutic encounter.

Feminists have, through the above sorts of arguments, exerted an immense impact on mental health treatment. Their campaign on violence against women, for example, has led to alternative models of service, such as rape crisis centres and refuges for battered women, in which women themselves are encouraged to take responsibility for their welfare in the context of achieving social and political change.

Gender differences in patterns of illness

Women are much more vulnerable to mental illness overall, and this is closely tied to marital, work and social roles. Studies have found marked gender differences in the rate for many psychiatric conditions. Women predominate in depression, both mild and severe, anxiety states including agoraphobia, other phobias and panic, and those states that manifest as bodily concerns. Men, on the other hand, show higher rates of anti-social personality and alcohol abuse. The reasons for women's greater vulnerability include:

- raising children and looking after the family is intrinsically frustrating;
- the role of homemaker is unstructured and her work invisible;
- working married women are under more pressure than married men and prone to greater role conflict.

Research bears this out. Married women show higher rates of psychiatric states compared to married men, whereas single women are similar to their single male counterparts. Marriage is associated with better physical health in both sexes but not with better mental health in women unless they are gainfully employed. The effect of a job on women's mental health depends very much on their husbands' or partners' attitudes and on their own satisfaction with arrangements for childcare. If good care is available and the fathers contribute to it, rates of mental illness are low. But employed mothers without available child care and with sole responsibility for children are particularly vulnerable. For non-working wives, children increase their vulnerability.

If we consider depression specifically, by far the most common mental health problem in women in Western countries, we see the immense impact of gender. For every man who comes for treatment, there are two women. Age is important. In children and the elderly there is little gender difference, but depression is much more common in women between these ages, reaching a peak in young mothers.

Biological factors may contribute to these differences, particularly in the case of severe depression after giving birth, but psychological and social factors are likely to play a role in milder forms. For everybody, clinical depression is preceded by a greater frequency of demanding life events. Women do not experience these events more often than men, and both rate their levels of stress similarly. But women react with more symptoms to the same stress—they show greater vulnerability to the effects of life events. Female vulnerability points to lack of a confidant, rearing young children, not having a job outside the home, and loss of one's mother in early life. Another factor may be a difference between the genders in appreciating and expressing distress, with women more inclined to acknowledge feelings, both positive and negative.

Mental health problems through the life cycle

The familiar female dominance in rates of depression, which becomes manifest from early adolescence, has stimulated the study of hormonal changes. There is a well-established link between childhood physical and sexual abuse and emotional neglect, and increased vulnerability to a wide range of psychiatric conditions.

Adolescence sees the development of a sense of identity and body image, and emerging sexuality. The enormous biological events around puberty drive physical and psychological change in a rapid and often perplexing way. It is also the period when the greater female susceptibility to psychological problems becomes evident.

Multiple social factors can exert long-term adverse effects on a growing girl's development—risky behaviour with sex and drugs, non-nurturing social relationships and interrupted education. Social influences, especially school, ideally provide an environment outside the family in which a girl can be extended both intellectually and socially, and her developing self-esteem consolidated. The opportunity prevails in these settings to compensate for families that have not offered good enough caring. Indeed, even girls who have been sexually abused as children can develop normally if they experience a trusting relationship with a role model during their teens. Social and sporting achievement also enhances self-esteem.

Kylie's parents separated when she was a toddler. She had no contact with her father thereafter and lived with her mother Josie, who abused drugs and suffered from depression. Josie was not only emotionally unavailable but also had numerous boyfriends, at least two of whom sexually abused Kylie. Not surprisingly, she felt anxious at school and was unable to trust anyone. This in turn led to ineffective study habits and to a belief that she was an academic failure. When she moved to high school she found comfort in the company of other adolescents who did not fit the mould; she forged the identity of a rebel. She began using illicit drugs, finding temporary relief from her emotional pain. At 13, Kylie was thrown out of home after a furious argument with her mother and began to work as a prostitute in order to fund what soon became an expensive habit. At 16, following a suicide attempt, she was admitted to a psychiatric hospital for the first time, but did not engage with social and health services as recommended until a year later when she became pregnant. The arrival of a baby girl motivated her to look at herself afresh, and enabled engagement with a therapist for the next four years. She managed to parent her child well with this regular support. A key factor that prompted progress was her attachment to an aunt who had been there for her throughout her childhood, as well as to a community psychiatric nurse who provided support and was always accessible.

Psychological problems in adulthood may be associated with menstruation and fertility—including pre-menstrual tension, conflicts over contraception and a sense of loss linked to infertility. Sexual difficulties range from poor communication to severe physical and sexual abuse, all of which increase vulnerability to psychiatric illness. Single or repeated pregnancy loss through termination, miscarriage or stillbirth has the potential to influence a woman's emotional adjustment. Psychiatric disorders occur more commonly in the year following childbirth. Depressed mothers can adversely affect their children, leading to a vicious cycle of family dysfunction.

Another difficult time follows surgery on female organs (hysterectomy and mastectomy). Alzheimer's disease affects older women disproportionately, both directly and as carers, because of their greater life expectancy; emotional disturbance is common among carers of the elderly mentally infirm.

The menstrual cycle

Menstruation has been shrouded in myth for centuries, and in many cultures misconceptions distort reality and influence the way a woman feels about herself, her body and her reproductive role.

Emotional and behavioural changes have been associated with the menstrual cycle since ancient times. About 50 per cent of women have one or more symptoms. Irritability, restlessness, anxiety, depression, insomnia and impaired concentration are experienced more frequently during the pre-menstrual and menstrual phases, while feelings of wellbeing are more typical of the middle of the cycle.

Hormonal changes during the pre-menstrual phase probably account for behavioural, cognitive, mood and sexual changes. These features are experienced by most women, and more markedly by those who eventually seek medical help. A hormonal sensitivity—the brain affected by rapidly altered oestrogen and progesterone levels—is assumed to explain why certain women are more severely affected than others, but no specific abnormality has been detected. We do know, however, that these symptoms disappear after removal of the ovaries or following a natural menopause.

Pre-menstrual dysphoric disorder, a mouthful, has been proposed as a label for these changes when they are severe. Its features tend to include sadness, tension, irritability, poor concentration, fatigue, sleep disturbance, bodily symptoms (with relief by the post-menstrual week); and of such degree as leads to marked psychological distress and disrupted social functioning.

Belinda, a young mother of three, requested counselling for her marital difficulties. She described frequent arguments, particularly over housework, finances and child care. Husband John complained of her incessant nagging, and irritability with the children. After a comprehensive inquiry it became clear that Belinda experienced these feelings in a predictable monthly cycle. Seven to eight days before each period she became tearful, over-sensitive, irritable and prone to outbursts over trivial matters. Sometimes she even hit out at the children, feeling quite unable to control herself. The aftermath was awful guilt about her behaviour. Once her period began, all these symptoms evaporated. Belinda admitted to being a perfectionist and high achiever, and having had painful periods during adolescence.

Treatment comprised explaining the nature of pre-menstrual dysphoria to both Belinda and her husband, and counselling to work out how they might as a couple cope more adaptively with stress. Belinda was also taught the rudiments of relaxation and given a tape to use daily. The couple responded well to these relatively straightforward measures, with family life becoming much more harmonious and fulfilling.

Motherhood
Giving birth and nurturing the newborn infant represents one of the most profound events in a woman's life. While community expectations point to

blissful motherhood, many women experience just the opposite—considerable distress in the year after childbirth. It is in fact the time of greatest risk for psychiatric illness in a woman (a six-fold increase compared to other phases of her life). Postpartum mental illness is a misnomer since in most cases, symptoms are experienced during pregnancy.

Postpartum psychosis (previously called puerperal psychosis) is a serious mental illness of women after childbirth, but fortunately rare (about one in a thousand births). On the other hand, the risk of psychosis in the first month after childbirth is a dramatic twenty times greater than in the two years before the birth. Whether postpartum psychosis is a distinct illness or a form of mood disorder remains an open question. The condition usually declares itself within a couple of weeks. This massively increased rate, combined with the brief period between the birth and the onset of symptoms, suggests that the illness is linked to as an yet undetermined hormonal imbalance in predisposed women, possibly a decline in circulating oestrogens that affects chemical messengers in the brain. Other related factors are prolonged labour, stillbirth, a past history of postpartum psychosis, and a family history of mood problems.

Typically, the affected woman has delusionary thoughts and hallucinations. These erroneous beliefs usually involve the infant, who may be regarded as the devil or worse and therefore in need of saving, with its death the only remedy. She also exhibits what is best termed perplexity—the sense that something has gone horribly awry—together with a feeling of helplessness about what to do. I still retain the image of a postgraduate student in her late twenties who tragically smothered her 4-week-old baby, her first, out of an unshakeable conviction that he was a demon with devilish plans; an accompanying voice commanded her to kill him before he could wreak damage on the world. There were no mother and baby units in those days, but more importantly the diagnosis had been missed until the infanticidal act.

Treatment is similar to that of psychotic illness generally but, as the case illustration screams out to us, the safety of both mother and baby is paramount; special consideration is also given to selecting medications that are safe for the baby if the mother is breastfeeding (see Chapter 11).

Postpartum depression occurs much more commonly than postpartum psychosis. About a quarter of women are affected by lowered mood in the first year after birth, with a peak period onset during the second and third months of the child's life. Despite obvious emotional distress in the mother and her consequent poor coping in caring for the baby, the condition may still be missed; what should be a joyous experience is suddenly clouded, indeed feared, and this totally unexpected response is explained away as the effect of interrupted sleep and associated exhaustion. Apart from her altered mood, she feels totally inadequate, unable to cope with even routine tasks and guilty over not caring enough for her baby. Other features, of varying intensity, usually worsen at the end of the day and include fatigue, insomnia and a fear of harming the baby. The mother's suffering interferes with her bonding to the baby and to its development, as well as with marital, family and social ties. Recognition, prompt treatment and, ideally, prevention therefore help to promote the mental health of mother, baby and family.

There is no way of guaranteeing to a woman who has had a past episode of postpartum disturbance of mood (or a psychosis) that a recurrence in a future pregnancy can be prevented. On the contrary, the risk of a recurrence is about a third to a half with subsequent births. I have known a number of women who desperately wanted another child but were immobilised by fear of suffering a postpartum mental illness again. In the end it is for the parents to decide and for the psychiatrist to monitor the pregnancy with utmost diligence and treat as the need arises.

As in the case of postpartum psychosis, the cause of depression in the new mother is something of a mystery. Biological, psychological and social factors all probably contribute in varying measure. A past history of menstrual problems or depression may predict vulnerability, as may a history of depression in the family (suggesting a genetic component). Psychological and social factors, including during pregnancy, are also relevant. Among the psychological factors that appear to play a part are lack of emotional support, stressful life events, a history in earlier years of sexual abuse, a childhood typified by uncaring parents and longstanding anxiety. Indeed, the descriptor 'postpartum' may be misleading, given that the onset of emotional distress is commonly during the pregnancy rather than in the wake of the birth.

The challenging question arises as to whether to prescribe anti-depressants during the pregnancy, especially in the first trimester. The main problem is safety; evidence from large Danish studies suggests an increased rate of cardiac defects (but still extremely rare), premature delivery and high blood pressure. Stopping anti-depressants in pregnancy also has its problems, exposing the woman with severe recurrent depression to a possible relapse. Treatment decisions require patient, spouse and psychiatrist to consider carefully the risks and benefits of medication and no treatment. This is not at all easy. I have had patients vulnerable to severe depression who have delayed the decision for years or gone ahead only to have a miserable pregnancy for one of several reasons.

Depression occurring in the postpartum period is in essence no different from that at any other point in the life cycle. But the fact of a newborn baby and its needs makes it a immense challenge to the clinical team.

The safety of both mother and baby is the biggest worry. Frighteningly, suicide is one of the most common causes of maternal death, especially in developed countries where obstetric care is advanced. Not surprisingly, a new sub-specialty has evolved in psychiatry, requiring sophisticated treatment programs, in which the mother and baby are seen as an integral pair.

Support that helps to cushion or even prevent postpartum depression involves a structured day, socially sanctioned rest, granting the woman privacy, assistance in daily tasks from relatives and friends, and recognition through various rituals of the mother's new social status. In many traditional cultures, the new mother receives this form of support explicitly— mainly from the family. For example, Jamaican women customarily enjoy ritual seclusion for the first week or so and spend the next month at home, with the baby cared for by grandmother. In traditional Nigeria, mother and baby are placed in a special hut within the family compound for several weeks; again the grandmother has a designated role. In Western society, by contrast, the previous practice of a six-week 'lying-in' period is a dim memory. Rituals are also far less common, reflecting perhaps a more secular age.

The *postpartum blues* is easily distinguishable from postnatal depression in that it is a mild temporary experience limited to the first ten days after birth. Features last only hours to days and then evaporate. These are typically weeping, changeable mood, insomnia, anxiety and irritability. About 70 per cent of new mothers experience the blues. Fortunately, explanation and support are invariably enough to alleviate the distress. On occasion, however, the blues are a prelude to more severe mood disturbance.

Sonia, a 26-year-old nurse and mother of two children, one aged two, the other eight months, went to her family doctor complaining of tiredness and apathy after the birth of the second child. The doctor suspected depression, despite Sonia's disclaimer, 'Isn't this the way all tired mums feel?' She described an initial feeling of joy at the birth, but soon after returning home from hospital had begun to experience gloom and pessimism, insomnia, utter exhaustion, loss of appetite and poor concentration. She was also constantly irritable with both children and with her husband, and felt unable to control this. She withdrew from friends, neglected housework and felt awful that she was 'such a bad mother'. She felt hopeless about the future and believed she would be better off dead. Her baby cried incessantly and would not settle. Sonia felt frustrated and angry with the baby and most disturbed by her lack of any feeling towards him. Just before seeking help, she had even thought of smothering him to stop him crying.

Sonia's mother had suffered from bouts of depression, one severe episode requiring hospital treatment. They had a poor relationship; Sonia regarding her mother as critical and unsupportive. In the remote past, she had been sexually abused by her godfather, which left her shorn of self-confidence and self-esteem.

Sonia and the baby were admitted to a mother and baby unit. An anti-depressant was prescribed, selected specifically because its transmission in breast milk was negligible. Individual psychodynamic therapy was instituted to help Sonia deal with unresolved matters such as the sexual abuse and the troubled relationship with her mother, and with current parenting difficulties. A mothercraft nurse counselled her briefly on breastfeeding and aspects of the mothering role. Couple counselling was also undertaken to improve marital communication. At first tentative about the benefits of a group for new mothers, Sonia became an active member both socially and in contributing medical information gleaned from the internet.

Infertility and pregnancy loss

Pregnancy loss is best seen as a form of grief, encompassing as it does a major loss. Whether the loss has been through spontaneous or induced abortion or stillbirth, it is compounded by an associated loss of the status of motherhood. And the woman's incapacity to rely on her body to give birth buffets her self-esteem. If an infant dies shortly after birth, numerous social practices aid the bereavement process, but these rituals have unfortunately not been extended to the premature end of a pregnancy (memorial services are a recent development). Initial numbness is followed by sadness, empti-ness, perhaps anger, a sense of inadequacy and a tendency to blame others. These feelings will wane and be replaced, if grieving is effective, with a renewed willingness to engage with life.

Although one in five pregnancies ends in miscarriage, health profes-sionals have tended to disregard this potentially distressing experience. Lack of sympathy for a woman who has miscarried has been widespread in societies past and present. In the Middle Ages, women were sometimes even burned alive. In some contemporary societies, repeated miscarriage is grounds for a man to divorce his wife—as is infertility. Although the general view is that the trauma is not great, miscarriage even when planned (for any one of many rea-sons) is a loss and therefore inherently stressful. It involves loss of the fetus, of energy invested in the pregnancy, and of a sense of control of one's health and fate. Lack of support and ritual deny women comfort and lead to feelings of isolation. Early pregnancy loss denies the mother an opportunity to fare-well a tangible body, which complicates the mourning process.

Death close to the time of birth produces longer-term psychological symptoms and disturbed family relationships. The well-recognised symp-toms include depression, insomnia, withdrawal, anger, guilt and marital strain. Although mothers usually show more symptoms than fathers, the toll can be heavy for both. Factors influencing outcome of mourning are the level of support from the extended family and of contact with the ill or dead infant, the length of time the infant lived, the type of communication between the parents, and the reactions of health professionals.

Many of these psychological issues are also relevant to the infertile couple. Although the many new technologies under the rubric of IVF (in-vitro fertilisation) have evolved dramatically, the success rate remains disappointingly low and the stress to those participating in the program high. Continuing infertility, and even failure to respond with the aid of technology, is harmful to the mental wellbeing of both partners and to the marriage. Because of this vulnerability, psychiatrists have become increasingly involved.

Lena, 28 years old and married, had symptoms of postpartum depression following the birth of her first child, a daughter, who was then four weeks old. This was her third pregnancy. She had had a termination at nineteen and a miscarriage two years previously—eighteen weeks after a three-year history of treatment for infertility. Lena had been extremely distressed at the time of the miscarriage and by the lack of support from the hospital. In particular, she was not allowed to hold the baby or proceed with any other mourning ritual. Her sister, however, had given birth to a 24-week baby, who had survived after being placed in intensive care and receiving extensive resuscitation. Lena was enraged about what she saw as an arbitrary decision that a loss of pregnancy before twenty weeks was considered a miscarriage.

Since Lena's family did not understand her feelings, she kept most of her grief to herself. She had not really overcome her loss when she conceived again a year later. The birth led to a reawakening of her grief, anger and guilt about both previous pregnancies.

Menopause

Women cease menstruation at around the age of fifty in Western societies. Since their life expectancy is approaching eighty years, women can expect to live more than a third of their lives beyond the menopause. The relationship between psychological symptoms and the menopause is unclear. Gynaecologists tend to focus on symptoms directly attributable to deficiency of the ovarian hormone oestrogen and thus amenable to hormone replacement therapy (HRT). But social scientists maintain that symptoms are more influenced by the expectations of a particular socio-cultural group or by demanding life events. Women face many of these in their middle years: a major illness in themselves or spouse or close relative, job uncertainty, 'mid-life crisis' or retirement of spouse, their own retirement, caring for an elderly parent, children leaving or returning home, and the ultimate loss—death of a spouse. There are of course positive countervailing forces: the advent of grandchildren, freedom from unwanted conception, and the opportunity to pursue new interests. Given their biopsychosocial perspective, psychiatrists generally straddle these two points of view.

Most menopausal women report positive or at least neutral feelings concerning the ending of their menses. Menopause has only a minimal impact on how they regard their status of health, both physical and mental. An exception is the surgical menopause group (that is, women whose uterus and sometimes ovaries have been removed); they have poorer health and use medical services more frequently prior to, as well as after, surgery. Any negative attitudes women harbour towards their menopause are related to the common experience of symptoms long before they cease to menstruate.

Elevated rates of depression are found among women attending clinics dedicated to menopausal problems and among middle-aged women attending gynaecology clinics. Depression in the menopausal years may be linked to a sense of loss of fertility and femininity, although these reactions are relatively uncommon in Western societies. More likely than not, depression relates to the ups and downs of middle age rather than to the menopause itself.

On the other hand, changes in mood may be linked to classic disabling menopausal symptoms like hot flushes and profuse sweating. These are arguably the only direct effects of the loss of ovarian hormones, with psychological complaints explained by the domino theory—that is, flushes and sweating cause insomnia, which leads to fatigue and irritability, and so on. In any event, these classic symptoms are the most responsive to HRT. We remain uncertain whether this type of treatment does its work by removing unpleasant physical symptoms, which in turn paves the way for emotional benefits, or whether there is a direct effect on the depressed mood. Prescribing anti-depressants is probably the better option when the mood disturbance is prominent. Issues of concern to the woman—for example, children leaving home, marital discord, the strain of caring for a frail parent—call for a psychotherapy approach, often in association with relevant medication.

Celia, aged 52 and married with three sons, required hysterectomy for heavy periods, during which she unexpectedly had her ovaries removed due to complications. She immediately received HRT, but a month later began to experience hot flushes, sweats, dizziness and swinging mood. She felt so low, anxious and lacking in confidence that she withdrew socially and neglected her domestic chores. She felt physically unattractive and lost interest in sexual relations with her husband.

Celia's mother had suicided at the age of 55, a loss that she had never fully grieved for. Her husband was not only extremely busy at his job, but had little capacity to express his emotions. All three of her sons were in their early twenties and living away from home. The youngest son had moved just before the surgery. Celia felt she had lost her identity as a woman and her role as a mother.

Treatment included anti-depressant medication and HRT. Psychotherapy was geared to explaining the role of the sex hormones in leading to the hot flushes and night sweats, and her emotional reactions to them. The therapist also provided her with the opportunity to deal with her losses and adjust to the next phase of her life. Brief couple counselling was added in order to promote a much deeper understanding in the husband of his wife's need for emotional support and more quality time as a couple. Celia spoke optimistically about new options, particularly resuming a long-dormant interest in the visual arts. Not only did she begin to attend courses in medieval painting, she also joined an art class using her 'favourite pastels'.

The elderly woman

In Western societies most women are widowed in their mid-seventies. For every 100 women aged over 80 years in Australia, for instance, there are only 47 men. Large numbers of women live alone; many of them lack a supportive family network. However, it is a myth that elderly women are a helpless, disease-ridden group. While some of the last years may be spent in partial ill-health, only a small percentage of elderly women is institutionalised. The increased ageing population has profound political and economic implications for health care, social welfare and economic support, as discussed in Chapter 16. Negative portrayal of elderly women as unattractive, dependent and physically decrepit has unfortunate psychological and social repercussions; we need to rid ourselves of stereotypes.

We must also consider the wellbeing of the caregivers, given that a quarter of the elderly over eighty-five, mostly women, have Alzheimer's disease or a related disorder. In the United States and Australia, three-quarters of the people caring for the elderly without pay are women. Men and women bring different expectations and coping strategies to this role and experience it differently—a subjective and objective sense of burden being greater for female than male carers of relatives with dementia. Women feel greater strain and in fact shoulder more of the burden than do men.

Three-quarters of the long-term mentally ill in nursing homes are women, mainly with depression and dementia. Older women are also vulnerable to alcohol and drug abuse (the benzodiazepines in particular) —above all those who are isolated, trapped in unhappy marriages, institutionalised in nursing homes or psychiatric settings, or lacking adequate resources to obtain treatment. Yet older women are often under-represented in the use of mental health services.

Quality of social activity and satisfaction in relationships are vital to the morale of elderly women (as to their male counterparts). Wellbeing is linked to support that provides acceptance, reassurance of worth, and opportunity to participate in recreational pursuits that contribute to quality of life.

The abused woman

A sad reflection on us all is the abuse of women since time immemorial, a pattern that still prevails. Abuse occurs throughout the life cycle, and includes child abuse (both physical and sexual), incest, wife battering, rape and abuse of the elderly.

Most people would think of violence towards women as being mainly perpetrated by strangers, as in the case of criminal rape. However, it is in the family that violence of all types is focused and, unhappily, tradition has tended to condone it. This social attitude may help to explain Freud's view that his female patients' accounts of sexual abuse in childhood were fantasies. Most violence is carried out by men, with the burden falling on women. The victim, of whatever age, develops a state of helplessness after repeated abusive experiences. She may even conceal the true source of her injuries from health professionals.

The impact of violence on a woman may be an immediate response (resembling post-traumatic stress disorder) of fear, withdrawal, emotional inhibition, disturbed self-image and sexual dysfunction. Longer-term effects include depression, which is the most common symptom in adults who were sexually abused as children.

Conclusion

Knowledge of the maladies of women and their treatment has seen enormous progress. We have come to appreciate, through an impressive research effort, that women are burdened at many critical times in their lives with a range of psychological stresses that contribute to mental ill health. Fortunately, psychiatry is well placed to offer effective treatments and progress is likely to continue. Contributing to these changes has been the high proportion of women within the psychiatric profession itself. They have taken a special interest in this burgeoning area of clinical practice and research as well as bringing a sensitive empathy to the sufferer.

CHAPTER 16

The Elderly

The world's population is ageing rapidly. In a typical developed country like Australia, the proportion of people aged sixty-five years and over will double by 2050. The number of years a person spends actively retired has gone up ten-fold over the last century. The picture of increased longevity in developing countries is even more extraordinary; in China, one in three of the population will be aged over sixty by the middle of the twenty-first century. These projections have huge implications for psychiatry when we consider the mental illnesses whose onset is mainly in older people. Thus, dementia will be much more common in decades to come. The number of cases worldwide is expected to increase from 25 million in the early 2000s to 80 million in 2040, with most new cases in the developing world. These are frightening statistics since we do not have a cure for dementia and treatments to slow it down are not that effective.

On a brighter note, we should hasten to proclaim that most elderly people are fit and active, and lead satisfying, productive lives. The Roman philosopher Cicero captured this well when he observed: 'So far from being listless and sluggish, old age is even a busy time, always doing and attempting something, of course of the same nature as each man's taste had been in the previous part of his life'. We have only to think of the artist Pablo Picasso, the cellist Pablo Casals, the playwrights Sophocles and George Bernard Shaw, the philosopher Bertrand Russell and the composer Giuseppe Verdi. Sophocles wrote his great tragedy *Oedipus at Colunus* at the age of 90, while Verdi composed his last opera at the age of 80, and the glorious choral work, *Stabat Mater*, three years before his death at 87. They are notable examples of the fact that age is no impediment to creativity.

As I myself have grown older, I have come to appreciate how much those in the last quarter of their lives benefit personally from their collected wisdom and are well placed to transmit the valuable lessons they have learned over many years to the next generation. My own father-in-law lived to 90 and had many valuable lessons to pass on to the family. We were thrilled when he agreed to write a memoir (reluctantly so; he thought it would be of limited interest). This turned out to be a wonderfully successful book entitled *I Rest My Case*. I always regret that I did not encourage my father to share his insights with us. He died relatively early, long before I came to the realisation that we can learn much about life from the elderly.

Old age is also a time of loss. The very elderly in particular are likely to be widowed, live alone and have physical or mental limitations that affect their independence. Many require the support of family, friends, neighbours and social services, and some repeated admissions to hospital or permanent residential care.

Society's attitude to elderly people is a crucial factor in how they adapt to old age. It ranges from respect, even reverence, for their wisdom to a negative view that they are a heavy burden on society, particularly as the health and welfare dollar is increasingly stretched. Plato puts forward a view in *The Republic* in the form of a dialogue between Socrates as a young man and Cephalus, an old one, who opens the conversation:

'I find that as I lose my tastes for bodily pleasures, I grow more eager than ever for discussion.' Socrates replied, 'I enjoy talking with very old men. I consider that they have gone before us along a road which we must all travel in our turn, and it is good that we should ask them of the nature of that road, whether it be rough and difficult, or easy and smooth. You Cephalus are now at that time of life which the poets call "old age the threshold", and I should particularly like to ask your thoughts on this question. Is it a painful period of life, or what is your news of it?'

Cephalus then said, 'You know how some of us old men are often together, true to the old proverb. Now most of the company whenever they meet lament their wretched lot. They long for the pleasures of youth, and some of them bewail the insults which their kinsfolk heap upon their years … in my opinion, Socrates, they don't really see what is wrong. If they were right, then I too, and all who have come to my time of life, would by reason of old age have suffered as they have; but, as a matter of fact, I have met many whose experience is different … But all these troubles, their complaints against their kinsfolk among them, have but one cause, and that is not old age, Socrates, but men's dispositions or personality; for old age lays but a moderate burden on men who have order and peace within themselves, but ill-governed natures find youth and age alike irksome.'

Cephalus' response is a wise reminder that the psychological ills of the elderly stem from a complex mix of factors. I will describe the features and treatment of the psychiatric conditions that affect the old, including dementia, depression, anxiety, substance abuse and personality problems. But first, I will briefly outline the psychiatrist's approach in evaluating these factors.

How do psychiatrists assess the elderly?

Since elderly people are usually reluctant to complain of emotional or memory problems, and when they do their relatives all too often put these down to the natural effects of ageing, health professionals who look after them have to take special note of any early changes in their psychological state. So, for example, many serious depressive states remain unrecognised, even though depressed elderly people respond to treatment as well as younger people.

The specialty of psychiatry of old age (also known as psychogeriatrics) provides assessment and care to old people with mental illnesses in community, hospital and residential aged-care settings. With expertise in this phase of the life cycle, they can offer appropriate medical and psychological treatments, liaise with aged-care services, and appreciate ethical, legal and practical issues that arise. Occupational therapists, social workers, psychologists and especially nurses also play key roles.

Assessments are done in a clinic or, more advantageously, in the person's home, particularly in the case of frail, deaf or confused people. Valuable information can be obtained at a glance. Is there food in the kitchen? Is the person clean, groomed, adequately clothed and nourished? Is the house clean? Is there evidence of hoarding? Are there physical hazards such as lack of heating, scatter rugs on polished floors or unsupervised pets, or evidence of failing domestic competence such as dirty surfaces, unopened mail or burned saucepans? They can also be seen with family or friends, who are always asked to comment on the nature and duration of symptoms if the elderly person is confused. Specific queries about the person's orientation in time and space, recall of recent events, attendance at appointments, payment of bills and so forth may be most revealing. Questions directed to the confused person are posed in as simple and clear a form as possible.

Mental and physical illness both increase in frequency with age, and the relationship between them is complex. One may lead to the other or they may occur at the same time. For example, if a person is gloomy and has an under-active thyroid, any mood change may well be due to this. The depression may respond to correction of the thyroid problem, or require treatment in its own right in addition to thyroid replacement medication.

Since our ability to handle drugs diminishes with age and our vulnerability to side-effects increases, particularly in dementia, the use of drugs is more risky in the elderly.

Once a diagnosis has been made, the psychiatrist considers the physical, psychological, social and environmental factors that may be playing a role. Consider the case of Mr Schmidt, aged 84, who emigrated to Australia from Austria in 1939; he became severely depressed for the first time a few months before being seen in the clinic. He had had his blood pressure tablets changed at that time, when his heartbeat became irregular. Although Mr Schmidt had coped well with life overall, he became vulnerable to even the mildest stress. He had lost his appetite and 8 kilograms in weight. The onset of the lowering in mood seems to have coincided with the third anniversary of his wife's death and the question of residential care being raised by his children, who had noted increasing memory lapses.

Many factors were considered in the assessment including:

- biological—change in medication, with potential side-effects;
- psychological—unresolved bereavement and worries about his future living arrangements;
- interpersonal—disagreement with his children over giving up his independence;
- social—the loneliness of widowhood and a reduced capacity to get to social events.

Elderly mentally ill people are particularly vulnerable to abuse. Relatives may see their difficult behaviour as a deliberate campaign to gain attention and may take retribution, and a few retaliate in kind. Intentional, sustained abuse is much less common. Children may squander parents' money or seek possession of their house; owners of residential homes may threaten residents' financial assets or behave cruelly and vindictively. Such abuse rarely comes to light, since the victims are either unaware of it or too frightened to complain. It may fall to the vigilant doctor to identify exploitation or maltreatment and intervene accordingly.

Most people regard quality of life in the elderly as more relevant than mere longevity. It is appropriate to treat remediable and distressing conditions like a urinary tract infection, bowel obstruction or fractured hip, as quality of life is thereby improved. On the other hand, many agree that vigorously treating severely demented people for, say, pneumonia or kidney failure only postpones the inevitable, and may well be unmerciful.

By far the most noteworthy mental illnesses that befall the elderly are the dementias and it is therefore to this group of conditions that we turn first.

Dementia

The word 'dementia' conjures up apprehension in many of us, given how prevalent it is as people live so much longer than at any other point in history. We tend to poke fun at the spectre of dementia as part of coping with the anxiety. We hear such comments as 'Oh dear, another senior moment' when someone struggles to recall a name of a familiar person or object. Although we associate dementia with the elderly, it can occur occasionally at an earlier age as a complication of a range of medical conditions. The rate mounts with every extra five years of life above 60, increasing from one in a hundred 65 year-olds to a frightening quarter of those aged 85. In Australia, the estimated figures are striking—25 000 newly diagnosed cases in the year 2005 compared to a likely 175 000 new cases in 2050. There is certainly a price to pay for growing old—for the unlucky person who loses their mind and identity, for their relatives, and for society, which has to support both the afflicted and family carers.

Alzheimer's disease (AD) is the most common form of dementia (about half the cases) and, alas, the one with an elusive cause and for which a cure is unavailable. Alois Alzheimer is a prime example of a psychiatrist who searched relentlessly for changes in the structure of the brain that might underlie severe mental illnesses. 4 November 1906 stands out as a key date in the history of dementia. On that day, Alzheimer described the case of a woman who, at the age of fifty-one, had begun to develop an array of mental symptoms—jealousy of her husband, hallucinations, trouble in reading and writing, forgetfulness, poor judgement and, at times, delirium. Alzheimer had observed her closely over five years until her death as she deteriorated severely, becoming bedridden, mute and incoherent. He found her brain, following her death, to be shrunken and withered. Four years later, his colleagues at Munich named the condition Alzheimer's disease in his honour.

Many theories have been proposed as to why amyloid, a protein, builds up between the brain's nerve cells, and fibrils in the cells themselves become tangled up. Advancing age and a family history of dementia increase the risk. The amyloid protein has been shown to be part of a larger protein (APP—amyloid precursor protein) that occurs in normal cells. It had been known for decades that these typical brain changes occur in all people with Down's syndrome who survive to middle age. Down's itself is a genetic condition due to an abnormal chromosome. This link between the two conditions is explained by the finding that a gene on Chromosome 21 controls the level of APP; the amyloid deposits in Down's result from increased concentrations of APP.

Vascular dementia, representing 15 per cent of the dementias, is the result of disease of the blood vessels in the brain leading to the death of nerve and other cells. Usually there is a history of high blood pressure or strokes or both. Unlike AD, the onset is typically abrupt and takes the form of episodes of sudden deterioration interspersed with periods of improvement.

Dementia with so-called Lewy bodies, occurring much more commonly in men, comprises about the same proportion of dementias as the vascular type. A principal component of the Lewy body (first described in 1914 by a German pathologist, Frederick Lewy) is a protein whose presence in brain nerve cells indicates that they will not survive. As with AD, cognitive decline is progressive (actually more rapid), with death occurring after an average six years compared to ten in AD.

Other causes of dementia include Parkinson's disease, AIDS, head injury and lack of oxygen to the brain.

In only very few cases is dementia potentially reversible or improved with relevant treatment. In that related to alcohol abuse (6 per cent of dementias), abstinence may be of benefit. Hormonal disorders—especially an under-active thyroid, vitamin B12 deficiency and certain infections of the brain—are other potentially reversible causes.

The clinical picture

Given how common the dementias are, most of us have known or do know a sufferer and are familiar with the changes that occur in the spheres of memory, intellectual abilities, behaviour and personality. Few elderly people complain explicitly to their doctor of forgetfulness and muddled thinking. More commonly, problems are brought to medical attention by relatives, and friends or doctors are alerted when their patients forget appointments or show self-neglect. However, family members, especially spouses, may delay seeking help through fear their loved one will need to be removed to a nursing home. Dangerous or bizarre behaviour, such as a fire in the kitchen, wandering away from home, aggressiveness, constant repetition of questions, accusing neighbours of stealing money or a spouse of being an impostor, are alarming and precipitate action.

Memory impairment is the key feature of dementia. People's ability to learn new information is reduced early and declines until they can retain virtually nothing for more than a few seconds. Their recall of events of the distant past also worsens over time, even to the extent of highly personal information like names of spouse and children. The process is akin to a malfunctioning tape recorder where the ability to record new information is steadily lost. Information already on the tape is wiped out at the same time, starting with recent material and progressing until the entire tape is wiped clean. Apart from memory, other mental functions deteriorate— intelligence, language, calculation, orientation in time and place, and judgement. In the advanced stage, the person becomes a shell of their former self, requiring assistance in every activity of daily living—feeding, toileting and dressing. A total reversion to childlike behaviour results. Shakespeare's seventh age in Jaques' famous speech in *As You Like It* sums up this end point most graphically:

> … Last scene of all
> That ends this strange, eventful history,
> Is second childishness, and mere oblivion,
> Sans teeth, sans eye, sans taste, sans everything.

Despite these unwelcome features, many demented people are only affected to a mild degree. Even those who exhibit more severe changes may spend their days sitting quietly or pottering aimlessly. A gentle elderly lady may need help from her husband but the full extent of her dementia may not become apparent until a dramatic incident points to the truth, and memory, orientation and day-to-day skills are challenged.

If the person had always been good-humoured this generally continues, whereas previous distrustful, argumentative or obsessional traits are magnified, often leading to friction with family and friends. A few people become fearful and agitated and require constant reassurance.

Assessing the patient

In examining the mental state, appearances can deceive. People living alone often look untidy whereas those living with a relative tend to be neatly groomed. Most people show little distress when errors in their stories are exposed, but those with greater awareness become anxious about their limitations. Discussion about family, hobbies or a recent activity may be revealing if descriptions are rambling, and recent and long-past events are interwoven. A clue is the person's tendency to reply in general terms to specific questions, so that the query 'What day is this?' is answered with a discourse on events of the previous week.

The psychiatrist always tests intellectual functioning if there are difficulties with memory, orientation, judgement or everyday skills. This is necessary because mildly demented people conceal deficiencies by off-handed reassurances or humour. Tests of orientation to time, and ability to recall three simple words or a fictional name and address are commonly used. Assessment of the capacity to copy a diagram or draw a clock face is a good indicator of global mental impairment in the absence of any other obvious cause such as a stroke or Parkinson's disease. Contrary to popular belief, non-demented old people are almost always aware of the day of the week and month, and most know the date within a day or two. The style of answers is often as revealing as the content. Glib responses ('I don't follow the news any more' or 'I was never any good at counting') are commonly used by people to conceal their deficits. These are similar to methods we all use in everyday life when our competence is challenged and we feel threatened.

Physical examination and special tests are necessary to ensure that no reversible cause of dementia is missed. Finding a cause that is treatable is unusual in the elderly.

About 5 per cent of demented people need treatment for depression—which is suggested by withdrawal, restlessness, insomnia and poor eating. Depressed, demented old people look tired and preoccupied, conveying a sense of unhappiness and hopelessness. Some of them decline abruptly following the death of a spouse or major change in their environment.

The personal dimension

Many published accounts of the experiences of families attest not only to the tragedy of dementia but also to the devotion and courage of relatives, particularly spouses and children. Sharon Aldrick witnessed her grandparents' experience:

> It was a strange day, the day she died. We were quite upset, but my grandfather, not a tear rolled from his eyes. I suppose he had accepted it a long time ago. He was happy she died peacefully in his loving embrace. Her pain and suffering from the past 25 years had finally ended.
>
> My grandfather used to work in the bakehouse, making his bread deliveries by horse and cart. My grandmother worked in a factory creasing tobacco papers. He earned £2, she earned £4, and when they married in 1939 she gave up her job, as was expected of a wife. They bought an orange orchard four years later and spent their days working hard on the farm and raising six children. She loved cooking and sewing and decorating the house with flowers from her garden.
>
> The first few years before the diagnosis of Alzheimer's Disease my grandfather spent in darkness, not knowing why his wife would break down and cry, argue and yell at him constantly. He watched her decline from a capable, competent woman to one unable to look after herself. She would hide her money and forget where she hid it. Her clothes were worn back to front. She was frustrated by tasks she could perform with ease just a few years ago.
>
> I suppose I look at my grandfather as heroic. When I think about it, I wonder could I do the same? Could I devote myself to caring for my spouse the way he did: total loyalty with no gratitude.

He would say, 'She was the best-fed. I would feed her strawberries all day, boiled eggs for lunch and Weetbix with warm milk in the morning'. He would change her sanitary pad and carry her from the bed they shared for 56 years and place her in her lounge. She would spend the day curled in a foetal position, with the television casting images that had no meaning to her. He spent the day working on his 200 hectare orange orchard from sun up to sun down.

Returning home, he would sit with her, holding her hand, feeding her chocolates and talking to her. It did not concern him that for the past 15 years she had not even known who he was. Alzheimer's had dissolved the memory of him from her mind.

It was sad to watch an intelligent, strong woman fade slowly. It must have been heart wrenching for my grandfather to watch and to have no control over her fate …

A heart-rending account of how Alzheimer's disease affects the lives of both its victims and their loved ones is that by the literary critic John Bayley. His wife, the celebrated novelist and philosopher Iris Murdoch, first showed evidence of mental impairment when contributing to a conference in Israel. Iris was unable to find the words she needed and seemed oblivious to the audience's discomfort. A similar speaker's block occurred a few months later at another conference. On her return to Oxford, Iris was troubled, unusually so, by a paucity of ideas for a new novel; she had enjoyed a long and productive career up to that point. For Professor Bayley, the signs were ominous. As he put it, the insidious fog that Alzheimer's resembles was a portent of things to come. Iris's mother had been similarly diagnosed years before. Three years after these conference difficulties, the full tragedy had also unfolded for her daughter as she sat in front of the television watching and enjoying *Teletubbies*, a children's program. Two years later she was dead, at the age of eighty-one. (*Elegy for Iris*, St Martin's Press, London, 1999 and *Iris and Her Friends*, Duckworth, London, 1999.)

Another personal account of great poignancy is that by Michael Ignatieff, a Canadian writer:

I remember how it began, five or six years ago. She was sixty-six then. She would leave a pot to boil dry on the stove. I would discover it and find her tearing through the house, muttering, 'My glasses, my glasses, where the hell are my glasses?'…

The deficits … are localised. She can tell you what it felt like when the Model T-Ford ran over her at the school gates when she was a girl of seven … But she can't dice an onion. She can't set the table. She can't play cards. Her grandson is five, and when they play pairs with his animal cards, he knows where the second penguin will be. She just turns up cards at random ... After a week with him, she looks puzzled and says, ' He's a nice little boy ... who does he belong to?

'Where are we now, is this our house?'

'Yes.'

'Where is our house?'

'In France.'

I tell her: 'Hold my hand, I'm here. I'm your son.'

'I know.'

But she keeps asking where she is. The questions are her way of trying to orient herself, of refusing and resisting the future that is being prepared for her ... She wakes in the night and lies in the dark by my side ... She turns and notices that I am awake too. We lie side by side. The darkness is still. I want to say her name. She turns away from me and stares into the night. Her nightie is buttoned at the neck like a little girl's.

'Deficits', *Granta*, vol. 27, summer 1989, pp. 163–72.

How does the psychiatrist help?

Ideally, people with dementia participate in decisions about their care. When diagnosed early, they can be invited to consider assigning an enduring power of attorney or making a will. Since patients may forget these discussions, written notes and brochures are useful. The diagnosis is explained to the person and their family sensitively, and the hope expressed that effective support services and medications can play a key role.

The psychiatrist's main task is to form a clear view as to how the person and family are coping, since this will determine where treatment is best carried out. How does the person manage with dressing, washing, bathing, cooking, housework, shopping and handling money? How much help is required and who provides it? Will neighbours assist in a crisis? What services are in place? Are relatives disturbed by any difficult or dangerous behaviour?

If the person can be cared for at home, then clear information helps carers to deal with disturbing behaviour that they might otherwise attribute to wilfulness or laziness. Advice that argumentative people should be humoured rather than challenged or that those who resist dressing or bathing should be left for a moment helps. Regular physical exercise, distraction, music and human touch all have their part to play to promote quality of life. Memory aides (for example, identifying the date and day prominently, keeping a diary or journal and simple word games) help to delay the next stage of the disease.

Most importantly, given the relentless nature of their responsibility, carers are encouraged to unburden themselves by ventilating their concerns, and to arrange breaks for themselves. Helpful interventions include home help, meals on wheels, respite care, dosette boxes to organise medications, nursing help with bathing, and carer support groups. Patients and carers are also encouraged to accept referral to self-help organisations for advice and support. As a group, carers experience elevated rates of distress, social isolation, physical ill-health and financial hardship. These can be diminished by early provision of education, advice and support, as well as by active treatment of any manifest psychiatric disorder.

Residential care comes sooner for people who live alone or whose carer is frail. Families and friends are nonetheless encouraged to persist while the person is content and enjoys adequate quality of life. Since the move from familiar surroundings is disruptive and often distressing, the nursing home is fully informed of the person's particular needs prior to the move.

Drugs have a limited role in dementia. Unfortunately, they are sometimes prescribed at excessive levels in nursing homes in order to quieten the agitated person. Used in this way they can worsen the person's mental state, and even cause death.

The introduction of a novel class of drugs known as cholinesterase inhibitors to reverse the process of mental decline instilled much hope in patients, relatives and psychiatrists, but its effectiveness varies. The rationale for their use in Alzheimer's disease—abnormal function of the choline messenger system—is overly simplistic, since other chemical systems are also disturbed. True, some people may become brighter and function better, and deteriorate when treatment is stopped, but any positive effects do not endure for long. Others do not benefit at all.

Other drugs play a very limited role since they all may increase confusion and impair the sense of balance, leading to falls. Short-term use of hypnotics may reduce disturbance during the night. Anti-psychotics in low doses may improve daytime anxiety, aggressiveness, delusionary thinking and hallucinations. Mood stabilisers may be used to reduce unpredictable aggressiveness and unstable mood, and anti-depressants to treat a persistent lowering of mood.

The Lamberts illustrate a typical program of treatment:

Mr and Mrs Lambert's family doctor, Dr George, visits their home following a request from their worried daughter. Mr Lambert is 83, has osteoarthritis and mild respiratory difficulties, but is mentally alert. Eighty-year old Mrs Lambert is, by contrast, physically well but has become increasingly forgetful. She had gone shopping the previous day but not returned home within an hour as was her usual custom. A woman had found her weeping in the shopping centre and brought her home after ascertaining her address from an invoice in her handbag.

On arrival, Dr George notes the house is dusty, the kitchen in disarray and the garden ill-kept—not at all the usual picture with which he is acquainted from past visits. Mrs Lambert is oriented to place but not to time. She does not know her date of birth and claims that she is 'about fifty'. She knows the names of her children but not those of her six grandchildren. She has no knowledge of recent events in her life or in the wider world and certainly does not recall getting lost the previous day.

Physical examination is normal though she smells of stale urine and does not appear to have bathed for a few days. Mr Lambert intimates that she refuses to shower and insists she has just done so. The doctor obtains a comprehensive history from the husband, evaluates Mrs Lambert's mental functioning and performs a physical examination. He also collects blood and urinary specimens to run special tests.

Dementia due to Alzheimer's disease is diagnosed. The couple and their children are put in touch with the local branch of a self-help organisation; the couple then enrol in a 'living with memory loss' course. Meals on wheels, home help and community nursing are arranged. A family discussion is held to decide on an enduring power of attorney and guardianship. A cholinesterase inhibitor is prescribed, with improvement noted over the next few weeks in Mrs Lambert's memory, alertness and mood.

Delirium

The elderly are especially prone to delirium, and more so when they are physically ill or under treatment with drugs. In fact, one in six patients aged over 65 who enter a general hospital are affected. Unfortunately, it may go unrecognised in a busy hospital given the staff's focus on physical disease and its treatment. The typical delirious person is disoriented in time and place, utterly confused, has very poor memory for recent events and misperceives the environment. They may misidentify, for example, the folds of the curtains as animals.

Prevention is by far the best approach in elderly people admitted to hospital, focusing on orienting them to their new surrounding, mobilising them soon after an episode of illness or surgery, minimising the use of drugs that affect the brain, ensuring night-time sleep and encouraging daytime wakefulness, attending to hearing aids and spectacles, and guarding against dehydration.

Mr Dakis, 72 years old and previously well, underwent hip replacement surgery. On the evening following the operation he became uncharacteristically abusive, began to shout incoherently and attempted to pull out his intravenous drip. Psychiatric assessment showed that he was totally disoriented in time and place, panic-stricken and could not remember anything about the surgery. Mr Dakis was convinced that the nurses were poisoning him through the drip. He saw and felt ants crawling all over his body and pointed to folds in the curtain as sinister figures plotting with the nurses against him. With appropriate treatment, correction of his electrolyte imbalance, Mr Dakis made a complete recovery to the immense relief of his family, and only vaguely remembered the 'weird' experience.

Mrs Roberts is an 88-year-old widowed, retired nurse living happily in an aged-care hostel. She has been forgetful for two years and sometimes thinks her daughter is her late sister, but a diagnosis of dementia has not been made. On the way to dinner she falls and is taken to the emergency department, where a fractured neck of femur is diagnosed. Because there are no spaces on the operation list she undergoes surgery three days later. While waiting, her fluid and food intake is poor and she receives several doses of pethidine for pain. She becomes increasingly confused, convinced that she is back in Japan, where she nursed Australian servicemen in 1945.

After surgery Mrs Roberts remains confused and is so noisy that she is placed in a room remote from the nurses' station. She is especially frightened and confused at night, and drowsy during the day. Food and fluid intake remains inadequate and several meal trays are removed untouched. A urinary tract infection is treated with an antibiotic. A low-dose anti-psychotic is used to treat her troubling delusions of persecution by the Japanese. After three weeks her confusion is less marked but she now has a large bedsore and urinary incontinence. She is transferred to a geriatric ward where she slowly improves and her bedsore starts to heal. Despite physiotherapy she fails to regain independent mobility and is transferred to a nursing home. Although forgetful, she continues to refer to 'that awful time when I broke my hip and was in the Japanese hospital'.

Management of delirium involves tackling its causes, supportive care, preventing complications, and treating behavioural symptoms. A quiet, evenly lit environment with minimal distractions and maximal reassurance are essential aspects of care. Maintenance of fluids and nutrition is vital. A soft light at night, familiar nurses and regular visits by family and friends contribute to the person's overall wellbeing. An anti-psychotic drug may be necessary to deal with any frightening hallucinations or delusions. Following delirium, people may have baffling, unpleasant memories of their experience, as was the case with Mrs Roberts, and feel embarrassed by reports of their behaviour. Families need support and information so that they can deal with the changes they witness in their relative. Recovered patients often need repeated reassurance that terrifying memories of the episode are akin to a bad dream and that the delirium has no bearing on their future mental health.

Mood problems

Before considering the lowering of mood that requires medical attention, we need to note that grief, a normal emotional process, is omnipresent in later life given the many losses that the elderly encounter: spouse, other relatives, friends and acquaintances, health, independence, the family home and neighbourhood, and social changes. Deaths of friends or family members often conjure up memories of earlier losses. Grieving takes diverse forms, from utter sadness through feelings of guilt or anger to poor concentration. Most bereaved people do resume full lives. In complicated grief, bereaved people are unable to accept their loss. They often have endured unusual sadness or trauma in their past or have a history of conflicted relationships.

Compared to the common experience of grief, depressive illness affects only 5 per cent of the elderly. Those at risk have had a bout of depression in the past, suffer enduring pain, physical or sensory incapacity, have experienced complicated bereavement or lack emotional support, among other things. Many medications can trigger lowered mood. Similarly, a range of medical conditions, such as stroke, may be associated with depression.

Depressive illness in the elderly is very like that for any other age group, with pessimism, loss of the capacity to gain pleasure, fatigue, poor sleep, loss of appetite and social withdrawal prominent. Suicide has classically been more frequent in older people, especially in men, but the risk has diminished in developed countries, possibly attributable to greater knowledge in the lay community that social and medical support is available, and to the widespread use of well-tolerated anti-depressant medications. Old men who do kill themselves have often lived alone and suffered from disabling, painful physical illnesses.

The mood change may be masked or present unusually. Complaints of pain or physical discomfort is one form of disguise. But physical ailments are so common in the elderly that the precise cause is often elusive. People who previously coped well with a physical disability may now weep and plead for assistance. As heart, lung and kidney disease, and cancer, also lead to anorexia, disturbed sleep and lack of energy, coexisting depression can easily be overlooked.

Spontaneous complaints of forgetfulness and muddled thinking strongly point to depression rather than dementia. When left to their own devices, demented people tend to be unaware of their lapses. Equally, depressed people may be so slow in their thinking and movement that they actually appear to be demented. They need help with dressing, bathing and feeding, and the simplest questions are countered with 'I don't know' or 'I just can't do it'.

Some elderly people interpret their gloom as a natural response to ageing while others fear that endless complaints will alienate relatives, friends and doctors. Many of those mildly to moderately depressed feel lonely and unwanted, fearing illness, dependency, moving to new accommodation and using up their financial reserves.

The opportunity to express such concerns is much appreciated, as is the doctor's attention to anniversaries of the death of a spouse, children or friends. Persistent and painful medical conditions must be treated, and various forms of home help arranged. Grief counselling and couple or family therapy may also help. Progress with these various psychological and social measures is monitored after a week or two, with the perspective of a relative or friend central to this review.

Depressed older people have a higher than average mortality because of the strong association between disordered mood and serious physical illness. Apart from this, the outlook is similar to that for younger age groups. For instance, two-thirds of people admitted to hospital for depression show substantial improvement, but recurrence is common and continuing treatment usually arranged, especially if there is a past history of depressive relapses.

Anti-depressants are most helpful, in smaller dosage, but side-effects such as dizziness are still problematic; falls are therefore a risk. People are cautioned to rise slowly from bed or bath, and to switch on a light when toileting at night. Electro-convulsive therapy (ECT) is an option in people who are markedly slowed down or present with psychotic features, in those who refuse to eat or drink, and where the risk of suicide is high. ECT can be used even in the presence of impairment of higher mental functioning, although the latter may be aggravated in the short term.

Older people were traditionally regarded as unlikely to benefit from any form of psychotherapy since they were insufficiently flexible in their thinking. Freud set the limit at 50 years for psychoanalysis when he himself was aged 49! In fact, a large proportion of elderly depressed people welcome the opportunity to learn more about themselves and how they can make positive changes for the future. Family counselling may assist in improving relationships.

If the target is complicated grief, therapists acquaint themselves with the diverse cultural patterns of grieving and act sensitively and compassionately in the face of expressions of mourning with which they are unfamiliar. Empathic listening to the person's story, encouraging expression of pent-up feelings and attempts to carry out avoided tasks (for example, sorting through the deceased person's belongings), help in most cases. Where marked depression supervenes, anti-depressants may well have a place.

Cognitive-behaviour therapy is suited to people of a more practical bent, focusing as it does on the daily recording of mood and activities, with the positive reinforcement of tasks achieved. Other practical strategies include regular exercise and social involvement.

Mr Bennet, a 74-year-old retired engineer with a history of high blood pressure, sought help from his family doctor after a three-month period during which he had stopped attending football matches and gardening—his two favourite pastimes. He found visits from his children and grandchildren tiring, hoping they would soon depart. He woke up in the early hours and had lost both appetite and weight. Life seemed hopeless; he sighed that he would be better off dead. On examination, he looked sad and spoke slowly and minimally. He had suffered a depressive illness requiring ECT in his early forties. When aged 59, he had plummeted again to the point of trying to hang himself. After another course of ECT, he was maintained on anti-depressants for two years. Between these episodes, Mr Bennet had been active and sociable with strong ties to both family and community.

He was regarded as 'safe enough' to be treated at home. Anti-depressants were prescribed, starting on half the usual dose because of his age and increased to a standard adult dose a week later. Within a couple of weeks, he felt a gradual lifting of mood. Resumption of his usual social links and leisure activities was encouraged. Given the severity and frequency of past depressions, medication was continued indefinitely. Had Mr Bennet failed to respond within these four weeks, he would have required referral to a psychiatrist, who would have tried various strategies including increasing the dose of medication, using a different anti-depressant or applying ECT.

Most elderly people with an abnormal elevation of mood have had bipolar disorder for many years, while some have been depressed and exhibit the manic state only more recently (often following treatment with anti-depressants or ECT). Very few develop pure mania for the first time in later life. An even smaller number become manic in response to a stroke, head injury or other brain damage. While over-activity, pressure of speech and insomnia are typical, people are more often irritable than elated. Grandiose delusions are common. One patient I knew believed he was Superman, another that she was a prophetess who had been selected by God to save the world from sin. Families are particularly distressed by any sexual disinhibition or financial indiscretion. Treatment in hospital is usually necessary, given how out of contact with reality the person is. There, treatment with modest doses of anti-psychotics is effective in most cases. Mood stabilisers may be prescribed to prevent further attacks of mania, or of both mania and depression in the case of a clear-cut bipolar pattern.

Anxiety

Anxiety, which affects around 10 per cent of the elderly, may appear dramatically in response to a physical illness, bereavement, financial or family concerns or a move to new accommodation. More commonly, people with longstanding anxiety worsen in the face of a threatening event. Typically, they experience insomnia, fatigue, irritability, tremor, palpitations, shortness of breath, forgetfulness and poor concentration. As always in the elderly, the psychiatrist attends to both emotional and physical factors. Heart and lung diseases present particular difficulties because their symptoms may closely mimic features of anxiety. Moreover, many anxious people have associated physical disease and it is not uncommon for them to fear its implications.

Irrational fears are much more frequent than generally thought. One or more falls, for instance, may frighten a person into refusing to leave their home. They move from room to room by grasping tables and chairs, and respond to appeals to walk unaided with protest and tears. Gradual encouragement to overcome such fears, perhaps in a day centre, promotes recovery.

Mildly anxious people simply require reassurance, care of any physical illnesses, referral to social services for financial benefits, and attendance at a social club or day centre. The long-term anxious need support as they lurch from crisis to crisis that to other people appear trivial. Angry retorts and stern warnings achieve little. On the other hand, relaxation training and simple psychological manoeuvers such as graded exposure to what they fear are helpful. Benzodiazepines and other drugs for anxiety may cause drowsiness, confusion, unsteadiness and falls, and so are used only if absolutely necessary, and then only for a circumscribed period.

Mrs Albert, aged in her seventies, was brought along by her daughter because she and her brother and sister found their mother 'intolerable'. She was described as 'demanding, self-centred and unpleasant to be with'. She was constantly fearful, especially worried about her 'memory lapses', and sought endless reassurance. It emerged through careful questioning that she had always felt fearful beyond her familiar environment, and tended to avoid any new encounters. Treatment involved meetings with Mrs Albert and her daughter initially, followed by individual sessions in which she was encouraged to face those things she feared very gradually. As she had a chance to reflect on her life, grieve for lost opportunities and feel affirmed as a person, she found herself a dancing partner and started dancing twice a week. She thrived, and looked and felt much younger. Her anxiety receded and the 'memory problem' evaporated.

Delusional disorders and other psychoses

Typical events befalling elderly people, like loss of a loved one, may lead understandably to an insecurity about the world around them. A few lonely, mistrustful people, particularly isolated women who are partially deaf or blind, conclude that others dislike, avoid or take advantage of them. They argue with neighbours and shopkeepers and abruptly take offence. Their beliefs fall short of psychotic thinking but result in greater isolation. Some live in squalor and resist help. When these beliefs become pronounced and are held unshakeably, we enter the territory of delusional disorders.

The delusions are usually banal—the person is convinced, despite all evidence to the contrary, that neighbours are banging on walls or hurling rubbish over the fence. Or bizarre strangers or secret investigators spy, tap the telephone or bombard the person with special gases or waves of electricity. In response to these ideas, neighbours may be cursed—even summoning the police for protection. In a case that I once assessed, the patient, previously a delightfully congenial woman, became convinced beyond any shadow of doubt that an elderly neighbour with whom she had enjoyed a long friendship had stolen money from her wardrobe. All attempts to disabuse her of this allegation tragically failed, leading to a permanent fracture of the friendship.

This form of psychosis may be confused with dementia. Dementing people who lose treasured items may cover these lapses by accusing others of stealing them. These ideas, unlike those in the psychoses, are rarely elaborated upon and quickly forgotten, at least by the person themselves.

Some people readily accept psychiatric help. Others are suspicious, refuse the staff entry and insist that treatment is unwarranted. Medications are introduced gradually to reduce the likelihood that side-effects are construed as a plot to harm them.

Substance abuse

Alcohol abuse is more common in elderly people than is generally appreciated. Some have always drunk heavily, others increase their intake through boredom, loneliness, anxiety or depression. Those who live alone are at particular risk, and even the disabled and housebound obtain supplies surprisingly easily. Their children and friends often fail to intervene or even collude in the abuse on the grounds that 'a drink keeps her happy'. It may take a serious fall or marked confusion after a temporary withdrawal to alert the doctor.

Treatment of underlying factors—loneliness, anxiety or depression—are tackled directly through such measures as attendance at a day centre, bereavement counselling or anti-depressants if indicated. People who resist may develop a severe memory disorder as a direct effect of alcohol poisoning of the brain, and then need nursing-home care for their own protection.

The elderly are the largest consumers of benzodiazepines, usually hypnotics. Insomnia results so commonly from tedium, loneliness, inactivity, pain, anxiety and depression that a doctor's response with sleepless patients may be to recommend a benzodiazepine. Or perhaps a hypnotic was prescribed for a person admitted to hospital for medical or surgical treatment. The snag in both situations is its continued use. Benzodiazepines are best avoided because they are highly addictive. However, in some elderly long-term insomniac people the benefit is such that it would be cruel to withhold the drug.

Personality disturbance

We quoted Plato earlier: 'old age lays but a moderate burden on men who have order and peace within themselves, but ill-governed natures find youth and age alike irksome'. Argumentative, suspicious or dependent behaviour may be due to anxiety, depression or dementia. However, some elderly people have always behaved in an abusive, dependent or reclusive fashion. These tendencies may have faded in middle-life, only to recur with mounting difficulties in the last phase of life. An insecure widow may telephone her children, friends and family doctor many times a day. She makes impossible demands of them and cannot cope with the simplest task since the death of her husband. A reclusive, suspicious man may respond with alarm to hospital admission. Enforced proximity to others may result in anger and irrational insistence on leaving the hospital.

A detailed inquiry by the psychiatrist helps to clarify the picture. Has the person always been anxious or demanding or suspicious? What has triggered this recent outburst? It is never assumed that a 'difficult' personality explains all. The person's demands are dealt with matter-of-factly, as anger and sarcasm worsen matters. If possible, a plan of care is mapped out in collaboration with the person, outlining the help that will be provided in particular circumstances. The distress of relatives and carers obviously also requires attention.

Abuse of the elderly

Elder abuse, a relatively new phenomenon dealt with by psychogeriatricians, probably affects about 5 per cent of the elderly. Physical, psychological, sexual and financial types have been identified. The typical case is a cognitively impaired and dependent woman. The abuser usually has lived with the victim for many years, may depend on her for accommodation or financial support, and may have a record of substance abuse or violence. Often the abuser is unable to cope with the demands of a person whose mental functioning is deteriorating and behaviour tricky to manage. Where abuse is due to such stress, providing emotional and practical support to the carer is invaluable. When the abuse is extreme, separating the pair is advisable through a guardianship or restraining order.

Meeting the needs of the family

The family's interests are commonly paramount in the context of old age psychiatry. The need for a close partnership between family and psychiatrist has been well recognised for decades in child psychiatry (for obvious reasons), but it is only since the 1980s that the experience of informal caregiving for the elderly psychiatric relative has been properly appreciated.

Relatives are often upset by the person's changes in personality and loss of interest in the family. Caring for a physically disabled but mentally intact person is difficult enough. Caring for a person who confuses a daughter with a sister, shows no gratitude, and wets and soils repeatedly is hard, relentless work. Even so, many relatives press on, regarding a request for outside help as a betrayal of trust.

However, we do have a range of services nowadays to assist carers, and they themselves have set up self-help organisations, support networks and political lobbies. On this basis, much can be accomplished. For example, an elderly spouse who wishes to continue caring for a partner with dementia can be supported through respite care, home nursing, meals on wheels, home aids, and the like.

A greying society, and the progressive closure of the old-fashioned and isolated mental institutions, have spawned a new era for the family carer. Indeed, carers have, in a sense, returned to centre stage, a role they played for centuries. Since their pivotal contribution will certainly continue, carers are often society's unsung heroes and deserve every support.

Conclusion

Goethe's remark that 'Age takes hold of us by surprise' was probably more true in his time than ours. With an increased life span and with elderly people making up a growing proportion of the population, there is greater recognition of the last quarter of life than at any other time in history. In response, psychiatry has developed a major sub-specialty that attends exclusively to the needs of elderly people who become emotionally troubled. And a worldwide research effort has been mounted to tackle the disorders that afflict this group at an especially vulnerable period in their lives. Foreseeable developments include even safer medications for depression and psychoses, increased use of psychological therapies, and more effective treatments for Alzheimer's disease and other dementias.

CHAPTER 17

Suicide and Deliberate Self-harm

There is but one truly serious philosophical question and that is
suicide.

Albert Camus

Suicide is undoubtedly the most challenging phenomenon for psychiatrists.
An estimated one million people kill themselves each year—one death
every 40 seconds. In the United States, for instance, 31 000 deaths are due
to suicide, in Australia 2200, in China 300 000, and in Canada 4000. Among
them have featured some of the most creative men and women. We examined the life and death of Vincent van Gogh in Chapter 2. In the twentieth
century the writers Ernest Hemingway, Primo Levi, Virginia Woolf, Sylvia
Plath, Robert Lowell and Theodore Roethke, and the artists Marc Rothko,
Jackson Pollock and Amedeo Modigliani, all took their own lives. Not only
are these figures, in both senses of the word, disturbing to psychiatrists and,
of course, to the community, but the inherent nature of suicide makes it difficult for us to confront—psychologically and ethically.

Suicide differs radically from other clinical circumstances. For most
mental health problems, psychiatrist and patient share the same goals,
but when it comes to suicide they hold diametrically opposed views.
Furthermore, it is not merely a clinical problem to which treatment strategies are applied but also an existential one—the question is not how to
achieve a better life but whether to live at all. That the starting point in
treating the suicidal person is seen so differently by psychiatrists and patients
means that we are required to persuade them to change a basic attitude to
life. The very phenomenon of suicide, which expresses a voluntary rejection
of the value of life, threatens psychiatrists' deepest convictions about the
sanctity of life. Moreover, we have trouble ridding ourselves of this sense of

threat because the dilemma of suicide is inherently puzzling: there are real problems in offering a rational justification for the value of life. In addition, the suicide rate among psychiatrists, as among doctors generally, is much higher than in the general population, and they are therefore vulnerable when treating suicidal patients. In other spheres of treatment, psychiatrists can more easily detach themselves. But since the possibility of suicide is considered by virtually all people at some stage or another in their lives, psychiatrists may have difficulty taking an objective view of their suicidal patients.

Suicide through history

Suicide has always been part of the human condition. In the Bible, suicide is mentioned only as a curiosity and indeed no word is used to cover the act. Only five cases are recorded in the Old Testament, with Saul and Samson the best known. Self-killing is described as a natural association with a reasonable intention, like avoiding torture by the enemy or wreaking revenge.

Suicide was more prominent in Greek and Roman times. Aristotle argued that killing oneself is against the 'right rule of life', and unjust to the State. Socrates' prohibition was based on the notion that it was an injustice to the gods: people were only the custodians of life provided to them by the gods. The Romans regarded suicide from the individual's point of view. The philosopher Seneca proclaimed that 'mere living is not a good, but living well' and argued that disturbed peace of mind or misfortune were adequate reasons to suicide. He also valued the ultimate freedom— the choice of how to end one's life. Pliny the Elder thought that in this type of freedom, human beings were superior even to the gods. And so it was that suicide in Imperial Rome was widespread, with no sanctions against it.

Christianity ushered in new attitudes. St Augustine argued against suicide by interpreting the sixth commandment as applying to self-killing as well as to the murder of others. Thomas Aquinas, in the thirteenth century, was the first to offer a comprehensive Christian argument against suicide. He claimed that it violated the natural law, which prescribes self-love; the moral law, because it hurts the community; and the divine law, since only God has the right to take life. This position affected European attitudes for generations and only shifted at the time of the Renaissance. The eighteenth-century philosopher Montesquieu, for example, strongly criticised the anti-suicide laws in Europe as cruel and inhuman. In his view, no one was obliged to work for society when he had become weary of life, and the State's laws had authority only over those who decided to go on living.

The reasoning used by Aquinas was challenged by the Scottish philosopher David Hume, using the same three levels of law. Firstly, suicide was not necessarily against a person's interests if misery, sickness and misfortune made life unbearable. Secondly, suicide did not harm others because in death a person no longer had a duty to society, and indeed suicide might reduce the burden borne by others. Finally, if God governed every aspect of the world, then suicide must also be seen as part of his will.

The first attempt to understand suicide scientifically was made at the end of the nineteenth century, when the French sociologist Emil Durkheim wrote of what he saw as a social phenomenon. He analysed the person's possible motives and his relation to society (see below). This launch of scientific inquiry came into its own in the twentieth century, and psychiatry has made the greatest contribution to studying suicide objectively. Beyond the attempt to explain suicide scientifically, psychiatrists have sought to treat the suicidal person effectively and to prevent actual attempts. They are also much involved with caring for survivors of failed suicides and bereaved families.

This effort to diagnose and prevent is, historically, a radical shift in the approach to suicide. Treating has replaced moralising and legislating. Like many other social phenomena, suicide has become thoroughly medicalised. The suicidal person is viewed as afflicted by psychological forces and thus in need of professional help. Moreover, the person is considered not to be morally responsible for the act. A more liberal position on suicide is one result of the evolution of this scientific and medical interest.

With this historical perspective in mind, we now discuss the contemporary psychiatric position regarding suicide and examine what we know about its clinical aspects. First, we need to define the term.

Defining suicide

The word comes from the Latin *sui-cidere*, literally to cut oneself. It applies to the intentional act of killing oneself, where the person knows that the act will result in death and is not coerced or encouraged by others to carry it out. This definition seems clear enough, but the complexities of suicidal behaviour soon emerge when we think about other kinds of self-killing— such as self-sacrifice in war, hunger strikes as political protest, some cases of heavy smoking or drinking, and hazardous pastimes like motor-racing and mountaineering.

A special conundrum is how we are to consider a suicidal act that seems rational given the person's circumstances. A classic case is someone in the terminal phase of a painful illness, with no realistic expectation of improvement, who has always taken pride in living independently, does not wish to burden others, and does not want to live in what for them are degrading circumstances.

The case of the author Arthur Koestler brings into sharp relief the issue of rational suicide. He had been a fervent believer throughout his life in the right to die in dignity and was active in associations that promoted voluntary euthanasia. When his own health deteriorated due to the combined effects of Parkinson's disease and leukemia, Koestler wrote an unambiguous letter explaining his suicide plan. He justifies the act in a compelling way that would be hard to challenge, at least on the basis of psychological factors such as impaired clarity of mind, incompetence in terms of being able to reflect on the implications of alternative decisions regarding continuing to live, whim, or external or internal pressure. Consider the penultimate paragraph:

> I wish my friends to know that I am leaving their company in a peaceful frame of mind, with some timid hopes for a depersonalised after-life beyond the confines of space, time, and matter, and beyond the limits of our comprehension. This 'oceanic feeling' has often sustained me at difficult moments, and does so now, while I am writing this.

By contrast, the news that his wife had joined Koestler's suicide (they were both found dead in the same room) raised doubts about the authenticity of her decision. Being young (49 at her death) and healthy, was Cynthia's choice of death unduly influenced by her husband's decision? An analysis of her suicide note suggests that Koestler did not try to dissuade her. She explicitly declares that the idea of a double suicide has never appealed to her and that she fears both death and the act of dying. In the same breath she mentions her inability to live without her husband, even though she feels she is the bearer of 'certain inner resources'.

These two cases reflect the arguments for and against the idea that suicide can be rational. Whatever view we take, the spectre of different categories of suicidal behaviour arises, revolving mainly around motive. It may be the product of a disturbed mind, or reflect a person's apparently coherent wish to accomplish what could be seen as a desirable goal—to be spared intolerable suffering. A further difficulty is what we are to make of a person who fits our definition but does not die because of miscalculation—for example, by overestimating the effect of a drug overdose, or by interruption when the family returns unexpectedly from a holiday. Or a person may miscalculate in the opposite way—feeling burdened by life, they overdose in order to 'have a long sleep', and unknowingly take a lethal dose (see deliberate self-harm below).

Suicide rates

Applying the above definition, we can study the rates of suicide in different societies and at different times. We can go further by teasing out psychological and social factors that appear to be associated with people who kill themselves and, in this way, determine who is particularly vulnerable.

In developed countries, suspected suicides are referred to coroners' courts and statistics on rates are based on their data. All coronial inquiries seek to determine cause of death but the criteria for different types vary between countries. In the case of suicide, evidence must relate to the act being self-inflicted and the intent being to die. Judgement as to whether these criteria have been satisfied is difficult, and is made on the balance of probabilities. If the evidence suggests that death was self-inflicted but no reasonable conclusion can be made as to intent, the case is recorded as accidental death of undetermined cause. This system, which may underestimate the rate of suicide, limits comparison of rates between countries.

Despite these limitations, rates have been determined since the twentieth century, at least in Western societies. The league table makes for frightening reading. The annual number of suicides in men per 100 000 inhabitants ranges from an average 20 in, for example, Canada, United States, Australia, Sweden, Iceland and Germany, to much higher levels in Sri Lanka (45), Ukraine (47), Hungary (45), Latvia (45), Russia (69) and Lithuania (74). These differences are difficult to explain, given the many factors likely to contribute to the final figure. Psychiatrists are especially interested in the so-called risk factors—those associated with high rates and that might possibly be changed through a program of prevention.

Whatever the actual rate, we must also note that for each person who suicides, up to 50 other people deliberately harm themselves without intending to die (it must always be an estimate since it is virtually impossible to detect all such cases). Moreover, many people other than the victim are severely affected by a suicidal death. Sometimes family members experience profound grief that endures indefinitely.

What leads to suicide?

Let us return to the risk factors. Many more men than women kill themselves (rural China is a notable exception, where the prevalence among young women using rat poison is disturbingly high). The sex difference could be explained by the methods used. Men are apt to resort to more violent methods, such as hanging, shooting, drowning and jumping, whereas women tend to poison themselves by taking excessive doses of prescribed or illicit drugs. The risk of suicide increases with age, those over sixty-five having the highest rate of any age group (the rate in the United States in the general population rises to more than double in those aged over eighty).

These patterns are not necessarily cast in stone. A horrendous increase among young men, but not women, between fifteen and thirty-five from the

1960s to the 1980s in many Western countries caused much consternation among psychiatrists and public health officials. Again, we must tread cautiously in trying to explaining this change, and investigate what other risk factors are linked to it. Meanwhile, where solid evidence is lacking, commentators speculated that potential influences included high levels of unemployment among the young, an increased rate of divorce and family breakdown, greater prevalence of substance abuse, and a sense of alienation.

Many of these factors are socially linked, a pattern that takes us back, as alluded to above, to the pioneering work of Durkheim. He speculated that suicide would be rare in a politically, economically and socially well-integrated society. Suicide for him was mainly explicable in the context of the society to which the person belongs. Two forms result from adverse social forces. The egoistic form stems from inadequate involvement with society: 'springing from excessive individualism'. The anomic form, by contrast, results from social change like loss of religious affiliation, divorce with its associated disturbance in community organisation, or political crisis (for example, the suicide rate in Vienna escalated dramatically on the eve of World War II). Social studies since Durkheim have moved away from theoretical models and focused on such factors as marital status and socio-economic status. So, we learn that the rate for single people is twice that of married, while the divorced and widowed have rates five times higher again.

Unemployment is an adverse influence, as is lower socio-economic status. Religious affiliation is usually regarded as protective and we do know that Judaism, Christianity and Islam all prohibit suicide as part of their ethos (while venerating martyrdom). However, this may be an artefact of reporting, which is possibly reduced through concealment in societies where religious belief prevails. Copycat suicide applies to young people, the rate going up in the aftermath of the media exposing a suicide. This poses a dilemma for the media, who have a duty to inform but may contribute to the problem they are reporting. The best option is for them to do so accurately and responsibly.

A possible genetic component in suicide is illustrated starkly in the American writer Ernest Hemingway's family. Apart from killing himself, his father, two siblings and a grand-daughter died by their own hand. Of course, they could all have inherited a vulnerability to mental illness. On the other hand, identical twins have a six-fold greater concordance rate compared to non-identical twins. Neuroscientists have been relentless in their research for abnormalities in the brain chemistry of suicide victims, but findings have been inconsistent. A deficiency of the chemical messenger serotonin in brain fluid is associated with a four-fold increase of death through suicide. The quest has practical implications. If an accurate test were available during life, psychiatrists could be especially vigilant regarding those who had low levels of serotonin, although reliance on a single result could never supplant the comprehensive assessment of suicide risk.

Suicide and mental illness

There is robust evidence of a link between suicide and a number of mental illnesses, especially depression, alcoholism and schizophrenia. Overall, the psychiatrically afflicted have a ten-times greater risk than the general population. In a classic English study, of 100 consecutive suicides taken from coronial records, 93 people were judged by a panel of psychiatrists to be mentally ill. Two-thirds were diagnosed as suffering from substantial depression and 15 per cent from alcoholism. A similar level of psychiatric disorder was found in a definitive American study of 134 suicides.

The close link between suicide and depression has been repeatedly confirmed. In follow-up studies of people diagnosed as suffering from various forms of depression, a consistent pattern emerges, with up to twenty times the death rate from suicide in these patients compared to people not suffering from mood disorders.

Hopelessness, a cardinal feature of severe depression, has an especially strong link with suicidal behaviour. As William Styron, the American author, wrote about his own harrowing experience of melancholia in a memoir aptly entitled *Darkness Visible*, 'the pain of depression is quite unimaginable to those who have not suffered it, and it kills in many instances because its anguish can no longer be borne'. I still find it difficult to imagine such depths of despair, even though I have treated hundreds of people with this malady and once plunged into a depression myself in which state I harboured suicidal thoughts. Surely, I surmise, they must realise somewhere in the recesses of their psyche that they are receiving professional care and that things will get better. Their level of anguish must be so pervasive and so profound that any seed of hope for improvement must be deeply buried and inaccessible. I am still haunted by the spectre of a colleague, a psychiatrist too, who jumped to his death from the seventeenth storey of an apartment block after struggling with treatment-resistant depression for several years. Transient remissions provided minuscule relief; he felt that the black dog would not only pursue him repeatedly but also attack more ferociously.

Imaginary voices ordering the person to kill themselves is an ominous feature of schizophrenia (and, rarely, of psychotic depression too), but more commonly it is the sense of a lack of career, social and intimate ties and therefore the anticipation of a barren life that leads to despair and the decision to suicide. Alcohol abuse entails a lifetime risk of about 4 per cent, usually after years of decline. As with schizophrenic patients, the alcohol dependent person loses all social and interpersonal links, feels isolated and forlorn. Suicide may also occur in response to psychotic phenomena experienced during intoxicated or withdrawal periods.

The details of this link between mental illness and suicide bear on the role of the health professional. This is the series of findings:

- suicide is frequently preceded by one or more acts of deliberate self-harm;
- the risk of suicide is high immediately after people are discharged from psychiatric hospital, possibly because they now have more energy to carry it out;
- suicide occurs among people who are resident in a psychiatric hospital;
- most suicidal people give a warning before carrying out their plan;
- many suicidal people consult their family doctor or a psychiatrist in the weeks before the act.

This research supports the view that the person at risk of suicide can be identified, a vital matter for prevention. Psychiatrists are emboldened to intervene when they know they stand a good chance of stopping a tragic outcome.

Assessing the risk of suicide

A key task for psychiatrists in assessing all patients is to determine the risk of suicide. This is particularly so when people harbor suicidal ideas. Suicide is usually well planned and a warning often given. About one in six people who have suicidal ideas has actually written a suicide note. It is difficult, however, to identify who will act on their thoughts and when they will do so. Previous suicidal behaviour is a crucial predictor. About three quarters of the people who suicide have attempted it in the past. The seriousness of those acts is a strong pointer.

But even in high-risk groups, prediction is complicated and unreliable. I have had occasion to make tricky decisions about how long to treat a suicidal patient in hospital. I once looked after a young man with enduring schizophrenia who responded well to treatment but became overly dependent on the therapeutic team over a period of several weeks. We feared that we were partly responsible for Rod's dependency and that we were doing him harm by not preparing him for his transfer to the community. We embarked on a plan to equip him with the psychological wherewithal to live in an apartment on his own. Two weeks later, Rod was still protesting that he was not ready for the move. We felt more confident and encouraged him accordingly. Rod left the ward reluctantly on a Friday afternoon. He was found hanging from a ceiling fan on Sunday morning. Needless to say, we were totally shattered by the tragedy. As is customary in this type of situation, we were assisted by colleagues not involved in Rod's care to deal with our feelings of grief and guilt. A sobering feature of orienting new professional trainees is to share with them one's own experiences of losing patients and to inform them that they are likely to encounter this before long.

Treating the suicidal person

The psychiatrist's aim in treating suicidal people is to reduce the risk of it happening. The first question is whether people recognise their difficulties and can accept the need for treatment. In deciding whether they should be helped as an in-patient or out-patient, voluntarily or involuntarily, much depends on the mental state, level of risk, presence of mental illness and availability of social support. Compulsory hospitalisation, if needed, is explained to patient and family as an essential dimension of treatment, arising out of a concern for safety and wellbeing. Irrespective of the diagnosis, a trusting alliance is pivotal since disruption of key relationships is commonly part of the story. Psychiatrists accept the demands suicidal patients may make but also tactfully point out their role in collaborating with the treatment program.

The suicidal person usually needs the safe environment of a hospital ward. A team approach is applied with clear agreement about the need for security, including the frequency of nursing observations. Restricting access to tablets, windows on upper floors, sharp objects, rope and so forth is essential. Any discovered mental illness and any contributing physical illness are treated vigorously. Notwithstanding these efforts, it is impossible to eliminate all hospital-based suicides. While reasonable precautions are called for, people must still be treated in the least restrictive manner. Any effort to prevent all suicides would fail and result in unacceptable constraints on the vast majority of 'at risk' people.

Society expects psychiatrists to prevent suicide. But this is unrealistic. We cannot chain people to their beds and observe their every move. Fortunately, only rarely do people treated in hospital commit a suicidal act and even fewer complete it. The problem of identifying this small group is sharply felt by staff, who can do no more than apply their most rigorous and informed judgements.

People not admitted to hospital are given detailed information about available supports. They are carefully told who is handling their care, as well as the place, dates and times of appointments and how to summon urgent help. Access to the latter might be by telephone to a clinic or hospital psychiatric unit, or through a telephone counselling service, a family doctor or the emergency department of a general hospital. Family and friends are pivotal in providing support for the person at risk. They are advised as to how to appreciate the gravity of the situation and are a source of information about the person's psychological state.

In all these circumstances, psychiatrists see their role as being to save the life of a person whose suicidal thoughts are probably the product of a disturbed mind. They would not hesitate, for example, to act vigorously in the following typical case.

Amy, a 40-year-old housewife and mother of three teenage children, has shown apathy, withdrawal and self-neglect over several weeks. During this time she has lost interest in family and friends, wakes at about two o'clock each morning and cannot return to sleep, and has lost over 6 kilograms in weight. She has also developed the unshakeable belief that she is worthless, has let her husband and children down, and deserves to die. Amy feels helpless and desperate and sees no future for herself. She suffered a similar episode three years previously, for which she was treated in hospital with supportive care and anti-depressant medication. She made a good recovery then and had felt content with her life until this time.

The diagnosis is undoubtedly severe depression, with psychotic features. Given the severity, the psychiatrist is obliged to assume a paternalistic role and, with the family's co-operation and support, take firm initiatives: admit Amy to hospital, even by compulsion if it proves necessary; repeatedly assess her mental state; closely supervise her daily activities; and energetically treat her psychiatric condition with anti-depressant drugs within a caring environment. Electro-convulsive therapy may be required if her condition deteriorates and/or the suicidal behaviour intensifies.

Suicide and the bereaved

Suicide is catastrophic for relatives and friends, particularly when the deceased person is young. Reactions encompass the whole range of emotions seen in grief, including depression, denial, anger and guilt. The guilt revolves around not having done more to prevent the death, particularly if there was a previous suicide attempt or if the person had revealed their suicidal intent. Blame is frequently attributed elsewhere by those unable to come to terms with their guilt. Counselling for the bereaved is always necessary in order to reduce the anguish and to prevent long-term adverse effects. Because grief may last indefinitely and lead to damaging repercussions for family members, professional intervention is always appropriate. But the professional helper must not intrude on the family's grief prematurely or they may be viewed as an interloper who violates family privacy. A careful approach using tact and discretion is called for. Clarifying that it was the result of a mental illness that had proved resistant to treatment provides comfort. Drawing an analogy between suicide following a severe mental illness and death from physical illness, or accepting the finality of death rather than grappling with the uncertainty of a chronically suicidal relative, also help. Some wish to know if genetic factors pertain; we can reassure them by stating that the link is negligible.

Self-help groups for those bereaved through suicide offer a safe forum to share feelings. Talking to other similarly bereaved people, at various stages of grieving, instils the hope of coming to terms with loss.

Preventing suicide

Given the convincing evidence of a link between suicide and mental illness, psychiatrists and the medical profession generally have a crucial role in reducing the rate. Prevention takes various forms. It is vital that family doctors are sensitive to early signs of severe depression in any patient, but especially if there has been a history of suicidal behaviour or any form of deliberate self-harm, or a family history of suicide. Doctors are particularly wary of depressed people who also have a physical illness, since the risk of suicide rises with incapacity, loss of independence or poorly controlled pain. Other preventative measures include effective treatment of any psychiatric condition in which suicide is embedded and, no less important, efficient follow-up care after the initial treatment program has ended.

Broader social programs have been considered, tried, but not adequately tested. Pioneering efforts go back to the early twentieth century, when the Salvation Army set up a Suicide Prevention Department in London and the National Save-A-Life League was established in New York.

Take the means to carry out suicide. When coal gas was replaced with non-poisonous liquid gas in the United Kingdom, suicidal death from this toxic source declined, but over some years carbon monoxide poisoning from car exhausts took over as an alternative way to kill oneself. In the United States, guns are used much more commonly in suicides than in many other countries and it is conceivable that better gun control could have beneficial effects. Education programs in schools would seem on the face of it to have merit but the best way to implement them remains elusive. Educating the public at large is another option but again questions about its effectiveness have not been resolved. One reason for the vagueness is the fact that in any particular community the rate of suicide is low, and any links between an initiative tried and change in that rate is difficult to pin down to a specific factor.

The alternative is to devise strategies for those who are at special risk. As we have seen, this means identifying risk factors in people with severe depression, and to a lesser extent those with schizophrenia and alcoholism.

The snag is the lack of a direct association between an individual case and the factors that have emerged from research on large groups. More likely than not, large-scale preventive programs will not succeed and we will need to continue to rely on the judgements of experienced and skilled clinicians.

The ethical dilemmas of intervention and prevention

Given the clear association between suicide and mental illness, psychiatrists agree that they are justified in asking or even forcing suicidal people to reconsider their attitude, to give themselves a second chance or to put off a final decision in case their circumstances change. This postponement policy is logically sounder than non-intervention because the intervention itself is a reversible act. If further study shows that suicide is indeed rational, or every effort at treatment fails to alter the person's frame of mind, or the person persists in their wish regardless of changed circumstances— then there is always the option of letting the person carry out that wish. Only in extreme cases such as, for example, a paraplegic who can be technically prevented from killing himself, can we question the moral legitimacy of prevention. The freedom to terminate one's life remains a basic consolation to human beings.

This is the moral justification of preventing suicide. What about the controversial issue of the psychiatrist's potential role in assisting a person to suicide. In the widely quoted case of Elizabeth Bouvia, a woman with incapacitating cerebral palsy, she declared herself to be suicidal when admitted at the age of twenty-six to the psychiatric unit of a Californian hospital in 1983. She refused nourishment and sought a court order preventing the staff from force-feeding or discharging her. Her wish to die was the result of a belief that her future prospects were grim.

The court ruled in favour of the hospital. While Ms Bouvia was competent in arriving at her decision, the requirement of the common good overrode respect for her wishes. The judge, in concluding that 'society's interest in preserving life and the medical profession's obligation to do so outweighed her right to self-determination', referred to the 'devastating' effects that assisting suicide would have on other patients and people afflicted with handicaps.

Even more ethically complex is the Chabot case. In 1991, Dr Boudewijn Chabot, a Dutch psychiatrist, was consulted by Hilly Bosscher, a 50-year-old retired social worker. She wanted him to assist her to end her tragic life. Three men had played a role in her life: her ex-husband had abused her physically, one son had died by his own hand, the other had lost a battle against cancer. Dr Chabot got to know his patient well over several months and concluded that she was not suffering from any diagnosable psychiatric disorder. Moreover, her contact with reality was consistently intact. Notwithstanding, he recommended anti-depressants and psychotherapy. Her response was emphatic: since life had no meaning for her, she sought help to achieve a foolproof and painless suicidal death. Having consulted several professional colleagues (none of whom interviewed Mrs Bosscher), Dr Chabot gave Mrs Bosscher a lethal drink in her own home.

The legal repercussions are noteworthy. In view of the significance of the case, the Dutch Supreme Court became involved and ruled that Dr Chabot was guilty of assisting in a suicide, but also concluded that he had adhered to the guidelines on euthanasia and assisted suicide set by the country's medical association by judging Mrs Bosscher to be a suitable candidate: she had suffered dreadfully, been mentally competent, and sought to die without any sign of external duress or coercion. Given these circumstances, Dr Chabot was permitted to continue his psychiatric career.

The Chabot case raises new issues in physician-assisted suicide. One factor that usually serves as part of the justification for professional cooperation with suicidal plans (as well as with requests for euthanasia) is the irreversibility of the condition from which the patient is suffering. In the present case, Mrs Bosscher is experiencing profound grief, which can be expected to persist for an extended period. On the other hand, it is not necessarily irreversible (let alone deteriorating), and one cannot judge her situation as hopeless. This by no means implies that there is no rational basis for suicidal choice, since the severe pain of the present may outweigh the prospects of a better future; but it does impose a special ethical constraint on the psychiatrist, who is expected to consider seriously the long-term interests of his patients.

Another element is the absence of a medically defined syndrome, usually the principal grounds for a medical intervention. It is noteworthy that Dr Chabot himself emphasises that he did not consider himself as a doctor and the woman as a patient in the circumstances. If that is true, it is not clear why a psychiatrist should assist in the act of suicide. Should not physician-assisted suicides be limited, by their very definition, to circumstances in which the relationship between the two parties is of a medical nature, that is, involving the attempt of a doctor to help their patient who is suffering from a clearly defined syndrome?

One could argue (as has been done in the debate on abortion and euthanasia) that even if actively causing death is morally justified under certain conditions, it should not be the function of physicians, whose primary professional role is to save life. Psychiatrists, according to this view, should not be expected to serve as 'executioners', mercy killers, sympathetic relievers of intolerable pain. They should cooperate with requests for help to suicide only when the basis for these are associated with a pathological (non-curable and irreversible) condition. Although many warnings of the threat of a slippery slope are overstated, it seems that the Chabot case, due to its qualitative distinction from other cases of physician-assisted suicide, calls for particular ethical caution.

It should be noted that the court did not recognise Chabot's defence, namely an irresolvable conflict between the duty to preserve life and the duty to do everything possible to relieve the patient from unbearable suffering. And, indeed, since the case involved a non-physical and non-terminal condition, the doctor could not be sure that there was absolutely no prospect of treatment or improvement. The question of evidence becomes crucial in such cases, and the Dutch court noted that Chabot failed to get a second expert opinion based on a thorough examination of his patient before making his decision to provide Mrs. Bosscher with the means for her self-inflicted death.

Psychiatrists, and the medical profession generally, are bound by legal requirements that to aid, abet or counsel suicide is an offence. The whole issue of euthanasia and assisted suicide is surrounded with intense controversy. Since the first edition of *Understanding Troubled Minds* (1997), noteworthy legal developments in a few jurisdictions around the world have shown that physician-assisted suicide is now more readily considered as a viable option than at any other time in medical history. Holland is at the forefront of these changes. Since 2001, doctors have been permitted to assist in acts of suicide as long as specified conditions of care are met. But psychiatric cases, like Elizabeth Bouvia, remain unclear, since the law is restricted to terminally ill patients afflicted with enduring and intolerable pain and other physical symptoms who freely, competently and repeatedly request that their lives be ended because of their suffering. Arguments against assisting a 'psychiatric suicide' are likely to prevail.

Deliberate self-harm

In this account of suicide I have referred to a range of behaviours whose hallmark is self-harm. We need to distinguish more clearly between a suicidal act and self-harm. In suicide, a person both intends to die and knows that the action taken will result in death, whereas self-harm is not intended self-killing.

Erwin Stengel was the first psychiatrist to highlight this second category of suicidal behaviour when he introduced the concept of attempted suicide in the late 1950s. Other terms used since include 'deliberate self-harm', 'self-poisoning' and 'parasuicide'. It is not surprising that we are struggling with semantics; we are dealing here with a form of behaviour that is not readily definable. Since Stengel's original concept, a consensus has emerged that people may harm themselves, even seriously, but in the belief that they will survive. Although their act was intentional, not accidental, and to some extent planned, their aim was not to die.

We can probably best think of suicidal behaviour as lying along a continuum. At one end, a person clearly wants to die and takes definite steps to achieve this result. At the other end, a person clearly wants to live but feels the urge to harm themselves—for a variety of reasons that we consider below. Along this continuum are people in a state of perplexity about their intentions and goals. For example, a man may be so overwhelmed by a predicament that he is incapable of facing it directly. While in an alcohol-intoxicated state, he compulsively takes an overdose of sleeping tablets prescribed by his family doctor. His motive is clouded by the alcohol, but he desires a form of oblivion—whether it is a period of temporary unconsciousness or death is left hanging. This uncertainty is sometimes thought of as a form of Russian roulette—'If I die so be it'. Even after waking from the resulting stupor, he is still baffled by what he should do, particularly as the original predicament is still pressing (which is often the case).

Another indication of this overlap between suicide and deliberate self-harm is that some people who kill themselves have made statements or left notes that clearly show they did not intend to die. On the other hand, a person whose wish to die is strong may survive through force of circumstances.

One way out of this murkiness of definition is to study the different forms of deliberate self-harm. This has been extensively done, with people interviewed as to their motives and thoughts building up to the act and their feelings about surviving it. What do these studies reveal about motive? People who deliberately harm themselves are often overwhelmed by pressing personal problems, whether in their family life, social relationships, work or health. A stressful life event in the six months before the act is four times more likely among people who harm themselves deliberately compared to the general population. Deliberate self-harm, then, seems to be a form of communication.

Among the messages commonly conveyed through the act are anger, frustration, revenge, defiance, an attempt to win sympathy or re-establish a broken relationship. Underpinning many of these is the proverbial cry for help: 'I feel awful; I am at the end of my tether; I am confused and don't know what to do; please help me!'

Alongside this, people often report a desperate need for relief from this state of mind, best achieved through lapsing into unconsciousness: 'All I want is a long sleep so that I can be free of the emotional pain'. Not unexpectedly, the most common form of deliberate self-harm, in 90 per cent of cases, is taking an overdose of a drug that is likely to 'knock me out'. The benzodiazepines and anti-depressants, widely prescribed by family doctors, are readily available for this purpose. People often take over-the-counter analgesics like paracetamol in the mistaken belief that they have a similar effect. People who cut their wrists or lacerate other parts of the body are often seeking relief from intense bodily tension.

This is what studies tell us about the characteristics typical of people who deliberately harm themselves. They tend to be late adolescents or young adults, women (in a ratio of three to one), single or divorced. They tend not to have a formal psychiatric diagnosis but instead have experienced longstanding problems of living with which they have struggled to cope—as their misuse of alcohol and drugs like benzodiazepines illustrates. Many have come from families marked by conflict and tension. They are likely to be facing a crisis at the time of the self-harm, and have recently sought help for it from their family doctor or other source.

About one in five of these people will repeat the self-harm in the following year. For a few, most of whom have an underlying psychiatric disorder (particularly mood disturbance, substance abuse or some form of disturbed personality), the behaviour becomes habitual in the face of even minor stress. One in a hundred people will actually kill themselves in the twelve months following an episode of deliberate self-harm, often in circumstances that leave doubt as to their true intent. Sharon's story is a typical example of deliberate self-harm.

Sharon, a 24-year-old clerical assistant, was brought to the emergency department of the hospital by her family following her overdosing with twenty-five paracetamol and ten benzodiazepine tablets. After her drowsiness had lifted, she cried profusely and expressed a wish to 'get away from it all'. This need to escape had been her original motive when taking the tablets.

She felt trapped in a longstanding conflict with her parents over how she should live her life. Their strict code of conduct for all four children included career plans and marital choice. One older sister had married at an early age and was living at a distance. Her younger brothers lived in fear of their father, a tempestuous man given to violent outbursts. Sharon had twice fled from her home because of her father's violence. She had only returned out of a sense of loyalty.

The current crisis had been provoked by her boyfriend's refusal of Sharon's ultimatum to become engaged (as a first step to leaving home with her parents' support). Sharon had taken an overdose once before, also when buffeted by parental pressures and feeling hopelessly stuck. Generally, however, she was an amiable, sociable and lively person, with friends and interests.

Sharon agreed to the psychiatrist's recommendation to spend a few days in hospital, because the family crisis seemed intense and the father's tendency to violence put her and other family members at risk. Moreover, she was unable to give any guarantee about her own safety. She soon responded to the supportive environment on the ward and was able to express her feelings of frustration and anger. She became quite animated in relating to fellow patients and staff. But, when visited by her family, heated arguments erupted and Sharon became extremely distressed.

As well as individual therapy, using principles of crisis intervention (see Chapter 19), a family meeting was held. This was emotionally charged, with her father threatening to disown her if she left home without his consent. The parental relationship was strained to breaking point and the other three children fearful of the father's threats. A later meeting was less fraught although the father's stubborn hold on the reins of power in the family dominated the proceedings.

However, Sharon and the family were encouraged to recognise the conflicts and to map out ways of resolving or at least defusing them. A program of family therapy was arranged as well as a series of counselling sessions for Sharon on her own.

Treatment and prevention of deliberate self-harm

Sharon's case illustrates many of the principles that psychiatrists adopt in dealing with people who deliberately harm themselves. They include a careful assessment of the person and their family, crisis intervention that may require brief admission to a psychiatric unit, and individual and/or family therapy. In more complex cases, continuing treatment is needed, usually in the form of long-term individual psychotherapy (see Chapter 19). We avoid posing direct questions that could be felt as critical, but rather offer empathic comments such as 'Things seem to have got on top of you recently' or 'You must have been very upset'; the latter facilitates rapport and sharing of concerns and difficulties. In the case of any resistance, the therapist manifests a willingness to listen actively and stresses the need to understand the person's story.

Preventing self-harm in the first instance would obviously be ideal. It was in pursuit of this goal that self-help organisations like the Samaritans (the first of its kind, founded in 1953 in London by the Reverend Chad Varah) and Lifeline were established. Trained non-professionals are available on the telephone around the clock to offer counselling to people who feel themselves in crisis and in immediate need of a sympathetic ear and advice. Like all self-help groups in the mental health arena, this type of counselling service fits extremely well with professional sources of help. Family doctors are a lynchpin in that they are well placed to identify people who harbour suicidal thoughts.

Conclusion

Suicidal behaviour is potentially preventable but saving every person from a suicidal death is not. Psychiatrists' ability to predict who will kill themselves is limited and is likely to remain so. Nonetheless, in tandem with societal policy-makers they need to do what they can to reduce the rate. As is noted in the earlier comments on treatment and prevention, a range of measures are required—from educating the community about their need to summon professional help promptly when they are distressed, to treating vigorously those we can identify who are at risk.

Although suicide rates have declined marginally in some countries since the 1990s, we have not reached that point at which mental health and related social services are sufficiently developed to meet the population's needs. Just as deaths on the road have tumbled with the evolution of a raft of well thought out initiatives, so society has the task to map out a multi-faceted program to lessen the tragedy of self-inflicted death.

CHAPTER 18

Drugs and Other Physical Treatments

Most people with mild psychological problems can be treated without medication. But for many with moderately severe conditions and for all of marked severity, drugs and other physical therapies acting on the brain are central to treatment.

Physical treatments—which include drugs, occasionally electroconvulsive therapy and very rarely psychosurgery—control symptoms by readjusting those chemical processes in the brain that we assume are disturbed in many mental illnesses. Much of our knowledge comes from looking at drugs that are effective to determine how they work in the brain. We know, for example, that all effective drugs to treat schizophrenia block a specific chemical messenger, dopamine. Working back from this observation, researchers postulate that dopamine activity is increased in schizophrenia.

This line of thinking provides a basis for the massive expansion of pharmaceutical research since the 1950s that targets a particular neurochemical system with a view to developing new drugs with the greatest therapeutic effects and the least side-effects. By contrast, treatments prior to the 1950s were non-specific and largely ineffective.

Past methods of dealing with mentally ill people reflect what to us now seem bizarre ideas about abnormal behaviour. Common practice in the old asylums included such crude methods as blood-letting, purging, mechanical restraints, twirling-stool therapy and sudden dunking in water (many designed to shock people back into sanity). Patients would risk dying because of exhaustion during excited states like mania, or from infections such as pneumonia due to immobility associated with severe depression, or from suicide.

In the twentieth century, psychiatrists embraced great and desperate cures. New treatments to induce a state of semi-coma or deep sleep, and indiscriminate operations on the brain in order to modify behaviour, had their vogue. The 1950s was the key decade for discovery of drugs targeted to specific disorders. Reports on the anti-psychotic properties of chlorpromazine (the first modern tranquilliser) and on the anti-depressant actions of imipramine (the first effective drug for depression) were published. Discovery of the effectiveness of the benzodiazepines in treating anxiety followed soon thereafter.

All these discoveries were based on serendipity rather than rational drug design. Dozens of drugs with similar activity have since been made, tested and introduced into practice to treat tens of millions of people worldwide. The impact of their use has been dramatic. Disabling symptoms are much more readily controllable and recurrent illnesses prevented or muted by long-term use of medication. Modern drugs have enabled many people who would otherwise have been treated in hospital to be cared for in the community. This is one factor in the change in health policies that has led to a massive reduction in psychiatric beds in many countries.

Principles of drug use in psychiatry

Sound treatment requires accurate diagnosis. Psychiatrists ensure that psychiatric symptoms are not arising from an underlying disorder. For example, patients with epilepsy and AIDS, or those who abuse drugs such as amphetamines, can present with psychotic features. Although anti-psychotics may still be required, the primary task is to treat the basic cause. Similarly, patients with schizophrenia or alcoholism may present with anxiety and depression, in which case treatment is focused on the principal illness.

In prescribing drugs, we consider how they are delivered to and removed from their sites of action in the brain, and the mechanisms by which they exert both therapeutic effects and side-effects. For example, anti-psychotics and anti-depressants remain active in the brain long enough to allow once-daily doses. Since drugs are variably absorbed and available in the blood-stream, selection of the correct dose has to be tailored to each person, taking into account age, gender, past patterns of response, any physical illness, and so on. Generally, two to three weeks are needed before the full therapeutic effects of many of these drugs are felt.

Several groups of drugs are used in psychiatry—the main ones are anti-psychotics, anti-depressants, mood stabilisers and anti-anxiety agents. These categories are based on their clinical effectiveness, but there is not always a direct relationship between the diagnosis implicit in their names and the type of drug used. Since people often have a variety of symptoms, drugs from more than one category may be prescribed, either at the same time or in sequence. Generally, however, the ideal is to use one drug at a time, and monitor its effect carefully. Let us now consider each category in turn.

Anti-psychotics

These were the first drugs to be used for specific mental illnesses. The prototype, chlorpromazine, was developed in 1950 as a new anti-histamine for use as a premedication in surgery. In initial trials, tranquillity was such a prominent feature that two French psychiatrists, Jean Delay and Paul Deniker, were encouraged to prescribe the drug for acutely disturbed patients. To their delight, it quelled their agitation and, even more excitingly, had the specific effect of dissolving delusions and hallucinations. Ever since then, anti-psychotics have been the mainstay of the treatment of schizophrenia and related psychoses (see Chapter 11), and of the prevention of relapse.

Neuroscientists have hypothesised that anti-psychotics exert their beneficial effects by blocking the receptors of the chemical messenger dopamine on the surface of nerve cells, thus increasing its concentration in the brain. We also know that more potent anti-psychotics have an affinity for what are called D_2 dopamine receptors as opposed to other dopamine receptors. These observations do not tell us what goes wrong in the brains of schizophrenic people. We need much more research to unravel what constitutes one of the most formidable challenges facing psychiatry.

In terms of effectiveness, there are few advantages of one anti-psychotic over another. One exception is clozapine, which helps a third of patients who fail to respond to other anti-psychotics. However, because of its association with potentially fatal suppression of the bone-marrow in 2 per cent of people, it is never used as a first-line treatment.

Since people presenting with psychotic features may not turn out to be suffering from schizophrenia but have a self-limiting episode lasting a matter of days, or a drug-induced psychosis after abusing a stimulant drug such as amphetamine, psychiatrists prefer to give them the opportunity to recover spontaneously and not use anti-psychotics. The proviso is when their mental disturbance and related suffering are intense.

When anti-psychotics are indicated, more modern ones are used, and in low doses. The dose is increased later if necessary. Specific anti-psychotic effects may not be detectable for weeks, although any excitement, aggressiveness and restlessness usually diminishes well before then. Anti-psychotics are more effective in treating the positive symptoms of schizophrenia, such as delusions, hallucinations and disordered thinking, than negative symptoms like social withdrawal, loss of interest, poor personal hygiene and restricted emotional expressiveness. Negative symptoms do respond, although more slowly and incompletely.

For people experiencing a first-episode psychosis, treatment is usually given for six to nine months after initial control of symptoms has been achieved. The dose is then gradually reduced and a close watch kept for any relapse. Unfortunately, about two-thirds of people do relapse in the first year after stopping anti-psychotics. Predicting who they will be is impossible. People experiencing several relapses may need anti-psychotics for years, even life-long. In long-term treatment, the lowest effective dose is prescribed in order to minimise side-effects.

Many people with schizophrenia, particularly during a relapse, do not see themselves as ill and therefore in need of medication and may refuse or neglect to take it. As this behaviour markedly increases the risk of relapse, psychiatrists stress the importance of sticking to the tablets. A growing number of anti-psychotics have become available in long-acting injectable form, which when given by (depot) intramuscular injection is slowly released into the blood stream for three to four weeks.

Anti-psychotics do not give rise to dependence and are safe when taken in overdose, but unfortunately side-effects, especially those associated with older forms, are numerous and troublesome. They include sedation, dry mouth, lowering of blood pressure and disordered movement. The latter include involuntary contractions of muscles in the tongue, face, neck and back, restlessness, and rigidity and tremor as seen in Parkinson's disease. These are treated once they appear or prevented in people at high risk by specific drugs (anti-cholinergics) used in conjunction with anti-psychotics.

By far the most worrisome movement disorder is tardive dyskinesia (TD). Typical features are smacking of the lips, protrusion of the tongue, purposeless chewing and puffing of the cheeks; the limbs and trunk may also be affected. One in five patients given 'first-generation' anti-psychotics shows TD, but very many fewer in those on newer type (second generation) medications. In the absence of any effective treatment, its prevention by using minimal doses is a foremost thought in the psychiatrist's mind.

New anti-psychotic drugs have been developed but they are not entirely trouble-free, producing sedation, weight gain and elevations of blood glucose and lipids. First-generation anti-psychotics resulted in a two-fold increase in the rate of diabetes in schizophrenic patients; second-generation medications have increased this by a further 50 per cent. Close monitoring of weight, blood glucose and lipids is therefore vital. Adjustment of the dose, as well as encouragement of exercise and healthy diet, are additional measures.

Neuroleptic malignant syndrome (NMS), a rare but serious complication of anti-psychotic use, develops idiosyncratically with fever, rigidity and fluctuating or elevated blood pressure. Treatment includes stopping the anti-psychotic immediately and emergency measures to lower body temperature and maintain steady blood pressure.

Many scientific comparisons of first- and second-generation anti-psychotics have shown the latter to produce more benefits, but the most comprehensive trial ever carried out, involving five anti-psychotics and over 1400 patients (the CATIE project), suggests that the differences are not that remarkable. Indeed, first-generation anti-psychotics may be used when patients fail to respond to newer medications.

Anti-depressants

The first compounds with a specific anti-depressant effect were discovered serendipitously in the 1950s. Imipramine, the prototype tricyclic anti-depressant, was recognised to be beneficial while under investigation as a potential anti-psychotic. Iproniazid, a monoamine oxidase inhibitor, was first used for tuberculosis and observed to elevate mood. Selective serotonin reuptake inhibitors were developed in the 1970s and are by far the most fre-quently prescribed anti-depressants. The chemical messenger, serotonin, was chosen as a focus in the light of the serotonin deficiency theory of depression. In the 1990s, a number of anti-depressants were introduced that act upon both serotonin and noradrenaline systems.

The distress of severe depression and the risk of suicide call for ener-getic treatment. The drugs are used both to treat the acute state and to pre-vent recurrences. The drugs also have a place in the treatment of other conditions—for example, obsessive-compulsive disorder.

Anti-depressants can be classified into three main groups: tricyclics (TCAs), monoamine oxidase inhibitors (MAOIs) and selective serotonin re-uptake inhibitors (SSRIs). They all appear to work by increasing levels of chemical messengers in the brain. SSRIs selectively affect the serotonin system, TCAs the noradrenaline system, MAOIs both these as well as dopamine. We cannot explain the anti-depressants' action in this way alone; it remains a mystery why despite their action occurring within hours or a few days, substantial benefit only follows two to three weeks later (though a measure of improvement may be felt earlier). The delay in response points to other neurobiological processes as part of their mechanism of action.

The psychiatrist's task is to match the drug to the person on the basis of, among other factors, degree of agitation or retardation, risk of suicide and response to past medication. No one group has been shown to be better or to act more quickly than any other. But the SSRIs cause far fewer side-effects and are safer than the other two groups—two distinct advantages—and are therefore the anti-depressants of first choice. TCAs are more effective in some severe cases of depression and are prescribed if there is no benefit from the SSRIs. MAOIs are kept in reserve as third-line anti-depressants since a small proportion of patients respond to them alone.

Tricyclics

So named because of their three-ringed chemical structure, the tricyclics (TCAs) were the first effective drugs in the treatment of depression. Since their effect lasts for fifteen to thirty hours they can be taken once a day (usually at night to exploit their sedating properties). They act on several brain chemical messengers, essentially normalising the disturbed brain function that underlies the modulation of mood.

However, they affect various chemical systems in the body at large, and thus produce unpleasant side-effects like dry mouth, constipation, dizziness, blurred vision, weight gain and tremor. Since these often precede the therapeutic effect, psychiatrists emphasise to their patients that they may feel worse before they feel better. Because of their strong effect on the body, overdose is dangerous and possibly lethal—death is usually due to heart complications.

Monoamine oxidase inhibitors

Introduced at the same time as the tricyclics, the monoamine oxidase inhibitors (MAOIs) are used much more sparingly because they can cause death through a stroke if people consume certain drugs, beverages (red wine and particular beers) or foodstuffs including cheese, meat and yeast extracts. However, a newer type of MAOI (Moclobemide) is largely free of this risk. Other side-effects include dizziness, weight gain, constipation and insomnia. Insomnia is a result of the MAOIs' stimulant effect, and necessitates them being taken early in the day.

Selective serotonin re-uptake inhibitors

Extravagant claims have been made for the selective serotonin re-uptake inhibitors (SSRIs)—that they are the magic bullet panacea for unhappiness. The first, Prozac (its chemical name is fluoxetine) has become a household name, and several others with a similar action have followed. This again typifies the pattern in psychiatry where a new medication is adopted with evangelical fervour and only later is assessed more soberly. In fact, the SSRIs are no more or no less effective than the tricyclics and MAOIs. Although they are better tolerated, they can cause side-effects like headache, gastric upset, anxiety and insomnia. A new version of the SSRIs is what are called the SNRIs. An attempt has been made to combine the effects of two chemical messengers—serotonin and noradrenaline. The first drug of this kind was venlafaxine. No special advantages result from this union but it adds to the psychiatrist's options in finding the anti-depressant that best suits a particular patient. It also has anti-anxiety effects. Given the drug's side-effect of increasing blood pressure, this has to be checked regularly.

Which anti-depressant and for how long?

Psychiatrists' choice of anti-depressants is partly linked to their practical experience with their use. In general, newer drugs are preferred, especially for people for whom safety and the avoidance of side-effects is a priority. Once an anti-depressant is chosen, whatever the type, an adequate dose is given. If no improvement occurs within four to six weeks, a drug from another class is tried.

People being treated and, where appropriate, their families, are made aware that the therapeutic effect of anti-depressants is usually delayed for two to four weeks. Before modern drug therapy, depressive episodes lasted several months. Given that anti-depressants help but do not cure, they are prescribed for a minimum of six to nine months to forestall a relapse. All anti-depressants are withdrawn gradually because a sudden stop may trigger a withdrawal syndrome (nausea, diarrhoea, abdominal pain, insomnia, light-headedness and cognitive difficulties). These features are not dangerous and usually disappear within two weeks.

People prone to repeated depressive episodes need continuing anti-depressant medication. Maintenance treatment for at least two to five years, and sometimes indefinitely, is given to patients who have had three previous episodes (two if recent and severe) or those with a family history of bipolar illness or recurrent depression. The rationale here is that these sorts of patients are most vulnerable because they have a genetic predisposition.

Many people respond better to combined drug and psychological treatments, particularly in terms of achieving sustained improvement and preventing recurrence. The need for such an approach is especially indicated by an incomplete response to either medication or psychological treatment on its own. The most illuminating account of the complementary roles of the two that I have come across is that by Kay Redfield Jamison, whom we met in the chapter on the highs and lows of mood. In her book, *An Unquiet Mind*, she writes:

> … I cannot imagine leading a normal life without both taking lithium [a mood stabiliser] and having had the benefits of psychotherapy. Lithium prevents my seductive but disastrous highs, diminishes my depressions, clears out the wool and webbing from my disordered thinking, slows me down, gentles me out, keeps me from ruining my career and relationships, keeps me out of hospital, alive, and makes psychotherapy possible.
>
> But, ineffably, psychotherapy heals. It makes some sense of the confusion, reins in the terrifying thoughts and feelings, returns some control and hope and possibility of learning from it

all. Pills cannot, do not, ease one back into reality; they only bring one back headlong, careening, and faster than can be endured at times …

No pill can help me deal with the problem of not wanting to take pills; likewise, no amount of psychotherapy alone can prevent my manias and depressions. I need both. It is an odd thing, owing life to pills, one's own quirks and tenacities, and this unique, strange, and ultimately profound relationship called psychotherapy.

Mood stabilisers

The mood stabiliser story has its origins in the late 1940s in the pantry of a mental hospital ward! John Cade, an Australian psychiatrist, conducted what he described as amateurish experiments there in the belief that the urine of manic patients contained a harmful chemical. He sought to identify it by injecting a number of substances present in the urine into guinea pigs in order to discover whether the adverse effects of manic urine could be replicated. Since one of these, uric acid, could only be injected when combined with another substance, he used lithium, a simple chemical similar to common salt. He then realised that it was the lithium that sedated the guinea pigs.

Buoyed by this serendipitous discovery, Cade carried out a pioneering experiment on his patients that demonstrated a dramatic therapeutic effect in mania (but not schizophrenia or depression). Lithium was thus shown to be valuable in an acute manic attack. Further research revealed that it decreases the frequency, severity and length of manic episodes and prevents recurrence of both highs and lows in bipolar patients. Those suffering two or more manic episodes within five years benefit from maintenance treatment. If mania could possibly cause harm to the self or to others (for example, a mother with young children), long-term treatment is seriously considered after a first episode. Since sudden discontinuation can precipitate a manic attack, the drug is always withdrawn slowly.

Lithium's mechanism of action is still unknown although complex biochemical theories abound. It is rapidly absorbed, and excreted through the kidneys. Since precise concentrations are needed for it to be effective, and high levels may actually be toxic, its level in the blood needs careful monitoring. Kidney function is therefore assessed before starting treatment, as is the thyroid gland because the drug may hamper production of thyroid hormone. If under-functioning of the thyroid does occur—as it does in 5 per cent of cases—it can be successfully treated with hormone replacement.

There are a number of side-effects of lithium. A tendency to produce excessive urine (polyuria), leading to thirst and a strong need to drink, may result from lithium's interference with kidney function. If severe, an alternative mood stabiliser may be used instead. Lithium can be dangerous when it exceeds its therapeutic level, resulting in tremor, slurred speech and vomiting. If not detected promptly, convulsions, disturbed heart rhythm and even death may follow. In these circumstances, measures to eliminate the drug from the body include, in the most severe cases, dialysis.

Two anti-convulsants, valproate and carbamazepine, also have anti-manic effects, both for the acute state and to prevent recurrence. As with lithium, the mode of action is unknown, but their role in mania suggests that brain processes that initiate the elevated mood may have something in common with epilepsy. Puzzlingly, lamotrigine, also an anti-convulsant, is effective in preventing the recurrence of depression rather than mania.

Because manic patients present as disinhibited and out of control, treatment typically begins in a hospital setting and, given the delay in therapeutic effect of one to two weeks, an anti-psychotic is given as well.

Anti-anxiety drugs

Anxiety is omnipresent as a result of life stressors and we all learn how to cope with it. When it becomes disruptive because of its severity or interference with day-to-day living, treatment may be required. Human beings have always looked to medicines for relief. A clutter of treatments punctuates the history of this search, most of which have turned out to have disastrous effects, particularly addiction. Psychiatrists nonetheless accept that anti-anxiety medication has a limited role in easing anxiety, but only once much safer psychological therapies have been tried (see Chapter 6). After criticism surrounding the use of barbiturates, the discovery in the 1960s of the purportedly safe benzodiazepines was seen as a major boon by both doctors and patients. Decline in their use after two decades of 'spectacular success' shows that no drug for the treatment of anxiety is trouble-free. Although the benzodiazepines are still commonly prescribed for anxiety, they should not be taken for more than four weeks at a stretch, with one exception—a small group of people who are disabled by severe and chronic symptoms.

Other drugs have a role to play. Anti-depressants such as the SSRIs and TCAs are effective in treating anxiety-related conditions such as panic attacks, obsessive-compulsive disorder, generalised anxiety and social phobia. Beta-blockers (used in medical patients for heart disease and high blood pressure) are effective for physical features of anxiety like tremor, sweating and palpitations, and are sometimes taken by actors and musicians to calm themselves before they go on stage. Buspirone does not lead to dependence, a distinct advantage over the benzodiazepines (to which it is structurally unrelated). It helps people with longstanding anxiety who need more than periodic treatment.

If benzodiazepines are prescribed, the clinician does so in the context of a primary psychological treatment like cognitive-behaviour therapy, relaxation therapy or stress management. Taking benzodiazepines only when symptoms are at their peak or before encountering a stressful situation is another strategy. Having medication at hand may suffice to quell anticipatory anxiety and render its use unnecessary. Other situations in which anti-anxiety drugs may be used are as adjuncts in treating psychoses that are otherwise difficult to control, and to treat problems associated with alcohol withdrawal.

A decision to use benzodiazepines is based on the duration of their effects. Whereas short-acting forms are preferred as a hypnotic when a hangover effect is unwanted, longer-acting forms are indicated when more continuous relief is required. There is a wide optimal dosage range. The dose is chosen patient by patient, always beginning at the low end of the recommended range and, if necessary, gradually increasing it until anxiety is controlled without inducing drowsiness.

This cautious approach is critical since the vast majority of people taking benzodiazepines are functioning in the community, and drowsiness is risky in activities such as driving cars or operating machinery. When on benzodiazepines, people need to minimise or avoid alcohol use because it also ultimately sedates. Apart from the sedation, and confusion in the elderly, benzodiazepines have remarkably few side-effects and are relatively safe when taken in overdose.

Were it not for the problem of dependence, the benzodiazepines would indeed be a most suitable treatment for anxiety. However, 40 per cent of long-term users experience unpleasant symptoms upon withdrawing from them. Underlying anxiety can rebound with even greater intensity. New symptoms of varying severity often occur, indicating physical dependence. Symptoms may occur within a day of ceasing short-acting benzodiazepines and several days after stopping a longer-acting one. To minimise symptoms, benzodiazepines are always tapered gradually. Those at particular risk—on prolonged, high-dose and short-acting benzodiazepines—benefit from an equivalent dose of a longer-acting type, and gradual withdrawal under cover of buspirone or a TCA.

Benzodiazepines and related drugs as hypnotics

> O sleep! O gentle sleep!
> Nature's soft nurse, how I have frighted thee,

That thou no more wilt weigh mine eyelids down
And steep my senses in forgetfulness?

Shakespeare, Henry IV, Part 2

Methought I heard a voice cry, 'Sleep no more!
Macbeth does murder sleep,' the innocent sleep,
Sleep that knits up the ravell'd sleave of care,
The death of each day's life, sore labour's bath,
Balm of hurt minds, great nature's second course,
Chief nourisher in life's feast.

Shakespeare, Macbeth

Insomnia has many forms and many causes. Whether occasional or long-standing, insomnia is not a medical condition but only a symptom. It has traditionally been classified into difficulty falling asleep (initial insomnia), remaining asleep (middle insomnia) and early morning awakening.

The role of hypnotics, or sleeping pills, is controversial. They do provide relief but, in other than short-term use, the risk of developing dependence is always present. A hypnotic taken during a long flight or a brief period in hospital is reasonable. The snag, however, is that a person may develop tolerance (the need to raise the dose in order to achieve the same effect) to a benzodiazepine within only two weeks.

A range of non-drug measures often improve sleep substantially, and are outlined here for convenience. Treatment is directed towards factors that have predisposed a person to insomnia, then trigger and sustain it. A behavioural program, which is the mainstay of therapy, involves practising healthy sleep habits (see the table below), relaxation methods and a focus on coping skills.

Healthy sleep habits

- Keep regular sleep hours:
  - go to bed and arise at consistent times;
  - maintain consistent sleep times, including on weekends;
  - use rituals involving washing, brushing teeth, pyjamas as behavioural cues.
- Exercise daily but not too close to bedtime.
- Avoid daytime naps.
- Ensure bedroom is comfortable (sound, light and temperature).
- Avoid alcohol, caffeine, tobacco, excessive liquid intake and heavy meals before sleep.
- Plan the evening to include a winding-down phase before retiring.
- Go to bed only when sleepy.
- Use bed for sleep, not watching television, reading or worrying.

- If unable to sleep, go to another room and engage in a boring activity (like ironing) and return to bed only when sleepy.
- If in bed for more than ten minutes without falling asleep, get up again; repeat this step as often as necessary during the night.

These healthy sleep habits make for sound sleep. If they are not followed, insomnia may continue or worsen. These strategies also tend to break the learned link between lying in bed and not sleeping. Reading, watching television, eating or worrying in bed are common associations. In their place the practice of relaxation, meditation and self-hypnosis can help by reducing anxiety. Worrying thoughts can be suppressed by imagining pleasant scenes such as waves gently rolling in to the shore. If these strategies fail, psychological treatment may be necessary to address factors like a continuing inner conflict. The person is helped to discharge emotions during the day rather than have them expressed through tension at night. Attention to relevant family and marital problems can help, as can assistance with relationships generally.

When insomnia does not respond to these measures, and especially when it is severe and impairs quality of life, short-term or intermittent benzodiazepines are warranted. They bring a quicker onset of sleep and reduce the number of awakenings. Newer alternatives, called cyclopyrrolones, zopiclone and zolpidem, appear to have less potential for dependence. Whatever type of hypnotic is prescribed, the lowest effective dose is aimed for. Drowsiness is a signal to reduce the dose or shift to a shorter-acting agent.

Electro-convulsive therapy

We now turn to a treatment wrapped in enormous controversy, despite over a half-century of its use as a mainstay therapy in psychiatric practice. Many people see it as a link to the barbarity they associate with treatments used long ago for the mentally ill—blood-letting, dunking and the twirling stool.

Before effective drugs were available, electro-convulsive therapy (ECT) was administered often, and at times indiscriminately. Undoubtedly, the procedure was primitive before the 1950s. Anaesthetics and muscle relaxant drugs were not used, with the result that people had convulsions of such severity that they were at risk of physical injuries, even fractures of the spine. This historical note is important because ECT continues to be depicted in the media in the most frightening fashion. Understandably, people including those who could most be helped, are left feeling frightened and distrustful.

Modern ECT in fact is safe and effective. I always recall a leading British psychiatrist declaring in a teaching session that, if he were unfortunate enough to suffer from severe depression, he would want to be hooked up to the nearest ECT machine without delay! I would do the same. In severe depression, when the risk of death from starvation, dehydration or suicide is prominent, or psychotic symptoms are present, or treatment resistance occurs, ECT is the treatment of choice. It is administered under anaesthesia; the person is asleep and unaware of having a fit that is induced by the passage of electricity between two electrodes placed on the sides of the forehead. It is given two to three times a week, usually for six to twelve treatments. Modern machines have a facility for calibrating the dose of current, as well as for monitoring the heart. The positive response rate for these patients is a striking 80 per cent, significantly more than for anti-depressants. Treatment is safe in virtually all situations. Even medically ill people can benefit, provided they can tolerate brief anaesthesia (a greater potential problem than the ECT itself). Apart from this, the main concern is memory impairment; this is common but mostly mild and temporary. Memory function returns to normal within days or weeks, and impairment rarely lasts longer than six months. Raised pressure within the brain, due for example to a tumour, is the only exception.

After ECT treatment, an anti-depressant and a mood stabiliser may well be prescribed to forestall another attack of a lowering of mood. ECT is not the preferred treatment for mania and schizophrenia, but may be applied for certain of their life-endangering forms, and then can have dramatic effects.

In animal studies, convulsive treatment results in consistent changes in the activity of chemical messengers, which provides an important clue to the way ECT works. We know conclusively that the effect is due to the induced fit and not to the passage of an electrical current through the brain. We now virtually eliminate the fit by administering a muscle relaxant drug—so that the brain fits but the body barely does.

Other brain stimulation therapies

In the newest physical treatment, repetitive transcranial magnetic stimulation (rTMS), powerful but entirely safe magnetic pulses are applied to the scalp (and thereby to the brain's surface). While depression scores might show statistical positive change, the clinical evidence for rTMS as a substitute for anti-depressants and ECT is limited. Only sophisticated controlled trials will eventually reveal whether it will have a role in the treatment of depression.

Psychosurgery

Even more disturbing to patients and their families than ECT is the fear of operations on the brain for psychiatric illness. Lobotomy was introduced in 1936 by Egas Moniz, a neurologist who won a Nobel Prize for his work thirteen years later. The procedure, which severed most of the nerve fibre tracts connecting the frontal lobes to the rest of the brain, was mainly used to treat schizophrenia. An estimated 50 000 people in the United States and 10 000 in Britain had the operation, the effectiveness of which for schizophrenia was never proven. This is yet another disturbing illustration of unbridled enthusiasm with good intention preceding proper scientific evaluation.

In contrast to the crudity of prefrontal lobotomy, subsequent psychosurgery techniques (more accurately called limbic system surgery) have targeted that area of the brain precisely and are used extremely sparingly. One of the most accurate is so-called stereotactic surgery, which can create lesions with a three-dimensional accuracy of one millimetre. These techniques are used for people with obsessive-compulsive disorder and depression that are severe and intractable and have not responded to other treatments despite persistent trials. Deep brain stimulation is another option for these two conditions and has the distinct advantage of being reversible. The surgeon inserts electrodes into specific parts of the brain and then activates them. Research trials show promising results.

The newer techniques, whatever their type, have many fewer long-term complications than did earlier operations. Changes in personality, and epilepsy, occur in less than half a per cent of patients. Notwithstanding, because of the controversial history of psychosurgery and its irreversible nature, in many health services the person's consent must be fully informed and supported by the judgement of an independent panel of experts.

Conclusion

When I began my psychiatric training in the late 1960s we had available to us newly discovered medications in all the classes we have covered in this chapter. It was an exciting time but also a frustrating one. The side-effects of the drugs we used were thoroughly unpleasant, even hazardous, and often led patients to stop taking them. The situation improved remarkably with the advent of second-generation anti-depressants and anti-psychotics, but not entirely so. New problems have accompanied their use. Psychiatrists nevertheless have at their disposal a diverse range of medicines from which to choose and the opportunity to identify the optimal drug for each person.

New possibilities in finding the best match of person and medication are likely as researchers discover gene–drug interactions. With the human genome mapped out, the burgeoning field of pharmacogenetics is focusing on ways in which we will be able to determine how a particular person will respond to various drugs in terms of both benefits and side effects. The day will dawn when we will know from people's genetic patterns which drugs suit them best.

Researchers in psychiatry will also tell us one day what the underlying causes are of the mental illnesses that currently require drug treatment. The pharmaceutical companies will then be well placed to design drugs that specifically target the causal mechanisms. Sound utopian? Not really; we can be confident that we will accomplish these goals. The only question is how long it will take.

CHAPTER 19

The Psychotherapies

Psychotherapy baffles the layperson. This is not surprising. Unless one has received treatment of this kind, it is difficult to imagine what actually takes place. Throughout my career, this is one area of mental health practice that I have found difficult to explain easily to prospective patients. Many misconceptions abound too, which adds to the confusion. My aim in this chapter therefore is to demystify the subject by covering its definition, the features the psychotherapies have in common and the different forms they take. I shall also add a brief word on research, given that controversy has dogged some of the therapies for decades.

I once wrote a book for the general reader entitled *What Is Psychotherapy?* and cannot hope to do justice in the space of a single chapter to all the themes I discussed there. If you wish to know more about a particular form of psychotherapy, I invite you to dip into *An Introduction to the Psychotherapies* (Oxford University Press, Oxford), a book I have edited since 1978; the most recent edition, the fourth, appeared in 2006.

What is psychotherapy?

Defining psychotherapy is tricky for at least four reasons. Firstly, many psychological treatments are available, each with its own rationale and methods. Secondly, however well planned, these treatments are to a varying extent unpredictable in their application. The reasons for this are obvious once you think about the nature of the process. Psychotherapy is influenced by many unique features, among them the patient's type of personality, the presenting problems, motivation for change and capacity for reflecting about oneself. Thirdly, treatment is also influenced by therapist's personal qualities and the values they espouse, in this regard, the therapist–patient relationship is all-important. Finally, goals of treatment range from relief of

symptoms (as in behaviour therapy) to radical personality change (as in insight-oriented approaches like psychoanalysis).

The task of definition is eased by referring to 'the psychotherapies', since we are concerned with an array of treatments, applied for varied purposes. (Counselling is related to psychotherapy but usually regarded as distinct from it—I shall address it briefly later in the chapter). All psychotherapies involve two foundational features. The first is a relationship between a trained health professional (psychiatrist, psychologist and social worker are the principal groups) and a person needing help to deal with psychological distress (for example, depression, anxiety, guilt, poor self-esteem, unresolved grief) and disturbed functioning (for example, failure in maintaining intimate relationships, marital strife, poor coping with stress). The second feature is the planned, systematic application of specific psychological principles.

Factors that unite the therapies

This succinct definition covers all psychotherapies, although the person's particular difficulties, and the psychological principles applied vary considerably. On the other hand, certain features unite the psychotherapies. These common basic factors were originally formulated by Jerome Frank, a pioneering psychotherapy researcher, in the early 1970s. Given the systematic studies of his group, we can conclude confidently that these factors are necessary but not sufficient for the practice of the psychotherapies, and that we also need to incorporate additional psychological principles.

An emotionally charged and trusting relationship   The therapeutic alliance between therapist and patient has hallmarks that distinguish it from the relationship it most resembles—a friendship. The agenda to be addressed is serious, often involving the ways in which people are failing to progress in their lives. The person is sufficiently distressed and dysfunctional to seek professional help and the therapist is committed to providing the relevant expertise. Given that issues raised in therapy are intensely personal—depressing, frightening, demoralising, embarrassing, shameful and the like—the person expects the therapist to be utterly trustworthy. The relationship calls both for qualities in the therapist best captured by the terms 'caring' and 'sensitive' and for definable skills (for example, to respond *empathically but still retain objectivity*—therapists place themselves in the patient's shoes, thus appreciating their internal psychological world, but remain detached enough to hear the story accurately).

Sharing a rationale   The therapist provides an explanation of the person's problems and of the intended methods for dealing with them that makes sense and is acceptable to the person in the context of their culture. Although unable to predict the precise course of treatment (Freud likened his own approach to a chess game), a coherent framework allows the therapist to apply psychological principles confidently. The explanation is often not subject to proof in a strictly scientific sense. After all, we are dealing with unique human beings, not predictable machines.

Consider a person who was adopted when five months old, has had much difficulty in forming intimate friendships in adolescence and adult life, and remains clingingly dependent on her adoptive mother. She may well not have developed a sense of basic trust as a result of being separated from her biological mother. This cannot be scientifically confirmed, but is nonetheless understood by both patient and therapist as a reasonable possibility since it rings true. Given that the person may feel perplexed at this point, the rationale helps her to appreciate that identifiable factors have contributed to her plight and that these are amenable to change.

Providing new knowledge   This arises out of the rationale and taps patients' potential to use new information about themselves, their problems and ways to change. This process is rarely encountered elsewhere, since patients are the very subjects of study and the mode of learning is correspondingly self-reflective (this differs from ruminating introspection that has often been the futile, stuck mindset in the past).

Learning may be about any aspect of one's internal psychological world and life relating to others, ranging from information about the origin of a symptom (for example, that emotional distress manifests as irritable bowel) to a profound experience of self-discovery (for example, acceptance that one must shape one's own purpose in living). 'Insight', the term used for such knowledge (hence, the aptly titled insight-oriented psychotherapy that we will consider shortly), reflects the process through which people look into themselves, ideally in a fresh and honest way.

Facilitating arousal and expression of emotions   The need for an emotionally charged relationship implies a forum in which the person can freely express feelings. Learning about oneself through experiencing what is happening in one's psychological world is hampered if it is an intellectual pursuit only. On the contrary, therapy encourages both emotional arousal and the expression of feelings, so that the person can get in touch with innermost grief, shame, gloom, envy, anger, frustration, anxiety, guilt, and many other emotional states. This enriches the learning process by stimulating self-reflectiveness (for example, 'I feel horribly guilty and wonder if it's tied up with my having left home when my widowed mother really needed my support'). 'Catharsis' (from the Greek, meaning purging) is the term used for release of pent-up feelings that commonly brings relief. However, we need to bear in mind that it also paves the way for posing the question: 'I wonder what lies behind the feeling I have just experienced?'

Instilling hope   This works on two levels—initially, as encouragement that the person can be understood and therefore anticipate benefit from treatment and, later, the person is buoyed by actual achievement of change as therapy evolves. The therapist's task in representing a professional group offering expertise and commitment is to convey optimism that the person can accomplish change (its degree is obviously a function of many clinical features, such as severity and chronicity of the problems tackled). In responding to each other's positive expectations, they forge a therapeutic alliance.

Experiences of mastery and success   Beyond instilling hope, therapy itself is a forum in which people can experience a sense of achievement and corresponding success. They often embark on treatment gloomily, dismayed by what they see as a record of repeated failure—in family life, social relationships, work and, generally, in coping with life's ups and downs. Although the story may not be so woeful, the person's own sense of failure resists any contrary evidence. As treatment unfolds, welcome shifts, however minor or mundane, often ensue. The person's tolerance of these experiences of mastery and achievement paves the way for a stronger sense of success. They no longer need feel like a powerless victim.

   I need to stress that the therapist's participation in this process is, as I have stated, akin to a friendship but also quite distinctive. The therapist is a participant–observer who also undergoes a powerful experience, particularly through the evolution of feelings, both positive and negative, to the patient. This experience needs to be monitored and addressed so that these feelings are marshalled for their productive value.

Classifying the psychotherapies

The key question in considering the potential role of the psychotherapies has at least three elements: what form of treatment, for what sort of person, with what type of problem?

One option is to distinguish between theoretical models, that is, in terms of *how* the therapies work. This approach is popular and leads to such well-known categories as Freudian, Jungian, behavioural, cognitive and existential. The snag is predictable: the list is fluid as new schools emerge, many of them only minor variations of a few core predecessors.

An alternative classification looks at the *target*—that is, where therapy is directed. Typical categories are couple, family, group and individual (short term and long term). As with the first option, this classification helps only partially. Apart from the obvious (for example, couple therapy, when a husband and wife or established couple present with relational problems), we are left in the dark as to which therapies help what sorts of patients.

Identifying the goals of therapy is the most useful approach to matching treatment and person. The resultant four broad categories are reasonably distinctive. Bear in mind, however, that more than one therapy may be applied at the same time (for example, couple and individual, individual and group), or one therapy may immediately follow on another. However, patients tend to work better in one form of psychological treatment at a time.

Therapies to deal with a crisis   A person overwhelmed by a critical life event (for example, the tragic death of a child) may need help to surmount the ordeal and to re-establish psychological stability. Crisis counselling (or crisis intervention) is usually short-term, up to several weeks, and may be provided individually or for a couple, family or other social group (for example, a school or community struck by tragedy).

Therapies for the long-term psychologically disabled   Some people are so incapacitated by their condition (for example, chronic schizophrenia and bipolar disorder, and severe borderline personality functioning) that they require long-term, indeed sometimes life-long, help. Supportive psychotherapy seeks the best possible adjustment, given that fundamental change is unattainable. People may be treated individually, together with one or more caregivers (usually family members), in a group of similarly disabled members, or with a combination of these.

Therapies to abolish or improve specific symptoms or problems This category covers a variegated assortment of symptoms and problems, from an irrational fear (for example, of spiders) through compulsive behaviour (for example, gambling) to inadequate social skills (for example, shyness). The therapies usually apply principles derived from various forms of learning theory to modify patterns of behaviour. Treatment is usually individually based but may involve couples or families.

Therapies to facilitate self-understanding These seek to promote greater self-understanding and so facilitate symptomatic improvement (for example, the cognitive approach to treating depression and panic attacks), shifts in attitude to oneself (for example, improved self-esteem) and, most ambitiously, personality change (for example, psychoanalytically oriented treatment for many forms of problematic personalities). Treatment is usually long-term and individually based, but variations include brief dynamic therapy (where an identifiable focus is targeted) and group therapy (where the group as a social microcosm provides a forum to learn about oneself and one's relationships).

A HERBAL Remedy for LIFEACHE.

you suffer from lifeache

your whole life is sore; it hurts when you move it.

HERBAL REMEDY.
Take one patch of grass, a mild day and two large green trees.

Lie on the grass beneath one tree and contemplate the other tree.

nap from time to time or gaze occasionally at the grass.

Pain will subside. Lifeache cannot be cured but you can learn to MANAGE THE SYMPTOMS.

leunig

Issues related to classification

Combining *medication and psychotherapy* is common and complementary, as discussed in the previous chapter; for example, anti-psychotics and supportive therapy in chronic schizophrenia, anti-depressants and psychodynamic therapy in depression, and mood stabilisers and cognitive-behaviour therapy in bipolar disorder.

An integrative movement has influenced the psychotherapies since the 1980s, in which previously sharp boundaries between theoretical schools have been redrawn. Combining one school with another has occurred, on the premise that in unity is strength, in terms of both reinforcement of theoretical concepts and added effectiveness. The most prominent example is cognitive-behaviour therapy. I have been involved in treatment trials of psychotherapy with patients with cancer over many years. Our group found that combining elements of cognitive and existential approaches was the best way to meet the needs of women having to adjust to early-stage breast cancer, and of men and their spouses coping with the demands of early-stage prostate cancer.

We need to distinguish carefully between this productive evolution in the psychotherapies and a practice in which a therapist borrows indiscriminately from two or more schools, usually in the face of a patient's failure to respond to a single therapy. This is akin to polypharmacy, in which drugs are added pell-mell to a condition that is ostensibly resistant to treatment.

To include Eastern practices such as transcendental meditation, yoga and Tai Chi in our classification of treatments would be stretching our definition of psychotherapy beyond the customary boundary. These methods, as well as Western-based forms of promoting relaxation or a state of inner calm, do have a place in psychiatric treatment but more in the context of promoting good mental health in all of us.

The same qualifications may apply to what are called the creative therapies—using the media of music, graphic art, dance, drama and literature. All of us appreciate the role of the arts in enriching our lives. There is no reason why they should not also have a place in psychiatric practice—mainly as a means of bolstering quality of life. We saw an example of this in the chapter on the psychoses—a poem entitled 'Psychotic Episode' by Sandy Jeffs. She has told me over the years how writing poems about her bewildering experiences has helped her profoundly to deal with the demands of her schizophrenic illness.

The graphic arts similarly serve many patients well. I have the good fortune to be involved in the Cunningham Dax Collection in Melbourne. Dr Dax was one of the first psychiatrists in the world to introduce art as part of mainstream psychiatric treatment. The 15 000 works, the largest collection of its kind, have allowed people with a mental illness or victims of trauma to express their complex psychological world and thereby to be better understood.

Music has always been valued for its healing effects, and musicians have applied their art to lift the spirits of the sick for centuries. Music therapy in the twenty-first century has found a place in diverse areas of medicine, including psychiatry. Research has shown that the mentally ill, even those with longstanding disabilities, can be encouraged to write original lyrics and offer suggestions for the melodic and rhythmic elements of the music. They can then gain much pleasure from what they sense is a creative process, feel they belong to a social group, and be pleasantly surprised that the group is able to produce a positive outcome such as an original song.

The internet is a new vehicle for providing certain psychotherapies, particularly more structured kinds. Given that psychological treatments are labour-intensive (compared, say, to drugs), available services will always outstrip demand. Compounding the overall limitation of resources is the maldistribution of therapists, with people living in regional and rural areas often short-changed. Treatment offered via the internet is burgeoning for these and other reasons.

An illuminating example is the application of an innovative program of cognitive-behaviour therapy (CBT) in which 300 patients diagnosed with a new episode of depression in one of 55 British general practices were randomly allocated to the computer-based option (which included a supportive role for therapists) or to two control groups. Improvement was much higher in the computer-based group than in those who did not receive this treatment over the ensuing months. Although a third did not complete therapy, this drop-out rate is still lower than computer-based CBT in which therapists play no role.

In a review in 2010 of 26 controlled trials of internet interventions (all CBT) for depression and anxiety, the results were promising, pointing to their potential role as a self-help treatment or as a part of conventional professional care. Similar evidence is also available in the case of children and young people. You may wish to try out some representative websites. MoodGYM was devised at the Australian National University in Canberra for mood disturbances (www.moodgym.anu.au); FearFighter in London for anxiety, panic and phobia (www.fearfighter.com); and Panic Online at Swinburne University of Technology in Melbourne for a range of anxiety states (www.swinburne.edu.au/lss/swinpsyche/etherapy/programs/registration). Not everyone will take to a more impersonal method of therapy; on the other hand, some people in need of help may feel less threatened by it compared to seeking out a mental health professional. Thus, it may well be a matter of horses for courses, and what a good thing that is.

APPLYING THE PSYCHOTHERAPIES IN PRACTICE

Psychoanalysis and psychoanalytically oriented psychotherapy

In the 1890s, Sigmund Freud founded what we now know as psychoanalysis. Beginning with his classic *Studies in Hysteria* in 1895, by his death it had developed beyond an innovative method of treatment into: (a) a theory of abnormal psychology, (b) an elaborate account of the 'normal' psyche, (c) a theory of culture and society (for example, the nature of civilisation, war and religion) and (d) a method to study mental life. By studying dreams, works of art, jokes, and apparently trivial events such as lapses of memory, as well as more clinically oriented phenomena like anxiety and depression, he argued for a continuity between normal and abnormal psychological states.

These ideas have now become part and parcel of Western culture. Indeed, in an elegy written after Freud's death, the poet WH Auden asserted that his contribution had been so monumental as to be the dawning of a new 'climate of opinion'. Psychoanalysis in general, and the writings and person of Freud in particular, continue to arouse extremes of admiration and attack—both within and outside psychiatry. In my view, the sensible psychiatrist adopts a balanced view, recognising that 'psychodynamic' ways of thinking are intrinsic to clinical practice, both psychiatric and beyond.

After qualifying as a doctor, Freud visited the celebrated neurologist Jean-Martin Charcot in Paris to study the use of hypnosis in conversion hysteria. His mentor in Vienna, the physician Josef Breuer, noted that hypnotised patients released intense feelings not expressed at the time of an original trauma but later linked to presenting symptoms. Freud further observed that when able to talk freely about innermost thoughts and feelings, without recourse to hypnosis, the person improved. He concluded that such repressed feelings were recreated in the person's unconscious relationship with the therapist (the so-called 'transference'). As Freud put it, the patient 'transferred on to the [therapist] mental attitudes that were lying ready in him and were intimately connected with his neurosis'. Moreover, the patient reproduces 'his intimate life history … as though it were actually happening'. Initially, Freud saw transference as an impediment to treatment; later, he regarded it as central. Accordingly, his emphasis shifted to eliciting and clarifying the transference relationship, thus illuminating how the past was still alive and influencing current mental life. Freud also described the therapist's potential to develop unconsciously held attitudes towards the patient, the 'countertransference'. While such transference–countertransference experiences influence all human relationships, Freud pioneered ways in which therapists might reflect upon these experiences between themselves and patients in order to help the latter to achieve better self-understanding.

Psychoanalytic therapy stems directly from Freud's work and that of his colleagues and, whether acknowledged or not, most Western therapies owe something to his theories and techniques. Many diverse concepts have emerged as part of this Freudian legacy. Here are just a few of them.

Carl Jung, who broke away from Freud, thought his emphasis on sexuality in child development too restrictive. From his observations, especially of dreams and artistic creations of patients with psychoses, coupled with the study of myths and symbols of ancient civilisations, Jung expanded Freud's notions of inner life. In particular, he developed the concept of the collective unconscious, that is, the repository of man's deepest psychological activity (he called it the 'true basis of the individual psyche').

The existential school has applied certain psychoanalytic aspects in its focus on a person's struggle to fend off anxiety linked to the threat of death and non-being, and to grapple with the awesome challenge of living an authentic life typified by purpose and meaning (see the existential approach below). Melanie Klein pioneered the use of play with young children as a means, not possible in words, for them to disclose their concerns and conflicts, and brought to light developmental anxieties that children experienced earlier in life. Erik Erikson applied Freud's ideas to a life-cycle model of human development, describing how the fulfilment of crucial tasks at each stage of the cycle requires an interplay between the individual's internal psychological life and society's institutions (family, peer group, religion, cultural practices), and helps to shape his emerging sense of identity. John Bowlby's attachment theory emphasises the infant's relationship to the mother as a key determinant of normal and abnormal psychological development, and specifies the particular role of attachment in achieving a sense of security. Self psychology, pioneered by Heinz Kohut, an American psychoanalyst, holds that narcissism is a critical, recurring, adaptive process in the evolution of a sense of self (for example, children should feel as if they are the apple of their parents' eyes, and then gradually face the inevitable and necessary disillusionment that such a special position cannot be sustained in reality).

The psychoanalytic approach to treatment

First described by Freud a hundred years ago and revised by him and his successors since then, the psychoanalytic approach explores the transference–countertransference relationship and the patient's resistance to change as central ideas. The goal is more mature personality functioning. Symptom relief follows the person gaining insight into unconscious factors that underlie their problems. This insight, in turn, arises from their emotionally charged experience of the relationship with the therapist, which invariably recreates past and current traumas and anxieties in the person's life, and the defences adopted against them. In the context of therapy, these are carefully and sensitively examined, and more adaptive responses sought rather than those adopted hitherto.

Despite a willingness at a conscious level to disclose their innermost thoughts and feelings, the person will inevitably resist the process at an unconscious level out of a fear of delving into deep waters (better the devil I know). This manifests in all sorts of ways—asking the therapist for advice, praise or validation, getting them to make concessions or special allowances, arriving late or not at all, disclosing important matters only in the last few minutes of a session, and deflecting the therapeutic conversation to an irrelevant topic are a few examples from my own work. If, on the basis of their own unrecognised countertransference, therapists *do* behave in ways that recreate for the patient traumas similar to those experienced in previous relationships, then any resistance is bound to be reinforced and therapy will stall.

So-called 'classical' psychoanalysis, applying the aforementioned features, is an intensive form of psychotherapy. Hour-long sessions are held up to five times a week, during which the patient lies on a couch, the analyst sits behind, and the patient is encouraged to freely associate and share whatever comes to mind.

A much more widely practised form is called psychodynamic or psychoanalytic psychotherapy. Here, the patient sits in a chair, opposite the therapist, and sessions take place once or twice a week. Again, the person is encouraged to talk about whatever thoughts or feelings come to mind. The therapist listens intently, monitors the feelings that the person expresses, pays heed to the thoughts and feelings in themselves that are aroused by the person and tries to understand both the verbal and non-verbal import of what the person is communicating. Kay has sought the help of a therapist.

Kay, aged 25 and single, presents with a childhood history of a conflicted relationship with her mother. She has not seen her father since he left the family when she was a 3-year-old. She is in a de facto relationship with Jim, who is described by Kay as loving and supportive except when he gets depressed, whereupon he tends to withdraw. They have a 2-year-old daughter, Kelly. Kay is seeking psychiatric help for recurrent severe headaches and abdominal pain for which no cause or effective treatment have been found. In one early session she is describing a recent incident when she left Kelly with her mother so that she (Kay) could attend a medical out-patient clinic for a specialist review. She was kept waiting for over two hours, whereupon she 'blacked out' and apparently had a fit.

The approach of Kay's therapist is underpinned by the following three elements:

Empathising   The therapist reflects back thoughts and feelings through a process of imagining what it is like to be in the patient's shoes; for example, 'Kay, it sounds as though you were sitting there for hours in the clinic, worrying about yourself, worrying about Kelly, and no one seemed to take any notice of your worries. You must have felt so alone and so frustrated!'

Kohut (see above) argued that empathy, rather than interpretation, is the vital ingredient in psychotherapy that enables optimal responsiveness and a matching sense in the patient of being understood; this process helps the person to gain a secure sense of self.

Clarifying   The therapist seeks to illuminate an issue so that its relevance in the person's mental life is highlighted; for example, 'Kay, can you describe what you were *feeling* as you sat there in the waiting room thinking about Kelly?'

Interpreting   The therapist links thoughts and feelings with a psychological experience of which the person is not aware but may appreciate once these links crystallise; for example, 'Kay, I wonder if you were getting more upset in yourself and angry at the doctors for keeping you waiting, but you couldn't criticise them or complain because you were afraid they might then not want to help you?' (Kay nods, appears close to tears and her hands tremble; a few minutes of silence ensue and she appears more composed.) 'Kay, you seem upset remembering that [empathic comment]. I wonder if you've also had that kind of upset with your mother when you felt angry with her but couldn't criticise her because you felt that she was also the only one who cared for you after your father left?'

The interpretation facilitates a cognitive and emotional link between the person's state of mind in the session and a current or past traumatic experience, thereby showing that presenting problems are meaningful and that the therapist is willing to help explore what the meaning might be. Until gaining insight in these ways, the person will tend to repeat faulty patterns of thought, feeling and behaviour (Freud called this the repetition compulsion). In the above example, Kay's anxieties about expressing anger lest it lead to rejection, and the resultant physical expression of this distressing dilemma, was a feature of her relationship with her mother, both in childhood and currently, as well as with Jim, and others, including the doctors at the clinic. It later emerged that Kay became excessively angry with Kelly, at which times she (Kay) feared being rejected; this in turn made Kay even more angry. At such times Kay considered hitting Kelly. These patterns were experienced and interpreted many times, a process Freud termed 'working through' (the playful word 'cyclotherapy' captures the sense of the process), which leads to deeper self-understanding.

Some therapists believe that it is the experience over time of not being abandoned by the therapist, and the feeling of being accurately and empathically understood in the moment-to-moment exchanges of therapy, that are more therapeutic than the insights gained from the therapist's interpretation. This question has engendered heated debate, particularly in the therapy of people suffering from borderline and narcissistic personalities (see Chapter 10). However, the distinction between empathic comments and a thoughtful interpretation is not always clear.

In addition to the above strategies, the need arises periodically for:

Confronting The therapist firmly presses the person to face and grapple with a particular issue; for example, 'Kay, I know it's hard for you to accept that you might feel angry sometimes, but you *did* say that you felt quite angry at the doctors for keeping you waiting'.

Who benefits from the psychoanalytic therapies?

People suited to psychoanalytic therapy, whatever its duration, accept a measure of responsibility to tackle their problems and work towards their resolution, even though they are not entirely cognisant of their origins or why their own past attempts to solve them have failed. A capacity to look into oneself and express thoughts, fantasies and feelings is necessary, since therapy works mainly through words. While a measure of anxiety is inevitable, the person is sufficiently robust to tolerate feelings generated by exploring unconscious forces ('ego strength' is the technical term). Appreciation that relating, both intimately and socially, is part of a mature personality, and experience of at least one significant tie, are two other desirable criteria. A person who stubbornly wants to make pivotal life decisions or seek immediate remedies is not suitable. Neither is the psychotic or severely depressed person.

Chris, a 38-year-old management consultant, sought therapy because he repeatedly failed to form a long-term relationship with a woman. He had adopted a lifestyle of brief, emotionally empty, highly sexualised relationships alternating with periods of dismal isolation. He came across as cynical and aloof. At first he was sceptical of the therapist's ability to help and poured scorn over his theories. The therapist interpreted the criticism as Chris's way of avoiding deep feelings; this led him to recall a similar attitude he had harboured towards his mother—a deeply religious woman whose need to avoid conflict had allowed his father to tyrannise the family.

Chris's contempt for people he perceived as weak, especially women, emerged during ensuing sessions. In this way, Chris had unconsciously identified with his tyrannical father while seeking to avoid behaving like him; hence his recurring pattern of short-lived relationships characterised by initial intensity followed rapidly by boredom, devaluation of the woman and various rationalisations to justify ending the relationship. Thus, one element of his presenting problem became clearer. This attitude towards women contrasted sharply with his conscientious work ethic on behalf of his 'needy' clients; this led to a discussion of his episodic anger towards those who did not live up to his expectations. With this insight he became less demanding of himself and his clients, and enjoyed his work more. A planned, brief form of psychoanalytic therapy may have ended here.

As treatment unfolded, another layer of conflict emerged: his anxiety about being seen as weak. This was the way his father had made him feel. Now, in the transference, the therapist was often put into the role of strong father with Chris his child-like victim. As the therapist interpreted this vulnerability, Chris became increasingly agitated. He missed sessions and criticised the therapist, again in his former cynical style. The therapist interpreted Chris's associated anxiety about a growing closeness to himself, and the fear of what might ensue. A slip of the tongue revealed this when Chris blurted out: 'I want to keep you at arms' length!'

Two themes crystallised. One was fear that the therapist would abandon him just as he believed his mother had failed to care for him. Chris then highlighted his intellectual prowess as a way of denying his emotional vulnerability. The second took the form of further criticism of the therapist concerning a variety of matters (for example, the therapist taking a holiday), even though Chris recognised that his resentment was irrational, and raising widely publicised scandals in the medical profession. This was interpreted as devaluing what the therapist had to offer because Chris felt the therapist was abandoning him during holiday breaks.

Chris became progressively more aware of how his profound neediness for nurturing, which he had never been able to acknowledge, had led to his contempt for people, especially women, and to an envy of those he saw as competent and able to offer him something he himself could not provide. This knowledge enabled him to approach personal and professional relationships with greater insight, and control over the anxieties that had affected his behaviour in the past. These insights paved the way for major changes of attitude and behaviour in his relating to others. Ultimately, Chris developed a stable relationship that led to an affectionate marriage, and entered into a more tender relationship with his mother.

Brief psychodynamic psychotherapy

Another aspect of psychoanalytic therapy concerns its *duration*. It is time-consuming, lasting years in people with deep-seated personality problems. A shortened form, variously termed brief or focal psychoanalytic therapy, has evolved for people with more circumscribed psychological difficulties. Although several variations have been described, they share the following properties:

- People are carefully selected, with these overlapping criteria to the fore: adequate resilience and ego strength; not being prone to psychosis, marked depression or overwhelming anxiety; ability to be self-reflective through a sufficient level of 'psychological-mindedness'.
- The number of sessions is restricted, with the limit imposed precisely (exactly twelve sessions in one approach) or kept to a predictable range, usually up to forty.
- Goals are specified in relation to an identified focus (such as unresolved grief), which is resolutely maintained (my advice to my students is to abide by the commandment 'Thou shalt focus on the focus').
- Transference is tackled head-on, although confined to the focus.
- The therapist may confront the person in a challenging, non-destructive way to a greater degree than in traditional psychoanalytic therapy.

The existential approach

Irvin Yalom, Emeritus Professor at Stanford University and with whom I had the pleasure of working when I was learning the ropes of psychotherapy, has written eloquently about the existential approach. He highlights our unavoidable confrontation with the four 'givens of existence': we have to accept the inevitability of our own death; we have the freedom and associated responsibility to make choices about how we shall live our lives; we are in the final analysis isolated in our lives in that we enter and leave the world on our own; and we have to determine a personal sense of purpose in the face of a cosmos that does not offer us meaning.

Human beings may find one or more of these ultimate concerns threatening and discomforting, become anxious as a result, and then attempt to ward off this anxiety by resorting to maladaptive defences. A wide range of clinical features may manifest, including a retreat into a feeling of helplessness, obsessive rigidity and associated compulsive behaviour, and a state of being driven to achieve at any psychological cost. We may suffer more directly from what has been called an existential syndrome by some and an existential vacuum by others (such as Viktor Frankl). The affected person feels empty, alienated, detached, dissatisfied, lacks spontaneity, and sees life as meaningless. Put another way, life is lived inauthentically. The tragic case of the poet Sylvia Plath, author of the illuminating *The Bell Jar*, illustrates many of these features. Consider these extracts from her diaries:

> I am afraid, I am not solid but hollow. I feel behind my eyes a numb, paralysed cavern, a pit of hell, a mimicking nothingness … I want to kill myself, to escape from responsibility, to crawl back abjectly into the womb. I do not know who I am, where I am going—and I am the one who has to decide the answers to these hideous questions. I long for a noble escape from freedom … Now I sit here, crying almost, afraid, seeing the finger writing my hollow futility on the wall … The future? God—will it get worse and worse? Will I … never integrate my life, never have purpose, meaning?

The aim of existential therapy is to wrestle unflinchingly with this sort of experience and to do so in such a way that the therapeutic journey becomes a search for authenticity. Another metaphor for the same quest is pithily encompassed in the title of Paul Tillich's contribution to existentialism, *The Courage To Be*. By facing up to existential anxiety, the traveller becomes more spontaneous, more responsible for their life, aware of personal meaning, open to new experience, and freed up to develop and exploit their creative potential.

The most crucial feature of the journey is aptly summarised in the word 'encounter'. The existential therapist accompanies the person in ways that differentiate the relationship from the typical one in psychoanalytic treatment, where the analyst serves as a blank screen for the person's irrational projections. In particular, the existential therapist is much more willing to share personal aspects of themselves in order to promote the notion that all human beings have to grapple with the four givens of existence. The therapist also relates in such a way that the encounter becomes as genuine as possible. The temporal perspective is present and future, so that more attention is paid to how attitudes and feelings have the potential to change. The person comes to accept a state of 'becoming'—moving into the future with a sense of commitment to the journey. Another key feature of the therapy is the process of understanding the person's life history in the context of their 'being-in-the-world', in contrast to an attempt to explain that history.

Cognitive therapy

The origins of cognitive therapy lie with the Greek Stoics, who held that 'men are disturbed not by things but by the view which they take of them' or, as Shakespeare put it later, 'There is nothing either good or bad, but thinking makes it so'. Aaron Beck, an American psychiatrist regarded as one of the most significant contributors to psychotherapy in contemporary times, noted in the early 1960s the rigidity of depressed people's pessimistic ways of thinking, which pervaded both their waking life and dreams. He saw this distorted thinking as the result of faulty information processing, concluding that negative thinking leads to depressed mood, not the other way around. Beck formulated an approach to challenge depressed patients dominated by negative thoughts. This was later combined with behavioural methods so that patterns of thinking and associated behaviour might be challenged concurrently.

Cognitive behaviour therapy (CBT) has become one of the most commonly used forms of psychotherapy. Having been devised as a treatment for depression, it has also been applied to a range of conditions from panic attacks to problematic personality. I had the pleasure of interviewing Professor Beck in 2003 in his clinic in Philadelphia, and asked him about this extension of CBT's use (and many other matters). His reply was characteristically candid: 'Originally, I thought that the formulation ... would suit about seven or eight conditions ... in essence, the neuroses'. He continued that if it could be demonstrated by strict scientific means to be effective for other conditions, including even the psychoses, that would satisfy him. CBT is in fact a heavily researched area, probably more so than any other approach in the entire history of psychotherapy research; dozens of treatment trials have been carried out.

How does the cognitive approach work? The therapist aims to help the patient examine assumptions, methods of reasoning and ways of processing information that lead to automatic, negative thoughts about themselves, the world and their future. More adaptive options are then sought and applied. Beck's approach in practice stresses identifying forms of irrational thinking and the contexts in which they arise. For example, depressed people are taught to recognise how they select only the negative aspects of a situation (selective attention), over-generalise from a single episode, personalise a situation by assuming they are the cause of a negative event, think dichotomously (seeing things in black and white or all or nothing terms), catastrophise by exaggerating the negative, apply self-critical labels ('I am a total failure'), and pepper their thoughts with 'shoulds' and 'oughts' ('I should have been a better mother').

In other psychiatric states, a person experiencing panic attacks misconceives physical symptoms as an imminent medical catastrophe, like a heart attack or stroke; socially phobic people are terrified they will lose self-control and expose themselves to the criticism of others.

Cognitive therapy posits that many erroneous beliefs and distorted thought patterns derive from childhood experiences, especially family life; these lead to patterns of thinking (cognitive schemata) that lie beyond immediate awareness (similar to Freud's concept of the pre-conscious rather than the unconscious), and that are tenaciously held and applied automatically. Therapy comprises:

- educating the person about the nature of symptoms (e.g. the physiological basis of anxiety and how this differs from an impending heart attack, and that misinterpreting symptoms may augment anxiety);
- recognising faulty thinking and its origins;
- formulating faulty thinking as a process that the person can test in day-to-day life;
- keeping a diary of negative thoughts and the situations in which they arise, and grading their severity;
- becoming aware of automatic negative thinking;
- learning, applying and recording attempts at alternative ways of thinking;
- incorporating these as homework tasks.

Patient and therapist identify problems, select goals and brainstorm alternative solutions, including their relative risks and advantages. The person may rehearse preferred solutions before applying them in their lives. The therapist, as collaborator and tutor, helps the person to test out ideas identified as the source of faulty thinking. Patient attitudes to the therapist are not explored as in psychoanalytic therapy; they are assumed to be positive and cooperative. However, they may be discussed if relevant, in the same way as other thoughts.

Consider now the story of Darren, which shares some features with Chris's story above. This will allow you to discern the differences in psychoanalytic and cognitive therapy.

Darren, 30 years old and unemployed, was despondent because of a failing relationship. He felt obliged to act cheerfully and worried that his girlfriend was disappointed in him. He was reluctant to state his needs for fear of burdening people, especially his girlfriend, whom he feared might leave him if he was 'too demanding'. This form of thinking was traced to his relationship with his enduringly depressed mother, whom he had sought to please and comfort after his father left the family when Darren was fourteen. The therapist suggested that his feelings of depression might be linked to his belief that he had insatiable needs; that his girlfriend would abandon him if he acted more assertively; and that were he to lose her, he would have nothing of value to offer in any other relationship.

With the therapist's support, Darren explored these assumptions, looked for alterative ways of thinking about himself and of testing whether they worked, and then rehearsed and applied them in his day-to-day life. He kept a daily record of his fears and the thoughts that underlay them, and of the responses of his girlfriend and others to his initiatives to express himself more clearly. His mood lifted considerably, as did his self-confidence. The relationship with his girlfriend improved, although it also became clear that neither of them was ready for a long-term commitment. She decided to move to another city for a few months. Darren was distressed, but it was not the catastrophe he feared. He was able to initiate new friendships in which, with the therapist's help, he continued to test out new ways of thinking.

The behavioural approach

According to this theory, symptoms derive from faulty learning or, put another way, symptoms are learned habits. The aim is to undo unhelpful patterns and replace them with more adaptive ones. Three models have been elaborated to explain how learning (and therefore faulty learning) occurs: classical conditioning, operant conditioning and modelling.

Classical conditioning is regarded as the substrate of normal and maladaptive behaviour. In Pavlov's well-known experiments, dogs were conditioned, for example, to experience fear on hearing a sound in the absence of the anxiety-provoking stimulus with which the sound had been paired. Similarly, symptoms develop when a neutral stimulus is linked with a fearful one. The resultant treatment is counter-conditioning, in which an opposite feeling to anxiety, namely relaxation, is paired with the feared stimulus (for example, thunder or flying). Relaxation, when successfully mastered, inhibits anxiety.

Systematic desensitisation takes this a step further, incorporating relaxation training and exposure to the frightening situation. A hierarchy is created from least to most anxiety-provoking. In phobia of flying, for instance, the minimal point may be the thought of glancing at photographs of an aircraft, the maximum an experience of actual flight. Images of increasing fearfulness are interposed between these extremes. Desensitisation succeeds as the person remains at ease in the face of the anxiety-provoking images. The process may involve the fearful stimulus as imagined or in real life. Treatment at an airport would reflect the latter in the case of a flight phobia.

A detailed hierarchy can be replaced by graded exposure on its own.

Another variant, response prevention, is applied to compulsive behaviour like hand-washing. The person, whose compulsion is precipitated by contact with an allegedly contaminated object, is exposed to it but prevented from reacting in their customary ways.

Operant conditioning posits that we repeat behaviour that elicits a positive response and avoid behaviour evoking the opposite. Reinforcement is regarded as a cogent feature of some forms of behaviour therapy in which desirable behaviours are rewarded, for example, in altering apathy in chronically disabled patients, but it is not often applied today. Positive reinforcers include praise and tokens. Negative reinforcement such as punishment has no role in treatment, given that it cannot be justified ethically.

Socially determined learning or *modelling* regards learning as derived from the observation of the behaviour of others. Thus, a person with a fear of snakes notes how the therapist, applying a graded approach, handles one. The person is encouraged to imitate this, with the effort rewarded through positive reinforcement. This is a simple method of learning but more subtle modelling occurs in all therapies. Freud pointed out in his essay 'Analysis Terminable and Interminable' that the therapist may on occasion assume the role of model. Group therapies lend themselves to social learning, since people may imitate behaviours of their peers that are relevant to their own difficulties.

Behavioural analysis consists of the assessment of identified problems: where and when they arise, what maintains them, under what circumstances they manifest and what repercussions they have. The purpose is to set appropriate goals and strategies in the form of a behavioural formulation. The person has to understand the program's rationale and become an active collaborator, with therapist as guide. Homework is emphasised, as is a requirement that the person monitor progress by use of daily ratings. A family member or friend may be invited to serve as ally; for example, acting as companion in graded exposure. Treatment is brief, weeks to a few months, with sessions conducted weekly. Intervals between sessions are gradually extended, culminating in one or two follow-up reviews.

Group psychotherapy

We are all members of many social groups, ranging from the primary one, the nuclear family, to the extended family, neighbourhood, various social groups, and beyond. In each case, we engage with others reciprocally, contributing to their wellbeing and receiving benefits from them. This natural process has been adapted in psychiatry to serve various purposes (see also family therapy below).

Membership of a social group may also go awry, with problems arising between people. The rationale for the group therapies recognises both the rewarding and adverse features of relationships, by providing a forum in which relational aspects of a person's difficulties can be dealt with, and the potential of a group harnessed to benefit all its members. Interaction and mutual influence are the planks on which the process operates. Long-term out-patient, short-term in-patient and self-help (or mutual-help) are the predominant forms of group therapy.

Long-term out-patient groups

Several models have evolved to help people with a combination of intrapsychic problems (for example, poor self-esteem, anxiety, depression) and interpersonal difficulties (for example, inability to express feelings, domineering, distrustful). A popular approach derives from the American psychiatrist Harry Stack Sullivan's concept that personality is mostly the product of one's interactions with significant other people. A group of six to eight patients and a therapist (or two co-therapists) meets weekly for about two years (if the group is 'slow open', new members replace 'graduating' members and the group continues indefinitely under the same leadership). It provides a forum in which participants explore their relationships with one another, gain insight into maladaptive patterns and experiment with other more effective ones, initially in the group and later in other social settings.

The common basic factors that unite individual therapies (outlined early in this chapter) operate in group therapies as well, but are supplemented by group-specific therapeutic factors, such as feeling a sense of altruism towards fellow members as they wrestle with their difficulties; identifying with, and learning from, the experience of others; a feeling of having much in common with fellow members; and, importantly, experimenting with new forms of interpersonal behaviour and obtaining group feedback about one's efforts.

Short-term ward groups

In contrast to the group in the community setting, psychiatric in-patients can only be members of a group during the period of their stay in the ward. They tend to be more disturbed and correspondingly less able to benefit from an experience of predominantly interpersonal insight. A useful model is labelled 'educative', since its chief purpose is to help people think in clinical terms about themselves, thus enabling more adaptive reactions to the effects of their condition. The therapist assists members to identify ineffective patterns of feeling, thinking and behaviour, and to avoid circumstances that provoke them.

Because of the rapid turnover of members, each meeting is planned as if it were the last, with patients urged to achieve what they can. Members and therapists set agendas that can be tackled in a limited time. Therapeutic factors have different emphases: interpersonal learning is supplanted by the acquisition of clinical knowledge; altruism and a sense of hope are particularly relevant.

Self-help (or mutual-help) groups

These terms are interchangeable. Although not strictly group therapy, in that professionals do not lead them (they may be invited to consult to the relevant organisation), the self-help group has considerable potential, especially for people disabled by continuing conditions like schizophrenia, gambling addiction and alcoholism, as well as for their relatives. Alcoholics Anonymous (AA), a forerunner, is a good example of people with a common problem setting up a group-based organisation whose chief purpose is to help one another. The process of self-help groups varies; prominent features are mutual support, a shared commitment to keep going whatever the odds (for example, even if a member has resumed drinking), and encouragement to lead as normal a life as possible.

A robust self-help movement is an invaluable complement to any contribution made by the mental health professions. We professionals need to remind ourselves to respect the expertise of patients and their families, which is obtained by direct experience.

Family therapy

That naturally occurring social group, the family (nuclear or extended), may be the most appropriate context for therapy. Psychiatry has tended to focus on the individual throughout most of its history, although we have appreciated that family factors may influence the onset and outcome of mental illnesses. The family has been seen as: (a) a possible cause (genetic or psychogenic); (b) a source of information about the patient; (c) a potential support to the patient, both emotionally and practically; and (d) an ally in monitoring cooperation with treatment and noting deterioration. Family therapy has also developed as a treatment to improve family functioning. While drawing on some of the concepts we covered earlier, family therapy also incorporates theories and methods devised by family therapists themselves.

Psychological principles were not applied to families until the 1950s, when Nathan Ackerman coined the term 'family therapy' and wove in psychoanalytic concepts to his work. Salvador Minuchin, another pioneer in the field, worked with delinquent youth whose behaviour resisted conventional treatment. He observed improvement when an under-functioning parent was recruited into the therapy process and encouraged to devise fresh ways of responding to the child. He then worked with families with an adolescent suffering from anorexia nervosa or uncontrolled diabetes, and noted tension between the parents and maladaptive alignments between a parent and a child. The child could be understood as carrying the family's unspoken conflicts and anxieties.

Emerging from this work came the distinction between the cause of a problem and what might be maintaining it. Systems theory, derived from the world of biology, was utilised to understand the latter and, more particularly, typical interactional patterns between family members. Regardless of its original cause, family dysfunction may be maintained because of the responses members make to their difficulties. Since it is frequently the case that the family is trying to help an ill relative, and indeed have coped with the problem for many years, the therapist asks 'Why now?' and seeks to clarify how family functioning has become compromised.

Various family therapy approaches have evolved since the 1970s, some of which continue to be influential. The Milan school, whose founders became frustrated by what they felt were the limitations of psychoanalytic methods, devised a clever and productive way of engaging families that they called circular questioning; this illuminates interactional patterns between members by asking one member about how others view an issue. For example, a depressed person may be asked what he thinks worries his wife most about his condition, or whether she spends less or more time with the children since his illness began, or whether she confides in her mother more than she does in him. An adolescent child may then be asked what the parents need to do to improve their communication. Changing the ways in which members relate to one another is assumed to alter the impact of the illness on the whole family, and to improve their functioning.

Another form of family therapy is the narrative approach. Its principal feature is that families regard an illness in a member, and their ways of responding to it, as reflecting the opinion of some professional authority or of the view the family members have of their own history. Such views exclude alternative stories about the problem, and ignore a time when the problem may have been better managed. The result is that other ways of thinking about dealing with the problem are inadvertently overlooked. A family that has lived through a civil war, for instance, may have an entrenched image of itself as always struck by ill fortune, and destined to face tragedy repeatedly in the future.

A form of family intervention termed 'psychoeducation' has been developed for people with enduring psychiatric conditions. In a supportive setting, the therapist uses training in communication skills and problem-solving methods, and provision of information about the illness and its treatment, to reduce their adverse effects. This well-researched approach has been found to reduce the rate of relapse in patients with schizophrenia (to which it has been most commonly applied).

Who benefits from family therapy?

Those people who benefit can be grouped as follows:

- The clinical problem manifests in family terms and family dysfunction is obvious. For example, marital strain predominates, with repercussions for the whole family; or tension between a father and an adolescent child dislocates family life, with everyone ensnared in the tension.
- The family has experienced a stressful event that has led to poor adjustment, or is on the verge of doing so. Such events, either predictable or accidental, include suicidal death, financial crisis, major physical illness in a member, the unexpected departure of a child from home, and so forth.
- Continuing and demanding circumstances are so taxing as to lead to poor family adjustment. The family's resources may be stretched to the hilt and external sources of support are scanty. Typical situations are a long-term physical illness or a persistent or recurrent mental illness.
- An identified patient develops symptoms in a poorly functioning family. For example, a mother's depression or a daughter's eating problem reflect underlying family difficulties.
- Mental illness causes adverse reverberations in the family. For example, a schizophrenic son affects his parents in ways that exceed their problem-solving capacity, or a severely anxious mother comes to rely excessively on her daughter's support.
- A thoroughly disorganised family, buffeted by myriad problems, needs help. For instance, one member abuses drugs, another is prone to violence and a third manifests anti-social behaviour.

Family therapy may be the treatment of choice in all these categories, but not necessarily on its own. Thus, in helping a disturbed family struggling to deal with a schizophrenic member, supportive therapy for the patient is also usually offered. A late adolescent striving to separate and individuate may benefit from individual therapy following family treatment, while the parents may require help to examine their own relationship.

Methods of treatment

Family therapists work on their own, or as part of a team with one member working directly with the family and the others observing through a one-way mirror. The latter is especially advantageous with complex families, when the therapist is often drawn into family conflicts unwittingly. The observers assist the therapist to clarify what may be going on and to plan corresponding interventions.

The following example illustrates family therapy in general, but one should bear in mind the multiplicity of theories and strategies available.

Zoe Jones, aged 16 and the youngest of three children, was brought by her parents to a psychiatrist because of rebellious behaviour and deterioration in her previously impeccable academic performance. As the parents' concerns mounted, they had become more controlling, to the extent that their worries dominated family life. In the first session, Zoe was sullen and unwilling to speak. After eliciting the parents' growing despair, the therapist turned to the family's history. The family had immigrated a few years previously at Mr Jones's behest, because of a job opportunity. His wife had been reluctant to leave her ailing mother, and her sister to whom she felt close. Mr Jones had recently lost his job and Mrs Jones's mother had died. Mr Jones had not been able to express his financial concerns or guilt at having separated his wife from her family. Likewise, she had not expressed her grief or her anxiety about the financial difficulty, lest this demoralise her husband further.

These matters were explored gently in the initial session, during which Zoe became more responsive and understanding. It emerged that she had 'flown the flag' for the family through her rebellious behaviour, in order to gain help for everyone. After two further sessions, she had improved considerably, both at home and school; Mr and Mrs Jones continued to attend to resolve salient issues for themselves.

Couple therapy

Counselling for couples developed after World War I, at a time of social change and hardship and of interest in the study of sexuality. The initial focus, often with moral overtones, was on educating people about marriage and sexual behaviour. Later, a *psychoanalytic approach* held that marital problems (about, for example, decision-making, intimacy, communication, sexuality) reflected unresolved problems from the partners' relationships with their own parents or siblings. Therapy aimed to identify these earlier conflicts and to show how they were recreated in the couple's interaction.

A *behavioural approach*, in contrast, emphasises how each partner shapes the other's current behaviour through positive or negative reinforcement; patterns learned in each family of origin may be played out repeatedly. Therapy charts areas of disagreement and devises new ways to approach them, including negotiation of responsibilities and effective communication.

A *cognitive approach* makes explicit the negative automatic thoughts and perceptions of partners about themselves and each other, examines how these are applied in the relationship, and then challenges them.

A *systems approach,* similar to the one I described in family therapy, has also been applied. The premise is that problems result from a cyclical pattern of interaction rather than from the actions of one or other partner only, and the therapist helps them to appreciate these patterns. Thus, instead of blaming each other, they take joint responsibility to find more constructive ways of relating.

Couple therapy may incorporate all these concepts, some of which address underlying causes and others the ways partners maintain patterns of conflict. For example, in domestic violence, the therapist identifies the sequence of exchanges leading to escalating tension between partners, specific strategies that the violent partner must adopt to break the spiral, and steps the abused partner may take to ensure her safety and that of her children (the behavioural approach). This may be followed by individual therapy to promote insight into deeper layers of their problem in terms of experiences in their families of origin, or family therapy to address current concerns once the risk of violence has abated.

A specific combination has been devised by an English colleague, Michael Crowe (see his chapter in S Bloch (ed.), *An Introduction to the Psychotherapies,* 2006), which he calls the *behavioural-systems approach.* The behavioural component concentrates on promoting open communication and ways of negotiating. The systems component is required when the situation is complex and relational dynamics rigid. For instance, the couple may be so enmeshed with one another that their capacity to act autonomously is jeopardised.

Sex therapy
I have covered sex therapy in Chapter 13.

Supportive psychotherapy
All forms of psychotherapy entail support but usually it is one of many therapeutic forces at work, not the dominant one. In supportive psychotherapy,

providing support is paramount. In essence, the therapist sustains people who have a longstanding inability to manage their lives. These people are so affected by their psychiatric state or the nature of their personality functioning, and prospects for psychological change are so limited, that they cannot cope satisfactorily without help, whether from health professionals, family carers or other sources. Furthermore, their vulnerability precludes insight-oriented forms of psychotherapy. In diagnostic terms, these patients suffer from chronic schizophrenia, recurrent or chronic depression or other severe mood disorders, chronic anxiety, or have features of marked problematic personalities.

The therapist's basic aims are:

- to promote psychological and social functioning by reinforcing the person's capacities to cope with life's demands;
- to heighten the person's awareness of reality: of their strengths (thus bolstering self-esteem) and vulnerabilities, and of the benefits and limitations of treatment;
- to monitor the clinical situation to forestall relapse, thus preventing or reducing deterioration.

While support is of the essence, related aspects of treatment are:

Reassurance First, the therapist dispels doubts and clarifies misconceptions—by, for example, reassuring people that they are not losing their mind, will not be permanently detained in hospital, and are not freaks. Second, the therapist records assets and achievements, however modest. The person may see nothing but failure. Invariably omitted in their self-appraisal are indisputable strengths and positive qualities; these are pointed out explicitly and repeatedly.

Explanation People usually need help to clarify problems and decide how best to deal with them. The focus is mostly on day-to-day issues. A key aspect is familiarity with the nature of the illness, and with the potential benefits and limits of treatment, including clarification about the role of any medication (e.g. benefits and side-effects), and what facilitates and prevents relapse.

Guidance Closely aligned to explanation is offering advice. The focus on practical matters, including budgeting, work, family and social pursuits, extends to exploring skills to cope with future challenges.

Suggestion This is similar to guidance but the therapist, confident of his or her ground, uses direct or indirect influence (for example, 'Wouldn't it be a good idea for you to rejoin the choir?' or 'Do you think taking up your sister's invitation to spend time with her and her husband on their farm would not be a terrific opportunity?')

Encouragement The therapist uses many techniques to combat feelings of inferiority (for example, urging the person to adopt a course of action about which they are wavering). Promoting confidence is best linked to specific circumstances, like asserting oneself justifiably at work with an insensitive manager. An action may seem trivial on the face of it, but for that person it constitutes a challenge. Since pushing people to pursue goals beyond their capacity may cause harm, constraints imposed by their clinical state are respected.

Permission for catharsis People with enduring difficulties are commonly burdened with frustration, regret, grief, envy, and other distressing feelings. The therapist provides a safe forum for these feelings to be expressed, so that they can be shared and better understood.

Influencing the person's environment These people are particularly vulnerable to the social environment. A clear example is the harmful effect on a schizophrenic person of a hostile and critical family. The therapist ensures that the social context contributes positively. Stressful factors are removed or lessened and potentially helpful ones suggested. It is easier to identify the former (for example, is a job too demanding, the family atmosphere too critical or financial circumstances too pressing?). Adding to the person's world might mean, for example, arranging participation in a self-help group to reduce a sense of loneliness. Since the family is usually the person's most crucial social group, special attention is given to their needs and how they might be best met.

Crisis intervention

In 1942, Erich Lindemann, an American psychiatrist, attended to the survivors of a nightclub fire in Boston in which 500 people died, and noted that those helped early fared better than those who were not treated for several weeks. Gerald Caplan, a member of the team, then developed a specific meaning of 'crisis', suggesting that it is an emotional state that occurs when people face hurdles that overwhelm their usual capacity to cope. A period of disorganisation ensues, during which they make abortive attempts to adjust. Eventually, a form of adaptation results, which may or may not serve their best interests. Caplan saw the crisis as a person's emotional state rather than the stressful situation itself (see Chapter 5).

A crucial factor in a crisis is the time during which the person is open to learning new ways of solving problems. Common stressors are loss, or threat of loss, of people or of things that give a person a sense of fulfilment, self-worth and identity. The loss may be of a spouse, family member or friend (for example, through death, divorce or migration); of valued possessions and home (for example, through natural disasters or migration); of bodily parts and function (for example, through injury and illness); of social role and financial security (for example, through retirement, unemployment or hospitalisation). Grief is a universal response to such loss. Transitions in the life cycle may also be marked by crises, since previous ways of dealing with stress must be revised.

A crisis is typified by: (a) anxiety with psychophysiological features, including insomnia, restlessness, over-activity, muscle tension and fatigue; (b) squandering attention on irrelevant aspects of the situation; (c) possible regression to a state of helplessness and dependence; (d) social withdrawal; (e) altered perspective so that past, present and future merge into the now; and (f) diminished capacity to reflect maturely, leading to behaviours that may provoke rejection by others.

The most suitable candidate for crisis intervention is a person who has functioned well but is now overwhelmed by a life stress. In a well-integrated person, both adjustment reactions including depression and/or anxiety, and grief reactions, respond well. The goal of relief from the effects of the crisis may be supplemented by learning new effective methods of coping and dealing with life's challenges. In effect, out of crisis may come a wider and richer psychological repertoire to call upon in the event of future stress. People with pre-existing personality problems may also benefit, but with the groundwork laid for more extensive psychotherapy at a later time.

Methods of treatment are:

Uncovering emotions   The person is encouraged to express feelings through the therapist posing questions gently and empathising strongly.

Making sense of the experience   The person's state of mind, including feelings, attitudes and beliefs about the current situation, is examined, as well as details of the stressful event. Links with significant other people are explored, together with their availability to provide support. This leads to an understanding of inner resources. Knowledge of the fate of fellow survivors (in the case of a group disaster) is crucial.

Regaining control   By discussing various courses of action and ways of implementing them, the person begins to regain a sense of competence. Emphasis on taking action, practical and symbolic, represents regaining control.

Brian, aged 52, had experienced irritability, decreased efficiency at work and lowered mood over several weeks. His effort to cope by immersing himself in his job only aggravated things. He resorted to alcohol in the evenings while attending, ineffectually, to paperwork. The problem had begun when his manager told him that the section he headed was to be reduced because of budgetary constraints. Brian held himself responsible, concluding that his life's work would be destroyed. He worried about how to inform subordinates, some of whom would have to be dismissed. He had always been proud of his independence and regarded reliance on others as weakness. In both his personal and professional life Brian defined areas where he carried responsibility, and then strove to meet it. Another source of stress was his teenager son's involvement in a near-fatal car accident several months earlier. He recalled his intense distress until told that his son was no longer on the critical list. The relationship between father and son had always been tense.

Therapy for Brian consisted of:

- encouraging him to express his anger, frustration and sense of impotence;
- challenging his pattern of assuming blame for the problems at work;
- involving his wife and children in a session in which he revealed his work pressures—their understanding and support contrasted with his expectation of derision for his weakness;
- devising a plan for family members to intercept him should he try to withdraw, and to engage him in discussion about his concerns.

The overall aim was to relieve Brian's distress and restore him to his previous level of functioning. His rigid, self-reliant style had blocked earlier resolution, but the crisis allowed the therapist to challenge his denial of a need to depend on others. There was limited exploration of the origin of his ways of coping (unlike in psychoanalytic psychotherapy) or of his views about himself and his relationships with others (unlike cognitive therapy). A year later, he did enter psychoanalytically oriented therapy to deal with longstanding traits he had come to realise made him feel vulnerable.

Counselling

Western society has become increasingly complex, with new forms of social relationships (for example, blended families, homosexual and lesbian partnerships), explosion of knowledge in many fields, rampant technology, and loss of confidence in solutions offered by religious traditions. Health care is correspondingly more complicated, often beyond the understanding of ordinary people. An array of counselling methods is available to help people make informed decisions in the face of these rapidly changing circumstances, and to deal with the impact of such decisions on their lives.

Although counselling shares many features with the psychotherapies, its focus is to assist people who do not warrant a psychiatric diagnosis but who nonetheless are grappling with a life-challenging issue.

Counselling may be vital, for example, for chronically ill people who, while adequately treated, cannot be cured (for example, diabetes, epilepsy, asthma), or who may require help to deal with life-long dependence on medical technology (for example, people on dialysis). Similar dilemmas occur for people whose treatment leads to considerable discomfort (for example, chemotherapy, mastectomy, amputation or colostomy), or where feelings and values may influence decisions about a procedure (for example, in-vitro fertilisation). With the evolution of clinical genetics, individuals or couples may need an expert to help them arrive at a reasonable decision regarding genetic testing, and to provide support in their decision-making.

Many forms of counselling have arisen in response to social needs, such as in couple relationships (though the overlap with couple therapy is obvious), in the educational sphere to deal with problems in vocational choice or study, and in the workplace to help those buffeted by conflict or retrenchment.

Whatever the area of counselling, its chief goal is to offer people an opportunity to reflect on an issue that they are not handling effectively. A pivotal assumption is that the person is, nonetheless, sufficiently well functioning to accept, at least in some measure, responsibility for the decisions or changes to be made. In general, the counsellor avoids telling people what to do but rather helps them to ponder over pertinent issues, including those that have been beyond their compass. Additional methods include providing relevant information (for example, about available resources), clarifying the person's beliefs about the problem, and correcting those that the counsellor knows to be erroneous.

Emma, a 17-year-old student, sought out the school counsellor three months into her final year with concern about falling behind in her studies. Her high expectations of herself and fear of failure stemmed from a view of success as rewarding her parents for the financial sacrifice they had made on her behalf (she had been educated in an expensive private school). The counsellor provided information about study methods and their effects on concentration. Emma used it constructively to justify her longstanding wish for leisure time. She remained a diligent student, but less driven. Emma also expressed concern at disappointing her parents, and became aware of her resenting the burden of obligation she carried. Counselling allowed her to express these feelings, following which she was able to modify her style of studying. Neither these emotions nor their childhood origins were explored (unlike in psychoanalytic therapy). Emma and the counsellor were satisfied with the outcome, and agreed on not examining deeper themes at that time. This could be a future option, depending on how she fared in the next stage of her life—her entry into tertiary education.

Researching psychotherapy

In 1952, Hans Eysenck, a Professor of Psychology in the University of London, threw down the gauntlet to psychotherapists by claiming that systematic studies showed psychotherapy to be no more effective than placebo. Considerable research has been carried out since then to examine not only the question of effectiveness but also related matters like cost-effectiveness (Do briefer forms help as much as longer-term treatments?); safety (Can therapies harm?); comparative effectiveness (Are some therapies more helpful than others?); and process (What elements of the treatment produce benefits?).

Much has been learned, both theoretically (theory is necessary to provide hypotheses for methodical study) and empirically (for example, randomised clinical trials, identifying selection criteria for different treatments, and establishing which variables are linked to patient deterioration).

We have impressive evidence—through sophisticated statistical analyses devised to make sense of treatment trials on effectiveness—that the psychotherapies provide worthwhile benefits for a broad range of patients. They are especially effective for those with maladjustment and post-traumatic stress disorder, as well as those with personality problems of mild to moderate severity. They are of less value to the severely mentally ill, including people with schizophrenia, unipolar and bipolar disorders and severe problematic personalities. However, intervening can be effective here, too; for example, psychoeducationally based family therapy reduces the relapse rate in schizophrenia, and intensive psychoanalytic treatment is helpful for borderline and narcissistic personalities.

Research suggests that psychotherapy of all types is potent, for good or for ill. Practised ineptly or prescribed inappropriately it leads to deterioration in up to 10 per cent of cases, paralleling clinical practice in psychiatry generally.

Relatively brief treatment (in the range of 8–16 sessions, usually weekly) with suitable patients leads to satisfactory outcomes, especially in cognitive, behavioural and couple therapies, certain forms of family therapy, and brief psychoanalytically oriented therapy. This knowledge has permitted more efficient deployment of specialist resources for people at the more severe end of the clinical spectrum, especially those with disabling problematic personalities.

Longer-term psychoanalyically based therapies for such patients have also been evaluated; the overall results indicate that they benefit substantially. In one analysis of 23 clinical trials, patients with complex problems were better off than 96 per cent of patients who did not receive therapy. The old criticism levelled against psychoanalytically based treatment that it is of minimal value can confidently be put to rest.

In terms of the therapeutic process, knowledge has accumulated on aspects of treatment that promote (or hinder) change. Research of this kind is crucial as a source of hypotheses relevant to outcome. For example, the customary trial in which two or more therapies are compared would be futile without assurance that a treatment was given in terms of its core concepts and could be readily distinguished from other treatments. The so-called fidelity study is commonplace in well-executed treatment trials in which audiotaped or videotaped excerpts of therapy are rated by 'blind' assessors for how faithful the therapists have been to the model of treatment under study.

Most therapists agree that psychotherapy is a blend of art and science. The art is the more intangible of the two, depending on features like empathy and sensitivity. This crucial dimension is elusive in the context of scientific exploration, but not impossibly so. The more amenable scientific dimension requires continuing scrutiny in the form of systematic research. Such factors as the therapist's commitment to the required properties of the model are carefully measured (for example, maintaining a focus on promoting family cohesiveness and emotional expressiveness in specific models of family therapy). Outcome, too, is scrutinised (for example, assessment of coping, depression, quality of life and the like, depending on the goals set for a treatment).

I concluded my book *What Is Psychotherapy?* in 1982 by quoting Judd Marmor, a prominent American psychotherapist; he expressed the hope that one day we would achieve 'a unified science of psychotherapy'. I echoed his hope and expressed optimism that we would reach the goal he had set. The subsequent three decades have witnessed that achievement and a flowering of the psychotherapies.

CHAPTER 20

Promoting Mental Health

The World Health Organization (WHO) has described mental health as:

> ... a state of well-being in which an individual realizes his or her own abilities, can cope with the normal stresses of life, can work productively and fruitfully, and is able to make a contribution to his or her community.

The WHO does not specify the abilities in its definition but may have in mind what Freud referred to many years ago—the ability to love (in effect, the ability to have affectionate relationships) and the ability to work (that is, to be productive). Many other criteria have been proposed over the years. They include flexibility, realistic appraisal and mastery of the world and its challenges, self-confidence, self-respect, self-fulfilment, self-realisation, capacity to deal with conflicting emotions, social consideration and the ability to think rationally. Clearly, many of these qualities overlap with one another. Promoting mental health as construed by the WHO is a formidable personal and collective challenge but one certainly worth considering.

We are accustomed to the idea of attending to our physical health and keeping fit. Keeping mentally fit warrants an equally important place in the way we view our health and wellbeing. Many elements are necessarily involved, and across the entire life span. They include, for example, empowering women, reducing work stress, exercising the mind, dealing promptly with bullying in schools, and organising social programs for the elderly.

The scope of this chapter does not permit us to delve into all these areas. Firstly, we consider general principles of promoting mental health—in other words, how to cope with life's demands as well as how to adopt specific strategies in the face of stressful circumstances. We follow this with other steps for people recovering from a mental illness or predisposed to recurrences of that illness. Finally, we discuss the needs of those who are markedly affected by their psychological problems over the long term. At each point there are implications not only for the individual but also for family members, friends and self-help organisations.

What is our context for these guidelines? In days gone by, psychiatrists assumed a paternalistic role in steering the course of therapy for people in need. The picture has changed radically, as in the whole of medical practice. The relationship between doctor and patient now resembles a partnership, with both people participating actively, though in different roles. Doctors offer relevant expertise. Patients take an active part by considering treatment options, weighing up their benefits and costs and, ideally, reach a consensus with their doctors.

As part of the partnership model, we recognise the power of knowledge to achieve a measure of control and mastery. This is particularly pertinent in psychiatry, where mental illness, which still carries stigma and a sense of shame, often leads to plummeting self-confidence. Any measure to counter these corrosive effects is welcomed, and there is a distinct advantage in being as aware as possible of the nature and treatment of the troubled mind. This knowledge is even more vital in psychiatry, where the mind and its aberrations are mystifying, even to well-adjusted and well-informed people. Experience certainly suggests that it is easier to acquire knowledge and mastery over a fracture of a bone than over a fracture of one's mind.

Despite the bewilderment, we value people taking responsibility for themselves and fulfilling their potential for autonomy. A balance is appropriate. On the one hand, the nature of mental illness is confusing and potentially disabling; on the other hand, it remains desirable that people take as much responsibility as they can for their welfare and fate. The picture is compounded by the role of family and friends, since they may be well placed to help relatives to be self-sufficient.

Principles and strategies—general and specific

Some principles and strategies to promote mental health can be applied across the life cycle, across a wide range of psychiatric ailments, and across the mental health–illness continuum. They are complemented by specific principles and strategies that professional knowledge and experience indicate are pertinent in a more focused way.

Let us use sleep deprivation to illustrate the application of general principles and strategies. We all know that our emotional wellbeing is adversely affected when we are deprived of sleep (by jet lag, shift work, preparing for an examination, sleeping inadequately). Effects of this deprivation include irritability, poor concentration, lethargy and emotional vulnerability. We can appreciate how the same physiological disturbance could more markedly affect people at risk of mental illness. So, people who have suffered recurrent depression or anxiety may relapse following a period when they run short of sleep. Commonsense suggests that maintaining stable sleep patterns is not only advantageous to a sense of wellbeing but also contributes to protecting and preserving mental health.

Complementing the general are a vast number of specific principles and strategies. They proliferate with time as new scientific knowledge and expanding community awareness help to identify their benefits to patients and their families. They tend to be associated with specific psychiatric states. Good evidence for this are the dozens of self-help organisations, each of them linked to particular conditions like autism, Tourette's syndrome, post-natal depression and anorexia nervosa. I have tried to highlight specific principles and strategies in earlier chapters. My focus in this chapter is on the general. This ties in with my aim—to inform people about ways of dealing with troubled minds overall.

Some useful general guidelines

The general principles and strategies I will now cover stem from the collective experience of myself and my colleagues in working with hundreds of patients and their families, and are a distillation of what we have found to work. I begin by setting out our ideas on promoting good mental health, then look at preventing slippage into mental ill-health.

We first need to acknowledge the relevance of basic public health measures—a foundation of mental health. For people to grow and develop with their psychological and physical faculties intact, such measures as good obstetric care, optimal nutrition and prompt treatment of infection are clearly vital. This is taken for granted in developed nations, but we should remember that for two-thirds of the world's population basic health needs are not met, with serious implications for both mental and physical ill-health.

The stability of the psychological and social environment complements these essentially biological needs. The most obvious illustration is 'good enough' nurturing at critical stages of development. Here, both family and the wider community play central roles in shaping conditions so that we can continue to fulfill our potential. While public health measures may see to the basic biological needs of people in the developed world, the same cannot often be said of their psychological and social needs. Indeed, at a time when family life has become more and more fragmented (a divorce rate over 40 per cent in many societies is one pointer), the picture is disconcerting. As noted in earlier chapters, contemporary society may indeed work against these psychological and social needs being satisfied. We all witness this in the frenetic pace of life, which takes its toll at home, at work and, more broadly, in the social environment.

Contending with life's stresses

All of us are familiar with life's stresses—those aspects of our lives and their emotional repercussions that we have to grapple with day by day. Given that stress is universal and inevitable, because of events we face across the life cycle, we can help ourselves by bolstering our effective coping strategies and altering those that have proved inadequate in the past.

The range of coping responses that may be adopted in the wake of stressful circumstances was set out in Chapter 5. I will highlight them once again. We must first distinguish between harmful effects of stress and its more motivating features.

Stress often entails an aspect of challenge that may bring out the best in us. Consider the value of deadlines in getting a task done. A degree of pressure at work may generate original ideas about how to deal with a thorny problem. A measure of family tension may yield solutions to under-lying difficulties and so benefit family life.

On the other hand, as we know only too well, stress has debilitating fea-tures; these are the ones that make us feel burdened and encumbered. It may be realistic to avoid the source of stress, perhaps temporarily, while we catch our breath and prepare to wrestle with the situation. We may take time out, immersing ourselves in other activities until a more propitious moment to face the music. These distractions may themselves entail an ele-ment of stress, but are of a different quality and, because we have chosen them, more tolerable.

The term we use to describe what we ultimately have to do is 'problem solving'—comprising a coherent set of maneuvers with a distinct sequence, and subject to rational planning and appraisal. We try to identify the problem at hand, then extend this by seeking to clarify its nature. What constitutes the problem? How has it come about? Does it resemble past problems?

Problem solving is not always easily accomplished, in that the distressed person may lack clarity of mind and good judgement may not flow easily. Mobilising other resources helps. The most common step is to seek help from family or friends who may be more objective in shedding light on the nature of the problems. With or without such external help, we attempt to tap other resources, usually of a personal kind, and mostly draw on our coping repertoire. Then follows the mapping out of options to deal with the problem and choosing the most appropriate. More than one problem may need attention, in which case it helps to tackle one at a time. We judge their merits in terms of potential benefits and costs. In general, Albert Einstein's dictum applies: 'It is impossible to get out of a problem by using the same kind of thinking that it took to get into the problem'. Having made our selection, we go ahead with its implementation but monitor its effectiveness closely so that we can judge whether to persist or to modify that option appropriately—or we may abandon it and replace it with something entirely new.

Given that many stressful situations recur and resemble one another, we do not need to reinvent the wheel on every occasion. Drawing on past experience that is relevant to the current stress helps. We are at an advantage if we can identify previous coping responses that led to mastery.

All these strategies are obviously part of a serious effort to surmount the pressures at hand, but there is a risk that too earnest an attitude may dominate our approach. A mature coping mechanism available to us is to inject a certain humour into the situation; its beneficial effects are to lighten the load and to bring a more realistic perspective. Roger McGough has captured these benefits delightfully in his pithy poem, 'Survivor':

> Every day
> I think about dying.
> About disease, starvation,
> violence, terrorism, war,
> the end of the world.
> It helps
> keep my mind off things.

Even in the face of dreadful circumstances, humour can be applied; we know, for instance, about the helpfulness of gallows humour. A marvellous example concerns two prisoners facing a firing squad. As the officer approaches them to apply blindfolds, one of the pair declares that he does not wish to be blindfolded under any circumstances. The other promptly sighs, 'For goodness' sake, don't make trouble!'

Anticipation is a key strategy in dealing with a stressful world. Indeed, a mature response is to anticipate and prepare accordingly. Many stresses are predictable, particularly events like the passage into adolescence or retirement, the birth of a baby or the death of a parent. By identifying stress as early as possible, we can marshal our proven coping strategies.

Distraction helps too. Although anticipation and distraction may seem contradictory, they complement each other. We may at one point confront the demanding situation looming and take action; at another point we may benefit from a break when we forget the pressures and turn to something less taxing. We all know about the respite of a vacation. Perhaps less obvious is the potential to be caught up in another activity that is engaging and draws on our full capacity. Consider a medical student who is jaded with studying the detail of the one hundred cysts of the mouth but also buffeted by a pending examination. While committed to preparing for the exam, the student also recognises the need to get away for a while, and takes the opportunity to work in a rural hospital for a week. This is not escapism, since the challenges and rewards encountered in this new setting revive motivation, even if it still means becoming acquainted with all those cysts! By chance, there is also an opportunity to talk through some of the frustrations of being a medical student with a newly graduated doctor, who not long before went through the same mill.

Such sharing brings us to another strategy that has proven beneficial since time immemorial. Although we tend, at least in the Western world, to value self-sufficiency, man is a social animal. All of us have a need to belong and to share parts of ourselves. When it comes to stress, the act of recruiting help facilitates the process of unburdening ourselves, with some relief from the pressure. As we feel less alone in facing problems, so they appear less daunting.

Another dimension of sharing relates to the adage 'two minds are better than one'. Even if explicit advice is not forthcoming, and it may well not be, exchange of ideas extends the range of options and boosts confidence to risk trying one of them out. An element of risk is inevitable. The philosopher José Ortega y Gassett reminds us of this when asserting that 'Life cannot wait until the sciences have explained the universe. We cannot put off living until we are ready'.

Society has recognised the need of people in crisis to unburden themselves and has responded in a most interesting way—through the use of technology. The Samaritans, Crisis Line and Lifeline are well-known examples of counselling, founded to support people with suicidal tendencies but then broadened to encompass anyone in crisis and with the need to talk it through. Fascinatingly, the internet has become another means of achieving similar ends.

These maneuvers may be all that is needed to deal with the stress—in which case emotional wellbeing is restored and lessons may be learned that help deal with similar demands in the future. But the stress may be of such quality or magnitude that its effects persist, leading to emotional dislocation. Other strategies then come into play.

Relaxation techniques

Many societies have known the value of various strategies to live more harmonious or bearable lives. Often associated with ancient religious practices, they include Yoga and Tai Chi. In today's more secular age, professionals have devised methods that resemble these practices, and given them names like anxiety management and stress management. Relaxation—achieving a calm and tranquil state—is the goal, which is the opposite of the worry and tension that result from hyperarousal.

Yoga has a rich history dating back thousands of years to an Aryan culture. The word comes from the Sanskrit, meaning to concentrate one's attention on. It also suggests a union. In one of the Vedas, yoga is described in the following way: 'When the senses are stilled, when the mind is at rest, when the intellect wavers not—then, say the wise, is reached the highest stage. This steady control of the senses and mind has been defined as Yoga'.

Another approach, like yoga in many respects, is meditation. Of the many versions, transcendental meditation is probably the best known. As the term suggests, its goal is achieving a sense of transcendence through a process of detachment. A key characteristic is a sense of inner calm and peace; this can be accomplished in a variety of ways, including focus on a word or phrase (mantra) or an image.

In recent decades, ways to reach this calm state have concentrated on the body. One popular method, progressive muscular relaxation, entails a systematic focus on sets of muscles, usually beginning in the feet and working up to the face. Muscles are clenched to the point of pain, followed by a rapid release of the tension. This induces a relaxed state not only within the muscles themselves but throughout body and mind.

Guided imagery may be added or used independently. The idea is to imagine a lovely tranquil scene such as a beach, a sunset or a glade, on the premise that the mind cannot sustain that imaginative process together with a state of tension. Akin to these more reflective approaches is the power of music to transfer us to another level of experience, typified by calm (music, of course, can do the reverse). Personal preference will guide the choice of calming music, although tapes are commercially available that claim to be particularly soothing.

Physical activity can be used to release tension or to prevent its development. Jogging and walking have proved popular, but pursuits of many types including swimming, cycling and working out at the local gym can have beneficial effects as people shed their bodily tensions; even spectator sports are useful in releasing physical and emotional tension.

People's preferred ways to relax are often linked to temperament. Some choose a meditational approach since they are more comfortable with a reflective mode; others opt for a physical outlet, while still others lean to music. These various ways are, of course, not incompatible; modes of relaxation can be combined. So, bushwalking produces a harmonious inner state by combining physical activity and communing with nature.

A sense of self and self-esteem

These key elements in promoting good mental health are the most challenging to write about. The concepts are nebulous and difficult to capture succinctly. Indeed, we enter the realm of the spiritual. In a sense, we are referring to how we choose to live our lives. The fact that these matters have preoccupied philosophers for centuries suggests that they are not amenable to ready analysis. But contemporary psychology and psychiatry do have useful things to say. Although the spiritual dimension is closely linked to the psychological themes I discuss below, it is beyond the reach of this chapter.

One central concept is a sense of the self, and its development through the life cycle. What do we mean by a sense of self? Many astute observers of the human condition have wrestled with it, and have teased out many dimensions. For our purposes, we refer to awareness of our identity: who we are, what meaning we give to our lives, what purpose and direction we take, what commitments we make to ourselves and others, what involvement we have in different facets of life. All these combine to provide us with a sense of coherence. This word is apt in that it conjures up the idea that the many parts of ourselves connect in a unifying way, leading to what Carl Jung called individuation. A closely related concept is self-esteem, which hinges on this sense of coherence but goes a step further in incorporating the idea that a person feels valued both in their own eyes and in the eyes of others.

The twin aspects of a sense of the self and self-esteem are intimately linked with another idea—personal development through the life cycle. Here, we are indebted to the psychoanalyst Erik Erikson, who showed us how a sense of identity that is central to a sense of oneself evolves from birth, becomes more or less established at the onset of adulthood (we may define adulthood as the achievement of a sense of identity) but then is moulded further by events like parenthood, the 'midlife crisis', retirement and the prospect of death. This developmental process has three aspects— our original inheritance (biological and genetic), the opportunities and challenges that come our way, and our responses to the first two aspects. We may contrast people who take many risks in life out of a conviction that every opportunity should be exploited, with others who passively sit by and accept whatever life brings along.

How do self-concept and self-esteem relate to our theme of promoting mental health? In one way, the answer is obvious—good mental health is synonymous with a coherent sense of the self and effective negotiation of the changes that make up the life cycle. But it is easier said than done, as the relevant concepts are often elusive and bewildering. How do I make my life coherent? How do I achieve self-esteem? Ultimately, it boils down to our searching for, and hopefully finding, a sense of purpose, direction and fulfilment. Each person's life has its unique stamp but for most of us it will include such domains as family relationships, friendships and work (see below) and religion. I mention religion last although it may be the most central for some people.

Oftentimes, we tend to neglect what under-girds our self-esteem—those aspects of ourselves of which we are proud—and worry about qualities we are less happy about. I would recommend an old Jewish saying that reminds us of the former:

> In every man there is something precious, which is in no one else.
> And so we should honour each for what is hidden within him, for
> only what he has, and none of his friends.

Yes, we should honour what is meritorious in others but also cherish what is meritorious in ourselves. The Roman emperor and Stoic philosopher Marcus Aurelius, who reigned in the latter part of the second century, also highlighted the need to reflect positively about oneself, and he added another dimension, namely the need to have a balanced attitude regarding our sense of positive self-appraisal:

> Think less of what you have not than of what you have; of the
> things you have select the best; then reflect how eagerly you would
> have laboured for them, if you had them not. At the same time,
> however, take care you do not through being so pleased with them
> accustom yourself to so overvalue them as to be distressed if ever
> you should lose them.

One corollary to Erikson's ideas about the life cycle is our acceptance that life does not stand still. Change is inevitable as we proceed through life, whether predictable events such as parenthood, retirement and death or accidents that are inevitable to a greater or lesser extent (a charmed life is a rarity, only occurring in fairy tales!). In terms of good mental health, we need to acknowledge that we constantly face new challenges and demands. As John Weakland, an American psychiatrist, once aptly put it, 'Life is one damned thing after another'. Again Marcus Aurelius hits the target perfectly with this advice:

> Observe constantly that all things come about by change; accustom
> yourself to reflect that the nature of the universe loves nothing
> so much as changing things that are and making new things like
> them. For everything that exists is in a way the seed of what will
> be … What is more pleasing or more suitable to universal nature?

Can you take a bath unless the wood underneath undergoes a change? Can you be nourished, unless your food undergoes a change? Do you not see that for yourself also change is the same, and equally necessary for the universal change?

The doctrine of the mean

We now turn to the concept, originating in Aristotle's *Ethics*, of moderation or, as he himself described it, 'the doctrine of the mean'. He argues that humankind benefits when it looks to the mean in action or feeling. The only exceptions are evil feelings like malice and evil actions like murder. Of feelings, Aristotle makes this claims:

> It is possible, for example, to feel fear, confidence, desire, anger, pity and pleasure and pain generally too much or too little; and both of these are wrong. But to have these feelings at the right times on the right grounds, toward the right people for the right motive and in the right way is to feel them to an intermediate, that is to the best degree … Similarly there are excess and deficiency and a mean in the case of actions.

Aristotle provides a series of examples in which a mean is preferable to either deficiency or excess. In the sphere of anger, the excess is irascibility, the deficiency a lack of spirit, and the mean patience. Implications for mental health follow logically. Although we should not stifle our feelings or limit our actions, we should have the capacity to modulate them. The alternative is to experience wild swings that have unfortunate repercussions. While striving for the mean may be a counsel of perfection, it is an identifiable challenge whose effectiveness we can monitor and evaluate.

Family, friends and mental health

As long ago as 1965, the World Health Organization published a volume, *Aspects of Family Mental Health in Europe*, which made the point that the mental health of each member of a family 'is inextricably bound up with that of other members, influencing it and being influenced by it both favourably and unfavourably'.

We all know that we cannot choose our family, but it is distinctly advantageous to be acquainted with features that typify the well-functioning family and are associated with the emotional wellbeing of its members. I dare not use the term 'normal family' since I find it eludes definition. I am in good company. Don Jackson, a pioneer of the family approach in psychiatry, concluded that there is no such thing as a normal family. Leo Tolstoy's contrary view, opined in *Anna Karenina*, was that 'All happy families are alike but an unhappy family is unhappy after its own fashion'. Whatever the case, it is intuitively appealing to do what is within our power to foster a psychologically healthy family environment. Together with three colleagues, I co-authored a book in 1994 entitled *The Family in Clinical Psychiatry*, in which we came up with six features linked to good functioning. Given their equal relevance, the following are not in any particular order.

- Clear delineation of the roles of family members, together with associated tasks and responsibilities (for example, a buoyant, lively youngest child may imbue his parents with a playful spirit, so promoting a sense of fun in the home).
- Warm and affectionate relationships, but also respect for each member's individuality and separateness. The useful term 'co-individuation' encompasses the latter aspect, and 'enmeshment' describes the family so tightly bound that it fails to provide for the independent growth of its members.
- Acceptance of explicit rules chosen (but changed when circumstances warrant it) to regulate the family's behaviour towards one another. These rules serve as a stabilising force and suit the needs and interests of all members.
- A shared ability to face challenges and deal with change, either predictable as part of the family life cycle (such as marriage of an adult child) or accidental (such as loss of a job, a car accident or illness). The family reacts adaptively and is prepared to assimilate new ideas from whatever source.
- Clear, open and direct communication of information, feelings and attitudes, so reducing the chance of misunderstanding; tolerance of conflict rather than recoiling from it; and readiness to grapple with differences when they arise. The family 'fights well and cleanly', thereby lessening the risk of psychological harm to one or more of the protagonists.
- A willingness to relate readily with other social groups, such as the extended family, children's schools, friends, work colleagues and neighbours. The bi-directional traffic permits members to benefit from creative contact with the external culture and to bring back what they have gained, so enhancing the family's functioning and development.

When it comes to friends we do, of course, have choice. Developing a genuine friendship is, however, far from straightforward; the same applies to sustaining it. So, what are the characteristics of friendship and how is a successful one linked to mental health? Aristotle is a splendid source of ideas in this regard; in Book VIII of his *Nicomachean Ethics*, he offers us virtually all we need to know. Friendship enables us to act benevolently (i.e., is based on goodness), serves as a refuge when misfortune buffets us, and 'holds communities together'. No one, he declares, would elect to live without friends.

Aristotle proceeds to outline three kinds of friendship—those from which we can obtain some benefit, others that give us pleasure, and yet others steeped in mutual affection. It is the third that is closely linked to mental health, since each person wishes good for the other for the friend's sake (not out of self-interest) and they please each other—'The good friend feels towards his friend as he feels toward himself, because his friend is a second self to him'. Moreover, giving affection is more satisfying than receiving affection. Aristotle then asks specifically whether friends are necessary for happiness (for our purposes here, the equivalent of mental health). The reply is an unequivocal yes. Why? Because man is a social being and would want to share any good things with others, particularly through shared activities. A solitary man by contrast has a 'hard life because it is not easy to keep up a continuous activity by oneself'.

Finally, the question arises as to how many friends we should have. Aristotle explicitly states that there is no correct number; a limit exists, namely a few whom we can 'love for their own sake and for their own goodness'. To be devoted to more than a few would tax us too much and also prevent the evolution of an intimate circle.

Many mentally healthy people will retort at this point that they value their own company and a state of self-sufficiency. Absolutely. But, appreciating solitude (that is, being on one's own—not loneliness) and enjoying it periodically is quite compatible with enjoying friendships. DW Winnicott, an English psychoanalyst and paediatrician, was one of the first, in 1958 in fact, to draw our attention to the capacity to be alone as a feature of healthy psychological development. He argued that the infant who has his needs met feels secure and therefore able to be alone in the presence of the mother; this experience enables him not only to develop further the capacity to be alone but also to 'discover his personal life.' A cherished psychotherapist colleague, Anthony Storr, wrote a superb little book called *Solitude*, thirty years after Winnicott's essay, in which he summarises the latter's key points: 'The capacity to be alone thus becomes linked with self-discovery and self-realisation; with becoming aware of one's deepest needs, feelings, and impulses'. Storr also explores other aspects of the subject, particularly the association between the capacity to be alone and creativity.

I cannot think of a more apt way of concluding our discussion of relationships and mental health than by quoting the Rabbinic authority Hillel (first century BC), one of the most revered Jewish sages:

> If I am not for myself, who am I?
> And if I am only for myself, what am I?
> If not now, when?

There are many interpretations of the original Hebrew text. Relevant here are the notions that we must esteem ourselves as a condition of mutual affection with family and friends; if we are totally self-preoccupied, relating to others is not possible; and we should not procrastinate when it comes to meaningful relationships.

Work and mental health

You will recall that the definition of mental health by the World Health Organization includes the criterion of working productively and fruitfully. Given that most adults spend a third of each weekday and roughly two thirds of their lives in the workplace, how we value our role there and how we benefit in psychological terms are crucial elements in contributing to our mental health. As mentioned at the beginning of this chapter, Freud highlighted the ability to work as one of the two essential criteria of the mentally healthy person.

We can tackle the links between mental health and working on three levels—the individual, the employing body and society at large.

If you have looked at Chapter 5 on stress and coping, you will appreciate that work may be a profound source of stress at the individual level. An employee may be subject to a diverse range of unnerving features, both internal and external. Bullying, sexual and other forms of harassment, pressure to perform, threat of retrenchment, anxiety of being found to be inept, striving for perfection, loss of satisfaction from the nature of the work, excessive responsibility, inability to keep up with technological change; the list is endless. The fortunate employee will be spared these sort of pressures and derive a sense of fulfilment and self-esteem.

Many of us will be content at one stage of our working life but encounter difficulties when circumstances change, whether through a callous new manager, the introduction of new demanding practices, the loss of job security, and the like. Then the individual should pay prompt attention to the problem by making efforts to identify its nature and options to deal with it, whether by turning to their own repertoire of coping strategies or seeking the assistance of any available human resources or other source of expertise. Millions of people do this, and more than once, in the course of their working lives. There is nothing to feel ashamed about in relying on others who are there for the very purpose of getting us through a rough patch.

Trying to accomplish change at the next level—that of the employing body—is more challenging, usually requiring collective action. As a 2007 WHO report concludes, a healthy workplace is typified by a relationship between employer and employee that is based on justice and decent conditions, such as a fair wage, protection from all forms of exploitation and the freedom to voice grievances. We all know of circumstances that are just the opposite, especially in the developing world.

A particularly unwelcome development is job insecurity. With the advent of a global economy, many employers have converted secure jobs to precarious ones, where a post is short-term or subject to unpredictable termination, and benefits like sick leave and paid leave are intentionally omitted from contracts. For example, a quarter of the workforce in Australia is employed on a casual basis. The WHO report notes the link between these arrangements and mental ill-health. Organisation consultants, often with a psychological background, have a role to play in these situations, but broader societal forces are also relevant in the face of obviously undesirable conditions.

The third level depends on society as a whole promoting values that in turn encourage respect for workers and treating them with dignity. Here, we are in the realm of human rights as manifest in the United Nations Declaration of Human Rights. Article 23 covers rights related to work.

1. Favourable conditions of work and to protection against unemployment.
2. Everyone, without any discrimination, has the right to equal pay for equal work.
3. Everyone who works has the right to just and favourable remuneration ensuring for himself and his family an existence worthy of human dignity, and supplemented, if necessary, by other means of social protection.
4. Everyone has the right to form and to join trade unions for the protection of his interests.

When things go wrong

No matter how diligent we are in pursuing the various strategies considered above, we remain emotionally vulnerable, in varying measure, and in one or more of many ways. Because of this vulnerability, and given related critical factors like genetic inheritance and family circumstances, we may experience mental ill-health. When this happens, commonsense dictates that we attempt to detect that something is going awry, face the changes that are occurring, and intervene without delay to minimise disruption to ourselves, our family and other relationships. Two factors make this problematic. Firstly, an immense overlap occurs between such disturbance and life experiences. All of our emotions are on a spectrum; think of feelings like anxiety, sadness and grief. Similarly, states of mind fall on a continuum; good examples are difficulties concentrating and remembering. Secondly, the organ responsible for judgement, the brain, is affected, with the capacity for thinking impaired. We can compensate for these impediments to early detection in ourselves or others by carefully noting the following five warning signs.

Excessive reaction to a life stress Although there are no set ways to deal with life pressures, we can usually determine if someone responds with exaggerated intensity. Take for example the response to the death of a friend. Individual cultures or ethnic groups have adaptive grieving patterns with recognisable features, like feelings of sadness, pining, transient social withdrawal and tearfulness (see the brief account of grief in Chapter 7). When experience exceeds these norms, in the context of a person's social group, this does not automatically reflect psychiatric disturbance but should alert that person or those around them that there may be more here than meets the eye.

Unduly prolonged response to a life stress We may use the same example of grief. Again, we have to bear in mind social custom, but the opportunity exists for the affected person or those who know them to question whether the grief has become entrenched.

Coping responses obviously or subtly deteriorate I have suggested that it pays to appreciate and reinforce our coping capacity by extending its repertoire and strengthening its constituent strategies. By contrast, our coping strategies may become unhelpful, even harmful. We may, for example, resort to the bottle, withdraw socially, sleep excessively, take undue risks, binge-eat, or any of dozens of other adverse activities. Little difficulty is encountered by the person or those around about in noting that coping has gone off the rails. But subtle changes tend to be camouflaged. The housewife who furtively consumes increasing amounts of alcohol to cope with a tense marriage may remain undetected until signs of self-neglect are observable.

Strange, bizarre behaviour Warning signs may be of this type. In the face of stressful circumstances, which are not always obvious, a person may begin to act inexplicably and may not be able to give a coherent account of this behaviour. Obvious examples include false thoughts of being hounded or self-starvation.

Impairment of a major mental function   This may involve one or more of what we call the higher mental abilities—concentration, judgement, memory and motivation. A common example is an ageing person who is unaware of beginning to show memory lapses, which her spouse recognises. What was originally dubbed as mere forgetfulness is now seen as a warning signal of a more serious mental change.

Detecting change early

With these five warning signals in mind, let us outline steps in discerning a disturbance in its early stages. A vital step is to acknowledge that something is wrong and that there is a need for action. What to do may not be clear—the situation is often bewildering and impervious to rational analysis.

The British author Robert McCrum describes in *My Year Off* how, having suffered a major stroke, he encountered much difficulty in thinking rationally about his experience:

> Sometimes it is difficult for me to acknowledge the importance of what has happened—to admit that the stroke was an irrevocable event in my personal history. I come from a tight-lipped culture in which the standard response to misfortune is to assert that one is 'fine', that one is 'perfectly OK'. It is, of course, a form of massive denial to claim that one is coping when, plainly, one is not. For me to admit that I have been scared and lonely these last several months is as difficult as it is to admit that I can sometimes feel a profound anger towards the world that has done this to me.

Testing out our intuitions and teasing out personal reflections is an appropriate response in the face of these puzzling circumstances. This is best done through sharing the experience of the worrisome change with trusted others, usually family members or close friends. If the intuitions and reflections are validated, systematic help is usually required. This may be provided by informal networks, if they exist and are appropriate. A good friend or a supportive spouse may be able to help to unravel the nature of the difficulties, and through such collaboration deal effectively with them. An alternative, or possibly the next step if the informal network proves insufficient, is to seek professional help. Help-seeking, however, can go wrong. Given that the organ of judgement is affected, vulnerable people may be so flummoxed that they fail to approach their needs rationally. I have had the repeated experience of assisting friends and acquaintances when they or their family members have lost their emotional anchorage and shown utter bewilderment about how to obtain help.

A word of caution—unfortunately, charlatans, quacks and gurus abound, many of them promising a quick fix, and sometimes charging accordingly. In general, it is wise to approach conventionally trained professionals, of which there is a wide assortment in the area of mental health care. Often family doctors are best placed to provide initial help, especially if they are familiar, trusted figures who have known the person and family over a long period. A variety of counsellors may be appropriate too. Some are easy to find; school counsellors or university counsellors (usually a psychologist or social worker) are good examples in that they are specifically trained to help people in these settings. But not all mental health professionals have had the relevant education. It is essential that they have been trained to respond to people with psychological troubles; asking questions about the extent of their clinical training and experience is entirely appropriate.

On occasion, and for diverse reasons, a good match between therapist and patient fails to evolve. The legitimate question then arises of whether to seek a more compatible healer. Neither participant should feel trapped—human beings do not automatically mesh with one another.

Medication has traditionally not been part of talking therapy. But do drugs have a place in treatment? There is no doubt that drugs have a scientifically confirmed role, and can markedly improve a person's mental state. In Chapter 18 we saw how, in the last fifty years, anti-depressant, anti-anxiety, anti-psychotic and mood stabilising drugs have come to play a pivotal role in alleviating distress. On the other hand, their indiscriminate use constitutes professional negligence and can pave the way for their abuse (I have referred particularly to the risk of abuse of the benzodiazepines).

With the help I have described, most people in acute distress will recover. They will be relieved of suffering or at least feel much better. But at this point there is much more to be done than merely sitting back and feeling self-congratulatory. The most vital extra step is to attend to the general principles for good mental health with which this chapter begins.

Indeed, once people have experienced psychiatric disturbance, the need to promote their own mental health becomes all the more critical. Unfortunately, despite all the best efforts, people with a basic predisposition to mental ill-health may experience recurrences. This brings us to the steps necessary to help people at risk over the long term.

People with continuing vulnerability

The reality of psychiatry is that many conditions, as in medicine generally, are apt to recur. The means to treat episodes of such conditions as obsessive-compulsive disorder, bipolar mood disorder, schizophrenia and panic disorder have improved vastly, but preventing their recurrence is still a challenge. For example, although lithium plays a crucial role in reducing the number of recurrences in bipolar as well as extending the period between attacks, total prevention, unfortunately, cannot be guaranteed. This points to a fundamental need on the part of patients and their families to accept that a continuing vulnerability prevails, and that this reality cannot be wished away.

Such acceptance is far from easy. With it comes an unwelcome recognition that an expectation we have always taken for granted—of good mental health—has to be radically revised. Moreover, the question arises about whether the vulnerability will be long-term, perhaps even life-long. A British child psychiatrist and past President of the Royal College of Psychiatrists, Michael Shooter, has highlighted just how demanding this transitional phase can be in an honest account of his own experience in coming to terms with mental illness. He also points out the benefits of genuine acceptance:

> The lessons for me have been hard learnt. I am no more immune than anyone else. I was depressed then and have been, intermittently, ever since. I will always remain vulnerable. But I have learnt to spot the warning signs—the vicious circle of overwork, disaster and drinking to relieve my sense of inadequacy. And when that is not enough, I have the knowledge that there is help available and that it will get me through.
>
> In the process, I'm convinced that recognising my own vulnerability has made me better able to help others—not by offering false 'hope' from my own experience but by being able to share the blackness in the middle of the tunnel when they cannot possibly see the light at the end.

We have looked at the idea of the partnership between psychiatrist and patient and highlighted its virtues. For a person who continues to be vulnerable, this partnership must have special qualities. Firstly, both participants should share a conviction that between episodes of illness the potential exists to boost resilience using the general principles and strategies for good mental health that I have outlined. In other words, even though a person is vulnerable over a long period, there will be opportunities to increase resilience.

Both people need to recognise the value of treatments that play a role in maintaining a symptom-free period, and also in nipping an impending new episode in the bud. Such treatment may well include medications of various kinds. Often, it is the psychiatrist and other mental health professionals who appreciate the place of these drugs even in the face of stiff resistance from patients, who may find them unpleasant to take because of troublesome side-effects and, crucially, because taking long-term medication is an unwelcome reminder of their status as patients.

A partnership of equal importance is that between the vulnerable person and family—the person's social support network. Ideally, there will be a triangular form of relationship, with the three parties—patient, family and health professionals—linked in a common purpose. In this ideal world the triangular partnership functions smoothly, but the nature of mental illness makes this difficult to achieve. Some tension is inevitable as patients may not be as aware of their needs as their doctors or families. Families may become over-caring, to the point of over-protectiveness. Health professionals are not always accessible to meet the needs of patient or relative.

The triangular partnership has several valuable functions, of which one of the most critical is the identification of early warning signs that something is wrong, that the vulnerable person is manifesting features of their illness albeit in a subtle form. The advantage of identifying symptoms is that the episode is caught before it overwhelms the person and becomes a full-blown breakdown. Accompanying the breakdown may be loss of insight into reality and, with it, possible failure to engage in treatment, with the potential complications of further deterioration.

A helpful strategy has evolved that may spare people from reaching this level of suffering. It uses the idea of a 'living will', signed by people requesting that, when they are terminally ill, no heroic measures should be adopted in trying to prolong their lives. In the case of psychiatry, a person with a recurrent illness reaches an agreement with their psychiatrist about the best course of action should they suffer a future episode and be unable to decide appropriately what treatment is in their best interest once they are in the midst of the episode. The 'advance directive' has been tried out in experimental settings and found to be helpful for those people who choose to participate in the scheme.

People with long-term mental problems

The final group of people in our mental health–illness continuum is relatively small, but most important because of their struggle to survive in a complicated world. In the past, they would have been placed in a remote mental hospital, there to be utterly forgotten about. While they have found their freedom and enjoy the benefits of citizenship in an era of community care, it comes at a price. For a person with an entrenched form of schizophrenia or unremitting depression, for instance, life can seem hard and demanding. A similar experience faces family members who are involved with their ill relative over a prolonged period. The most critical need for both groups is to accept the reality of their situation, similar to having severe diabetes or epilepsy or multiple sclerosis.

But much can be accomplished. People can be helped to reach their best possible adjustment by reinforcing their abilities to cope with the challenges of life. And self-esteem can be bolstered by highlighting assets and achievements. Relapses can be forestalled, with prevention of deterioration or re-hospitalisation. The concept of recovery has evolved in this context; at its core is the potential to regain control over one's life. A consensual position on recovery highlights the capacity of people to retain hope, feel empowered, deal effectively with internalised stigma, foster resilience, lead satisfying and meaningful lives, and participate in their own care.

These general strategies may be complemented by more specific ones. Here is a splendid example of how a person with eighteen years' experience of managing her own schizophrenic illness developed coping strategies to deal with her 'voices', which failed to respond to medication or other treatment. Anne Warnes offers these ideas:

- physically relaxing when the voices are at their worst;
- returning to a time when the person was free of voices;
- keeping busy with things that are automatic and do not require concentration;
- releasing feelings, even crying freely;
- chattering back at the voices (best when no-one else is present!);
- trying to talk about the voices with a sympathetic listener;
- playing music;
- planning interesting and pleasurable events regularly;
- going for a walk or taking exercise;
- joining in on activities with other people.

Anne Warnes had the talent to develop this coping repertoire. Other people may be less capable of thinking out these skills but can, through their membership of a self-help organisation, learn from the experiences of people with problems like their own.

Family and friends as caregivers

Families and friends may play a part at all points in the mental health–illness continuum. They are obviously vital in identifying early features of a first episode of mental illness, preventing recurrences, and providing support to people who are afflicted over the long term. Their effectiveness lies in personal qualities like motivation, sense of altruism, coping potential and empathic understanding. The job is not easy. The particular problems have been highlighted since the 1980s, with the aim of identifying their range and nature, and mapping out helpful strategies.

Research reveals a range of difficulties, covering personal, coping, family and social dimensions. One example of a personal problem is the sense of grief in parents who feel saddened by the missed opportunities of their adolescent child. Another is concern about not doing enough for an ill relative. Problems in coping include difficulty in dealing with a relative's excessive dependency, or confusion about whether any bizarre behaviour is due to the illness or to basic personality traits. Family tensions may be stressful as they entail, for example, conflicts about how best to care for the ill member, or a sense in the principal caregiver of criticism by other family members or of filling several competing caring roles. Beyond the family, caregivers often feel dissatisfied with mental health services, and troubled by society's stigmatising attitudes towards the mentally ill.

A psychiatrist colleague, Arthur Kleinman, has courageously shared his experience of caring for his wife, a tragic victim of Alzheimer's disease. In two articles in *The Lancet* (5 January 2008 and 24 January 2009), he highlights the stresses of functioning as a family caregiver. After a particularly frustrating encounter, he blurts out:

> 'Joan, you have Alzheimer's disease. You're not healthy. You have a brain disease. A serious problem.' I can barely conceal the frustration in my voice.
>
> 'Why did God do this to me? I've always been good. I never did anything to cause this. Should I kill myself?' She says it in such a way as to signal to me, as she has before, that this is a statement of pain and a cry for help, not an earnest question to discuss or to make plans. In fact it means the opposite: because, as in the past, she quickly changes tone. 'If you love then you can do it! We can live and love.'
>
> 'We can do it' I repeat, each time a little more weakly, enduring the unendurable. And so another morning begins, another day of caregiving and care-receiving between a 67-year-old man and a 69-year-old woman who have lived together passionately and collaboratively for 43 years.

Some of these issues can be dealt with in self-help groups, where caregivers share feelings and exchange ideas about how best to manage difficult experiences (see below). Mental health professionals are also well placed to offer expertise, and their research has confirmed a number of ways in which they can help families:

- listening actively (with a 'third ear') to family's underlying difficulties;
- acknowledging their demanding experiences;
- clarifying that their situation is not unique and that they are not freaks in responding the way they do to their ill relative;
- providing a safe forum for sharing intense feelings;
- praising their strengths and achievements;
- acknowledging and legitimising their personal needs;
- helping to identify and clarify specific concerns;
- collaborating with them in problem-solving;
- offering explicit advice;
- providing information about the illness and its treatment.

Self-help (mutual help) organisations

A major development in mental health care, the self-help organisation, is a response to the trend for people with mental illnesses to take more responsibility for their care, combined with an expanding role for their social support network. There is a similar pattern in medicine overall.

The first such self-help group, Alcoholics Anonymous (www.aa.org.au), was founded in 1935. Since then, they have mushroomed in many countries. Some cover mental health care generally—for example, MIND (www.mind.org.uk) in Britain, the National Alliance for the Mentally Ill (www.nami.org) in the United States, and SANE (www.sane.org) in Australia. These broad-based organisations lobby governments, advocate for the mentally ill and their families, and raise funds for innovative services and research. They also strive to reduce the stigma so typical of the experience of mentally ill people and their families. Other organisations focus on particular psychiatric conditions. Two eminently effective bodies in Australia, which deal principally with mood disorders, are Beyondblue (www.beyondblue.org.au) and the Black Dog Institute (www.blackdoginstitute.org.au).

Resourceful self-help organisations play a pivotal part in assisting both patients and families, particularly over the long haul. The coming together of fellow sufferers (and of their families) provides a sense of mutual support, as well as recognition that they are not alone in their plight. Not only this, people benefit by receiving advice about how to manage and cope with the demands of the particular illness. The term 'self-help organisation' is commonly a misnomer, since professional staff may be involved in one form or another. For example, many organisations employ trained counsellors to help people and their families with information and support, and professional staff produce educational booklets, videos and other forms of information.

CHAPTER 21

An Ethical Dimension

Psychiatrists have to grapple with many vexing ethical problems. Although these differ according to the type of psychiatry practised, certain themes are pervasive. These include how to assess the costs and benefits of a treatment; how to maintain confidentiality in the face of competing loyalties; how to define the boundaries of the profession; how to strike a balance between the ethos of a contractual partnership and paternalism; how to satisfy the interests of patients, their families and society when they clash; how to advocate for patients, many of whom are disenfranchised and powerless; suicide; patients threatening to harm others; the implications of impaired reasoning for informed consent; involuntary treatment; therapists imposing their personal values; use of treatments with potentially irreversible side-effects, and many more.

Furthermore, psychiatry has been buffeted by external pressures that derive from its unique role in society in tandem with its blurred professional boundary and flaky diagnostic criteria. The asylum as essentially a custodial institution and form of social control for over three centuries; the abuse of psychiatry to suppress dissent as occurred in the former Soviet Union; the stigma of suffering from a mental illness, and the perversion of psychiatry in Nazi Germany when it metamorphosed into a profession governed by an abhorrent racist ideology—these are but a few of the events or realities that have shaken the profession to the core.

One way to appreciate the scope of these ethical dilemmas is by noting the chapters that make up the text *Psychiatric Ethics* that I have co-edited since it was first published by Oxford University Press in 1981. Now in its fourth edition (2009), the book has covered tens of subjects over the years.

A few stories from my practice and that of my students will give the reader a good impression of the range of ethical challenges encountered by psychiatrists.

Josh, aged 7, is being treated for disruptive behaviour at school. His parents are separated and share custody; they have agreed that he will live mainly with his father, where he seems more stable, and alternate weekends with the mother. This is an informal, short-term arrangement, but his father has told Dr Grant, the treating psychiatrist, that he intends to apply for full custody through the family court since he feels that he can provide Josh with a more stable environment, a judgement echoed by Dr Grant. However, it is clear Josh does not want to hurt his mother's feelings by choosing his father, and he has shared this 'secret' with Dr Grant. So, when the father asks Dr Grant what Josh has told him, the ethical dilemma is whether to breach confidentiality on the grounds that this would serve the boy's interests (the information would probably assist the father to gain the court's support) or whether respect for confidentiality is a hallowed principle that should not be violated.

Mr Harris, a 67-year-old married retiree, is being treated for cancer of the colon, which has spread to the liver but is responding to chemotherapy. He has developed a severe melancholia, showing all the classical features. Treatment has included anti-depressants and electro-convulsive therapy. The latter has been stopped because of anaesthetic complications. Mr Harris now tells the oncologist that 'there is no point' in the chemotherapy. A psychiatrist has been invited to assess the patient and concludes that his pessimistic thinking is a feature of the depression. Mrs Harris has always harboured strong views about the value of alternative medicine and supports her husband in his decision to cease the chemotherapy. The treating team faces a dilemma—respect the couple's wishes or use leverage to get them to agree to persist with treatment for both the cancer and the depression. The psychiatrist is asked to clarify whether the disordered mood is affecting Mr Harris's ability to think rationally about what is in his best interests.

Tanya, aged 24 and single, is living on the streets and supporting herself through prostitution. She is brought to the hospital by the police, who found her acting bizarrely and heard her describing herself as 'saviour of the people'. She had been diagnosed as schizophrenic two years previously but soon dropped out of treatment because of her itinerant lifestyle. She has abused heroin and stimulants for several years. Given the severity of her psychotic symptoms, Tanya is made an involuntary patient and treated with anti-psychotics by injection. Her symptoms improve dramatically. She is therefore transferred to an open ward. She soon absconds, and is brought back by the police a day later in a deteriorated state. The same pattern occurs on two more occasions. The decision is therefore made to place her on a compulsory community treatment order; a social worker begins to search for suitable supervised accommodation. Tanya balks at the idea, protesting: 'I've lived on the streets since I was eighteen. You can find me a place but I'll go back to my street life after a week' (no doubt to earn money from prostitution in order to fund her heroin habit). Tanya is cooperative for four days and then carries out her threat. The team feels frustrated, helpless and confused about how to deal with what they see as her self-destructive behaviour.

Karen and Hugh have been married for thirteen years and have one child, Lucy, aged 9. Karen has experienced low self-esteem for several months and feels that she has failed as a mother and wife. She is receiving psychotherapy from Dr Davis. Hugh has a drinking problem, the result of the marital tension, and has also seen Dr Davis to assess his need for treatment. They both face the emotional burden of being on an IVF program. Lucy has always wanted a sibling. Then, quite unexpectedly, Karen conceives naturally. All three are overjoyed and the marriage changes for the better. A few weeks later, Karen asks Dr Davis to keep secret the 'horrible' news that she is carrying a baby with Down's syndrome. She is devastated and feels she could not possibly cope with raising a child with a disability. She knows that Hugh will want to keep the baby because he is a committed Christian. She asks the therapist to advise her as to what is the best way to deal with the situation.

Psychiatrists have, frustratingly, not yet managed to agree on a framework that can facilitate coherent ethical decision-making and lead to corresponding action. Diverse theories have been available, some for centuries, but they remain problematic when applied to the clinical sphere. Indeed, they often confuse rather than illuminate, and may even contradict one another. In this chapter I shall focus on ethical aspects of clinical practice that are especially challenging to psychiatrists, and then briefly offer a preferred theoretical framework to deal with them.

Ethical aspects of making a diagnosis

Conferring a diagnosis of mental illness on a person has significant ethical repercussions since the act may embody profound adverse effects, notably prejudice and discrimination (for example, limited job prospects, inequitable insurance cover). Furthermore, those deemed at risk of harming themselves or others may have their civil rights abridged.

Psychiatrists strive to diagnose by using as objective criteria as possible and information gained from previous clinical encounters. The process is relatively uncomplicated when findings such as gross defective memory and life-threatening social withdrawal strongly suggests dementia and severe depression respectively. Other situations are not so obvious. For instance, the distress experienced by a bereaved person may incline one clinician towards diagnosing clinical depression whereas another may attribute the picture to normal grief.

As we saw in Chapter 3, specified criteria on defining and classifying mental illness in the American Psychiatric Association's DSM-IV and the World Health Organization's ICD-10 do not preclude debate about the preciseness or legitimacy of certain syndromes, like attention deficit hyperactivity disorder (ADHD) and sexual orientation disturbance. Concern about the intrusion of value judgements into classifications has led to the contention that some diagnoses reflect pejorative labelling rather than scientific decisions. For example, charges of sexism were levelled against DSM-III on the grounds that masculine-based assumptions shaped criteria resulting in women receiving unwarranted diagnoses like premenstrual dysphoria.

The issue central to this debate is whether certain mental states are grounded in fact or value judgements. American psychiatrist Thomas Szasz takes a radical position, arguing that disorders of thinking and behaviour are due to objective abnormalities of the brain, whereas mental illness per se is a myth created by society in tandem with the medical profession for the purpose of exerting social control. The 'anti-psychiatrist movement' asserts that mental illnesses are social constructions reflecting deviations from societal norms. This argument is supported by the role of values in first defining homosexuality as a psychiatric disorder, then reversing that position through a ballot among members of the American Psychiatric Association in 1973.

Consequences of these sorts of disputes can be considerable (for example, exposing children erroneously labelled as ADHD to long-term dexamphetamine medication with its attendant risks). Psychiatric diagnosis may also mitigate legal and personal consequences of one's actions (for example, interpreting excessive sexual activity or repeated stealing of useless objects as variants of obsessive-compulsive disorder rather than wilful behaviours).

Ethical aspects of psychiatric treatment

Assessing and treating patients require a working alliance and informed consent. Many psychiatric patients are in a position to understand and appreciate the nuances of treatment options, to express an informed preference, and to feel comfortably allied with a therapist in their collaborative work. When the process of informed consent is responsibly handled, particularly with reference to benefits and risks of therapeutic options, people undergoing psychiatric treatment are in a comparable position to their counterparts in general medicine. This comparability is grounded in two concepts—competence and voluntarism. Competence covers the required criterion that the person facing choices in treatment enjoys the critical faculties to appreciate the implications of each course of action. Voluntarism refers to a condition whereby the process of consent is devoid of any coercion. Obviously, given that the organ of decision-making is the same one that is impaired in many psychiatric conditions, profound ethical complications may ensue when seeking informed consent.

Ethical issues arise once therapist and patient embark on treatment. At the outset, the patient is bewildered, vulnerable and distressed. Dependency bolsters the authority already vested in the therapist, and may be reinforced if the therapist divulges little about the nature of treatment, believing this would undermine the transference (irrational feelings and attitudes patients develop towards therapists), regarded by dynamically oriented schools as central to the process.

As noted above, informed consent is one means to dispel this air of mystery. One model invokes the concept of a therapeutic partnership, its cornerstone being an agreed on plan, subject to regular review. Among its elements are: identifying goals and methods to reach them, monitoring effectiveness, and permitting either partner to voice dissatisfaction. The partnership does not imply an equal share of power but rather an agreement about how power will be allocated. A person in the throes of an intense crisis, for instance, may lack the wherewithal to appreciate what is in their best interests. In collaboration with the therapist they may agree to assign that therapist a more paternalistic role. As the crisis wanes, so is there restoration of the patient's state of autonomy.

In reviewing models of informed consent, my colleague Allen Dyer and I have proposed an approach in which the therapist works to earn the patient's trust over time, and is not a one-off negotiation at the outset of treatment. The relationship also enhances a sense of responsibility in the therapist, who responds to patient's particular needs. Although autonomy in the patient is always a desired goal, it is not the therapist's sole preoccupation.

Values and psychotherapy

Treatment is permeated by values, and this is another ethically based feature that must be addressed, since the problems for which people seek help are bound up with the question of how they should live their lives, and therapists may impose values intentionally or unwittingly.

Tristram Engelhardt, an American moral philosopher, posits that psychotherapy often paves the way for ethical decision-making by patients, but that the aim is not for them to adopt a particular set of values. Indeed, the therapist avoids recommending how patients should live their lives. Instead, they are helped to reach a point where they can make their own choices, unhindered by psychological conflict and unconscious influences. Freud, also intent on promoting value-free treatment, argued that a therapist 'should be opaque to his patients and, like a mirror, should show them nothing but what is shown to him'. He insisted that therapy was limited to 'freeing someone from his neurotic symptoms, inhibitions and abnormalities of character' through making conscious the unconscious. On the other hand, he also pointed out an educative role, suggesting that the analyst 'in certain analytic situations … can act as a model for his patient and in others as a teacher'.

It is difficult to conceive of this hybrid role of mirror, model and teacher as value-free, even if the ultimate goal in analysis is to achieve autonomy, free of the influence of irrational forces. Thus, if therapy amounts to ethical intervention, the question arises as to how the therapist should handle this.

The therapist could make every effort to minimise the ethical role, but the likelihood of success is slim, since unavowed values will be manifest non-verbally. Another option is to accept the ethical intervention function but recognise this as the therapist's problem, not the patient's. The therapist must be aware of this potential role as moral agent and regard their own values as a factor in the encounter—thus being sensitive to these values and monitoring any impulses to influence the patient.

A third option has the therapist declaring their own values as a value in itself. The argument runs as follows: psychotherapy is a form of social influence; the therapist influences patients; the therapist acknowledges this state of affairs; and is transparent regarding the values he or she espouses. Some homosexual therapists, for example, have aligned themselves with the gay movement when treating homosexual patients. A distinguished psychotherapist and committed Christian, Alan Bergin, has evolved a school of 'theistic realism' in which the therapist shares values derived from a Judeo-Christian tradition, including forgiveness, reconciliation, spiritual belief and love. A group of therapists who functioned in the context of apartheid South Africa not only declared their repudiation of racism but also demonstrated their support for traumatised Blacks, especially those who had been victims of detention and torture. Particular groups are being served in these three illustrations. Avowal of values can also be applied generally. A therapist may decide to strive to be transparent with all patients about the values he or she holds.

The right to treatment

The emphasis on society providing adequate resources brings us to the right to treatment where liberty is restricted. The asylum era was marked by tragic neglect of patients' needs. The overcrowded institution became little more than a warehouse. Its custodial nature persisted even after the advent of drug and psychosocial therapies. It took a plaintiff to determine that a person committed involuntarily had the 'right to receive treatment that would offer him a reasonable opportunity to be cured or to improve his mental condition'. Diagnosed with schizophrenia in 1957, Kenneth Donaldson received minimal treatment for the next decade and a half. The US Supreme Court concluded in 1975 that a patient who does not pose a danger to himself or to others and who is not receiving treatment should be released if able to live safely in the community.

The right to effective treatment

The right to treatment has been revisited in subsequent judgements, predominantly in the United States (*Wyatt v Stickney*, 1971, 1972). However, the right lacked a guarantee that patients would receive effective treatment. This opens up a Pandora's box, reflected vividly in *Osheroff v Chestnut Lodge* (1984, 1985). The plaintiff, a 42-year-old doctor, sued a private psychiatric hospital for failure to provide anti-depressants in the face of his deteriorating depression. Gerald Klerman, a leading research psychiatrist, subsequently argued that the clinician is duty-bound to use only 'treatments for which there is substantial evidence' or seek a second opinion in the absence of a clinical response. Alan Stone, a leading academic psychiatrist, countered the Klerman position, which he proposed was tantamount to promoting 'standards of treatment ... based on ... opinion about science and clinical practice'; instead, we should depend on 'the collective sense' of psychiatry, as well as use the 'respectable minority rule', namely that a subgroup within psychiatry could legitimately develop new therapies.

The right to refuse treatment

As a voluntary patient, Dr Osheroff could have refused treatment of any type as part of informed consent. His lawsuit pinpointed Chestnut Lodge's alleged failure to offer him an alternative treatment in the face of his deterioration with the therapy offered. If principles of informed consent had been applied correctly, his freedom to choose one treatment over others, and to withdraw consent at any stage thereafter, should have prevailed.

The situation differs radically when the person is committed involuntarily to hospital or community treatment. The right to refuse treatment then looms large. A key event was another US legal judgement, when a court ruled that detained patients had a constitutional right to refuse treatment (*Rogers v Okin*, 1979, 1983). This coincided with changing commitment laws in many jurisdictions of the United States, from criteria linked to need for treatment to those highlighting the danger posed to the person themselves and/or others. The ethical repercussions are profound. If psychiatrists are empowered to detain patients, is it not a contradiction if they are then powerless to administer treatment should the patient refuse it? The argument rests on the premise that a person sufficiently disturbed to warrant involuntary admission is axiomatically entitled to treatment, and the consulting psychiatrist suitably placed to provide it. Without this arrangement, the psychiatrist's functions are reduced to custodial.

A countervailing argument is grounded in constitutional rights. Merely because people are committed does not mean they are incapable of participating in the process of informed consent. In the event they cannot understand or appreciate the rationale for a course of action, a form of substituted judgement should be employed, thereby ensuring that rights remain prominent. An assortment of legal remedies has emerged in response to this ethical quandary, ranging from a full adversarial process to reliance on a guardian's decision. American psychiatrist Paul Appelbaum has offered a lucid account of the options and his predilection for a treatment-driven model in which patients are committed because their capacity to decide about treatment is lacking as part of a disturbed mental state. His own research demonstrates that most refusing patients voluntarily accept treatment within twenty-four hours.

Involuntary treatment

A consensus has prevailed for generations that some psychiatric patients lose the capacity for self-determination. They become vulnerable to harming themselves and/or others, acting in ways they will later regret (for example, a manic patient's sexual indiscretions); and suffer from self-neglect (for example, schizophrenic patients who are homeless, malnourished and physically ill). What is not universally agreed is how best to deal with such vulnerable people. Society has, generally, called on the law to respond to the thorny issue of when and how to protect this group. However, variations in legislation and its application are legion, reflecting in part the ethical underpinnings of the process.

Psychiatrists and society need coherent arguments concerning the moral principles we should heed. A good start is the British philosopher John Stuart Mill's contention that the 'only purpose for which power can be rightfully exercised over any member of a civilised community, against his will, is to prevent harm to others. His own good, either physical or moral, is not a sufficient warrant.' Mill's caveat that an exception must be made in children and mentally disturbed people (for example, 'delirious' or in a 'state of excitement or absorption incompatible with the full use of the reflecting faculty') suggests they can legitimately be assisted.

My colleague Paul Chodoff has addressed the awesome question of compulsory treatment on the grounds of mental illness. He proposes a 'chastened and self-critical' paternalism, one 'willing to commit to strong safeguards against abuse'. This humanism is epitomised in a concluding sentiment: involuntary treatment is not a conflict of right versus wrong but one over the right to remain at liberty against the right 'to be free from dehumanising disease'. This notion of being imprisoned by illness would resonate with all psychiatrists who have treated psychotic patients.

Our discussion so far has referred to patients as a homogeneous group. Loss of critical faculties may be a unifying feature but ethical factors will vary according to particulars of the clinical state. One obvious example is suicidal behaviour. Thoma Szasz sees suicide as the act of a moral agent. The State should therefore not assume power to prevent self-killing although it may opt to advise for or against. This libertarian argument has the corollary that everyone should have the right to end their life. Szasz has, however, neglected Mill's point that when respecting a person's right to liberty, a possible exception is the loss of his critical faculties. This is not to claim that all suicidal behaviour is the product of a disordered mind. Suicide in the wake of long-term debilitating illness and a longstanding commitment to euthanasia seems rational—for example, the renowned author Arthur Koestler left a suicide note demonstrating that he arrived at his decision authentically and with his critical faculties intact.

The suicidal patient epitomises the psychiatrist's dilemma in having no choice but to impose treatment in various circumstances and having to declare a person's incapacity, by dint of mental illness, to make rational judgements about what is in their best interests. Two South African psychiatrists, CW Van Staden and C Kruger, cover this topic by highlighting its dimensions, namely the failure to understand relevant information, to choose between options, and to accept that the need for treatment prevails. They refer to the utility of a 'functional approach' in determining capacity, especially concerning the temporal factor, so that a patient incapable of consenting at one point in their illness may well become capable at another. Ethical arguments to justify detention in a hospital can be extrapolated into the community setting, as similar restrictions on liberty lie at the heart of the moral dilemma and the psychiatrist again has to consider the patient's competence.

A framework to deal with ethical challenges

We saw how ethical challenges exist at several levels in the clinical scenarios at the beginning of this chapter. A combination of two ethical approaches, principlism and care ethics, can be gainfully adopted in wrestling with these challenges.

Principlism (or principle-based ethics) relies on a set of well-established moral principles to identify and analyse ethical problems. These are:

first of all, do no harm (non-maleficence); act to benefit others (beneficence); respect a person's autonomy; and treat people fairly (justice). The approach holds that these four principles provide a useful starting point to aid ethical decision-making. They can be applied in conjunction with other pertinent information, such as scientific knowledge and repeated clinical observations, as well as being used flexibly.

The essence of care ethics is a reliance on the natural inclination of human beings to extend care to dependent and vulnerable people, and to react sensitively with such moral feelings as compassion, love and trustworthiness. The approach fits well with psychiatry, since its practitioners depend significantly on empathy in order to understand the wishes and needs of patients and their families.

Let us see how we can apply the care ethics and principlism in relation to the following case.

Emma, a 22-year-old secretary, began to exhibit restlessness, perplexity and remoteness from her husband, Tim, following the birth of her first baby ten weeks earlier. I was summoned after she had visited several neighbors without obvious purpose. I found a reticent, detached woman complaining that 'They have been out to get me from the beginning', and alluding to 'world famine and starving children'. My examination of her mental state revealed vague, paranoid thinking, but firm denial of suicidal and homicidal impulses; she was not obviously delirious. Emma resisted my recommendation that she be admitted to the local psychiatric hospital. Tim supported her, insisting that he did not regard his wife as mentally ill; moreover, he feared that she would deteriorate if placed alongside genuinely disturbed patients.

Buffeted by frightening internal forces, Emma's withdrawal and bizarre behaviour since her baby's birth point to the question of whether or not she is competent to appreciate her circumstances. Above all, can she protect her infant? Extending care to a deeply distressed woman who has lost her psychological anchorage (as well as to her anxious husband and the vulnerable baby) directs the psychiatrist to respond in accordance with the tenets of care ethics, particularly the goal of promoting trust. It remains an open question whether this means advising Emma (with Tim's support) to enter hospital, or committing her to involuntary treatment, or arranging for her rigorous supervision by family and friends.

What is vital is that the psychiatrist adopts a caring attitude. However, his options must be considered in the context of basic ethical principles; for example, is respect for Emma's autonomy possible or must the psychiatrist necessarily act in *loco parentis*, in accordance with the principle of beneficence? And given the entitlements due to the three participants— patient, husband and baby, what role does justice play? How can we ensure that we deal fairly with each of them? What must the psychiatrist do or not do to avoid harming any of the trio?

A synthesis of care ethics and principlism permits sound moral reflection by highlighting moral emotions when psychiatrists are presented with ethical conundrums.

The role of a code of ethics

This chapter would be incomplete without raising the question of whether a code of ethics has a role in psychiatry. Judith Lichtenberg, an academic philosopher, believes that 'codes of ethics can increase the likelihood that people will behave in certain ways', in part by making them more aware of the nature of their actions and also by 'getting [them] to behave in ways that have been determined ... to be morally desirable'. She also makes the point that codes are devised and applied by groups of people in order to pursue shared goals, considered worthy of attainment. Thus, the psychiatric profession as a corporate entity may elaborate ethical standards that its members judge contribute to the common good—by fostering desired moral actions in relating to the patients they try to help, to the colleague-ship of which they are a part, and to the society they serve. A code cannot, in and of itself, guarantee that the interests of these groups will be safeguarded, but it can certainly contribute to such a desirable goal as well as 'inform professional conscience and judgement'.

Conclusion

Perhaps I have erred in placing this chapter at the end of the book. In some ways, it should come at the beginning. Without a solid ethical foundation, anything else carried out by the psychiatrist seems futile to me. On the other hand, for the reader who has delved into other chapters, you will, I hope, appreciate how the ethical dimension applies to everything we do. In the mid-1990s I struggled to find a suitable symbol for my profession, and with ethics uppermost in my mind I came up with a three-legged stool. This simple item of furniture reminds us that humility is a hallmark of a good psychiatrist. The three legs must be of equal length and stature for the stool to be stable. What do the legs represent? Science, art and ethics. Conducting research to advance objective knowledge is essential. The art is more elusive, but cultivating empathy so that we can better understand what patients are experiencing is at its heart. The third leg represents the ethical dimension—the need to respect the humanity and dignity of our patients and to safeguard their interests. There is nothing like a picture to capture the

essence of what I am trying to convey (with apologies to my women colleagues, but a single stool cannot accommodate two practitioners!), and to bring *Understanding Troubled Minds* to an end.

A Select Guide to Further Reading

In mulling over how to compile this list, I toyed with various options, including one book for each psychiatric condition, a formal set of texts covering every topic, poignant accounts by patients or their families, and material prepared by self-help organisations. Rather than bombarding you with lengthy lists, let me offer a personal selection based on what I have found helpful or illuminating. I hope it will prove equally so for you.

I must immediately point out that books are but one means of acquiring information and knowledge. A range of other media—film, television, radio and the internet—are equally rich sources, with the latter steadily overtaking the other forms. Anyone with access to the web can readily locate sites providing topical and useful information about all aspects of mental health, but it is wise to remember that many contributions are of dubious quality. Try to stick to established government and self-help organisations. An excellent example is the website of the National Institute of Mental Health, the pre-eminent research organisation of the United States government, which offers a comprehensive account of developments in psychiatry (www.nimh.nih.gov).

This sort of material is widely available nowadays, its introduction having been spurred on by the advent of the self-help movement. A host of mental health organisations see the preparation and dissemination of information in the form of booklets and manuals as a core function. The organisations themselves are easily reached through the family doctor, psychiatric clinic, telephone directory and the internet. Their material is generally informative and user-friendly.

Let us now turn to books that I have valued over the years. The first group centres around personal experience of mental illness, through the eyes of patients, relatives or observers (in some instances, psychiatrists themselves). Sometimes, psychiatrists have linked up with patients or relatives. And some observers go beyond the clinical story and provide advice and guidance on how to deal with a particular mental illness.

Of what we might call testimonial literature, this is only the tip of an iceberg:

Mary Barnes and Joseph Berke, *Mary Barnes: Two Accounts of a Journey through Madness*, Penguin, Harmondsworth, 1973. The account of a psychotic experience co-written by a patient and a psychiatrist.

Ross David Burke, *When the Music's Over: My Journey into Schizophrenia*, Basic Books, New York, 1995. This personal account of schizophrenia was published after Ross Burke's death by suicide and covers the last six turbulent years of his life.

Anne Deveson, *Tell Me I'm Here*, Penguin, Melbourne, 1991. The well-known Australian broadcaster and filmmaker relates her poignant story of battling to help her son, Jonathan, to survive the torment of schizophrenia.

Janet Frame, *An Autobiography*, Random House, Auckland, 1994. A trilogy by the New Zealand writer who spent many years in a mental hospital; the film *An Angel at My Table* is a brilliantly directed rendering of her experience.

Hannah Green, *I Never Promised You a Rose Garden*, Holt, Rinehart and Winston, New York, 1964. The account of the psychotherapy of a psychotic young woman.

Kay Redfield Jamison, *An Unquiet Mind*, Knopf, New York, 1995. A psychologist's personal battle with manic-depressive illness.

——, *Night Falls Fast: Understanding Suicide*, Knopf, New York, 1999. A comprehensive account of suicide, especially in young people.

David Karp, *Speaking of Sadness*, Oxford University Press, New York, 1996. Personal testimony of an American sociologist, and material from his interviews of fifty other people who have experienced depression.

Kathy Kronkite, *On the Edge of Darkness: Conversations about Conquering Depression*, Doubleday, New York, 1994. A description of her own experience of depression, and comments from several other sufferers, including William Styron, Rod Steiger and Jules Feiffer.

Daniel McGowan, *Living in the Labyrinth: A Personal Journey through the Maze of Alzheimer's*, Delacorte Press, New York, 1993. A personal account of the experience of the early stages of Alzheimer's disease.

Spike Milligan and Anthony Clare, *Depression and How to Survive It*, Arrow, London, 1994, A collaboration between the famous British comedian and a professor of psychiatry; Milligan is searingly honest about his four decades of disordered mood.

Judith Rapoport, *The Boy Who Couldn't Stop Washing*, Dutton, New York, 1989. Patients and their families share their experiences of suffering from, or living with, a sufferer of obsessive-compulsive disorder.

William Styron, *Darkness Visible*, Jonathan Cape, London, 1991. The American novelist's vivid description of his devastating descent into depression.

Stuart Sutherland, *Breakdown*, Weidenfeld and Nicholson, London, 1987. An honest revelation of a mental breakdown and attempt at recovery by a professor of psychology.

Fuller Torrey, *Surviving Schizophrenia*, Quill, New York, 2006. A psychiatrist's
  effort to convey his patients' experiences of schizophrenia, coupled with a
  description of the disorder and its treatment.
Irvin Yalom, *Love's Executioner*, Basic Books, New York, 1989, A psychiatrist
  conveys most vividly the psychotherapy he conducted with ten of his
  patients.

For details of the life of Vincent Van Gogh, which has been highlighted and
is of enduring interested, see:
D Sweetman, *Love of Many Things: A Life of Vincent Van Gogh*, Hodder and
  Stoughton, London, 1990.
ME Tralbaut, *Vincent Van Gogh*, Viking, New York,1969.
V Van Gogh, *The Complete Letters of Vincent Van Gogh*, Thames and Hudson,
  London, 1958.
www.vggallery.com is a website very much worth a look.

I highlighted in the Preface the contribution of great writers to deep-
ening our understanding of mental illness. Indeed, among the most sensitive and astute observers of human nature are novelists, poets and dramatists.
As with the testimonial literature, examples here are unlimited, but note-
worthy are Shakespeare's *King Lear*, *Macbeth* and *Hamlet*, Chekhov's *Uncle
Vanya*, Balzac's *Louis Lambert*, Flaubert's *Madame Bouvary*, Hardy's *Far From
the Madding Crowd*, Scott Fitzgerald's *Tender Is the Night*, Ken Kesey's *One Flew
Over the Cuckoo's Nest*, Sylvia Plath's *The Bell Jar*, DM Thomas's *The White Hotel*,
Sebastian Barry's *The Secret Scripture*, Philip Roth's *Patrimony* and Pat Barker's
Regeneration trilogy.

You may seek a more scientific account of an aspect of psychiatry. I
hesitate to recommend formal textbooks since they are obviously technical,
commonly laden with jargon and, given their need to be objective, the
human dimension tends to be overshadowed by hard scientific data. Bearing
this in mind, two texts are popular among psychiatrists and regarded as
authoritative. The most commonly quoted American text is the *Comprehensive
Textbook of Psychiatry*, edited by B Sadock and colleagues (9th edition,
Lippincott, Williams and Wilkins, Baltimore, 2009). Another widely used
reference is the *New Oxford Textbook of Psychiatry* by M Gelder and colleagues
(2nd edition, Oxford University Press, Oxford, 2009).

To these must be added what psychiatrists have come to adopt as classics.
They include the work of obvious figures like Freud and Jung. A handy com-
pilation of Freud's main writings is *The Freud Reader*, edited and introduced by
Peter Gay (1989). Selected writings of Jung were brought together by Anthony
Storr and published as a pocket reader, *The Essential Jung* (1983).

Another classic is *Man's Search for Meaning* by the Viennese psychiatrist, Viktor Frankl (1962). The British psychiatrist and psychoanalyst, John Bowlby, devoted almost his entire career to preparing a trilogy entitled *Attachment and Loss* (1969–80); the books cover key themes like loss, sadness and depression. I have been very much influenced by another psychoanalyst, Erik Erikson, whom I have mentioned as the developer of the notion of stages of psychological development throughout the life cycle. *Childhood and Society* (1963) is one of his several classics.

Other contributions that have attracted the attention of psychiatrists include Arthur Kleinman's *Rethinking Psychiatry* (1988), in which he highlights the relevance of a cross-cultural perspective for mental health practice, a counterweight to the pendular swing towards the biological emphasis since the 1990s. Erving Goffman, in his book *Asylums* (1961), also adopts a social science approach when examining the social circumstances of the mentally ill in institutions. Another Goffman classic is *Stigma* (1964).

If you are interested in the history of psychiatry you have a broad choice. I would recommend *The Faber Book of Madness*, edited by Roy Porter (1991), an anthology covering a vast panorama. A more focused book by the French scholar Michel Foucault, *Madness and Civilization* (1965), attempts to explain the history of insanity from 1500 to 1800.

I may have already violated my own call for self-restraint in providing too many titles. I also end up feeling frustrated, since dozens of other books vie for your attention. So, in conclusion, let me reiterate that this reading guide is based on personal preferences and comprises books that are both accessible and digestible.

Index

abortion, 267
Ackerman, Nathan, 309
addictions
    addiction cycle, 166
    drug, 163, 164, 180; opiates, 175
    to electronic media, 29–30
    gambling, 33, 309
    sexual, 29
    see also alcoholism
adolescents, 10
    and cannabis, 178, 212
    girls, 223–4
    and mental illness, 91, 95, 117, 119,
        162, 209, 210, 217; psychoses, 213–14
    and personality changes, 129
    psychological development problems
        in, 33
    separation anxiety, 192
    and transition, 194, 209, 210
    see also children
ageing population, 232, 253, 254
    implications of, 234
agoraphobia, 66, 67, 68, 70, 71, 73–4,
    78, 80, 212
    and women, 222
AIDS, 163, 239
alcoholism, 96, 163, 164, 167, 169; and
    suicide, 261–2, 265
Aldrick, Sharon, 241–2
Allport, Gordon, 124
Alzheimer, Alois, 238
American Psychiatric Association
    (APA), 29, 30, 32, 76, 219, 347
anti-depressant drugs, 51, 52, 86, 100,
    101, 119, 212, 231, 232, 248, 249, 274
    effectiveness, 279, 285, 338,345
    monoamine oxidase inhibitors

(MAOIs), 277, 278
    selective serotonin reuptake
    inhibitors (SSRIs), 9, 10, 81, 211, 277,
        278, 281; Prozac, 278
    and side-effects, 227, 278
    tricyclics (TCAs), 81, 277, 278, 281;
        imipramine, 274
anti-psychiatry, 27, 145, 347
anxiety
    as adaptive response, 64
    as problem of life, 25, 211–12, 281
anxiety disorders, 9, 32, 65–7, 97, 306
    causes, 67–8, 75
    in childhood and adolescence, 212
    and dependency, 78–9
    existential, 302–3
    general anxiety disorder, 68–70
    and medical conditions, 66, 107
    misdiagnosis, 69, 71
    panic disorder, 68, 70–1, 339
    performance anxiety, 72
    phobic disorders, 71; social, 72–3, 81;
        specific, 71–2
    social anxiety, 33, 68
    see also agoraphobia; panic; phobia;
        post-traumatic stress disorder
Appelbaum, Paul, 351
Aquinas, Thomas, 256
Arataeus, 84
Aristotle, 256
    Nicomachean Ethics, 331, 333
Asperger's syndrome, 29, 202–3
asylums, 4–5, 6, 10, 11, 273, 344, 349–50
    deinstitutionalisation, 9, 10, 153, 253
attachment theory, 190, 297
attention-deficit hyperactive disorder
    (ADHD), 204–6, 347

Auden, WH, 296
Augustine, St, 256
Australian and New Zealand Journal of Psychiatry, 216
autism, 29, 33, 202, 203, 324
  adult, 203–4

Balzac, Honoré de
  Louis Lambert, 3–4
Bancroft, John, 188
Barker, Pat
  Regeneration trilogy, 75–6
Barry, Sebastian
  The Secret Scripture, 220–1
Bayley, John
  Elegy for Iris, 242
  Iris and Her Friends, 242
Beauvoir, Simone de, 219
Beck, Aaron, 97, 304
Beckett, Samuel
  Endgame, 133
  Waiting for Godot, 133
behaviour
  biological factors in, 220
  deviant, 26; in children, 206–8
  'illness behaviour', 103
  and problematic personality, 127, 206
  unconventional, 26
behavioural syndromes, 32–3
behavioural theory, 97
Bergin, Alan, 349
Bleuler, Eugen, 6, 148
Bloch, Sidney
  The Family in Clinical Psychiatry (co-author), 332
  An Introduction to the Psychotherapies (ed.), 288, 313
  Psychiatric Ethics (co-editor), 344
  What Is Psychotherapy?, 288, 320
Bosscher, Hilly, 266–7
Boswell, James, 74–5
Bouvia, Elizabeth, 266, 268
Bowlby, John, 130, 297
brain, the
  brain damage, 31, 41, 129; and alcohol, 171–2; Wernicke-Korsakoff syndrome, 172
  brain dysfunction, 14, 21, 24, 68, 203, 205, 209

development, 146, 148
  infections of, 239
  plasticity, 131
  see also electro-convulsive therapy; psychosurgery
Breuer, Josef, 104, 296
Bunyan, John
  The Pilgrim's Progress, 74
Burton, Richard
  The Anatomy of Melancholia, 85

Cade, John, 7, 8, 280
Caplan, Gerald, 58, 315
Cartwright, Samuel, 26
Casals, Pablo, 234
case studies
  acute stress reaction, 61
  alcohol abuse, 172
  amphetamine abuse, 178
  anorexia nervosa, 120–1
  bulimia nervosa, 121–2
  children, 195–6, 197, 198, 202, 205, 207–8, 212, 214, 224
  clinical depression, 86–90
  conversion disorder (hysteria), 109, 110; psychogenic amnesia, 111
  counselling, 318–19
  drug abuse: benzodiazepines, 174–5; opiates, 176; polysubstance abuse, 180
  elderly people, 237; anxiety, 250–1; delirium, 246; dementia, 242–3, 244–5; depression, 249
  ethics and psychiatry, 345–6, 353
  general anxiety disorder, 70
  hypochondriasis, 107; body dysmorphic disorder, 108
  mania, 91–3
  obsessive-compulsive disorder, 75
  panic disorder, 70–1
  phobic disorders, 71–4
  post-traumatic stress disorder, 78
  problematic personality: anti-social, 135; avoidant, 139; borderline, 137; dependent, 139; histrionic, 137; narcissistic, 138; obsessive, 140; paranoid, 133; passive-aggressive, 140–1; schizoid, 134; schizotypal, 134
  psychotherapy: cognitive, 305–6; crisis

intervention, 317; family, 312; psychoanalytic, 298–9, 300–1

psychosis: delusional disorder, 157; psychotic mood disorders, 155; reactive psychosis, 156; schizoaffective disorder, 156; schizophrenia, 152–3

psychosomatic (psychophysiological) disorders, 112

self-harm, 270–1

sexual problems, 183, 184, 185–6, 187

somatisation (somatising response), 105, 106, 113

suicide risk, 264

transsexualism, 182

Van Gogh, 12, 14–22

women: post-partum blues, 228–9; pregnancy loss, 230; premenstrual dysphoria, 225; surgical menopause, 231–2

Catherine of Sienna, St, 116

Cattell, Raymond, 125

Chabot, Boudewijn, 266–7, 268

Charcot, Jean-Martin, 296

Chesler, Phyllis

Women and Madness, 221

children, 10

abuse or neglect, 45, 46, 113, 131, 136, 137, 138, 147, 202, 214, 216, 219, 224, 229; emotional deprivation, 130, 131; incidence of, 215; paedophilia, 189, 190

assessment, 196–7, 201

attachment problems, 202

attachment theory and, 130–1

development (normal), 193–4, 199, 204, 209, 210, 212, 215, 217

and mentally ill parents, 78, 194

psychiatric disorders, 192–3, 199; and abuse, 214–15; behavioural, 33, 129, 194, 196, 204–8; developmental, 193, 195, 199–201, 208; emotional, 33, 129, 196, 198, 200, 210–11

psychological development disorders, 33, 193, 194–6, 197; and prevention, 216–17

Chodoff, Paul, 351–2

Churchill, Winston, 144

Cicero, 234

Clare, Anthony

Depression and How to Survive It, 92–3

Cloninger, Robert, 125

community-based care; 48–9, 161, 162, 274, 340

conversion disorder (hysteria), 102, 108–10, 296

depersonalisation, 110, 110

psychogenic amnesia, 110–11

psychogenic fugue, 111

counselling, 34, 80, 101, 318–19, 327

crises, 58

accidental 54, 60, 315–16

developmental, 54, 60

crisis intervention, 62, 100, 271, 292, 315–17

Crowe, Michael, 313

Cullen, William, 32

culture, 210, 290

and communication barriers, 36

cultural conflict, 44, 111, 198

cultural values, 24, 228

and personality styles, 124–5

and social conventions, 166, 336

Darwin, Charles, 220

The Expression of the Emotions in Man and Animals, 64

Dax, Cunningham, 294

defence mechanisms, 55–8, 102, 103

Defoe, Daniel, 5

Delay, Jean, 275

delirium, 31, 32

delusional disorders, 32, 40–1, 42, 105, 154

see also psychosis; schizophrenia

dementia, 31, 41, 238

from alcohol abuse, 239

Alzheimer's disease, 9, 31, 224, 238, 239, 342; incidence of, 232

causes, 238–9

incidence of, 238

with Lewy bodies, 239

and personality change, 129–30, 238, 239

vascular, 31, 238–9

see also elderly people

dementia praecox. See schizophrenia

Deniker, Paul, 275

depression, 7, 11, 19, 25, 32, 44, 47, 51, 84, 107, 118, 165
   accounts of, 83, 87–90
   and anxiety, 66, 94
   and appearance, 91
   and biological changes, 2, 90
   in childhood and adolescence, 210, 211, 223
   clinical/severe, 83, 84–5, 86–7, 88, 91, 96, 261, 264, 265
   and dependency, 132
   described, 88, 90–1, 94
   dysthymic disorder, 94–5
   melancholia, 21, 84, 88–9, 345
   and physical illness, 98, 105, 114, 265
   psychotic, 85, 91, 154
   recurrence of, 248, 249
   and stress, 97
   and women, 222, 223, 231, 232, 233
Deveson, Anne
   Tell Me I'm Here, 161
Diagnostic and Statistical Manual of Mental Disorders (DSM-IV; APA), 28–9, 31, 93–4, 128, 199, 347
Dickens, Charles, 127
Dickinson, Emily, 26
dissociation, 110–11
Donaldson, Kenneth, 350
Down's syndrome, 33, 238
drug and alcohol abuse and misuse, 32, 66, 69, 131, 134, 164, 166
   in adolescence, 210, 211, 213
   alcohol abuse, 32, 42, 51, 66, 69, 70, 78, 131, 163, 169–70, 180, 270; effect on families, 166, 170–1; and the elderly, 252; and genetics, 165; and psychological complications, 171–2, 239
   amphetamines, 32, 164, 177, 275; and psychosis, 146, 147, 157, 160, 178
   benzodiazepines, 32, 70, 81, 163, 174, 252, 270, 338
   caffeine, 78
   cannabis, 32, 147, 163, 165, 178
   causes, 165, 166–7, 179
   cocaine, 164, 177
   hallucinogens, 163, 164, 165, 179; LSD, 146, 147, 179, 213; and psychosis, 179

   and the international drug trade, 180
   and mental illness (dual diagnosis), 146, 147, 165–6
   nicotine, 78
   opiates, 163, 175–6, 345
   outcomes, 167, 169, 176
   polysubstance abuse, 179–80
   stimulants, 164, 177, 345
   solvents, 163, 179
drugs, 114, 142, 146
   oral contraceptives, 98
   recreational use, 163, 178; adolescents, 212
drug treatment (medication), 273
   acamprosate, 172
   anti-anxiety, 274, 281; benzodiazapines, 281, 282; buspirone, 281–2
   anti-psychotics, 92, 100, 146, 153, 157, 159, 209, 250, 251, 274, 275–7; chlorpromozine, 274, 275; clozapine, 275
   chemical aversion, 172
   cholinesterase inhibitors, 244, 245
   effectiveness, 274, 275, 280, 338
   and elderly people, 237, 244, 252
   hormonal, 182, 191
   hypnotics (sleeping pills), 244, 252, 282, 283, 284; benzodiazapines as, 282, 283, 284
   mood stabilisers, 100–1, 250, 274, 280; lithium, 7–8, 100, 101, 279, 280–1
   naltrexone, 172, 177
   reserpine, 95, 98
   side-effects, 38, 48, 51, 98, 114, 123, 159, 247, 250, 275, 276, 280–1, 282, 286; treatment, 276, 280
   sildenafil, 187
   stimulants, 205, 206
   tadalafil, 187
   tranquillisers, 8, 172
   see also anti-depressant drugs
Durkheim, Emil, 257, 260
Dyer, Allen, 348

eating disorders, 32, 210
   anorexia nervosa, 29, 33, 43, 44, 116–20, 123, 209, 324; and

osteoporosis, 118
binge-eating disorder, 122
bulimia nervosa, 29, 116, 121–2, 123, 209
obesity, 122–3
ego, 23, 67
and id, 67
and superego, 67
Einstein, Albert, 325–6
elderly people, 36
abuse of, 237, 253
and caregivers, 232, 238, 241–2, 243, 244; support for, 253
fit and active, 234–5
and loss, 235, 251; and grief, 247, 249
physical illness in, 236, 237, 246, 247, 248, 250
psychiatric conditions: anxiety, 236, 250–1; assessment, 41–2, 236, 237, 240–1; bipolar 249; delirium, 245–7; delusions, 250; dementia, 234, 237, 238, 241–2, 245, 251 (care), 243–4 (clinical features of), 129, 239–40, 248; depression, 91, 95, 223, 236, 237, 241, 247–8, 249; factors in, 236; personality disturbance, 236, 252–3; psychoses, 251; substance abuse, 233, 236, 239, 252
in residential care, 232, 244
role of health professionals, 245, 246–7, 250; psychiatrist, 236–7, 238, 240–1, 243, 246, 248–9, 251, 252–3, 254
society's attitude, 235
women, 232–3
electro-convulsive therapy (ECG), 248, 284–5, 345
described, 284
legal protections, 50
and severe depression, 7, 86, 87, 99, 100, 249
and suicidal behaviour, 211
Eliot, TS, 180
Ellis, Albert, 63 n.
emotional (psychological) problems and physical symptoms, 102–15
Engelhardt, Tristram, 348
Epictetus, 53
epilepsy, 109, 158, 196, 203, 281

Erikson, Erik, 130, 204, 297, 329, 330
Childhood and Society, 194
ethics and psychiatrists, 11, 35, 255, 266–8, 307, 344–6, 352–4
and diagnosis, 346–7
and treatment, 119, 347–8; involuntary, 351–2; and rights, 349–51
and values, 348–9
euthanasia, 258, 267, 352
exercise, 80, 328
existential theory, 68, 297
Eysenck, Hans, 125, 319

families, 111, 250, 252, 309
as carers, 50, 148, 241
dysfunction in, 39, 117, 190, 193, 194, 198, 200, 201, 207, 270–1, 310, 311
divorce in, 194, 195
effects of a mental illness, 36–7, 78–9, 315
genetic background, 43, 86, 134, 201, 238, 242, 260, 279
help for, 48, 161, 201, 202, 247, 253, 342–3
relationship problems in, 38, 44–5, 51, 99, 100, 119, 132, 148, 197, 229, 233, 284, 299, 301, 346
supportive, 119, 120, 158, 191, 244, 264, 323
feminism, 219, 220, 222
fire-setting, 33, 207
Fitzgerald, Zelda, 221
Frame, Janet, 221
Frank, Jerome, 289
Frankl, Viktor, 303
Freud, Anna, 216
The Ego and the Mechanisms of Defence, 56
Freud, Sigmund, 56, 204, 305, 307, 322, 334
on anxiety, 64, 67
case histories, 80, 104
on personality, 130
and psychoanalysis, 296–7, 299, 300
repression, 8
and sexuality, 181
Studies in Hysteria (with J Breuer), 104, 296

and value-free treatment, 349
  on women, 221, 233
Friedan, Betty, 219
Fromm-Reichmann, Frieda, 147

Galen, 2
gambling, 33, 309
Gaugin, Paul, 18, 20
Gautier, Theophile, 87–8
George III, 3
gender identity, 181
  gender dysphoria, 181
  disorder, 204, 209
gender roles, 220, 221, 223
Global Burden of Disease, The, 11
Goethe, Johann Wolfgang, 254
Goffman, Erving
  Asylum, 9
Gogol, Nikolai
  Diary of a Madman, 4
Greer, Germaine, 219
grief, 96–7, 267, 316, 336
  in the elderly, 247, 249
  pregnancy loss and, 229–30
  following a suicide, 259, 263
Grigorenko, Pyotr, 26
Gull, William, 116

health system
  and elderly people, 235
  and mental health programs for the
  young, 217
  and mental illness, 11, 160
Hemingway, Ernest, 255, 260
hepatitis, 163
Hill, Sir Denis, 129
Hillel (Jewish sage), 334
Hippocrates, 2, 84, 108
Hippocratic oath, 35
Hobbes, Thomas, 2
Horney, Karen, 221
human rights, 335
Hume, David, 256
Hyland, MJ, 170–1
hypochondriasis, 9, 70, 102, 106–7
  body dysmorphic disorder, 107–8
hysteria. *See* conversion disorder

identity, 111

crises, 209
  loss, 110
  sense of, 130, 135, 136, 159, 297, 329
  see also gender identity
Ignatieff, Michael, 242–3
intellectual disability, 193, 203, 204
International Classification of Diseases
  (ICD-10; WHO), 28, 29, 30, 31, 32,
  77, 127–8, 199, 347
internet, 79, 327
  and psychotherapy, 295

Jackson, Don, 331
Jamison, Kay Redfield
  An Unquiet Mind, 93, 279–80
Janet, Pierre, 110
Jaspers, Karl, 144
Jeffs, Sandy, 145, 151–3, 294
  Poems from the Madhouse, 151–2
Johnson, Samuel, 74–5
Johnson, Virginia, 181
Jones, Ernest, 64
Jonson, Ben, 58, 59
Jung, Carl, 297, 329

Kanner, Leo, 202, 203
Kempe, Henry, 214
Kernberg, Otto, 136
Klein, Melanie, 297
Kleinman, Arthur, 342
Klerman, Gerald, 350
Kline, Nathan, 8
Koestler, Arthur, 257–8, 352
Koestler, Cynthia, 258
Kohut, Heinz, 297, 299
Kraepelin, Emil, 6, 84, 148
Kruger, C, 352

Laing, RD, 27, 145
Lasègue, Pierre, 116
Leupnitz, Deborah
  The Family Interpreted, 219
Levi, Primo, 255
Lewy, Frederick, 239
Lewis, Sir Aubrey, 26
Lewis, CS
  A Grief Observed, 96–7
Lichtenberg, Judith, 354
Lima, Almeida, 7

Lincoln, Abraham, 88–9
Lindemann, Erich, 315
lobotomy, 285–6
Lowell, Robert, 255

McCrum, Robert
  My Year Off, 337
McGough, Roger, 326
malingering and factitious disorder, 113
mania, 32, 38, 40, 48, 84, 85, 91–2, 94,
  281
  described, 92–3
  and psychosis, 154
Marcus Aurelius, 330–1
Marmor, Judd, 320
Mary Magdalen de Pazzi, St, 116
Masters, William, 181
Maupassant, Guy de: *La Horla*, 4
medicine
  classification of illnesses in, 28
meditation, 79, 294, 328
men
  and alcohol abuse, 222
  anti-social behaviour, 134–5, 222
  and opiate abuse, 175
  and paraphilias, 188–91
  sexual problems, 183, 185–6, 187
mental health (and its promotion), 83,
  294, 322–3
  assisting the vulnerable, 338–41; drug
  treatment, 339–40
  and change, 330–1, 334
  described, 322, 334
  doctrine of the mean, 331
  and law, 49–50, 350, 351
  and long-term mental illness, 340–1
  and psychological and social needs,
  324
  public health measures, 324
  responding to signs of mental ill-
  health, 335–9; drug treatment, 338;
  seeking professional help, 337–8
  role of family and friends, 323, 325,
  330, 331–4, 337, 340; as caregivers,
  341–3
  sense of self and self esteem, 329–30
  stress: coping strategies, 325–8,
  334–5, 336
  and work, 322, 334–5

mental illness (psychiatric disorder)
  classification of 27–34, 43, 199
  course of, 50–1
  defined, 25
  diagnosis, 26, 30–1, 34, 188
  and disability, 11
  early accounts and practices, 1–7,
  273, 284
  factors in: biological, 6, 31–2, 46, 51,
  68, 114, 190, 227; psychological, 43,
  44, 45, 46, 47, 51, 114, 227; social, 44,
  45–6, 47, 51, 114, 117, 190
  long-term, 340–1
  nonconformity as, 26
  and physical illness, 37, 38, 42, 51, 86
  social stigma of, 5, 11, 92, 151, 162,
  323
mentally ill people, 273–4
  and competence, 48, 351
  and danger to others, 49
  and dignity, 35
  isolation, 10, 90
  rights of, 47, 50
  and stigma, 11, 35, 344
  vulnerability of, 49
mental retardation (intellectual
  disability), 33
Mill, John Stuart, 89–90, 351
Miller, Arthur
  The Crucible, 220
Milligan, Spike, 92–3
Minuchin, Salvador, 310
Modigliani, Amedeo, 255
Molecular Autism (journal), 203
Molière
  Le Malade Imaginaire, 106
Moniz, Egas, 7, 285
Montesquieu, 256
mood disorders, 2, 8, 32, 34, 41, 46, 83,
  84, 93, 130, 145
  adjustment disorder, 95
  in adolescence, 210–11, 213
  bipolar, 19, 20, 84, 85, 86, 93, 100–1,
  149, 165, 209, 292, 339
  causes, 95–8, 99
  cyclothymia, 95
  unipolar, 84
  see also depression; mania
Morris, Jan

Conundrum, 182
Munchausen syndrome by proxy, 216
Murdoch, Iris, 242–3
music, 79, 84, 294, 295, 328

nervous breakdown, 37–8, 61
neuropsychological testing, 41, 43
neurotic disorders, 32, 34
  symptoms, 68

obsessions, 67, 81
obsessive-compulsive disorder (OCD),
  32, 66, 67, 68–9, 74–5, 81, 307, 339
occupational therapists, 50
On Golden Pond (film), 54
organic disorders, 31–2
  thyroid disorders, 31, 66, 78, 95, 158,
  239; and depression, 86, 98, 99, 236
  see also brain
Ortega y Gasset, José, 327
Ovid, 138
Owen, Wilfred, 76

panic, 9, 32, 65, 66
Parkinson's disease, 239, 258
Pavlov, Ivan, 306
personality traits and types, 24, 124–6,
  165
  see also problematic personality
pharmaceuticals
  and pharmacogenetics, 286
  research, 273, 287
phobia, 9, 32, 64–5, 67, 306–7
Picasso, Pablo, 234
Pilowsky, Issy, 103
Pinel, Philippe, 3
Plath, Sylvia, 221, 255
  The Bell Jar, 303
Plato, 252
  The Republic, 235
Pliny the Elder, 256
Pollock, Jackson, 255
post-traumatic stress disorder, 30, 62,
  69, 75–8
  and alcohol abuse, 171
  in children, 214–15
problematic personality (personality
  disorder), 33, 34, 124, 126–9, 142
  anti-social, 96, 129, 134–5, 206

avoidant personality, 40, 72, 139
borderline, 130, 131, 132, 135–7, 292,
  300; and childhood abuse, 215
dependent, 132
factors in, 129–30, 135, 136
histrionic, 130, 132, 137
and maladaptive behaviour, 129, 132
and mental and physical illness, 131
multiple personality disorder, 111
narcissistic, 130, 138, 300
obsessive, 139–40
paranoid, 130, 133
passive-aggressive, 140–1
and the psychiatrist, 131–2
schizoid, 133–4
schizotypal, 134
and stress, 142
Prichard, John, 127
psychiatric nurses, 50
psychiatrists
  training, 37
  work with patients, 22, 23;
  assessment, 34, 38, 39–40, 41–2, 98–9,
  158, 167–8, 197–8, 201, 213, 240 (and
  suicide risk), 262; diagnosis; 42–3,
  105–6, 108, 118, 132, 153, 154, 198–9,
  216, 243, 274; formulations, 43–7,
  184, 307; interview, 34, 35–9, 40, 41,
  78, 132; as partnership, 323, 339, 348;
  prognosis, 43
  see also ethics; psychiatry;
  psychotherapy; treatment
psychiatry
  as branch of medicine, 25
  child and adolescent psychiatry, 192,
  196, 206, 218
  community-based, 10
  and confidentiality, 35
  diagnostic practice in, 27;
  biopsychosocial approach, 27, 36,
  196, 231; differences, 30
  drug use in, 274, 277, 278, 286
  and empathy, 13, 233, 299, 300, 353,
  354
  history of, 1–11, 143, 148, 273, 344
  old-age, 236–7, 238, 240–1, 243, 246,
  248–9, 251, 252–3, 254
  perspectives, 23–4; dimensional, 23;
  explanatory, 13–14, 20, 22–3, 24;

understanding, 22, 24, 43, 127
and sense of self and self-esteem, 329
and suicide, 255–6, 257, 260, 261–5, 272; assisted suicide, 266–8
and women, 219–22, 233
see also ethics; psychiatrist
psychoanalysis, 8, 9, 23, 100, 104, 296, 298
and the ego, 23
psychoanalytic theory, 55, 67
self-psychology, 130, 297
psychological development disorders, 33
psychology, 50, 329
psychosis, 20, 21, 36
causes, 145–6, 147; and life experiences, 8, 22, 61, 147
defined, 32, 143
drug-induced, 31, 146
genetic predisposition to, 8, 20
and substance misuse, 21, 160
see also psychotic disorders; schizophrenia
psychosomatic (psychophysiological) disorders, 102, 112–13
psychosurgery, 7, 50, 81, 221, 273, 285–6
psychotherapy, 101, 115, 141, 211, 231, 232, 279–80
behavioural, 80, 306–7, 320
classifying the therapies, 292–4
cognitive, 80, 294, 304–6, 320; cognitive-behavioural therapy, 9, 10, 46, 80, 82, 99, 122, 141, 249, 282, 294, 304; computer-based, 295
and counselling, 232, 318–19
couple therapy, 52, 114, 248, 292, 312–13, 320
and the creative therapies, 79, 84, 294–5
crisis intervention, 315–17
existential, 294, 297, 302–3
family, 10, 81–2, 100, 119, 141, 161, 193, 212, 213, 248, 271, 309–12, 319
features of, 23, 288–91, 320
group, 9, 119, 141, 142, 191, 207, 307–9
individual, 51, 52, 114, 120, 141, 142, 193, 229, 271, 292, 308

insight-oriented, 111, 291
interpersonal, 99–100
psychoanalytic, 80, 296, 297–302, 303, 319, 320; brief, 302, 320
research in, 319–21
supportive, 294, 311–12, 313–14
see also treatment
psychotic disorders, 144
classification, 148–9
delusional disorder, 156–7
diagnosis, 144
drug-induced psychosis, 157
psychotic mood disorders, 154
as public health problem, 144
reactive psychosis, 156
schizoaffective disorder, 154, 155
schizophreniform disorder, 154
and self-harm, 270
see also psychosis; schizophrenia

Quakers, 3, 5

Rainman (film), 203–4
Ramsay, Melvin, 109
relaxation, 79, 80, 282, 327–8
Richardson, Henry Handel
  The Fortunes of Richard Mahony, 5–6
Rivers, WHR, 76
Roethke, Theodore, 255
Rollin, Henry, 6–7
Rothko, Marc, 255
Russell, Bertrand, 234
Russia's Political Hospitals (Bloch and Reddaway), 27

Sacks, Oliver
  An Anthropologist on Mars, 204
Sakel, Manfred, 7
Salinger, JD
  The Catcher in the Rye, 54
Santayana, George, 1
schizophrenia, 6, 7, 32, 57, 84, 97, 134, 145, 161, 273, 275, 292, 339, 341, 345
in adolescence, 209, 213
and diagnosis, 31, 149, 153
factors in, 146, 147; drug use, 146, 147, 165, 213; genetic factors, 146, 148; stress, 148
incidence of, 144

and recovery, 145, 153
symptoms, 151, 275; delusions, 149,
152; disorganised thinking, 40, 118,
149, 150; hallucinations, 149, 150;
'negative symptoms', 149, 275
(cognitive impairment), 150, 151
Schneider, Kurt, 127
self-esteem, 45, 46, 98, 115, 176, 213,
229
low, 94, 100, 107, 121, 122, 123, 139,
147, 166, 178, 194, 201, 346
self-harm (deliberate), 137, 262
incidence of, 259
by laceration, 33, 34, 131, 135, 270
motives, 269
by overdose, 37, 45, 86, 131, 258, 269
suicidal behaviour, 211, 268–9, 272,
352
self-help organisations and support
groups, 10, 50, 79, 123, 160, 265, 309,
324, 341
Al-Anon, 169
Alateen, 169
Alcoholics Anonymous (AA), 163,
167, 169, 173, 309, 343
Beyondblue, 343
Black Dog Institute, 343
for carers, 244, 253
Crisis Line, 327
Headspace, 217
Lifeline, 271, 327
MIND (UK), 343
Narcotics Anonymous (NA), 169, 176
National Alliance for the Mentally Ill
(US), 343
Reach Out, 217
Samaritans, 271, 327
SANE, 343
TRANX, 175
Weight Watchers, 123
Seneca, 256
sexual dysfunction, 32, 33, 182–7
sexuality, 188, 347
in adolescence, 210
homosexuality, 29, 188, 347
and paraphilias, 181, 188–90
transsexualism, 181–2, 189
Shakespeare, William, 127, 304
As You Like It, 240

Hamlet, 54, 87
Henry IV, Part 2, 282–3
Macbeth, 283
Othello, 169
Shaw, George Bernard, 234
Shooter, Michael, 339
Silence of the Lambs (film), 135, 189
sleep
disturbance, 118, 247, 323; in
children, 200, 210
healthy sleep habits, 283–4
sleeping disorders, 32; insomnia, 241,
250, 252, 283, 284
social workers, 50
somatisation (somatising response),
105–6, 112–15
and families, 105
Sophocles
Oedipus at Colonus, 234
Soviet Union
dissent in, 26–7
psychiatry in, 27, 344
stealing, 33
Steinem, Gloria, 219
Stengel, Erwin, 30, 268
Stoics (Greek), 304
Stone, Alan, 350
Storr, Anthony
Solitude, 333
stress, 51, 53–4, 63, 97, 142
acute stress reactions, 60–1, 62
adjustment disorders, 32, 60, 62, 98
coping mechanisms, 55–8, 60, 325,
334
and eating binges, 121
management, 282
and physical illness, 59–60, 112
and psychosis, 145–6, 147–8, 156
see also crises
Styron, William
Darkness Visible, 90, 261
suicide, 36, 88, 352
in adolescence, 211
assisted suicide, 266–8
and the bereaved, 257, 264–5
copycat, 260
defining, 257–8, 268
in history, 256–7
incidence of, 255, 259, 272; among

psychiatrists, 256, 261
means of, 259, 265
men, 259–60
in mothers, 228
and mental illness, 258, 261–2, 265, 266; anorexia nervosa, 117; borderline personality, 135; depression, 247, 261, 265; schizophrenia, 150, 153, 261, 265
prevention, 263, 264, 265–6, 272
and religious affiliation, 260
risk factors, 258, 259–62, 265
and substance abuse, 171, 260, 261–2, 265
see also self-harm
Sullivan, Harry Stack, 107, 308
syphilis
neurosyphilis, 5, 6, 7
Szasz, Thomas, 27, 347

Tai Chi, 79, 294, 327
therapy. *See* psychotherapy
Tillich, Paul
The Courage To Be, 303
Tolstoy, Leo, 331
Anna Karenina, 332
Tourette's disorder, 33, 324
in children, 204, 208–9
treatment
alcohol and drug abuse, 164–5, 167–9, 172–3, 174, 175, 176, 178, 179–80, 309; dual diagnosis, 165–6, 168; and family, 169; and substitution therapy, 176, 177; supervised heroin injection, 177
anorexia nervosa, 118–19, 123
anxiety disorders, 66, 70–1, 77, 78–81, 281, 286, 319
bulimia nervosa, 122, 123
childhood psychiatric disorders, 193, 200, 201, 202, 203, 205–6, 207, 208, 210, 211, 212, 213, 216, 297
compulsory, 49–50, 92, 99, 100, 159, 161, 263
counselling, 114, 119, 176, 289; family, 193, 205, 248, 264–5; and trust, 168
depression, 46, 49, 51, 52, 86, 98–100, 101, 248, 279, 286

diversity of settings, 48
and elderly people, 241
emotional problems and physical symptoms, 113–15; psychogenic amnesia and fugue, 111
hospitalisation, 48, 51, 99, 250, 270
length of, 50–1, 153, 162, 168, 275–6, 279, 280, 292, 293, 302, 308, 320
mania, 7, 48, 100, 101, 281
multidisciplinary approach, 48, 50, 115, 118, 176, 263
obesity, 123
paraphilias, 190–1
problematic personality, 141–2, 293, 319, 320
psychotic disorders, 155, 157–9, 161–2, 189, 226; and support, 159–60
schizophrenia, 146, 150, 153, 158, 159, 262, 286, 309, 311; tests, 158
sexual dysfunction, 183, 185, 186–7, 313
self-harm, 271; and prevention, 271
sleep disorder, 283–4
stress, 61–2
the suicidal person, 255–6, 257, 261, 262–4, 267; and trust, 263
and women, 2, 3, 220–2, 233; infertility, 230; menopausal symptoms, 231, 232; postpartum, 226, 227, 228
see also anti-depressants; drug treatment; electro-convulsive therapy; psychotherapy

United Nations Charter on the Rights of Mentally Ill People, 11
United Nations Declaration of Human Rights, 335

vaginismus, 184–5
Vaillant, George, 56
van Gogh, Theo, 16, 21
van Gogh, Vincent, 12, 14–22, 24, 88, 255
Crows over the Wheatfields, 21
Van Staden, CW, 352
Varah, Reverend Chad, 271
Verdi, Giuseppe
Stabat Mater, 234

von Feuchtersleben, Ernst, 143

Wagner von Jauregg, Julius, 7
Warnes, Anne, 341
Weakland, John, 330
websites, 217, 295, 343
Winnicott, DW, 131, 215, 333
women
  abused women, 233
  and anorexia nervosa, 116, 123
  and bulimia nervosa, 116, 121–2
  as carers, 224, 231, 232
  and conversion disorder (hysteria), 108
  elderly women, 232–3, 251; in nursing homes, 232; wellbeing, 233
  and infertility, 229, 230
  menopause, 230–1; and life events, 230–1
  and mental illness, 2, 3, 219–20, 222;
  factors in, 222–4, 233
  and the menstrual cycle, 224–5, 347
  and motherhood, 225–9
  post-partum blues, 228–9
  post-partum depression, 200, 219, 224, 226–8, 324
  post-partum psychosis, 226
  pregnancy loss, 229–30
  and self-harm, 270
  and sexual problems, 184–5
  and societal values, 219–21
  and somatisation, 113
Woolf, Virginia, 255
World Health Organization (WHO), 11, 28, 31, 77, 174, 199, 322, 334, 335
  Aspects of Family Mental Health in Europe, 331

Yalom, Irvin, 302
yoga, 79, 294, 327, 328